The Mind and Art

of

HENRY ADAMS

The Mind and Art
of
HENRY ADAMS

BY J. C. LEVENSON

ILLUSTRATED WITH PHOTOGRAPHS

HOUGHTON MIFFLIN COMPANY BOSTON
The Riverside Press Cambridge
1957

In memory of my father

Preface

IN THE COURSE of writing this book, I contracted many obligations of gratitude. For my awareness of Henry Adams' existence apart from the written word, I owe thanks first of all to the vigorous personal testimony of his nieces, Mrs. Robert Homans and Mrs. Ward Thoron. I am also grateful to Mrs. Homans for letting me use the Adams manuscripts which she has deposited in the Houghton Library at Harvard University, including the correspondence of Brooks and Henry Adams, and I thank the Houghton Library for access to these and other Adams materials. I am doubly indebted to the Massachusetts Historical Society—for use of the enormously rich Adams Papers deposited there by the Adams Manuscript Trust, and for access to the basic collection of Henry Adams' personal library. Professor William A. Jackson of the Houghton Library and Mr. Stephen T. Riley, Librarian of the Massachusetts Historical Society, extended kindness to me beyond the measure of official hospitality.

In the questions I have put to my subject matter and the ways I have tried to understand it, I am indebted to Professors Paul Herman Buck, Perry Miller, Kenneth B. Murdock, and Henry Nash Smith. I have a special debt to the late F. O. Matthiessen. I should also like to express my gratitude to those fellow scholars whom I know indirectly through their work on Adams. Thanks to the researches of Max I. Baym, Harold Dean Cater, William H. Jordy, and Ernest Samuels, my own tasks were greatly lightened. Joseph H. Summers and Katherine Simonds Thompson, by their devoted and exacting criticism, kept me aware of the book I wanted to write even when I did not know how to meet their high standards. Many others who contributed to my work—scholars, teachers, firsthand informants about Adams, students with whom I read his work, and friends with whom I talked about him—remain anonymous in order that a shorter list might possibly be read; all, named and unnamed, have taught me that any work of the mind, while it is the responsibility of the individual, is the product of a community.

For the opportunity to start this book, I owe thanks to the United States government and the G.I. Bill of Rights; and I am grateful to the American Philosophical Society and the University of Minnesota for generous grants which helped me bring the book to completion.

My wife wisely knew how to combine the gifts of aid and comfort. There is no thanking her.

J. C. Levenson

Author's Note

MOST READERS do not like to be interrupted by bibliographical citations, and for their sake I have eliminated superscript numbers from the text and put my list of references at the back of the book. In quoting, I have adhered to the original spelling without comment. When I have adapted quotations to my own sentences, I have freely changed initial capitals or lower-case letters and final punctuation and omitted without note words that precede or follow the quoted fragment.

For permission to quote unpublished materials, I acknowledge permission from the persons and institutions mentioned in the Preface. For permission to quote copyright materials, I make the following acknowledgments.

To Houghton Mifflin Company, for: *A Cycle of Adams Letters, 1861–1865* and *Letters of Henry Adams, 1858–1891* and *1892–1918*, all edited by Worthington C. Ford; *Henry Adams and His Friends*, compiled by Harold Dean Cater; *Letters to a Niece and Prayer to the Virgin of Chartres*, edited by Mabel La Farge; and *Mont-Saint-Michel and Chartres*, *The Education of Henry Adams*, and *The Life of George Cabot Lodge*.

To The Macmillan Company, for *The Degradation of the*

Democratic Dogma by Henry Adams, edited by Brooks Adams.

To Charles Scribner's Sons, for *The Letters of Henry James,* edited by Percy Lubbock.

To Alfred A. Knopf, Inc., for the Phillips Bradley revised translation of *Democracy in America* by Alexis de Tocqueville.

Contents

(Illustrations follow page 162)

The Mind and Art
of
HENRY ADAMS

Chapter I

THE MAKING OF AN HISTORIAN

HENRY ADAMS offers to his fellow Americans the richest and most challenging image of what they are, what they have been, and what they may become. If it were not for Adams the historian and artist, Adams the public man would be worth scarcely a footnote in the study of politics. The private man would have disappeared except for the handful of people who can claim he was part of their lives. The theorist of history would never have come into existence. We are aware of these and other Adamses because of the writer, and to know him better, we are obliged to look more closely at what he did. For the story of a serious artist's work tends to be the essential story of his life. That is the assumption on which this book has been written, but it was Adams' assumption, too. He himself recognized that for the man deeply committed, art virtually becomes life. Midway in his historical career, he observed his own commitment and declared with simple candor that "if I felt a perfect confidence that my history would be what I would like to make it, this part of life — from forty to fifty — would be all I want." No man gets, or can even name, all that he wants, and Adams wanted more than he said. Unable to take satisfaction in his history, he came to dwell almost obsessively on the waste of physical nature, the losses in social "progress," the mortality of human life. Yet he survives because he defied laws he thought of as absolute and universal. Making history into art, transforming the dead records of the past into a living possession for the present, he won a victory over oblivion.

Since the historian's own testimony about his calling conflicts with his reputation for gloom, we would do well to recall how often Adams has been seen through the looking-glass. Readers know him mostly from *The Education of Henry Adams*, which is wrongly called *An Autobiography*, and the image which they identify with the man is a projection partly of Adams, partly of themselves. The *Education*, published posthumously in 1918, led the best-seller lists in "nonfiction" for two years and became the special property of the postwar era. Debunkers saw the iconoclast who used President Grant to define the pre-intellectual, archaic man; the politically disillusioned found him to be the spokesman for a country "mortgaged to the railways"; doubters approved the protestant against the great secular faith in progress who asserted that "all he could prove was change"; the spiritually restive admired the man who looked upon the dynamo as an occult mechanism and yet insisted that "all the steam in the world could not, like the Virgin, build Chartres." Those who looked for Adams the artist appreciated the starved New Englander's response to the "delicate grace and passionate depravity" of the Potomac spring and the narrator's mask of a tired old man who knows too much about life to find it worth living; but they tended to see him merely as one who had gone through life with the sensibility of a septuagenarian, and they could hardly remain content with an Adams they made in their own image. The image lingered, but the attitude of the perceivers changed and the posthumous Henry Adams was outgrown. Yet the writer who offered so many things to so many different readers could not have been simply an unreal image, reflecting his audience and providing no genuine substance himself. Now that time has begun to free us from our coercive memories, our own age has been trying more seriously than ever to interpret the signs of Adams' enduring value.

An obvious way to start reseeing Henry Adams is to keep in mind that his earlier writings are not mere appendices to the *Education*, his late "Essay on Twentieth-Century Multiplicity." By taking seriously the first modern historical scholar in America, the brilliant biographer of Albert Gallatin and John Randolph, and the author of America's finest masterpiece in history, we begin to restore the powerful symmetry of an abundant literary career. The first and fundamental half of that career occurred between 1870 and 1891, between Adams' call to Harvard to teach medieval history and the publication of the final volume of his *History of the United States during the Administrations of Thomas Jefferson and James Madison*. In two decades as a professional historian, he produced a variety of works which show separately the elements of historical art, insofar as the elements of an art can be separated for critical consideration, and then he fused these elements in a work which, alone in the language, stands comparison with Gibbon's. The craft of history, as the one technical discipline to which Adams ever fully submitted, set its mark on his later writing. The well-known author of the *Education*, who made history his subject, was not a phenomenon created out of nothing, but the experienced writer who had successfully made history his literary form. Only when we have taken the measure of his earlier work can we intelligently turn to the traveler and thinker, the heresiarch against American optimism, and the connoisseur of art and sense with whom we have a deceptive familiarity.

Unusual personal circumstance led Henry Adams into the labor marked out for the historian by Sir Thomas North, the Renaissance translator of Plutarch — "to teach the living and revive the dead." His own past, never having died, needed no reviving for him: his life extended vicariously over four generations. When he was born on February 16, 1838, not quite ten years had passed since his grandfather John Quincy Adams had been displaced from the Presidency of the United States by Andrew Jackson and the rising tide of a popular democratic movement. A generation before, his great-grandfather John Adams had been supplanted by Thomas Jefferson under much the same conditions. The family, though smarting with such wounds, remained devoted to classic statesmanship and to the republic they had helped to found; and they still had much to give. During Henry Adams' boyhood, his grandfather was already established as a leading Representative in Congress, the spokesman for independent conservatism and the great defender of civil liberties for the unpopular radicals of antislavery. The boy's father, Charles Francis Adams, became a leader of the "Conscience Whigs" and then of the Free-Soil Party, served as a congressman during the Secession Crisis and as Minister to Great Britain during the Civil War, and, among Reform Republicans of the postwar years, constantly loomed as a presidential possibility — though never quite a candidate. Even the generation of Henry Adams was to be active and influential in public affairs, although at one remove farther from the center of power. The family saga was complicated, but its direction away from political authority was clear. For the historian-to-be, it was fortunate that membership in a distinguished family made the past very much alive for him. On the other hand, his fortune entailed the need to understand the past as it affected him and his own times. As the first in a line of four generations and the only one of four brothers never to hold public office, he had to face the intellectual necessities of his position. The penalty of not understanding his historical situation could have been foolish petulance or egoistic despair. Indeed, there are charges aplenty which make his chief motive as a man and writer either a naïve disappointment at not inheriting the highest office of the land or an equally naïve disgruntlement with the breakdown of American politics in the post-Civil War age of violent business expansion. But the books by which Adams still teaches the living and revives the dead bear witness to his intellectual mastery of the past as well as his keen sense of its aliveness. He devoted the most energetic years of his maturity to the social concerns of his fathers, and in the practice of history rather than politics he indirectly fulfilled the personal ideals he derived from their hundred years' experience.

The derivation of particular ideals was not an accident, for the founder of the dynasty laid down a pattern of education which the family followed. John Adams, though he gave up schoolteaching for the law, never ceased to drive at the task of educating himself and his children. He worked out a schedule of attainments that was much like his friend Jefferson's, but, unlike the founder of the University of Virginia, he made the household rather than the state the main object of his efforts. He had thought that his practice at the bar might establish the family's economic status so that his sons might serve society the better and his grandsons, benefiting from the progress of family and state, might cultivate the gentler arts. Such a division of labor through time did not go into effect as planned. Speedily thrust forward by his own capacity and the revolutionary circumstances of his age, he changed only a little the ideas he held for posterity. Writing home from his wartime ministry to Paris, he reported the spell of artistic magnificence and his own refusal to be hurried:

> I could fill volumes with descriptions of temples and palaces, paintings, sculptures, tapestry, porcelain, etc., etc., etc., if I could have time; but I could not do this without neglecting my duty. The science of government is my duty to study, more than all other sciences; the arts of legislation and administra-

tion and negotiation ought to take the place of, indeed to exclude, in a manner, all other arts. I must study politics and war,
that my sons may have liberty to study mathematics and philosophy. My sons ought to study mathematics and philosophy,
geography, natural history and naval architecture, navigation,
commerce, and agriculture, in order to give their children a
right to study painting, poetry, music, architecture, statuary,
tapestry, and porcelain.

The stern conscience of John Adams helps account for Henry
Adams' being the historian of Jefferson and Madison before
he could become the author of *Mont-Saint-Michel and Chartres*.
The pristine American will that resisted the temptations of
Paris was strong enough to shape other lives; despite his pat
arrangement of the future, John Adams produced offspring
who recapitulated his own course.

The education of the Adamses bred a triple ideal in young
men — to be lawyers, statesmen, and men of letters. The
youth of each generation were prepared for the family calling,
which implied, in the way of institutional training, undergraduate study at Harvard College and the reading of law in
the office of a first-rate lawyer. John Quincy Adams read
under Theophilus Parsons, Charles Francis Adams under
Daniel Webster, and Henry Adams twice began his studies
under Horace Gray, only to be twice called, in 1860 and 1861,
to postpone the law and become his father's private secretary.
His not returning to legal study after the war was to mark
another divergence from the family norm, for he was once
again the first in a line of four generations and the only one of
four brothers not to become a lawyer. (Again, however, his
individual situation jibed with the history of the family; of
his brothers, only Brooks achieved any prominence at the
bar.) During the war years when their future had not yet
taken shape, Henry and his older brother Charles revealed
their shared possession of the family ideals even as they

anticipated a falling off to come. Charles wrote: "I would
be a philosophical statesman if I could, and a literary politician if I must; but to command attention as either I must
have a certain position of my own. A lawyer's would have
done, if I could have won it, but I failed in that . . ." Henry,
who had once planned his legal career in great detail, answered all too readily: "Only one fact I feel sure of. We are
both no longer able to protect ourselves with the convenient
fiction of the law. Let us quit that now useless shelter, and
steer if possible for whatever it may have been that once lay
beyond it." The brothers honored their inherited trinity of
aims even though they foresaw the coming breach in the
family rule. Henry gave up his belief that "to become more,
the law must be my ladder," but in the long run, he did not
stray so very far. His first serious work as a professional historian was a monograph on "The Anglo-Saxon Courts of
Law," and his major effort was in American political history
where he searched out the nature of statesmanship and analyzed the declining opportunities for its practice. Law and
politics, although a matter of speculative rather than practical
knowledge, were still to be the basis for his career as a man of
letters.

The family culture of the Adamses was far more than a
habitual calling to law and politics or a standard pattern of
professional training. Education began at home, and in each
generation the father tried, as Professor Samuel Flagg Bemis
observes of John Quincy Adams, "to give the young men an
education like his own — so far as it could be done in America
— as preparation for the call of public service." The education of an Adams could not be supplied by institutions, but
could be supplied by parents. In fact, it demanded extraordinary family cohesiveness. In a nation where sons have
usually attained at once their majority and their independence
of family, home, and past, the Adamses kept their promising

sons in a subordinate relation to the head of the family long past the usual age. Each father in turn personally initiated his son into the family culture: John Quincy served as private secretary to John Adams, and a second John served John Quincy in the same role forty years later, some thirty years before Henry Adams assumed the filial duty. Also, each father took his sons abroad to share the family's diplomatic experience firsthand. There was considerable difference, however, in the sons' experience: John Quincy Adams spent the years from eleven to seventeen in Europe amidst great affairs and then, true son to his iron-willed father, insisted on going home to get started at Harvard on schedule; Charles Francis Adams was in Europe with his father from the age of two until he was ten and, having received some indelible lessons about the English from his miseries in a British school, returned home while his reactions were still simple; Henry Adams was his father's secretary in England from 1861 to 1868, from twenty-three to thirty. When he gave up legal study to accompany his father to Washington in 1860 and to London the year after, he was reversing the usual process, slipping back from a more or less independent life to a renewal of subordinate status. The upside-down order of his education within the family was not likely to give Henry Adams the outgoing qualities of the political man and did in fact cut him off from his last chance to become a lawyer. Curiously, his Civil War experience was at once his fullest participation in the family scheme and the occasion of his breaking away from the ancestral pattern.

A close look at the emerging individuality of Henry Adams during the Civil War years may show the temperament, the ideas, and the intellectual character he brought to the craft of history. When Adams himself faced the problem of accounting for individuality, he was willing to trace his own as far back as an attack of scarlet fever at the age of three. He did not believe in neglecting biological explanations — or in overestimating them — but in his reflections he was primarily trying to do justice to the fact that historical processes go on a long time before they meet the eye. His childhood sickness gave him a chance to mention as possible consequences the short stature of which he was acutely conscious throughout his life, the general "fining-down process of scale" which he could not otherwise note without immodesty, and a habit of withholding himself somewhat from the burly activities of normally aggressive boys. Still, his own recollections of snow-fights in winter and the woods in summer, of nursery rhymes (in a critical edition, to be sure) and resistance to school suggest that the scarlet fever was more important in the imagination of the old man than in the life of the boy. Variation from type was hardly noticeable in his school or college career; even his literary interests while at Harvard made him no more promising than most class orators are said to be. Upon graduation in 1858, he took a different turn from his older brothers by proposing a two-year sojourn in Berlin in quest of the civil law. When this solemn expedition had evidently become a junket through Europe in general, his situation was still far from unique: other young men found their New England consciences stimulated by the necessity of explaining themselves to the parents who paid. Besides, he managed by his application to German to look the part of a student and, by a series of letters to the Boston *Daily Courier*, to appear also in the role of apprentice journalist. The family stamp showed when he turned, almost with embarrassment, from artistic attractions, and when, having contrived to meet the great Garibaldi, he found that "the Washington of Italy" was not up to his American original. Back home, he did start seriously to read law, though twice diverted to his father's service. Not until the second term of his apprenticeship, during Minister Adams' seven-year tenure in London, did his individuality become really apparent. Reversion to filial status was probably as painful to the young man as scarlet fever had been to the child, but the course of recovery from the direst pangs of adolescence proved to be the education of an historian. When the diplomatic private secretary learned to accept the limiting of his practical possibilities in life, he underwent an intellectual change from bewilderment to self-understanding and a temperamental change from youthful pretentiousness to quieter self-assurance. For the first time, his own image of himself markedly began to converge with the picture we can draw from the available facts. In the ample family correspondence of the Civil War period, the part of Henry Adams seems slight when measured against his father's gradual success in what was for the Union the most important foreign capital or, in the slowly mounted victory at home, the rise of Charles Francis Adams, Junior, from lieutenant to regimental commander. The younger brother, caught in the trying passivity of his private secretary's role, was careful not to set a higher value on inward experience than on public action. Nevertheless, the story of his personal growth is appropriately bound with that of the Minister's and the soldier's patient victories and, in larger terms, with the historic crisis of the nation.* Coming of age within his particular inherited culture, Henry Adams became the man to carry the family's greatness into new areas in a new age.

*My argument here and hereafter finds its chief support in the work of Worthington Chauncey Ford, whose brilliant editing of Henry Adams' letters laid down lines of development which further scholarship has confirmed and supplemented without substantially changing them. On the Civil War years, I follow in the direction pointed by his edition of *A Cycle of Adams Letters, 1861–1865* (2 vols., Boston, 1920). The inconspicuous form-giving quality of his modest labor can be seen in the shape he gave to the *Cycle*. Although the trend of the correspondence is that of a rising action for all three writers, the last letter from the father dwells on the appalling news of Lincoln's assassination, the last letter from the younger Charles describes the troubles of commanding a

What youth and maturity meant in the Adams family appears in the contrasting tones of father and son as they wrote from London on Independence Day, 1862, to young Captain Adams, a brigade staff officer with the Union Forces at Hilton Head, South Carolina. Although the father's letter occasionally verges on ambassadorial pomposity, it principally shows the firm grasp of the historical present which comes from constantly working a rich knowledge of the past for its ever-changing instructiveness. The senior Adams spoke, even to his family, in the carefully measured language of statesmanship:

> This is the 4th of July. Eighty-six years ago our ancestors staked themselves in a contest of a far more dangerous and desperate character. The only fault they committed was in omitting to make it more general and complete. Had they then consented to follow Thomas Jefferson to the full extent of the first draught of the Declaration, they would have added little to the seven years severity of their struggle and would have entirely saved the present trials from their children. I trust we shall not fall into any similar mistake, and if we are tempted to do so, I trust the follies of our enemy will avert us from the consequences of our weakness. This is the consideration which makes me most tolerant of the continuance of the war. I am not a friend of the violent policy of the ultras who seem to me to have no guide but their own theories. This great movement must be left in a degree to develope itself, and human power must be applied solely to shape the consequences so far as possible to the best uses. . . .

Negro regiment on Reconstruction duty (and is followed by an editor's note on his being retired because of a physical breakdown), and the last letter of Henry Adams tells of his indefiniteness of plans. The second volume thus ends with a dying fall, with all three writers sounding the family's and the nation's somber entrance into the postwar era. The Henry Adams who had so recently come to terms with himself would still have to come to terms with the Great Barbecue.

The Minister's scope of historical reference and his touch-stones of political sagacity take the letter back to the eighteenth-century rationalistic world in which the principles of the Adamses were revolutionary, where John Adams sat with Jefferson on the committee which presented the Declaration to the Continental Congress. Minister Adams was referring to Jefferson at a time when Southern appropriation of Jefferson's name had virtually eclipsed his reputation in the North, but the Adamses had long maintained their eminence in American life by holding to their convictions regardless of popular currents. The unhesitating reference to principle and practicality in the same breath accounts for Charles Francis Adams' depreciation of the "ultras" who, blinded by their own rightness, took no measure of the political possibilities. The mixture of high-principled intransigence and impatience with others' impracticality, like the constant reflection on past and present, was typical of the mature Adams mind. As for the ability to let historical movements develop of themselves, Henry Adams was one day to judge this his father's greatest talent as a diplomat.

The Minister's twenty-four-year-old son and secretary had not yet notably acquired his father's coolness or detachment. The father was a statesman's statesman, showing scarcely any but public sentiments; the son was a private, confidential employee at the legation, holding no governmental position himself and resented by those who did. Doubly an outsider, Henry Adams observed great events in which he could not participate and remained three thousand miles from great events in which he might have had a share. His tone was as personal as his father's was civic. Talking of the English cotton famine, he lacked the ring of authority, but when he reported the pressure of inactivity on youth, he began to sound convincing: "Hard as your life is and threatens to become, I would like well to share it with you in order to escape in the consciousness of action a little of the struggle against fancied evils that we feel here." Young and friendless in the greatest city of the world, anxious to do almost anything for relief, Henry stuck to his back-room writing desk or lingered at the edge of diplomatic parties with little to think of but the muddled tensions on which he was powerless to act. He might well leave the historical Fourth of July Addresses to his father; writing to his brother was an occasion, not for oratory, but for self-release.

Crossing the path of the two letters from London came a letter from the younger Charles which certainly must have fostered the envious illusions of his brother. He told of a hard four-hour engagement on James Island, off Charleston, from which the Union forces had to retire with severe losses. "I would not have missed it for anything," he wrote. "I had never really been under fire before and the sensation was glorious." While Henry struggled with his "fancied evils," Charles discovered that he had physical courage. The contrast was not new. Earlier, Charles had proudly sent word that no one in camp would believe in his reputation at home as "rather an old Betty," while Henry labored to express his uneasiness with the sensations of a double consciousness: "Do you understand how, without a double personality, *I* can feel that *I* am a failure? One would think that the *I* which could feel that, must be a different *ego* from the *I* of which it is felt." When Henry wrote, "You are so fortunate as to be able to forget self-contemplation in action, I suppose," Charles replied, "The mind is perfectly fallow." One thing the exchange made clear: caught between his brother's youthful breeziness and his father's unshakable gravity, the private secretary had to find a mode of being that expressed itself neither in oratory nor in action.

Despite his qualms, Henry Adams had almost from the beginning of his secretarial duties regarded himself as bound to his post. He did not quite think himself indispensable, but he resolved not to "leave the Chief and the family in the lurch." He took his consolation the easy way, vicariously feeling a ministerial importance and confounding his personal responses with national triumphs and disasters. In March of 1862, when the tide seemed to have turned in favor of the Union, he wrote to Charles: "I feel like a King now. I assert my nationality with a quiet pugnacity that tells." By April he could add: "There is, too, a certain grim satisfaction in the idea that this people who have worn and irritated and exasperated us for months, and among whom we have lived nearly a year of what was, till lately, a slow torture, should now be innocently dancing and smiling on the volcano, utterly unconscious of the extent of hatred and the greediness for revenge that they've raised." His country's greed for revenge seemed especially directed at the London *Times*, which had satirically exposed the American Minister's private secretary for doubling as a newspaper correspondent. In May, when good news was rarer, Henry's tone became a little more defensive: "As for this country, the simple fact is that it is unanimously against us and becomes more firmly set every day. . . . It is a sort of dogged English prejudice, and there is no dealing with it." The sensitivity which led in hard times to ugly vindictiveness turned thereafter into crude exultation. In the first flush of the report that New Orleans had been captured, the apprentice diplomat let himself go: "Indeed the effect of the news here has been greater than anything yet. It has acted like a violent blow in the face of a drunken man." War-engendered anxieties, intensified by having no vent in outward action, were beginning to be dangerous; partial relief through violence of language did less to restore equanimity than to confirm a deep-lying malaise.

Floundering in the psychological difficulties of his situation and his awkward age, Henry Adams could scarcely maintain communication with either of the people he was closest to. As a son, he would not discuss his troubles with his father — not, so he thought, because he was timid and the Minister formidable, but because he was considerate and his father overburdened already. As a brother, he was dismayed to find that personal effusion did not evoke the sympathy he was looking for. Charles was all too ready to undertake the role of therapist.* He had little patience, for example, with the precocious ennui of a boy who grumbled, "I am tired of this life." On Henry's extravagant emotions he came down hard:

> *You* "tired of this life"! *You* more and more "callous and indifferent about your own fortunes!" Pray how old are you and what has been your career? You graduate and pass two years in Europe, and witness by good luck a revolution. You come home and fall upon great historic events and have better chances than any young man to witness and become acquainted with them. You go abroad while great questions are agitated in a position to know all about them. Fortune has done nothing but favor you and yet you are "tired of this life." You are beaten back everywhere before you are twenty-four, and finally writing philosophical letters you grumble at the strange madness of the times and haven't even faith in God and the spirit of your age. What do you mean by thinking, much less writing such stuff? . . . We shall come out all right and if we don't, the world will. Excuse me if I have been rough, but it will do you good.

Charles's prescription for recurrent morbidity was a strenuous outdoor year. Having once been law clerk to

---

*Charles was especially zealous in administering a cold-water cure to Henry because, a couple of years earlier, Henry had tried to usurp the older brother's right to dispense advice. When, in 1859 and 1860, Charles was chafing at the narrow routine of a legal clerkship, Henry had written superciliously, "You haven't even used the chances you have," and "Your letter is healthier than usual," and other such galling condescension disguised as helpful encouragement. When Charles left the law for the army at the end of 1861 and Henry was feeling the constrictions of his position in London, the elder brother resumed his prerogatives with better humor than his supplanter had shown.

Richard Henry Dana, he complacently suggested going to sea
before the mast as an ideal cure. He might as well have advised his brother to grow six inches taller and ten more inches
around the chest. Still, his roughness taught a lesson as valuable as his proposed treatment was worthless. Henry could
no longer retort, "Physician, heal thyself," as he had in the
days when the studious purposes of his European trip were
crumbling and Charles' resolution to be a lawyer was being
sapped by the experience of becoming one. What counter-
criticism could be devised against the cavalry officer whose
baptism of fire was his authority to be judge and counsellor?
There was no answer to "Don't get into this vein again, or if
you do, keep it to yourself." What Henry could learn from
Charles's cumulative roughness was the need of a new
language. A simple cry of loneliness did not enlist the older
brother's sympathy, and an elaborate posturing seemed entirely to lose it. But if he could not exploit his self-pity, he
could make good use of another attitude which was just as
much a part of him. Accepting the detachment he could not
lose in self-effacing action, he learned to make his loneliness
interesting. By the fall of 1863, he could write Charles with
confidence that he would be heard:

> It is astonishing, even to me, how long I may remain in a
> place without growing to it. Friends! I have none, and my
> temper is now too bad ever to make another. Society! I know
> it not. Laziness, stupidity and self-distrust have shut its doors
> to me. It is wonderful, stupendous to consider, how a man
> who in his own mind is cool, witty, unaffected and high-toned,
> will disgust and mortify himself by every word he utters or act
> he does, when he steps out of his skin defences. Thus it has
> happened that now, after five years of uninterrupted travel and
> mixing with the world, and after a steady residence of half that
> time in this place, surrounded by the thickest of the rush of
> society and fashion, I now find myself in London alone, without

a house I care to go to, or a face I would ask to see. Melancholy, is it not! And yet I never was so contented since the last time I was in love and fancied, like an idiot, that man was a social animal.

In learning to write better, Henry Adams learned in a way to write fiction. Circumstance had dispelled his social isolation, and he gradually attained his old wish "quietly to slide into the literary set and leave the heavy society." In the spring of 1863, he was taken into a literary club where he could hobnob with "the cultivated radicals of England." He then began his lifelong friendship with Charles Milnes Gaskell, the son of a distinguished political and literary family whose public career was to be a constant reminder of the difference between the English and the American situation of the ambitious young intellectual. Drifting into literary and social life proved a more effective cure for morbidity than Henry Adams' conscious efforts to follow prescription. He had halfheartedly tried to arrange a military commission for himself, should he go home, but by the manner of his asking for an "invitation," he made clear the amateur quality of his military interest. Insistence on amateur status may have been a half-conscious answer to Charles, who had recently been trying the notion of an army career; it was more seriously the expression of a new-found point of view from which he could regard his worldly affairs with condescension.* Putting aside

*It was obviously not just chance which made Henry Adams a confidential secretary and not a cavalry officer. Even at the legation, his amateur standing could eventually have been changed by an appointment as Second Secretary — not a great distinction, but still an official appointment which he chose to decline. By the time the opportunity presented itself, he had found the advantages of his detached position. His ultimate opinion, delivered in the *Education*, still bore the marks of his youthful attitude: "He was at least no public official, like the thousands of improvised secretaries and generals who crowded their jealousies and intrigues on the President. He was not a vulture of carrion — patronage."

the temptation of a military career at about the same time as he was giving up the illusion of a legal one, he turned from tentative plans and actual frustrations to the engrossing activity of a speculative life. He came to see that his escape from anxiety must be through intellectual exercise rather than physical strenuousness. His was a monastic nature, he declared in a fine historical mixed metaphor; he preferred to be a Melanchthon and "those who choose to play the Luther may try it for all of me." Self-discovery went hand in hand with his engaging in a frantic course of study which, from his description, might by itself have taken all his time. "I jump from International Law to our foreign history," he told Charles, "and am led by that to study the philosophic standing of our republic, which brings me to reflection over the advance of the democratic principle in European civilization, and so I go on till some new question of law starts me again on the circle." His apparent going in circles was the surest progress he had yet known, as may be measured by the undramatized simplicity with which he could now talk to his brother:

> My candles are seldom out before two o'clock in the morning, and my table is piled high with half-read books and unfinished writing. For weeks together I only leave the house to mount my horse and after I ride, come back as I went. If it were not for your position and my own uneasy conscience, I should be as happy as a Virginia oyster, and as it is, I believe I never was so well off physically, morally and intellectually as this last year.

The young monk of Portland Place burned his candles for two authors especially, John Stuart Mill and Alexis de Tocqueville. He discovered, during that crucial year of the Civil War and his own youth, that these men were truly the "high-priests" of his faith. With their help, he could give shape to the ideas of aristocratic liberalism to which he was heir. Mill combined the talents of a hard-thinking logician with the political and economic interests of a classic liberal, and in general struck the young American as "about the ablest man in England." Tocqueville, recently dead (1859), still had a rising reputation. In his life he had symbolized the marriage of French rationalism with the English reformist spirit. His writing caught an eighteenth-century tone which would have been familiar to his newest reader, and his blind spot for Andrew Jackson would not have disturbed an Adams. Tocqueville's unequaled study of the American democracy criticized the developing republic by aristocratic standards, while his work on the Old Regime and his role in the Revolution of 1848 attested his dedication to the world-wide democratic movement. He was a born nobleman who believed in the rule of the naturally best and in the right of the democratic majority to select those best. Tocqueville, the young student of democracy who became a Deputy and, eventually, a Cabinet Minister, had an even greater appeal for Henry Adams than did Mill. The British philosopher, "very retiring and embarrassed in his manner," lacked the appearance of a public figure, although, as Adams would later see, English electoral customs allowed even Mill to win a seat in Parliament. Adams recognized him as "a mighty weapon of defense for our cause in this country," but he could not find in the unassuming Mill the hero of a fascinating political biography like Tocqueville's. To him, the Frenchman was a model as well as a teacher. Like the historian he was one day to become, he responded most deeply when concrete example and theoretical exposition could be contemplated at once.

In the choice of Tocqueville as model and high priest, Henry Adams once again was simultaneously honoring and departing from a family pattern. He saw in Tocqueville the projection, in a new historical setting, of ideals and experience with which he was thoroughly at home. His own way of looking at politics and society, virtually bred into him, derived from eighteenth-century American liberalism, as expressed by figures like John Adams and Thomas Jefferson; the Adamses habitually combined the French rationalists' method of referring all questions to "natural" abstract principles and the English empiricists' insistence on limiting social objectives within the narrow area of historical continuity. Furthermore, the Adamses had known in America a coincidence of birthright, natural fitness, and majority choice like that which favored Tocqueville's political career and conditioned his political thought. The descendants of John Adams were deeply conscious of their distinguished birth, but thought it was their merit, rather, which should win them the official responsibilities that the people assigned. Their notions of personal merit and political good were blended with a sense of family that could hardly be avoided. When Charles Francis Adams wanted to instruct his sons, for example, he tried to find, between his abstract consideration of virtue and his empirical examination of history, some one individual in whom his political ideals had proved viable; admitting the likelihood of bias, the Minister did not conceal his judgment that his father John Quincy Adams presented "the only picture of a full-grown statesman" yet produced in America. This was not a singular judgment, but for all its plausibility, it suggested that even justifiable family pride could be a narrowing influence. Tocqueville helped rescue Henry Adams from a limited vision of his own family which, though it included great men and deeds within its purview, might have become a real confinement of the mind.

Tocqueville counteracted a tendency to confuse merit and inheritance which was abetted by the Adams family custom of memorializing their own past. John Quincy Adams set the precedent when he began to write a biography of his father. Political obligations kept him from finishing the job, but later generations did not have the same deterrent. Charles Francis Adams completed *The Life of John Adams* and edited from his father's famous diary the *Memoirs of John Quincy Adams.* In the next generation, Charles Francis Adams, Junior, wrote the biography of his father, and Brooks Adams wrote a life of John Quincy Adams which he suppressed, as well as "The Heritage of Henry Adams," a biographical introduction to the posthumous edition of his brother's late essays. Henry Adams' own historical work necessarily touched upon his ancestors' worth, but it did so with deliberate casualness. Except in passages of the *Education*, he skirted direct treatment of the family's exploits whenever he could. He seemed consciously to exorcise the tempting sin of family pride when he had the heroine of his satirical novel *Democracy* deride the trait as one that clashed with the manners of American equalitarianism and the mores of a society in which high status is won by merit only. But if he avoided the usual family way of acknowledging their birthright, he did not do so from ignorance. In his college days, he had proofread his father's edition of the works of John Adams, and by the time of his stay abroad, he knew enough of his grandfather's unpublished papers to realize he did not want the task of editing them. Deep attachments and wide knowledge went into the family feeling on which he drew when he responded to the great liberal spokesmen of his own time.

Ability to find outside his family the most provocative examples of political integrity and achievement was part of the intellectual and moral breadth that made Henry Adams a great historian. He did not cease to be his father's son when he looked beyond his immediate inheritance, any more than he stopped being himself after getting over the worst problems of his ego. A step-by-step defense of inherited opinions may indeed be read in the progress of his historical career. In his edition of *Documents Relating to New England Federalism,*

1800–1815, he put his grandfather's and the family's case against their right-wing opponents, but as an editor rather than a pleader. With his satirical biography *John Randolph*, he gave retort courteous to the Virginian's denunciation of the "old bear" from New England, John Adams, and "the cub," his son; even so, his choice of subject revealed the indirectness with which his family feeling worked. By the same working of inheritance, the Adams suspicion of contemporary applause reappeared in his innuendoes on Jefferson, whose political success depended on an ability to appeal to classes whom the Adamses could not reach. His father's phrases about his President-grandfather defined the future historian's attitudes, but Henry Adams' youthful discovery of Tocqueville prefigured his mature judgment that the American who had most "thoroughly constructed a foundation for his public life" was Albert Gallatin. The political virtues of Jefferson's Secretary of the Treasury were much like those of John Quincy Adams, and in *The Life of Albert Gallatin* Henry Adams elaborated his father's argument that statesmanship begins in morals and from that firm base proceeds to practical applications "in a continuous and systematic way." In looking for a man who met the standards to which he was brought up, he thrust himself into a world that was bigger than his family. Gallatin, not his grandfather, gave him the occasion to set forth the Adams principles in concrete detail and to picture with quiet exactness the Adams situation wherein birth, merit, and status were tightly bound together. In the *Gallatin*, he could objectify his inherited idea of Massachusetts and Virginia in the relation of Geneva and France; the matching of the Old Dominion and the Old Regime was close enough for his satiric purposes, and his image of an eighteenth-century heavenly city was the more believable for not having Boston as its subject:

In any other European country a family like this would have had a feudal organization, a recognized head, great entailed estates, and all the titles of duke, marquis, count, and peer which royal favor could confer or political and social influence could command. Geneva stood by herself. Aristocratic as her government was, it was still republican, and the parade of rank or wealth was not one of its chief characteristics. All the honors and dignities which the republic could give were bestowed on the Gallatin family with a prodigal hand; but its members had no hereditary title other than the quaint prefix of Noble, and the right to the further prefix of *de*, which they rarely used; they had no great family estate passing by the law of primogeniture, no family organization centring in and dependent on a recognized chief. Integrity, energy, courage, and intelligence were for the most part the only family estates of this aristocracy, and these were wealth enough to make of the little city of Geneva the most intelligent and perhaps the purest society in Europe.

By looking forward from the Civil War years to 1879, when Adams' first big work of history appeared, we can see more clearly the direction which the young man was taking. While earlier Adamses wrote as public men even in their private correspondence, Henry Adams wrote as a private citizen — whether he was a private secretary or a professional scholar who put his work before so limited an audience that publication served to conceal. Between the isolation of high diplomatic officials and the isolation of the artist toward which Henry Adams was moving, there was a temperamental difference which we can see in the Minister's generalized advice and the historian's more vigorous setting forth of a concrete historical situation. The difference between the father's Fourth of July letter and the son's representation of eighteenth-century Geneva ran deeper than style. It implied contrasting attitudes toward history. Charles Francis Adams, and his father and his grandfather before him, treated history as the sum of political experience, any segment of the past contributing its equal share to a single universal system of practical statecraft; they silently assumed that in a changing world political problems were eternally the same. Henry Adams subscribed with qualification to this idea of the presentness of the past. Though he wrote the *Gallatin* as a handbook of statesmanship, such as John Adams might have written about Pericles, he made clear in the same work another, almost opposite conception of the past in terms of its larger continuities. Insofar as he conceived the past as genetically making the present, the situation and opportunities of the past by definition could not recur; he had to assume, however silently he did so, the fundamental irrevocability of the past from which the present has evolved. At the same time that he drew the practical lessons from Gallatin's life, he was implying that his story was practically irrelevant to his own very different age. He did not give up his father's view that the use of historical study was to teach an individual through models, but he focused equally on the social group and the totality of the past, conceived as together making an evolutionary pattern according to inexorable law. The shift from "rationalist" to "historicist" was neither complete nor clear-cut, but it proceeded far enough by 1879 to transform the ideology of Charles Francis Adams into the utopia of his son.

The longer view of Henry Adams' coming of age may still keep 1863 at the center of the picture. His historicism had two facets: it expressed both a personal nostalgia and a conscious purpose of making reason dominate experience. The sense of possibilities forever lost, which is a part of anyone's becoming fixed in his mature character, was to be projected by Henry Adams upon the historical past, and he was to search his own past, his country's, and the world's for patterns of development that might be taken as necessary laws. Not only his nostalgia, but also the scientific interest which would inform his best historical writing and receive elaborate exposition in his late essays can be traced to the young student in London. For his purpose, he went behind Tocqueville and Mill to more abrasive philosophers like Spinoza and Hobbes, valuing the tough qualities of mind which made their names "known only as terms of reproach by the vulgar." Moving toward a determinism that conceived an exact science of social affairs in terms of the already existent physical sciences, he wrote to his brother Charles:

> [I firmly believe] that the laws which govern animated beings will be ultimately found to be at bottom the same with those which rule inanimate nature, and, as I entertain a profound conviction of the littleness of our kind, and of the curious enormity of creation, I am quite ready to receive with pleasure any basis for a systematic conception of it all.

The emotional flavor of young Henry Adams' interest in a future social science was obviously a reassertion of his old "contemptuous view of the world in general," except that in 1863 he was able without a qualm to dismiss his theorizing as "unpractical experimento-philosophico-historico-progressiveness." He had an inkling that even if he should get the science he wanted, it would have to be a descriptive science rather than a practical one, for he shortly declared that "fatalism" would work "very well for a theory of existence so long as it has no occasion to regulate the relation between one man and another." Even making that very restrictive condition, he preferred a sardonic fatalism to the scarcely more encouraging faith of his brother. Hazy belief in the spirit of the age and bland confidence that things would come out all right in the end had, after all, the same limitations as a reasoned determinism. He put himself on the side of the tough-minded.

Adams' ideas of social science and the moral order, even in their germinal stage, contained profound ambiguities. He treated social phenomena as the data of systematic knowledge, as if their relation to the observer's interest and desire had nothing to do with what would be observed. He thus implied that society develops by laws of its own, independent of the values and the will of men. Already he was reducing his estimate of the human ego, moving toward the idea of the merely passive manikin and the mask behind which he concealed himself in the *Education*. In one sense, his reduction of the ego was only a step toward the making of a science or the rendering of a complex social picture: he was arguing for a wise passiveness which was, in his case, richly creative. But by his own judgment, whenever he mistook the figure of the manikin for a sufficient symbol of the nature and capacity of man, he was letting himself be taken in by the illusion of hard-boiled logicality. Although he distinguished between the social theory of a scientific observer and that of an ethical agent, he did not see how fine the distinction is — and he sometimes did not even keep the distinction in mind. The ambiguities of his theory were resolved less by active reason than by the circumstance of his becoming an historian: the past, being determinate, lent itself to his determinist assumptions in a way that the present or future would not. It was not in him to make history as his ancestors had, but to contemplate it. Through giving expression to what he saw, if not through public action, he managed to get beyond passivity to the positive assertion of value.

In his dedication to science, as in his other characteristics, Henry Adams represented the continuity and the mutation of family tradition. His own account, in the *Education*, of his becoming an historical evolutionist, makes him out too narrowly a creature of the nineteenth century; he said then that he should "by rights" have been a Marxist and that he became in fact "the next best thing," a Comteist. But his inveterate tendency to social positivism was far older in him than his awareness of Auguste Comte. What he learned from

Comte or Marx a little later in his life, like his reading of
Spinoza and Hobbes or Tocqueville and Mill, became part
of an education already in progress. These authors enlarged
his mind without changing the basic form in which family
influence had shaped it. Behind Henry Adams we can make
out quasi-scientific views of society much like his own:

> The mutability and mutations of matter, and much more of
> the intellectual and moral world, are the consequences of laws
> of nature, not less without our power than beyond our compre-
> hension. While we are thus assured that, in one sense, nothing
> in human affairs will be perpetual or at rest, we ought to re-
> member at the same time, that the duration of our lives, the
> security of our property, the existence of our conveniences,
> comforts and pleasures, the repose of private life, and the tran-
> quillity of society, are placed in very great degree in human
> power. Equal laws may be ordained and executed.

The qualification that specifies the range of human power
within the limits of necessity spells the difference between
John Adams and his great-grandson. The second President's
beliefs reflected, and in turn encouraged, the socially engaged
interests of a practicing statesman; the future historian's
search for unalterable law reflected and encouraged his tendency to passive observation and lonely disinterestedness. The
Adams trait they shared was a scientific turn of mind with a
clear history for four generations — and something beyond
that, an obscure love of cosmic necessity that seems to reach
into the Calvinist Puritan past with its central, compelling
interest in the providence of an inscrutable, omnipotent
God.* Henry Adams' attempts to write scientifically of

---

*Yvor Winters' chapter on Adams in *The Anatomy of Nonsense* develops the
analogy between Adams' theories of history and Puritan cosmogony with enough
evidence to make clear why this unprovable thesis is so plausible. See also
Chapter VIII below, on Adams' late essays.

political, economic, and social development never became
coldly mechanical because a personal relation to the past
underlay his intellectual formulations; he could not help
reviving the dead even when he conceived his aim of instruction most narrowly. The ideas and attitudes of his enduring
character, as they became articulate during the Civil War
years, pointed not only to the future but to a long history
of their own.

The decisive years in London bore a more tangible fruit
than the characteristics which can be seen by hindsight. As
hopes for a public career at the bar and beyond died of
attrition, young Adams adjusted himself to his long held idea
of a happy alternative. "A quiet and a literary life" had
been the goal he set himself as far back as his graduation from
Harvard. Casually to announce a modest goal had been easy
enough for the ambitious boy who knew the value of appearing indifferent; settling to have his wish come true was quite
another thing. Even at the height of youthful exuberance,
Henry Adams felt a serious New Englander's aversion to
becoming "one of that butterfly party which New Yorkers
seem to consider their literary world." His ambivalent feelings toward a mainly literary career were calmed at the war's
end, when new opportunities offered themselves. Work
slackened, but his father's mission and his own secretaryship
hung on from month to month until the spring of 1868. In
the relative quiet of these later years in London, he made a
good start toward becoming a most unflighty man of letters.
Before he was done, he had placed four learned articles with
that organ of New England orthodoxy, the *North American
Review*. First came a debunking piece on the John Smith
legend. He had done most of the work and a complete draft
of this essay during his first year abroad, going every step of
the way from conception to publication under the guidance
of a family friend, the historian John Gorham Palfrey. What

he did on his own in 1866 was to rewrite and rewrite until
his prose was as solid as the research behind it. Besides his
latter-day epistle from Massachusetts to Virginia, he did
painstaking studies of British fiscal policy during the Napoleonic Wars which turned out to be, in effect, a pair of hard-
money homilies on the greenback question. Finally, he took
an excursion into the newest evolutionary science and did a
careful review of Sir Charles Lyell's tenth edition of his
Principles of Geology. He had good reason to be content with
the range and quality of his achievement and he began to
think about a career in the political press on his return. He
felt safe in giving up the threefold ideal he had once cherished.
Looking about the family, he decided that in postwar America
a functional division of labor would be the practical course.
In a letter to Charles, he announced his long-term plan:

> John is a political genius; let him follow the family bent.
> You are a lawyer, and with a few years' patience will be the
> richest and most respectable of us all. I claim my right to part
> company with you both. I never will make a speech, never run
> for an office, never belong to a party. I am going to plunge
> under the stream. For years you will hear nothing of any pub-
> lication of mine — perhaps never, who knows. I do not mean
> to tie myself to anything, but I do mean to make it impossible
> for myself to follow the family go-cart. . . . I shall probably re-
> main under water a long time. If you see me come up, it will
> be with an oyster and a pearl inside. If not, why — so!

The idea of plunging under the stream was a recurrent
one with Henry Adams, but happily the young man who
came home in 1868 gave himself a couple of years in a lighter
element. Without particular encouragement or approval
from his family, he turned his back on Quincy and set off for
Washington. Having established himself at the confluence of
American political currents, he postponed his dive beneath

the surface and prepared instead to "bask in the sun if it shines." He ceased to sound like his own grandfather in scorning the butterfly existence of the New York literati; his new voice expressed a will to hang on tight to his late-found youth. As late as 1870 and within a few months of his removal to Cambridge, he reported a lively, unanchoritic life to his English confidant, Gaskell:

> Our season has begun here, and I am prancing and flirting every night more or less, and every morning I am lazily political. The life amuses me as you can imagine it would. It is in fact a brilliant sort of butterfly existence, which cannot last very long, but may pass for some years still. . . . The only real trouble is that one is here eaten up in one's self-conceit, and wants that taking down which is so necessary for one's good.

Despite his words on the good of being taken down, the young man about Washington was radically changed from the boy who guiltily enjoyed his European tour a decade earlier. The younger Henry Adams really asked for rough treatment and got it from his brother, whereas an older Henry bluntly wrote to Charles, "For God's sake, let us go our ways and not try to be like each other." In his second campaign for independence, he knew what he was after.

As a gentleman-reformer, dressed in the intellectual trappings of a London clubman or even a Continental dandy, Adams cut a rare figure in Washington. Cultivating the look of irresponsibility with the casualness of an expert, he also applied himself to his first advanced course in writing. His political articles, covering legislative and financial developments with a weight of detail and a sharpness of style to match, gained him a notoriety which he enjoyed to the full. Indeed, they almost won him the crowning pleasure of a libel suit. Acting on a corollary to the family belief that popularity did not confer merit, he sought in his writing to "do something obnoxious and do it well." The desire to do it well became more important than the desire for influence, and to satisfy the aim for excellence, he had to develop his skills at satire and at storytelling. Against attacks he met with in the press, he hoped to "retaliate with a Dunciad." He congratulated himself for the "intolerably impudent political abuse" of his article on "The Legal Tender Act." He recognized his brashness in risking comparison with Aristophanes, but he could not resist making Thaddeus Stevens into a latter-day Cleon. With the straight scholarly exposition of his first economic articles behind him, he now proposed, with "The New York Gold Conspiracy," to subordinate discussion of the currency question to "telling a story which has no parallel." Story and satire advanced together, as the serious amateur theorist of finance gave way to the young man who had known Lord Houghton and Swinburne and the dazzle of literary life abroad. The Adams suspicion of popularity took on a new look: "*Epatez les bourgeois!*"

To be the dandyish wit of the heavy quarterlies was not the sum of Henry Adams' ambition. He was determined to write well, "to polish away [his] stilts and get down to firm ground," and he progressed toward his object in private correspondence even faster than in his published articles. Aware that he must cure "that lechery for publicity which always marks our young men," he found the best remedy to be his habit of writing to his English friend Gaskell. With Gaskell he could write freely to a contemporary and yet be mindful of a reader whom he might alienate by pompous affectation or, at the other extreme, by excessive informality. Writing in simpler language than he used for the press, he began to show a dramatic style of unusual subtlety. When he got on the old topic of his solitude, for example, he could do much more than make himself the butt of an expansive joke. For his

new audience, he added new dimensions to his story of loneliness:

> I sit down to begin you a letter, not because I have received
> one since my last, but because it is one of the dankest, foggiest,
> and dismalest of November nights, and, as usual when the sun
> does not shine, I am as out of sorts as a man may haply be, and
> yet live through it. Do you remember how, on such evenings
> we have taken our melancholy tea together in your room in
> Stratford Place? My heart would rejoice to do it now, but soli-
> tude is my lot. This season of the year grinds the very soul out
> of me. My nerves lose their tone; my teeth ache, and my cour-
> age falls to the bottomless bottom of infinitude. Death stalks
> about me, and the whole of Gray's grisly train, and I am afraid
> of them, not because life is an object, but because my nerves
> are upset.

Adams kept the tone of the sympathetic season and the mood
of reminiscence from becoming banal because he used these
rather conventional props in a fresh and complicated dramatic
monologue. Adapting the cadences and the chief device of
Hamlet's "What a piece of work is a man!" speech, he conveyed both the poignancy and the irony of his situation. He
portrayed the grand terrors of his isolation as if he were imitating Hamlet, and then underscored the incongruity that so
vast a picture of chaos should proceed from the illusions of
bad nerves. The final twist of irony, the suggestion that this
modern terror is rather thin in being so largely a mere nervous
illusion, points forward to Eliot's "My nerves are bad tonight.
Yes, bad," in *The Waste Land*.

The loneliness that remained so important a theme in
Henry Adams' letters indicates that for him there was something drastically wanting in a career of free-lance journalism.
Enjoyable as he found his "Bohemian" life, he could not,
while living it, discover any purpose for his existence. "Bohemian" was a just adjective, not because the District of

Columbia bore any resemblance to the *quartier latin*, but because rootlessness characterized his life there. Equally pleased
and dismayed, the young man felt within himself a conflict
between stern provincialism and cosmopolitan taste. His
discomfort can easily be emphasized: he had an honest
"foolish weakness for combining social and literary success."
He certainly had no intention of quitting journalism when
he wrote in the spring of 1870, "I have wasted the winter
writing for newspapers and dabbling in politics, and am only
deeper and deeper in them as time goes on, but except for
the experience there is little satisfaction in it, though it suits
my blackguard tastes. . . . I want nothing and fight only for
the amusement of fighting."

The following summer's trip to Europe made clear how far,
in his second youth, Henry Adams had advanced beyond the
boy of ten years earlier. From his first European journey, he
could claim a vague initiation in sense and sentiment. Now
he received "the last lesson — the sum and term of education."
At Bagni di Lucca, he attended his sister's deathbed through
her ten days of agony from lockjaw. His final report on this
introduction to tragedy turns upon himself the image of
bodily violence that he had so lightly used as a boy in England:

> He had passed through thirty years of rather varied exper-
> ience without having once felt the shell of custom broken. He
> had never seen Nature — only her surface — the sugar-coating
> that she shows to youth. Flung suddenly in the face, with the
> harsh brutality of chance, the terror of the blow stayed by him
> thenceforth for life, until repetition made it more than the will
> could struggle with; more than he could call on himself to
> bear.

What he later called accidental education, unplanned and of
no obvious use to the mind or society, bore its fruit more
slowly than his education as an Adams. But the capacity for

felt experience and immediate involvement in sense and emotion lay quietly behind all his work. Historically to revive the dead was not just a process of intellectual reconstruction, and for this reason his sister's death was indeed the last lesson of his preparatory years.

In the midst of his ordeal as a helpless witness to suffering, he received a letter from Charles William Eliot, offering him an assistant professorship at Harvard. He would not be shaken from his chosen career, pointless though it might seem, and he therefore declined to exchange political journalism for medieval history. When, on his return to Boston, the offer was renewed by Eliot and urgently supported by his family, Henry Adams capitulated. "For the first time since 1861 his father interposed," and once again a period of independence came to an end. This time, however, there was no reversion to the role of private secretary.* He was about to enter upon a new kind of freedom in the enjoyment of a career that fully satisfied him, at least while he pursued it. Writing surreptitiously to Gaskell during an official faculty meeting, he demonstrated genuine pleasure in his complaints:

> My happy carelessness of life for the last ten years has departed, and I am a regular old carthorse of the heaviest sort. As for society, I have not seen the hem of a female garment since I came out here. Life has resolved itself into editing and professing. I always swore I would never descend to work, but it is done. Lo! the poor fallen one!

His happy carelessness of life was replaced by something better. The twenty years of his career as an historian are omitted from close scrutiny in the *Education*, and the omission is right because the two decades of his great imaginative contributions to the art of history require examination of his work

---

*The following year Charles Francis Adams went to the Geneva Arbitration Conference with Brooks Adams, aged twenty-three, as his private secretary.

rather than of the details of his living. Halfway through that distinguished career he wrote Gaskell in the tone of one whose youth had passed into calm, productive maturity:

> ... If I felt a perfect confidence that my history would be what I would like to make it, this part of life — from forty to fifty — would be all I want. There is a summer-like repose about it; a self-contained, irresponsible, devil-may-care indifference to the future as it looks to younger eyes; a feeling that one's bed is made, and one can rest on it till it becomes necessary to go to bed for ever; in short, an *editio princeps* quality to it, with a first class French binding, which only a Duke, or a very rich Earl of ancient foundation, could feel at twenty-five.

The years of Adams' middle life included his final migration to Washington and, in the terrible suicide of his wife, his final confrontation of tragedy. They were also the years in which he found fulfillment through mastery of his calling. As an historian, he put himself in intellectual command of the fields of law and statesmanship to which he had been brought up and from which his temperament and his times seemed to have cut him off. Attaining the third of his ingrained ideals, he became the man who exists for us today. As a man of letters he achieved his work, found his serenity, and endured his fate.

Chapter II

INTERPRETIVE SCHOLARSHIP

HENRY ADAMS' career as an historian began in the fall of 1870, when his appointment as Harvard's first professor of medieval history stirred the placid Cambridge atmosphere with mild surprise. He did not care to stir it more and restricted his Cambridge activities mainly to his college study in Wadsworth House and to his classrooms. Even such brilliant colleagues as the younger Holmes and William James did not provide a society he particularly craved, although he seemed to enjoy participating in their "club" of young intellectuals in the days before he had an independent establishment. Having been brought into the Harvard community, he still resisted becoming a full-fledged member of it. After his marriage to Marian Hooper in 1872, he moved across to Boston. The distance to his home on Marlborough Street was less than that from Boston to Quincy, but the effect of psychological removal was much the same. For an Adams, the Charles River served as well as the Neponset to objectify the personal barrier between the man and the scene of his worldly affairs. A long day of teaching, study, and editing chores for the *North American Review* (the editorship of which had been tied in with his appointment) was quite enough of the university. He took his duties seriously, but he had little time, less desire, and no obligation to exploit Harvard as a social milieu.

Some critics have reproved Adams for neglecting his colleagues, but none has suggested that he neglected his work.
The work was essential, for whatever his assets of intelligence
and imagination, every great historian must found his labors
on empirical scholarship. Fact-finding is in large part drudg-
ery, but to the creative mind it is also both the stimulus and
the consequence of new ideas. As information, fresh facts
turn stale all too quickly, but as discoveries they continue to
give evidence of eager search and the honest attempt to speak
with genuine authority. In scholarship, the hope of glory
matters less than plainer virtues. It was industry and the
energy of a fully committed mind which took Adams through
the hundreds of volumes that made him expert in the field that
he claimed to approach as a perfect amateur. The novitiate
of historical study he had served in Germany had seemed a
painfully blind digression, but the boy's waste of the 1850's
was redeemed in the 1870's by the man. He became one of
the innovators who introduced the German seminar method
in American education, even as John Quincy Adams had been
the first to bring home from Germany the lecture method of
teaching. As an editor, he established the criteria of German
historical scholarship for his reviews of the important histories
then being published. And as a student himself, in pursuit of
the Middle Ages, he read prodigiously, sometimes four books
a day (or night). His ability to cut through the bristling exterior of German scholarship to its vital contribution to learning cannot easily be traced to his quasi-academic sojourn in
Berlin: removal in place and time proved to be what he
needed, as though some infrared register of his mind required
slow development in the dark. In the country where learning
was most professional he had apparently been sensitized
with an ideal of competence that now showed through his easy
love of amateurism. As he said to Gaskell, he had descended
to work.

Adams' diligence quickly brought him to the vanguard among historical scholars. His colleagues may have seemed provincial to him even when they weren't, but his aversion to provincialism worked entirely for the good when it helped him to form his rigorous intellectual standards. In teaching undergraduates, he introduced the materials of cultural history as essentials for any picture of the Middle Ages, but he still felt the primary basis of scholarly understanding to lie elsewhere — in the painstaking mastery of fundamentals like the history of institutions, for which his seminars provided a training ground. The immediate literary result of his professorial years was *Essays in Anglo-Saxon Law*, a collection of monographs that grew from the work of his first graduate seminar. The book appeared in 1876 as the first American monument of German research technique and of the co-operative approach to scholarship which Adams regarded as appropriate to any advance in civilized accomplishment. It contained the theses of three promising graduate students, Henry Cabot Lodge, Ernest Young, and J. Laurence Laughlin, and a general essay of introduction by Adams himself. From the weighty bibliography at the beginning to the seventy-five-page appendix of "select cases," the volume conspicuously displayed the new learning. It was even dedicated to the godfather of the new scholarship, Charles William Eliot. Eliot's recruitment of Adams to the Harvard faculty had obviously produced "results."

Production in scholarship, as in anything else, implies a set of ideas of which the producers may or may not be fully aware. Behind its academic paraphernalia, the *Essays* presented an interpretation of history which, though still new in America, bore a sound English and German pedigree and was safe enough to become the prevailing academic pattern of the rising generation. Very simply, the "germ" theory of history furnished historians with the thesis that modern democratic institutions could all be traced genetically (and hence causally) back to the wilderness assemblies of Tacitus' Germany. It was a synthesis of many strains in nineteenth-century scholarship — the research of the Grimm brothers in comparative philology, studies of primitive institutions like those of Sir Henry Maine, the evolutionary theory of Herbert Spencer, and the racism that was corollary to all these disciplines. In America, Herbert Baxter Adams of Johns Hopkins became the most active proponent of the theory. An evangelist of institutional history, he had inscribed on the wall of his seminary study and the cover of the learned journal he founded a credo taken from the English historian Edward A. Freeman: "History is past politics and politics is present history." Freeman confirmed the international popularity of the new approach when he visited Johns Hopkins in 1882 and spoke on behalf of Herbert Baxter Adams' favorite ideas:

> . . . American institutions are part of the general institutions of the English people, as those are again part of the general institutions of the Teutonic race, and those are again part of the general institutions of the whole Aryan family.
>
> . . . The two main ties between the motherland and her great colony are the two main results of community of stock; that is, community of language and community of law.

Historians exchanged mutual congratulations as they found themselves united on a theory which enhanced their popular value in a nationalistic and evolution-conscious age. Their synthesis had the advantage of being both primitivist and progressive: it put the golden age both in the past and in the future and, so long as community of stock could be assumed as a central value, the present gleamed attractively, too.

Henry Adams took on the ideology of his profession. In 1876, the year of the *Essays*, he addressed himself to the general public in a Lowell Lecture on "The Primitive Rights of Women." Beginning with the premise that the works of

Homer could be read as treatises on ancient marriage law, he developed the theme of women's rights among the Achaeans to the full-stop chord of his conclusion:

> ... The institution of marriage, the law of descent in the male line, the importance of the family and the authority of the father, are characteristics so distinct in the whole Aryan group as to countenance the idea that this was in fact the real origin of the race, and that the primitive Aryan stock broke away from the original communal society with no other distinctive principle. Perhaps the institution of the family was the means of their extraordinary success, and of the domination which they established wherever they set their feet. Historically, the family is but an example of the energetic realization of those natural affections and that passion of property which lie deepest of all passions in humanity. The race which followed this path with the most vigor must have been the strongest race and the best fitted to conquer. Such a race had a natural instinct for law; its taste for the acquisition of private property required development of legal principles; its faculty of adopting reforms in society proves its intellectual versatility; and what are all these but the same characteristics which appear again ages afterward, in the greatest of all the works of their descendants, — in the civil law of Rome, and in the common law of England?

Experience of men and the world was to change Adams' mind about many of the Victorian shibboleths he pronounced in 1876. Nevertheless, these ideas about home and family, the rule of law, the competition of races, and the beneficence of acquisitiveness were part of the intellectual equipment he used in the practice of research. The enthusiastic statements of the Lowell Lecturer give a clue not only to the popular currents of thought, but also to the morale of the disciplined historical worker. The "germ" theory was indispensable to an authority on "The Anglo-Saxon Courts of Law," for along with its intellectual content it carried a set of demanding technical requirements. Adams might keep the rhetoric of the public forum when he entered the chambers of legal history, but he had to adopt a more conservative line of argument. He could not freely exploit a single document like the *Odyssey* from which a whole world might be deduced; he had to build his essay on the whole corpus of Anglo-Saxon documents, even though the increase of data would limit the range of possible conclusions. The genuine academician might be pleased to settle just one small point of controversy, to prove, for example, that the "hundred," as court and as territorial district, was the administrative unit of the Anglo-Saxons as it had been for all the primitive Germans. Sifting all the evidence and the learned commentaries on that evidence, Adams showed how the new theory led to careful research as well as public oratory.

Rigorous exercise in the conventions of his craft energized the whole mind of Henry Adams and brought to the point of formulation ideas which went far beyond the conventional. In the process of scholarly research, he began unconsciously to blend his inherited way of thought with that of his own time. The general ideas which informed his best historical work and gave rise to his extensive speculations on the theory of history began as limited perceptions — perceptions at which he arrived only after profound immersion in the facts of a particular historical situation. This immersion made the difference between Adams' way of testing political precepts in the actualities of history and an approach that could be more simply labeled as utilitarian. The utilitarian method can be seen in most of Adams' early essays, written as they were to help with political questions of the moment. The Washington journalist's two annual articles on "The Session" were at once reports on Congress and pleas for reform, as his earlier pieces on British finance had been pointed at the current American problem of greenback inflation. There were dangers in his double interest in past politics and present history: the assumption that the present can easily profit from study of the past is a common incentive to historical investigation, but it has the frequent result of making the past a sort of mirror which returns only as much light upon the present as is directed to it. When the past is conceded no chance of generating a light of its own, the interaction of past and present which makes history interesting as well as useful fails to take place. The utilitarian in history usually misses the complexities which would make it hard for him to prove whatever he wants. Rigid adherence to present purpose may work the same effect as its opposite, the altogether disinterested quest for the past: it may blind the historian to the ultimate paradox, that history never, as well as always, repeats itself. Because Henry Adams could not eradicate his deep moral commitment to his own society, his professional commitment to finding the past as it really was could not be other than fruitful. In "The Anglo-Saxon Courts of Law," he plunged for the first time into the almost unlimited details of the past; the ideas which then freely floated to the surface are what distinguish his piece from the countless others which, in the coming generation, used the same historical techniques to advance the same outmoded thesis.

Adams began by asserting that the early Germans organized their state by "popular" institutions, "embracing rich and poor alike." Later scholarship takes a less simple view, but in 1876, Adams could push at once into the intricacies of judicial history with a confidence bred of conventionality:

> The student of history who now attempts to trace, through two thousand years of vicissitudes and dangers, the slender thread of political and legal thought, no longer loses it from sight in the confusion of feudalism, or the wild lawlessness of the Heptarchy, but follows it safely and firmly back until it leads him out upon the wide plains of northern Germany.

The thread he chose to follow was not simply the existence of the "hundred" court, but the modern idea of the democratic state. He argued that the hundred was a geographical as well as a communal entity, that the "state" was the political unit of the Germans, the hundred its territorial and administrative subdivision in which all free men participated. His stated purpose, and perhaps his only conscious one, was to show the factual accuracy of statements like these. Once he established what the Anglo-Saxon courts were, his students could discuss the laws of property and family and the "due process" which rounded out the picture. The whole collection of essays would then offer a scholarly version of the professor's Lowell Lecture.

Interesting complications set in at once. Taken together, the institutions Adams described made up a primitive federal system. His hypothetical Anglo-Saxon democracy, with its territorial state and federal principle, might expand on American lines if conquest brought several such states into an enlarged federation; on the other hand, if a military victory were prosecuted in the true Teutonic manner, grimmer possibilities were at hand:

> . . . It is obvious that if military conquest, under the influence of foreign example, ever took the shape of consolidation, so that two or more states were united in one, and their popular assemblies ceased to exist independently, and became merged in one great assembly of the entire nation, such a change might easily give birth to a military monarchy, a territorial aristocracy, a feudal anarchy, or almost any other form of transition.

The scholar was referring to the Frankish consolidation of national power under Charlemagne, but he spoke as a first-hand witness to the aftermath of violent unification through civil war. The same autumn of 1876 saw publication of Adams' monograph and the election of President Hayes, whose advent to power meant the removal of the last occupation troops from the South and the end of Radical Reconstruction. Adams' own convictions showed in his choice of language here, for despotism, oligarchy, anarchy, and feudalism had since the time of John Adams been interchangeable terms for the family's conception of political evil. The historian concluded that the fusing of several sovereign states might account for an immense growth of power, but must inevitably do so at the cost of democratic institutions: "From the moment the small state became merged in a great nation, the personal activity of the mass of free men in politics became impossible, if for no other reason than for the mere difficulties of distance."

Adams seemed to back Montesquieu in the eighteenth-century theorist's classical explanation for the failure of geographically extended democracies.* It was also Montesquieu's belief, as Hamilton cited it in the Ninth *Federalist*, that the problem of extending popular institutions had been historically solved by the invention of the "confederate republic." The French philosopher adduced the Lycian Confederacy as the "model" by which to argue his point; the nineteenth-century historian, however, found models from ancient Greece less rewarding than cases from the relatively nearer history of western Europe to which he traced modern institutions. Just such a case emerged when Adams described English development from the primitive Anglo-Saxon states to the federal system of Alfred the Great.

These large political issues stemmed from Adams' proof that the hundred of the Anglo-Saxons had always signified a district as well as a group. He marshaled evidence from the entire body of early charters to show that courts with the hundred procedure and districts of the appropriate size existed as far back as the records go, even though the hundred went by

*Adams qualified his adherence to Montesquieu with one of his most patent Americanisms. Having made it clear that the organization of a consolidated government necessarily left out the freemen, he took solace in adding that at least the national assembly would retain its function as a supreme court!

other names, principally "shire," in the earliest times. Under
the unified kingdom of Alfred (871–899), skin-deep legal reforms changed the terminology, but little else: "The State of
the seventh century became the Shire of the tenth, while the
Shire of the seventh century became the Hundred of the
tenth." The verbal changes that came under Alfred had
masked the previous existence of the hundred and the shallow-
ness of Alfred's reforms. Most historians thought the English
king tried to copy the Frankish example and missed the point
of Charlemagne's hundred constitution; deliberately or not,
Alfred neglected to abolish the state governments which inter-
vened between the nation and the local district. Rather, he
pushed to a new height the pristine federalism he had found.
Shire and hundred, state and district, were preserved, while
the Witan, as the judicial assembly of the nation was called,
developed rapidly along traditional lines. Adams admitted
that on the level of the Witan, at least, the complement of the
assembly was thoroughly aristocratic, but he noted a germinal
separation of powers, whereby the king or the king's agent
was merely presiding officer and not a member of the court,
and felt that this made up for the aristocratic trend: "All
these courts — the hundred, the shire, and the Witan — were
mere adaptations of the primitive organic type of popular
assembly. Nor did the Anglo-Saxons ever entirely lose sight
of this, their original democratic starting-point." The kingdom of Alfred the Great still qualified as an example of republican confederacy. In thus bringing Montesquieu up to
date, Adams made his peace with the authors of the *Federalist*
papers and with his own family conscience.

Even in a professional monograph, Adams aimed to do
more than argue. He had a story to tell, and he was able to
manipulate the difficult details of his subject matter so that
the intricacies of his argument became the complications of
his narrative. At the heart of his dramatic interpretation
was the telling flaw of Alfred's "typical" English conservatism.

The king was indifferent not only to the reforms of Charlemagne which would have undermined popular government, but also to the positive changes toward administrative efficiency which might have ensured the lasting vitality of free institutions. Alfred brought in neither the system of appeals nor the equity procedures with which Continental jurisprudence had improved the crude stiffness of German legal structure. He introduced no devices but names to modify a system "which, by common consent, even in his time, was utterly unequal to the public wants." With the great chance to be that original lawgiver whom the Anglo-Saxons never were to have, Alfred did nothing to assure coherence in his "confederate republic." The only ground of unity was his strong personal leadership. His failure to rise to the needs of his time provided a discouraging lesson in statesmanship, for if the state did not make good on its judicial obligations, private interests would be quick to usurp its functions. The gradual shift to extra-legal arbitrations did not change the letter of the constitution and the manorial lords did not yet exercise official power, but society had lost confidence in its unreformed institutions, its judges, and its law. In the long run, difficulties of geographical extension were less important than the human failure to devise adequate instruments of self-government. The Henry Adams of the *History* was foreshadowed in the scholar who showed, in the barely civilized world of the Anglo-Saxons, not just the germination of modern democracy, but also the enigma of whether "democratic power" is "a contradiction in terms."

Adams' story did not end when Alfred missed his chance to forge an adequate governmental machinery, for the unified state of the Anglo-Saxons gave no signs of immediate breakdown. On the contrary, England entered upon a flourishing time never equaled in her past and destined to last almost a century — this in an era when the Continental German state was disrupted by war and the crumbling of public institutions.

The Franks had had the advantage in the organization of power because they had taken the path of consolidation instead of confederation, but their uncompartmented state seemed amidst a sea of troubles to capsize all at once. Following his history into the tenth century, Adams worked variations in the "germ" theory which his fellow scholars were to make in the coming generation. First, his emphatic distinction of Anglo-Saxon history from the main course of Teutonic development was to be taken up in the 1890's when German and British imperialism began to clash and belief in the happy family of races came up for reconsideration; his own motive was not to choose among empires, but to contrast democracy and military autarchy.* Far more important was his version of the hundred years' grace that England enjoyed in isolation from the Continent. Here, even more than in his other Americanisms of interpretation, Adams points toward the historiographical revolution effected by Frederick Jackson Turner. Turner, who took his Ph.D. under Herbert Baxter Adams at Johns Hopkins, put a "grass-roots" interpretation on the existent theory and began the movement which traced all valuable American institutions back to our own wilderness democracies. For compelling historical reasons, Americans quickly preferred their own frontier to the wide plains of northern Germany as a source of democratic virtues, and a host of scholars crowded into the path which Turner first opened. Henry Adams was to face the problem of this interpretation in his own way in the *History*, but in his essay on the Anglo-Saxon courts he foreshadowed his later answer. The seeming exception to European history proved to be only a delay. The influence on England of Continental develop-

---

*It must be pointed out that the "germ" theory was never much taken up in the Latin and eastern European countries, though to the north and west it was overwhelmingly popular. Until the beginnings of imperial conflict in the nineties, few devotees of the theory objected to identifying the playing fields of Eton with those of Teutoberger Forest. Their main object was to connect national origins with the primitive, rather than the Greco-Roman and Catholic, past.

ments was sure, however slow: "Both consolidation and dis-integration came at last, only in forms somewhat less mis-chievous in their immediate effects, and much more beneficial in their ultimate results, than was the case in the Empire and in France."

The consequences of Alfred's tragic failure of statesmanship were subtle, often invisible to naked observation, but they loomed into plain sight at last. Adams dated the disintegra-tion of the Anglo-Saxon state from a grant of official jurisdic-tion to the Abbey of St. Augustine shortly after Edward the Confessor (1042–1066) came to the throne. Asserting that a private jurisdiction was first conferred at so late a date, Adams had to prove his point against the undivided opinion of con-temporary scholars. To do so, he showed that charters before 1042 did not bestow *sacu* and *socn* on anyone ("sac and soc" being the conventional phrase in grants of jurisdiction), but only *socn*. Legalistically and philologically, that term could be proved to mean not a right to judge, but a right to the pro-ceeds of litigation and to freedom from entry by the king's agents into one's own lands. In his purely technical approach, Adams made two dubious assumptions — that the administra-tion of justice was a coveted privilege rather than a necessary burden, and that the perquisites of office might be given away when the functions of office had not already gone. The nice point that there was no perfect grant of jurisdiction before 1042 overrode for Adams the whole tendency of circumstantial evi-dence. Admitting that extra-constitutional developments had for at least a century been going in the direction of feudalism, he still clung to the advantage of technicalities whereby he could assign the constitutional revolution to a specific time and agent. Not that he wanted to blame the denouement of Anglo-Saxon history on Edward alone. He held lords and commons responsible, too. In the last analysis, the people brought their fate upon themselves by overlooking the little point that mattered most to a constitutionalist:

It mattered not so much to them whether the king's, the abbot's, or the lord's reeve presided over their court, as it did that whoever presided should not abuse his power. But the theory of the constitution was irretrievably lost. Justice was no longer a public trust, but a private property. The recognition of the legality of private tribunals for the church was a recognition of the legality of private tribunals in general. . . . The entire judicial system of England was torn in pieces; and a new theory of society, known as feudalism, took its place.

"The Anglo-Saxon Courts of Law" was the first and in many respects the only work Henry Adams ever undertook with a purely professional purpose. The book which his essay introduced was by and for historical scholars, written in accordance with specifications laid down by the guild. There were dangers in professionalization, and Adams sensed how narrow a margin existed between virtuoso scholarship and pedantry. He took time from his teaching and research to compose an epitaph for himself in twelfth-century Latin. Embarrassed, as he later put it, "at shedding his lifeblood for the sublime truths of Sac and Soc," he remained proud of the Latin which showed his mastery of other than barbarian sources of his culture:

HIC JACET

HOMUNCULUS SCRIPTOR

DOCTOR BARBARICUS

HENRICUS ADAMS

ADAE FILIUS ET EVAE

PRIMO EXPLICUIT

SOCNAM.*

*Here lies
a little man who was a writer
a master of barbarian lore
Henry Adams
son of Adam and Eve
who first explained
socn.

Despite his anxiety, the *homunculus scriptor* had proved that the scholarly protocol of the doctors had its uses. How great they were may be measured in the difference between Adams' monograph on the Anglo-Saxon courts and his tour de force on "The Primitive Rights of Women." In a popular lecture he was free of strict professional requirements; reverting to the easy generalizations of popular science, he proclaimed the Aryan "the strongest race and the best fitted to conquer," partly because "its faculty of adopting reforms in society proves its intellectual versatility." Closer application to his craft had led Adams to question the popular thesis and come to an opposite conclusion, that the tragedy of the Anglo-Saxon era was that it offered "not one example of an original and progressive lawgiver." The scholar-critic in Adams spoke with a deeper, more commanding voice than the dilettante-reformer. His tone was solemn and occasionally pedantic, but it was the tone of thoughtfulness and intellectual authority.

Adams' questioning the conclusions but not the premises of conventional scholarly theorizing marks the point to which his historical imagination had now developed. Intended to fill a very small niche, at best, "The Anglo-Saxon Courts" did a lot more than establish facts and put them together in a usual way. His essay went beyond the "germ" theory to become an exposition of federal republicanism more comparable to Hamilton's Ninth *Federalist* than to other such reconstructions of past institutions. It shows its descent from John Adams' *Dissertation on the Canon and the Feudal Law*, which, in the robust voice of eighteenth-century liberalism, asserts the authority of the civil government against all usurpers whatever. As a critique of administrative fossilization, it resembles Brooks Adams' *The Theory of Social Revolutions*, published almost four decades later. But if placing the work in the family line suggests its richness, fixing the moment of its composition reveals another side. With due respect for the complexities of honest scholarship, Adams tried to avoid making his story a fable to serve his own political platform, but the professional historian was also the amateur politician. At a time when the Granger Movement was pressing its battle against the power of railroad monopolies, Adams joined with like-minded friends at Delmonico's Hotel in New York to organize a third party dedicated to the reform of party machinery and the civil service. His analysis of public institutions apart from the social developments to which he assigned final historical responsibility was not due merely to the scholarly conventions within which he worked. He transcended the limitations of his accepted form, but not of his own mind. The mind could grow, however, and meanwhile he used his habits of political observation and judgment to see responsively the details of the past. Naturally, his habitual way of perceiving a past situation affected his ultimate conception of it; objectivity on either score is always only approximate. His lively perceptions proceeded in what seemed an order dictated by the past, and his over-all conception shaped a work of imaginative excellence on a moral and esthetic level where "objectivity" does not exist. Among the legal remains of Anglo-Saxon society, he had found not only facts, but a story with a beginning, a middle, an end, and an important relevance. On the chosen ground of his profession, he had mastered the techniques of critical investigation and proved his ability not only to test historical facts, but to organize his knowledge.

☆   ☆   ☆

Adams enjoyed charting a new path but chafed at following it once the period of exploration was over. With the same indifference with which he had given up the utilitarian historical essay, he turned from the history of ancient institutions and the standard research monograph. The same trait showed in his teaching as in his writing. After a couple of years of giving the basic courses in medieval history at Harvard, he dropped all but his seminar and moved on to the field of American colonial history. Two years later, he dropped this also, in order to undertake a course in American history from 1789 to 1840. In each of the areas he first penetrated, he left handpicked students of his own in charge: Ernest Young got the post of teaching medieval history and Henry Cabot Lodge, colonial American. On the eve of his resignation in 1877, he was planning a course on American history to be given jointly by Lodge and himself: Lodge would present the Federalist and he would present the Jeffersonian point of view. The literary evidences of this course which Adams never gave throw light on his effectiveness as a teacher, his authority as a scholar, and his convictions as a citizen.

In proposing to speak for the Jeffersonian side, Adams was not merely nominating himself a devil's advocate. The boy who called on Garibaldi had, despite a Bostonian squeamishness, seen the Italian democrat as heroic and unpretentious, not at all "vulgar or demagogic." The young private secretary recognized that his country's democratic cause had its true allies among the stolid middle classes and depressed workers of Great Britain, rather than in the elegant London society where he should have liked to cut a figure. In postwar America, where differences between the parties were slight and a superficial program of reform constituted the only independent cause he was aware of, Adams' liberalism could not effectively be distinguished from political gentility. Earlier times gave clearer issues: extreme Federalists, Hamilton for one, had read John Adams out of the party when he made peace with revolutionary France in 1799; they gave the same treatment to John Quincy Adams when he supported Jefferson's Embargo in 1808. In the actualities of political controversy, the Adams conception of national good several times took them from the party of their class and renewed the collaboration with Jefferson that dated from 1776. Henry Adams was now concerned with an epoch in which his vicarious past was most alive. The American interpreter of Alfred the Great might run the risk of pedantry; the dialectical opponent of Henry Cabot Lodge ran the risk of being too deeply committed.

The partner to Adams' historical dialectics was twelve years his junior, a student in his very first class at Harvard. Lodge had a temperament much more worldly than reflective and an excellent mind that pretty much made up in training for what it lacked in delicacy. As an ideal complement to Adams' own personality, he was the kind of student whom the professor tried hardest to reach. The casual undergraduate found himself confronted by a teacher who roused not only interest, but opposition; as Lodge afterward recalled, his faculties suddenly awakened, he "discovered that it was the keenest of pleasures to use one's mind." While a law student, Lodge wanted to do graduate work in history too. Asking his teacher's opinion, he learned that Adams gave stimulation more freely than advice. The master told his would-be follower that the question to ask about "the historico-literary line" is, "Can you make it *pay*? either in money, reputation, or any other solid value." Adams continued by drawing in some ironic perspectives on his own calling:

> Now if you will think for a moment of the most respectable and respected products of our town of Boston, I think you will see at once that this profession does pay. No one has done better and won more in any business or pursuit, than has been acquired by men like Prescott, Motley, Frank Parkman, Bancroft, and so on in historical writing; none of them men of extraordinary gifts, or who would have been likely to do very much in the world if they had chosen differently. What they did can be done by others.

Further, there is a great opening here at this time. Boston is running dry of literary authorities. Any one who has the ability can enthrone himself here as a species of literary lion with ease, for there is no rival to contest the throne. With it, comes social dignity, European reputation, and a foreign mission to close.*

Since this letter has earned Adams a certain disrepute in quarters where the boundary between irony and cynicism is not clearly marked, it is well to place beside it the more straightforward letter he wrote to Lodge a year later. When his pupil was totally discouraged after a first "wallowing" in historical knowledge, Adams responded in complete seriousness. Discussing the intellectual equipment which the history student should try to develop, he enjoined Lodge to be patient in the quest for basic skills. The ultimate aim was for quality. As to "making it pay," the man who later computed the cost of his passion for history as about equal to keeping a good racing stable defined the place this question always kept at the bottom of his moral scale:

> . . . I thought, and still think you were trying to cover too wide a field of mere fact. For the present I was much less inclined to trouble myself about the amount you learned than about the method you were learning. I have, no doubt, more respect for knowledge, even where knowledge is useless and worthless, than for mere style, even where style is good; but unless one learns beforehand to be logically accurate and habitually thorough, mere knowledge is worth very little. At best it never can be more than relative ignorance, at least in the study of history. So I wanted you only to read a few specimen books, not large ones either, which would give you an idea of

---

*Of the historians whom Adams listed as exemplars of his literary calling, he never became as close to any of the famous Boston trio as to George Bancroft, the Göttingen-trained scholar and Jacksonian politician from western Massachusetts. Bancroft was to be a help to Adams in his researches and one of the select critics to whom Adams sent the privately printed draft of his *History*. Ernest Samuels suggests that it may have been Bancroft who got Adams the chance to edit the Gallatin papers.

historical methods, and I wanted you to learn to use Latin and German with facility, and I suggested Anglo-Saxon, which I am studying myself and which is quite amusing. Nor do I see the necessity for your working very laboriously even at this. You will work hard enough one of these days if you ever get interested in the study; if not, what does it matter? The question for you is not by any means whether you can do a great deal, but whether that which you choose to do, be it much or little, shall be done perfectly, so as to give you credit worth your having. . . .

But I suppose you are pestered by the question which bothers us all when we are at the beginning of a career, especially if, as is usually the case with Americans, we are a little inclined to thinking too much about ourselves. I mean the question of whether a given line of occupation is going to pay, whether you are really ever going to make your scheme work. I am not going to enter into any argument in favor of the course you selected. I don't care to take such a responsibility as that of giving advice to anyone on a matter which involves the occupation of a life-time. If you have seriously become so far discouraged as to think of changing your line of work, and if you have found any other profession or occupation which satisfies you, I have nothing to say against it. But if, in spite of all discouragements you still think a literary life best suited for you, then I hope that we may begin work next term with rather a more definite aim and better defined instruments.

Lodge not only joined in the project on Anglo-Saxon law, but also became Adams' assistant on the *North American Review*. His initiation into historical criticism went hand in hand with daily instruction in the art of plain writing. The young man showed amazing energy. While teaching, preparing his doctoral dissertation, getting ready for his bar examination, clerking in the law offices of Ropes and Gray, tending his job as assistant editor, and heading a household that already included two children, he also began collecting and examining documents for a biography of his great-grandfather George Cabot! This biography, published in 1877, was one of the intellectual landmarks of the Adams-Lodge relation. Vigorously setting forth the Federalist view of our early history, Lodge argued that John Quincy Adams' switch to the Jeffersonian ranks in 1808 was his "fatal blunder," and that the Hartford Convention, at which Cabot played a leading role, stood as a great monument to the tradition of resistance to oppression. No matter how respectful he might be as a student, Lodge could not defend his Tie-Wig Federalist ancestor and still pull his punches against the House of Adams. Disinterested fact-finding did not necessarily mean neutral history, and Lodge was ready to enter the forum against his master when a question of family was involved.

Lodge's overt pleading helped renew the urgency of such questions for Henry Adams. Godkin's *Nation* offered him the chance of hot rebuttal in a critical review, but his full-dress reply was to be far more temperate and oblique than his immediate comment. *Documents Relating to New England Federalism, 1800–1815* was a scholarly collection of evidence that ran over four hundred pages. Adams took for his own words little more than the four-page preface in which he began and ended with disclaimers of partisan commitment:

> This volume has no controversial purpose. Under the ashes of half a century the fires of personal and party passion still glow in these pages; but only curious students in history care any longer to stir them. For such as these this volume is printed; not with a view to controversy, but to place before them historical matter which there is no further reason to withhold.

He entered a fact brief against the Tie-Wig Federalists and then, with the laconic irony of a prairie lawyer, declared his own disinterestedness. If he did not take sides, it was because he did not see how there could be two sides to the question.

The chief exhibit in Adams' collection was the hitherto unpublished "Reply to the Massachusetts Federalists" by John Quincy Adams. The complicated history of this document began in the national election campaign of 1828 when President Adams, accused of being a turncoat to his original party, replied with the countercharge that New England Federalists had sporadically engaged in treasonable conspiracies against the Union from 1804 until the climactic Hartford Convention of 1814. The countercharge brought out indignant cries of defamation and an "Appeal" for particulars which was printed over the signatures of thirteen leading citizens of Massachusetts, survivors from the Federalist leadership of 1804 or heirs defending their own good names in their fathers' reputations. The President decided against continuing the controversy at the time, but in the days after his defeat and retirement from office, he returned to the issue of his long-term justification. The "Reply" he prepared was so strongly vituperative, even to his own inflamed judgment, that he thought better of publishing and quietly filed the manuscript among the family's private papers. By the time his grandson deemed it judicious to have the pamphlet printed, the circumstances of the controversy had been transformed. By 1877 the abundance of extant Federalist writings had already led to an equal abundance of Federalist biographies, many of which glossed over and some of which omitted altogether the incidents and documents that might have supported John Quincy Adams' accusations. Simply to counteract the growing myth of Federalist sanctity, it was high time the public be reminded that another side had existed in the politics of the early nineteenth century. Catholicity of scholarship demanded as much, just as it suggested that the too-long-suppressed pamphlet be published amidst a collection of relevant documents. The original pamphlet had weak spots because its author lacked evidence that could now be supplied by his opponents' published letters and because he depended in part on information that later researches were to discredit. Henry Adams assembled the historic materials which made his grandfather's point better than the President had been able to make it himself.

Adams' fact brief leaves the reader still perplexed as to one major problem that recent history has uncomfortably revived, whether or not there might be a difference between contemplating overthrow of the constitution and actually conspiring to execute such vague designs. At a time when the outcome of the American constitutional experiment was truly unsettled, slight forces were clearly dangerous and disaffected men were dangerously present in many of the most powerful councils, public and private, through the land. Half a century later, the national-minded Henry Adams on his scholarly bench arrived at a severe judgment on the facts. He spurned the argument of his friend Lodge that, unduly influenced by the Civil War, he saw treason too easily. To his mind, legalism seemed a more decent error than relativism. His review of Lodge's *Cabot* had explicitly stated the historical judgment which lies tacitly behind the collected evidence of the *Documents*. Lodge had used for his biography not only the still unpublished "Reply," but also many of the Timothy Pickering manuscripts that Adams later printed — manuscripts which showed that Pickering at least, long before the Hartford Convention, had looked for the national crisis which would make separation of the northeastern states politically practicable. Adams commented:

> From the papers published by Mr. Lodge, it is now an easy task to settle the long-standing controversy in regard to the purposes of that body, and to see why it might be looked upon as a conservative and patriotic measure by Mr. Otis, and by Pickering and his friends as merely a stepping-stone to their long-expected "crisis."

Lodge had scarcely intended to prove the existence of a nearly consummated plot against the constitutional government, but Henry Adams allowed no extenuation. He wrote off the Federalists with an ironic flourish: "It is amusing to observe that not one of these correspondents or principals ever raised, or seems ever to have thought of the objection, that the scheme proposed was treason." When Lodge got his turn to review Adams in the *Nation*, he admitted himself *touché* on the question of an 1804 conspiracy, but he did not capitulate to his master on all points. Just as Adams shied away from *his* point about the definition of treason, so Lodge declined Adams' inferences about later events and insisted that there was no "plan" of secession in 1807 or 1814. The issue between the two debaters remained alive for Henry Adams till his dying day: to have a confederated republic, he believed, one must first have a republic.

Adams made his case by giving facts, and facts only, and stopping at the first stage of critical scholarship, the establishment of primary sources. In his earlier professional effort he had claimed a competitive victory over high-ranking European scholars like Schmid, Maurer, and Stubbs, each of whom he managed to correct; aiming now to set straight his former student and his protégé, he refused to enter an essentially provincial quarrel in the panoply of the full-fledged, internationally-recognized historian. Some of his restraint may even have come from his sympathizing too well for words with the despair of John Quincy Adams at the time of his defeat. As an editor, he noncommittally explained to his readers the bitter tone of his grandfather's pamphlet, from which, after fifty years, he still felt obliged to delete a particularly violent passage:

> His diary tells how, at this time, the sense of personal abandonment, caused by a rapid desertion of his former friends and

followers, had gained so strong a hold upon his mind that scarce
a day passed when his ears did not ring with the old refrain: —

> "*O Richard! O mon roi!*
> "*L'univers t'abandonne.*"

This passage from the Grétry opera which John Quincy
Adams had once attended in Paris, was to persist in Henry
Adams' imagination as in his grandfather's. If citing it
showed the historian's personal involvement in his materials,
clearly he could not satisfy his feelings simply by reviving
"hereditary enmities." He did suggest to the "new generation
in our universities and elsewhere" that history could throw
light upon such enmities, and his list of recommended readings
was headed by Alexander Hamilton's pamphlet *John Adams*.
He did not press along this line himself because his concern
was with New England Federalist conspiracies and he could
hang on Hamilton a sentiment no more treasonable, though
no less unpalatable, than many of his party held — "that
dismemberment of our empire will be a clear sacrifice of great
positive advantages, without any counterbalancing good;
administering no relief to our real disease, which is Democracy." Adams took seriously the complication whereby the
fate of the American democracy and that of the national republic had become permanently joined, but he needed a different and a larger subject before he could grasp the full
meaning for himself of this great theme. Privately he argued
Hamilton's motiveless quest for consolidated power with
Lodge, who was to become the biographer of the Federalists'
intellectual leader; publicly, he could continue the debate
only after he himself had become the biographer of Albert
Gallatin. To confront the issues raised by his own extended
past, he had to travel a longer way around than he could trace
in the *Documents*.

The surest way Adams had of doing things well and only

once was never to leave any bridges standing behind him. Chafing at the dignified security of his professorial position, he now began his detour from academic conventionality. He wrote to the president of his university proposing a rival course in American history to clash with his own — "to counteract, within its range, the inert atmosphere which now pervades the college, at least the portion with which I am best acquainted." His impolitic language did not prevent his proposal being accepted, but he still found reason to complain. He felt that the growing popularity of his college courses threatened to drive him away. True to the family temperament, he was as suspicious of success as he would have been wounded by failure. As with the professor, so with the editor. He began his last year with the *North American Review* by publishing a centennial survey of American progress in half a dozen fields, solid, sober, and authoritative; he ended with an equally thorough survey of the American political failure, throwing into the 1876 campaign a barrage of disconcerting reformist articles. This October number included his last venture into political journalism, a fine abusive piece on which he collaborated with his brother Charles, "The Independents in the Canvass."* He paid for his fun with peculiar readiness, letting the publishers edge him out of his editorial job. He had been gradually closing down his Cambridge career well before he got the invitation to edit the Gallatin papers. When the invitation came, he seized the chance to "cut loose" from the felt constrictions of academic

---

*"[The Republican Party] mustered, of course, its train of camp-followers and stragglers and adventurers, — those who joined its ranks at the eleventh hour, and even just before the striking of noon, — who were as loud-mouthed and repulsive a set of political vagabonds as ever canted about principles or hungered after loaves and fishes. For a number of years this element, as a whole, retained its proper position at the rear. In proportion, however, as the objects for which the party was organized became accomplished facts, it assumed a greater and greater prominence, until at last it secured for itself an almost undisputed ascendancy. This was not unnatural." *North American Review*, CXXIII (1876), 426.

and of New England life and resigned from Harvard. The volume on the Federalists was datelined Washington; Henry Adams had returned to the scene of his earlier liberation.

☆   ☆   ☆

In less than two years, Adams published three volumes of Gallatin papers and a weighty biography to go with them. The event marked Adams' start on the classic course which historians supposedly follow, from the compilation of data to special studies to more general history. The easiest path would have led in just the opposite direction, for nineteenth-century progress in the practical science of research had effected a technological revolution in history as in more obviously industrial callings. As Arnold Toynbee has observed, division of labor led to what might be called an overproduction of information and a neglect of the large general undertakings which might integrate the vast new accumulations of fact. Toynbee points to the great German historian Theodor Mommsen as his prime example of the movement from general synthesis to the editing of documents, for Mommsen "became almost ashamed" of his early masterpiece, *The History of the Roman Republic*, and "made it his life work to organize the exhaustive publication of Latin inscriptions and the encyclopaedic presentation of Roman Constitutional Law." The great collections of source material and monographic studies, the English historian concedes, "are monuments of the laboriousness, the 'factual' knowledge, the mechanical skill, and the organizing power of our society. They will take their rank with our stupendous tunnels and bridges and dams and liners and battleships and skyscrapers, and their editors will be remembered among the famous Western engineers." Industrialization of historical learning may keep men so busy with technical activity that they never question the ends of knowledge, and the individual may become so absorbed in his specialized part in the process that he never tries to grasp the whole of any subject. Humanity requires historical works of art as well as encyclopedias, but the need can be stated more readily than it can be satisfied. Henry Adams' work on Gallatin lets us see the slow, and the only, way in which the stages are passed between scholarship and art.

Even a minor question of sectional history had demanded the compilation and editing of documents. The biography of a national figure like Gallatin required the same first steps. In fact, since the subject was bigger, the initial excavations had to be deeper and the foundation of factual knowledge more firmly laid. A *Life of Albert Gallatin*, to be at all complete, would almost have to give the national political history of two or three decades. When the Jeffersonian party was forming in the 1790's and beginning to challenge Federalist supremacy on the floor of Congress, Gallatin was the leader of his party in the House of Representatives. When the Republicans came to power in 1801, Gallatin became Secretary of the Treasury, first member of the Cabinet on domestic affairs. And when, in the course of events, "diplomacy had become more important than finance," Gallatin changed his role again and became chief American negotiator of the Treaty of Ghent. The three successive periods in the history of Jeffersonian democracy and in the life of Albert Gallatin marked out for Henry Adams a possible structure for his book: framed by brief sections to be entitled "Youth" and "Age," sections on "The Legislature," "The Treasury," and "Diplomacy" might be fitted into a dramatic five-act composition. Hindsight sees a happy chance in the natural disposition of historical materials to fall into place, but only because the biographer worked an intractable mass of data until it yielded the clue to a seemingly organic narrative form. By the exacting labors that went into *The Life of Gallatin*, Adams entered upon the last stage of scholarship and the first of historical art.

Adams did not try to push at once beyond this transitional stage. Instead of dramatically exploiting the symmetrical composition he had envisaged, he deliberately made the body of his work too heavy for its well-articulated skeleton. The would-be historian crossed the biographer. He could either scale down the treatment of some events and judiciously omit others, in order to focus properly on the key dramatic episodes, or he could make the *Gallatin* a basic work of reference for future writers in the field, including himself. Divergent literary and scholarly aims created a real dilemma; there could be no satisfactory compromise between dramatic economy and scholarly fullness, at least within the limits of a single volume. He constantly found how "hard it is to decide that any particular letter or episode is not possibly important to somebody." His decision was to make the book a compendium of documented statements of fact, such as he might one day conveniently cite in order to spare himself the longer demonstration from evidence that would slow an historical narrative. The *Gallatin* was geared to the low speed of relentless, painstaking demonstration so that the *History* might move at a faster clip. Its usefulness to the historian proved to be the same as its interest for the reader. In a strict and solid order, it refers the facts about a long generation in American life to the single life of an eminent public man and offers a consistent, if not always a dramatic, view of that historical span. It is a baseline from which to survey an age.

The method of inclusiveness, which curtailed the possibility of relating events dramatically to a unified action, compelled Adams to strive for an analytic coherence that would make up for the lack of narrative unity. He therefore made the three stages of Gallatin's career into categories of political inquiry — legislation, administration, and the conduct of foreign policy — rather than acts in a personal and social drama. Even so, he ran the danger brought on by his method and tended to treat events as self-enclosed units, exploring the significance of each rather than of all. What he did becomes clearer if we note the precedent in American historiography for tough empirical examination of the detailed national record. Richard Hildreth had developed the method in his anti-Puritan, anti-Jeffersonian, anti-slavery *History of the United States*, which was published in six volumes from 1848 to 1852 and set the biases of American historical writing for half a century thereafter. The lonely apostle of Benthamite utilitarianism in America, Hildreth tried to bring science into his craft by subjecting to minute and systematic inspection his wide knowledge of his country's past. The result was an intellectual vivacity in the treatment of single episodes — and an atomizing effect that makes sustained reading difficult. In an acute essay on the "scientific" historians of the generation before Adams, Donald Emerson has contrasted the methods of Hildreth the Benthamite and John W. Draper the Comteist, two "sports" of the mid-century when "romantic" narrative history was in vogue. Draper, with a keen sense for complex evolutionary patterns in history, wrote the prospectus for what might have been our classic history of the Civil War, but the execution of his work betrayed the brilliant introduction. Draper's ideas sometimes coerced, sometimes altogether missed the facts with which he filled his volumes; his history sank to oblivion while Hildreth's became "standard" and shaped the nation's opinion of its past. The revival of interest in Adams' historical writing which works backward from the *Education*, tends to emphasize the monumental Draper-like generalizations and to ignore the spirited, quasi-utilitarian handling of details that encourages a close reading. In the *Gallatin* at least, Adams was closer to Hildreth and avoided his structural looseness by putting more complicated questions to the facts. An inductive method is always only approximate, since generalizations come from the observer and not from the facts themselves. What matters in the distinction being made is that Adams' first order of generalization was concerned with relatively minute details so that his larger ideas, the result in great part of putting more specialized ideas together, lent themselves to empirical verification more readily than Draper's. In this way, the *Gallatin* served Adams as a conceptual as well as a factual preparation for his work on the *History*.

A number of themes emerged from Adams' handling of the biographical data, for, to the politician *manqué*, the record of Gallatin's public life provided a manual of "the highest practical statesmanship." In his earliest political role, that of legislator, Gallatin did not allow himself to be deluded by success in debate but knew, by the same instinct that spoke to three generations of Adamses, that "the essentials of power in a deliberative assembly are only to be secured by labor and activity and by mastery of the business in hand." During the ten-year apprenticeship that prepared the Jeffersonians for assuming power, Gallatin made an education of political adversity. As Adams saw it, even out of power Gallatin contributed directly to good government since "the duty of an opposition is to compel government to prove the propriety of its measures, and Mr. Gallatin's incessant watchfulness gave the party in power a corresponding sense of responsibility." The man who raised the level of political responsibility in the bitter days when American parties were first forming brought unusual personal qualities to equally unusual opportunities. For Gallatin was an outsider to American society, a Genevan who had emigrated in 1780 at the age of nineteen, and he also bore the onus of being connected (albeit honorably) with the famous Whiskey Rebellion of 1794:

> That a young foreigner, speaking with a foreign accent, laboring under all the odium of the western insurrection, surrounded by friendly rivals like Madison, John Nicholas, W. B.

Giles, John Randolph, and Edward Livingston . . . that such a man under such circumstances should have at once seized the leadership of his party, and retained it with firmer and firmer grasp down to the last moment of his service; that he should have done this by the sheer force of ability and character, without ostentation and without the tricks of popularity; that he should have had his leadership admitted without a dispute, and should have held it without a contest, made a curious combination of triumphs. Many of the great parliamentary leaders in America, John Randolph, Henry Clay, Thaddeus Stevens, have maintained their supremacy by their dogmatic and overbearing temper and their powers of sarcasm or invective. Mr. Gallatin seldom indulged in personalities. His temper was under almost perfect control. His power lay in courage, honesty of purpose, and thoroughness of study. Undoubtedly his mind was one of rare power, perhaps for this especial purpose the most apt that America has ever seen; a mind for which no principle was too broad and no detail too delicate; but it was essentially a scientific and not a political mind. Mr. Gallatin always tended to think with an entire disregard of the emotions; he could only with an effort refrain from balancing the opposing sides of a political question. His good fortune threw him into public life at a time when both parties believed that principles were at stake, and when the struggle between those who would bar the progress of democracy and those who led that progress allowed little latitude for doubt on either side in regard to the necessity of their acts. While this condition of things lasted, and it lasted throughout Mr. Gallatin's stormy Congressional career, he was an ideal party leader, uniting boldness with caution, good temper with earnestness, exact modes of thought with laborious investigation, to a degree that has no parallel in American experience.

For the ideal to become actual, the times as well as the man had to be right. Adams asked what conditions let a Gallatin rise, and for answer he pointed to the radical division on principle of the two major parties. A statesman who lacked the faculty for histrionics or for trafficking in promises and spoils might be advanced by a party anxious for the execution of a program, even though he would be neglected by a political machine interested only in votes and offices. In short, men of principle once belonged to parties, as Henry Adams did not, and men of independence at one time were not "as independent of each other as they were of the party 'machines.' " Not only did honest men have a party, but in the age of Gallatin, "when party feeling ran higher than ever since, there was no such party tyranny as grew up afterwards in American politics." Adams was once more at an issue he had faced as a journalist and an amateur politician, finding, wherever he turned, that Gallatin the outsider had enjoyed favoring situations that the insider Henry Adams never approached. His notion that there had been an age of statesmanship and that it was over became fixed in his treatment of Gallatin's career during the 1790's.

Strongly as he might suggest his preference for the politics of the eighteenth century, Adams had no intention of portraying the past as idyllic or the age of statesmen as an age of saints. The issues of democracy and positive national government were real and difficult, and in his treatment of the Jay Treaty debates of 1796, he showed how hotly abstract questions could be argued. He insisted that sharp conflict of principles be made out through the haze of patriotic historiography:

> In recent times there has been a general disposition to explain away and to soften down the opinions and passions of that day; to throw a veil over their violence; to imagine a possible middle ground, from which the acts and motives of all parties will appear patriotic and wise, and their extravagance a mere misunderstanding. Such treatment of history makes both parties ridiculous. The two brilliant men who led the two great divisions of national thought were not mere declaimers;

they never for a moment misunderstood each other; they were in deadly earnest, and no compromise between them ever was or ever will be possible. Mr. Jefferson meant that the American system should be a democracy, and he would rather have let the world perish than that this principle, which to him represented all that man was worth, should fail. Mr. Hamilton considered democracy a fatal curse, and meant to stop its progress. The partial truce which the first Administration of Washington had imposed on both parties, although really closed by the retirement of Mr. Jefferson from the Cabinet, was finally broken only by the arrival of Mr. Jay's treaty. From that moment repose was impossible until one party or the other had triumphed beyond hope of resistance; and it was easy to see which of the two parties must triumph in the end.

Adams thus struck out at once against both Federalists and pallid neutrals in historical interpretation. In establishing the dynamic situation of 1796, he made clear his position as a Jeffersonian and a realist. He upheld his position with skill, cited Federalists against themselves with a diabolical accuracy, and even dared excoriate the untouchable Washington himself on an issue of constitutional interpretation. In the context of violent controversy, Albert Gallatin, who "at every period of his life required the spur of sincere conviction to act a partisan part," was vigorous in the democratic cause. Had he lacked the external conditions of deep-rooted conflict, his cautious scientific cast of thought might indeed have left him sceptically disengaged from politics. As it was, the chief literary endeavor of Gallatin out of power, his *Sketch of the Finances of the United States*, had a fate quite unlike that of Henry Adams' "Session" two generations later: instead of becoming a campaign document for a party to which he could not belong, it served Gallatin's direct purpose — "to educate his own party and to plant his own principles deep in popular convictions." The issues were real, the political battles were hard-fought, and the fruit of Gallatin's diligent years of opposition was his appointment as Secretary of the Treasury when Jefferson became President in 1801.

In the first third of his book, apparently a straightforward account of Gallatin from the runaway boy of Geneva to the leader of his party in Congress, Adams still made choices which affected both his narrative and his analysis. Before discussing the Republican program, he had to decide just when it became well enough defined to be discussable. By taking as his critical episode the debate on the Jay Treaty, which "thrust a sword into the body politic," he passed over Jefferson's leaving the Cabinet in 1791 or the conflict over the French war and the Alien and Sedition Acts of 1798–99. In effect, he concentrated Republican indignation against the administration of Washington rather than that of John Adams. Focusing on the parliamentary scene, he kept attention on Gallatin rather than on Jefferson, the intellectual leader of the democratic movement, and he was incidentally enabled to argue that the Alien and Sedition Acts were the work of a Congress far ahead of its presidential leadership. This whole development, rendered with a density of detail that could for most scholars have made it a sufficient and indeed an exemplary work by itself, was for Adams merely introductory. In the opening paragraph of Book III, "The Treasury," with its four times repeated phrase "the highest practical statesmanship," he immediately reduced all that had gone before to the status of preliminary action. Jeffersonian political theory could only be assessed when the Republicans themselves held power, but even then the Genevan immigrant from Pennsylvania could hold the center of the stage.

In the *Gallatin* for the first time, Henry Adams gave voice to his lasting opinion that the basic practical questions of government were economic. Even when his interest later came to center on an economy of forces, in which natural resources and the production of harnessable energy had greater importance than pecuniary capital, he still used trade as a yardstick for his incessant calculations. At the time of his writing Gallatin's biography, he used more conventional terms, by which the fiscal policy of government might be minutely analyzed, but he was already concerned to relate his narrower economic approach to the entire scheme of society:

> In governments, as in households, he who holds the purse holds the power. . . . Washington and Jefferson doubtless stand pre-eminent as the representatives of what is best in our national character or its aspirations, but Washington depended mainly upon Hamilton, and without Gallatin Mr. Jefferson would have been helpless. The mere financial duties of the Treasury, serious as they are, were the least of the burdens these men had to carry; their keenest anxieties were not connected most nearly with their own department, but resulted from that effort to control the whole machinery and policy of government which is necessarily forced upon the holder of the purse. . . . There are, to the present time, in all American history only two examples of practical statesmanship which can serve as perfect models, not perhaps in all respects for imitation, but for study, to persons who wish to understand what practical statesmanship has been under an American system. Public men in considerable numbers and of high merit have run their careers in national politics, but only two have had at once the breadth of mind to grapple with the machine of government as a whole, and the authority necessary to make it work efficiently for a given object; the practical knowledge of affairs and of politics that enabled them to foresee every movement; the long apprenticeship which had allowed them to educate and discipline their parties; and finally, the good fortune to enjoy power when government was still plastic and capable of receiving a new impulse.

The promise to show Gallatin handling "the machine of government as a whole" implied that there would be such a

machine and that, for Adams, the essence of Jeffersonianism
was the democratic principle and not the opposition to
positive national powers. It was easy to show how accession
to office changed Republican ideas of "strict construction"
and limited government in case after case. The Louisiana
Purchase in 1803 is the traditional example. That Gallatin
urged Jefferson in that instance to solve constitutional difficulties by ignoring them was but one sign of how practical
his high statesmanship could be. When Jefferson outlined to
his Secretary of the Treasury a subtreasury plan that would
make it possible to dispense with Hamilton's United States
Bank, Gallatin briefly replied that against the Bank there
were "none but political objections"! Henry Adams at this
time interpreted Jefferson's yielding on these questions to be
the flexibility of political genius. The seeming contradiction
of Republican principles weighed less in the scale than
Gallatin's skilled execution of the original Jeffersonian program — reducing the debt, cutting expenses, making government economical by making it efficient. For a long time,
Gallatin's "passion for organization" was devoted to effecting
this negative policy, although neither he nor his party intended
to economize the government out of existence. The accomplishment of five years, which, Adams pointed out, reduced
the debt no faster than the Federalists themselves had planned,
freed the Republicans from what they felt to be the shackles
of the past. At that moment they paused to gaze at the vista
of the future. The detailed mapping of that future would be
Gallatin's job, but the wondrous vision was peculiarly Jefferson's and for once he was given the stage alone. It was the
high point of the book:

> Nowhere in all the long course of Mr. Jefferson's great career
> did he appear to better advantage than when in his message
> of 1806 he held out to the country and the world that view of
> his ultimate hopes and aspirations for national development,

which was, as he then trusted, to be his last bequest to mankind. Having now reached the moment when he must formally announce to Congress that the great end of relieving the nation from debt was at length within reach, and with it the duty of establishing true republican government was fulfilled, he paused to ask what use was to be made of the splendid future thus displayed before them. Should they do away with taxes? Should they apply them to the building up of armies and navies? Both relief from taxation and the means of defence might be sufficiently obtained without exhausting their resources, and still the great interests of humanity might be secured. These great interests were economical and moral; to supply the one, a system of internal improvement should be created commensurate with the magnitude of the country; "by these operations new channels of communication will be opened between the States, lines of separation will disappear, their interests will be identified, and their union cemented by new and indissoluble ties." To provide for the other, the higher education should be placed among the objects of public care; "a public institution can alone supply those sciences which, though rarely called for, are yet necessary to complete the circle, all the parts of which contribute to the improvement of the country and some of them to its preservation." A national university and a national system of internal improvement were an essential part, and indeed the realization and fruit, of the republican theories which Mr. Jefferson and his associates put in practice as their ideal of government.

Gallatin's "Report on Internal Improvements," to which Adams immediately turned, declared the positive content of the Jeffersonian "dream." Its impressive list of specific proposals included a national turnpike from Maine to Georgia and better roads to the distant cities of Detroit, St. Louis, and New Orleans; improvement of the great rivers that flowed east and west from the Appalachians and turnpikes to link these rivers; canals from the Hudson to Lakes Champlain and Ontario and a great Inland Waterway along the Atlantic Coast. The details of costs and budgeting for this immense program did not discourage Gallatin; on the contrary, "he wished to fix the policy of government for at least ten years, and probably for an indefinite time, on the whole subject of internal improvements, as he had already succeeded in fixing it in regard to the payment of the debt." A broad ten-year plan would eliminate "the whole business of annual chaffering and log-rolling for local appropriations in Congress, and all its consequent corruptions and inconsistencies." (What proposal could have had greater appeal to a dedicated reformer in politics?) Although Gallatin's report was not presented until April 1808, Adams linked it to the Presidential Message of 1806. Foreshortening his time scheme, the historian reinforced the sense of climax and prepared for the dark contrast of foreign complications that demanded attention at once from Gallatin and from Gallatin's biographer.

Adams had early stated that "the condition on which alone the principles of the Republicans could be carried out was that of peace." The tranquil prosperity which the nation enjoyed during Jefferson's first administration had been due to respite from the violent party quarrels and foreign disputes of the previous decade. In peace, defense costs could be cut and the national power could help the developing country as a whole, instead of burdening the poor with taxes from which they drew no benefit. Not government, but the onus of government was to be minimized. The country was to be given over to the pursuit of happiness instead of the quest for power. It was natural that men who thought peace so necessary should think peace to be possible, and from that premise they worked out their foreign policy. They thought it better to endure minor abuse from the great warring powers of Europe than to put their great experiment to the hazard of war. They waited patiently for Britain and France to realize that infringement of American rights brought no advantages; if simple patience should not be enough, they would then wait for embargoes to persuade the offender through his pocketbook. Henry Adams regarded this foreign policy, connected as it was with the reduction of armaments and the general economic program, as part of a rigid Jeffersonian system which he "confessed" to find "a system of doctrinaires":

> Far in advance, as it was, of any other political effort of its time, and representing, as it doubtless did, all that was most philanthropic and all that most boldly appealed to the best instincts of mankind, it made too little allowance for human passions and vices; it relied too absolutely on the power of interest and reason as opposed to prejudice and habit; it proclaimed too openly to the world that the sword was not one of its arguments, and that peace was essential to its existence.

Adams summed up what he called the dogmas of the Jeffersonians in half a dozen words, "Government must be ruled by principles," and added, "to which the Federalists answered that government must be ruled by circumstances." The antinomy of these two propositions became the central problem of his handbook of politics. It also provided the basic dynamic tension of his narrative, since he conceived the theoretical opposition to have been completely worked out in American history. The Federalists had had their chance first. According to Adams, their belief was that the existence of government depended on the concentration of force by those who wielded the most power in society, that the object of government was its own perpetuation through gathering more and more strength to itself and to the class which gave it existence, that the function of government in attaining this end was simply to apply force in automatic response to the stimuli of either opposition or opportunity. The historian offered his own judgment that "there never was a time when the political formulas of Hamilton, George Cabot, Fisher Ames, Gouverneur Morris, and Rufus Griswold could have been applied even in New England with a chance of success"; government by and for the propertied classes had inevitably to fail on the American scene, and the election of 1800 marked the end of its unsteady career. Yet he qualified his judgment and remarked that it was "none the less certain that a small knot of such men, with no resources other than their own energy and will, practically created the Constitution, administered the government under it for ten years, and at last very nearly overthrew it rather than surrender their power." Beginning on the third of March 1801, the Jeffersonians put to practical test formulas which were the reverse of Federalist doctrine. They held that the existence of government depended on the consent of the governed, that the end of government was the promotion of humane objects, that the function of government was essentially negative — to keep its power at a minimum and avoid the application of force at home or abroad. In Adams' view, the Jeffersonians governed on these principles with results so encouraging that a transition from negative to positive government could at last be entertained. At the peak of success, Jefferson proposed his master plan for America's future. Then came news that in American waters the British frigate *Leopard* had fired without warning on the U.S.S. *Chesapeake*, forced her to strike her colors, and taken four members of her crew as British deserters. If the Federalists had ignored Jeffersonian principles to their own disadvantage, the Republicans' unconcern for circumstance had brought them up short on the threshold of national disaster.

Adams handled his denouement less well than his rising action, slipping frequently into a rather lurid tone. At this stage of his personal development, the only kind of pathos he could convey was that of melodramatic disillusionment. "Even the American who reads the history of the year 1807," he commented, "seeing the brutal directness with which Mr. Canning kicked Mr. Jefferson's diplomacy out of his path, cannot but feel a certain respect for the Englishman mingled with wrath at his sarcasm." He could fairly show how the violence of international relations made Jefferson's foreign policy look naïve, but he had not prepared the reader for the callousness with which he dismissed the Republicans' farsighted domestic hopes along with their shortsighted diplomacy of "interest." He argued that Canning's program for getting back British commerce and British sailors left America "no alternative but submission or war, and either submission or war was equally fatal to Mr. Jefferson's Administration." His moral seemed to be the futility of will and the vanity of human wishes: the "honest and reflecting mind" now learned at last that "circumstances must by their nature be stronger and more permanent than men." Gallatin, having just such a mind, did learn from the event "how to accept defeat and adapt himself to circumstances, how to abandon theory and to move with his generation." He had a lot of adapting to do. The United States was to go through a protracted period of neither war nor peace, in which disorganized expenditures for preparedness nullified the plans for national economic development, and the uncertainties of politics made a rational defense program impossible. The direction of planning passed from the Treasury Department, and the Secretary, who had vowed never to act as "a mere financier," "a contriver of taxes, a dealer of loans, a seeker of resources," found himself reduced to that very unleaderly role. To meet the demands of circumstance became increasingly complicated, since his stand for rationalization of the country's economic efforts brought him into conflict with Congress; the harder he fought for the rule of intelligence in politics, the more

he made himself a political liability to the Madison administration. The time came when Gallatin saw that he could be
of more use to the nation as a diplomat. Adams put it somewhat sensationally: "The past was a failure; he might fling
it away, and still rescue his country and himself by this change
of career." The rescue was accomplished and the Peace of
Ghent clinched a triumph that our arms had not won, but
Adams portrayed Gallatin's life from this point as a progress
into disenchantment. In the period after 1815, staggering
growth of material wealth gave new importance to speculative
interests and the slave power on the national scene. Despite
the transformation of the country's political and moral sentiments, Gallatin felt neither old enough nor philosophical
enough to retire from public affairs. In a series of minor,
almost offstage roles, he tried to be, as Henry Adams later
was, *inactively* concerned, neither in nor out of politics. The
comedown of his later career was not more striking than its
dignity, but, according to his biographer, "he had outgrown
the convictions which had made his strength."

The Life of Gallatin was not merely an occasion for Henry
Adams to project the "O Richard! O mon roi!" attitude to
which he was constitutionally susceptible. At forty he was
outgrowing the world-weariness he had prematurely known
at twenty-five, and his feeling for the wiser and sadder Gallatin
of old age was partly based on his seeing a more positive side.
He recognized that his subject's education by defeat taught
not only the omnipotence of circumstance but also the deeper
lesson that "the failures of the past were not due to the faults
of the past only." What is more, Gallatin's earlier successes
had, despite the interruption of war, fixed for America traditions of democratic growth and peaceful prosperity resting on
popular strength rather than force of arms. The Hamil-
tonians had not after all been right; they misjudged circumstances in not seeing the national character to be essentially

Jeffersonian. Jefferson, Madison, and Gallatin had their victory, even though, putting "too high an estimate on human nature," they had failed of their ultimate object: "Since the day when foreign violence and domestic faction prostrated Mr. Gallatin and his two friends, no statesman has ever appeared with the strength to bend their bow, — to finish their uncompleted task." Nor did Gallatin's regrets unman him. He had to revise some of his early beliefs, but he refused to admit that circumstance could ever outweigh principle. Despite a chastened confidence in human nature, he expressed hope that the people would "themselves ultimately cure the evils under which we labor." When most tempted to bitterness, he still affirmed the ultimate Jeffersonian faith, a trust in the right of a new time to its own methods:

> The energy of this nation is not to be controlled; it is at present exclusively applied to the acquisition of wealth and to improvements of stupendous magnitude. Whatever has that tendency, and of course an immoderate expansion of credit, receives favor. The apparent prosperity and the progress of cultivation, population, commerce, and improvement are beyond expectation. But it seems to me as if general demoralization was the consequence; I doubt whether general happiness is increased; and I would have preferred a gradual, slower, and more secure progress. I am, however, an old man, and the young generation has a right to govern itself.

The Gallatin who endured disillusionment "and yet became neither a cynic nor a transcendental philosopher" evoked Henry Adams' deepest response. However circumstance might force either the biographer or his subject to reconsider beliefs about progress, it was force of conviction which made the dramatic interest of the story. Though hopefulness might dwindle, a man could stick to his unfinished task. For beyond the failure or achievement of an individual, there were larger questions to be asked. With the completion of his book, Adams left at once for Europe, a confirmed scholar out to plunder archives for his projected *History*.

Chapter III

SATIRIC VIRTUOSITY

HENRY ADAMS announced his solemn farewell to reform
in *The Life of Albert Gallatin*, but not his farewell to
politics. He had too much vitality as a political man
to stay in the early grave to which Grantism had consigned
him. On first moving back to Washington he had observed,
"The fact is I gravitate to a capital by a primary law of nature." But he returned in a new role: as an historian, he made
politics his subject, not his career. Like Henry James, who
could neither accept the life of the British upper classes nor
remove himself from it so far as to lose sight of his materials,
Henry Adams gave up active participation in the reform
movement only to become a "stable-companion to statesmen." The note of stoic resignation on which the *Gallatin*
ended partially described the way he took up his role as
private critic, behind-the-scenes adviser, and confidential
contributor of funds. But the Bohemian journalist of a decade
earlier also survived, however transformed in the literary
gentleman who established himself at the pinnacle of respectability with the charming wife who made his house
one of the most pleasant in Washington. One witness to
the happy arrangement was James himself who, in the mid-
eighties in his story "Pandora," drew a good-natured portrait of the Adamses. He caught the high spirits by which

conscious search for amusement leavened their social exclusive-
ness: he had the fictional Adams protest to his wife as the
social season approached its end, "Hang it, there's only a
month left; let us be vulgar and have some fun — let us invite
the President." James's insight is confirmed by reality:
Adams made his appropriately formal valedictory to the hot
struggles of the political arena in the full-dress scholarly
biography of Gallatin but, while bowing gravely, got in a
parting salvo. Without acknowledging his authorship, he
published his novel *Democracy* in 1880, just a few months after
the "ponderous" biography — a biting satire, the sharpness
of which is tempered by the gaiety of its irreverence. It was as
though, gracefully retrieving his hat and gloves at the vesti-
bule of the White House, he paused to tweak the butler's nose.

His youthful iconoclasm of the 1860's does not alone account
for the satiric humor which Adams mastered in the decade of
labor that produced his *History*. In *Democracy* and two years
later in the *John Randolph*, which he prepared for the American
Statesmen series, he showed a new, more sophisticated deri-
siveness that expressed his assurance in the métier of historian
and his contentment with his position in society. The scholar
who labored diligently all morning and the gentleman who
gave his afternoons to riding and then to the company of
friends were on good terms. As James rightly portrayed him,
Adams did not suffer from the lack of resource which generally characterized the Americans whom one heard "invoked, again and again, with the mixture of desire and of
deprecation that might have attended the mention of a secret
vice, under the name of a leisure-class." Actually, that "class,"
as it then existed, gathered in other centers than Washington:
the new-rich migrated to larger cities and the old wellborn of
the East went, if anywhere, to Europe. In Boston Adams had
been the member of a class; in Washington he belonged,
rather, to a circle. As a professor and a reformer, he had

moved among people who shared his assumptions and opinions to a degree which bored him, but as a gentleman of
letters he associated with men and women with whom his
bond was taste and imaginative liveliness. The innermost ring
of his Washington circle included John Hay, a dedicated
Westerner who had been Lincoln's secretary, the famous
author of *Pike County Ballads*, and a successful businessman and
politician in Cleveland before going back to the capital as an
Assistant Secretary of State. Another member was Clarence
King, head of the United States Geological Survey and possibly the best conversationalist in the country, a scientist, ex-
plorer, public servant, and private speculator as well as a
raconteur and wit. Among such friends, Adams felt himself
rescued from the provincialism of place and class and culture
which he had feared at Harvard. The titillating sense of im-
propriety which James observed in him was the effect of
liberation; it did not consist in any departure from impec-
cable conduct and manners, but in the exhilarating free play
of mind.

Democracy shows how far the enjoyment of skillful play
entered Adams' character as a writer. The irony of the
Gallatin had been deadly serious: the reversal by which
Federalists moved to a Jeffersonian attitude on states' rights
and the Republicans to more than Hamiltonian assumptions
of national power had deprived Adams' hero of his going convictions, and we are meant to feel appalled. But the conundrum of whether "democratic power" is a "contradiction in
terms" could be set forth as a comic theme, too. Having accepted the conditions of democratic politics and his own relation thereto, Adams made the exclusion of virtue and talents
from power the basic story of his novel. His fable was simple:
Madeleine Lee, a young widow "bent upon getting to the
heart of the great American mystery of democracy and government," finds out that the two things are not the same. She

moves to Washington to conduct her inquiry and there carries
on a highly spiritual flirtation with the Honorable Silas P.
Ratcliffe, Senator from Illinois and Secretary of the Treasury
and would-be President thereafter, the archetype of post-Civil
War politicians; finding him to be the essence not of statesmanship but of corruption, she turns him down as a suitor and
flies from the scene of her near mistake. With such a plot,
Adams fell into some obvious dangers — self-indulgence in
drawing a heroine who combines the qualities of being good,
wellborn, able, and decidedly out of place in modern America
and moral oversimplification in putting this ideal woman into
an iniquitous Washington jungle. On the other hand, he produced a variety of character that counteracted the tendency to
egoism and a variety of situation that counteracted the
tendency to naiveté. His inventiveness helped make good his
ironic thesis that democracy had better not take its definition
from what he observed at the capital, so that the book became
more than a document of biography and calls for serious consideration as a novel.

Adams' heroine, Mrs. Lightfoot Lee, comes to Washington
as footloose as her author. Bored equally by business and
philosophy and social work, paths she has found to "lead
nowhere," she is consumed with ennui and an ambition that
can discover "no one object worth a sacrifice." Her venture
into the political world is but one episode of a pilgrimage to an
unknown destination, a quest for an unknown grail which, if
it exists, may give meaning to her journey. Although pilgrimage is ordinarily an act of faith, hers is testimony to a want
of faith. The way of temptations is so much the harder when
each tempter speaks a seeming truth that must be taken as a
tentative hypothesis. Each hypothesis found wanting leaves
the pilgrim with dismay at one more lost possibility, instead of
with joy at one more obstacle passed. Bunyan's Christian
robustly sang as he strode along the narrow road to the certain

gate; Adams' wanderer has many roads to travel, none of them lighted and all leading to Vanity Fair. The action is a satirical prototype of that in the *Education*.

Just because it is so easy to read Henry Adams into the character of his heroine, we have to read carefully what his imagination had to report about her. She lacks durable faith, it is true, but she has affirmative qualities. Once she accepts a hypothesis, she accepts with her full energy in a way that is hardly distinguishable from faith itself. Judged by her practical commitments, she has a belief in America far deeper than ordinary patriotism, since what she does believe she tries to make something of. She cannot detach herself from her native country: Europe can give her spoils, but education must begin at home. The total yield of her touring has been a Corot landscape and a few "bales" of assorted bric-a-brac:

> With this she declared Europe to be exhausted, and she frankly avowed that she was American to the tips of her fingers; she neither knew nor greatly cared whether America or Europe were best to live in; she had no violent love for either, and she had no objection to abusing both; but she meant to get all that American life had to offer, good or bad, and to drink it down to the dregs, fully determined that whatever there was in it she would have, and that whatever could be made out of it she would manufacture.

This is weaker language than Thoreau's vow to "drive life into a corner and find out the good or meanness of it," but the resolution personally to measure the possibilities of American life is substantially the same.

Mrs. Lee's determination to "manufacture" something out of the national resources suggests the course of her unconscious discoveries. From her initial resolve to "touch with her own hand the massive machinery of society" to her final sense of a narrow escape from "being dragged under the wheels of the machine," a persistent line of imagery implies that mechanization has taken command and human reality has departed from politics. Public life becomes a dehumanized charade. At her first White House reception, she finds herself confronted with the image of "two seemingly mechanical figures, which might be wood or wax, for any sign they showed of life." The President and his wife stand ungainly and stiff, "their faces stripped of every sign of intelligence, while the right hands of both extended themselves to a column of visitors with the mechanical action of toy dolls." As though caught in an opium dream, Mrs. Lee envisages an eternity in which "we shall all wander round and round the earth shaking hands." Invited to witness "the droll aping of monarchical forms," we find ourselves watching a horde of automata in "the slowly eddying dance of Democracy"; and when the heroine has to be taken home on the verge of hysteria, we recognize that an excessive sense of horror has wrecked the novelist's and the reader's satiric detachment. When Mrs. Lee finally leaves politics, "glad to quit the masquerade, to return to the true democracy of life," the implied affirmation is less believable than the recollection of the American dream turned nightmare.

The satire of lost values, as better novelists than Adams have proved, is a self-destructive literary form, since it depends on reason when reason fails. Melville's *The Confidence Man: His Masquerade* and Twain's late bitter satires likewise show irony turning into monstrosity. In none of these cases does the author succeed in implying a world that makes sense as a criterion for a world that does not. The writer's subject overwhelms his positive values and destroys the place of security from which alone he can control the creatures of his imagination. Unable to comprehend the meanness he discovers, the satirist seems to argue that the world he represents is hallucinatory instead of real. The point is that neither satire nor history, the literary forms which make the most distinctly intellectual demands, can express the overthrow of reason in a

chaotic world. The author's ethical uncertainty is a question
not simply of bad morals but of bad literature — a failure to
organize the data of fiction or history. No one can say that
Adams ought to have been a first-rate novelist or that anyone's
first novel should demonstrate mastery of form, but it is worth
while to mark the nature of his failure, since an author's unsuccessful efforts indicate the dangers which his better work
overcomes and may therefore conceal.

If we remember (as Adams did not always himself) that Mrs.
Lee is self-deceived as well as victimized, there is much to
enjoy in *Democracy*. The amateur novelist, despite a certain
amount of stumbling, did manage to produce a satire. Once
the heroine decides to take the "Prairie Giant of Peonia,"
Senator Ratcliffe, as her test case of American politics, she goes
about her business with something more than pitiable innocence. In her first social exchange with the Illinois statesman,
she unblushingly calls a speech of his "both for language and
imagery quite equal to anything of Webster's." The irony
exists for her alone:

> The Senator from Illinois rose to this gaudy fly like a huge,
> two-hundred-pound salmon; his white waistcoat gave out a
> mild silver reflection as he slowly came to the surface and
> gorged the hook. He made not even a plunge, not one per-
> ceptible effort to tear out the barbed weapon, but, floating
> gently to her feet, allowed himself to be landed as though it
> were a pleasure.

Feminine cunning may flatter itself that it has caught one of
that Washington species who live in "gaunt boarding-house
rooms, furnished only with public documents," but Ratcliffe
can counter with his own political brand of weapon, unbarbed
but effective. As acquaintance ripens, he keeps Mrs. Lee informed of what he does, constantly asking for advice and
gradually committing her to his point of view; he manipulates

her in much the same way as he works on the President-elect, newly arrived in the capital to organize his administration. The "web of intertwined influences" which recalls "the lost art of the Roman retiarius, who from a safe distance threw his net over his adversary, before attacking with the dagger," wins Ratcliffe the post of Secretary of the Treasury. Applying his political technique to courtship, he tries to confuse the right and wrong of any issue beyond all recognition, persuade Mrs. Lee that the question is one of power and not of principle, and let the lure of power do its work. A tone of candor is essential: he admits having rigged an election during the Civil War, but that was to save the Union by keeping his party in power; for so high an end, he would "do it again, and worse than that." He points out that a Cabinet Secretary may decline his share of the patronage but wonders when ordered to find jobs for the President's friends whether he ought to save his purity by deserting his post. With such ingenuousness in the face of moral complications, he cultivates in Mrs. Lee a sense of her duty to help him administer power. He almost succeeds despite the opposition of all her genteel friends, but one of them knows the only secret Ratcliffe has kept to himself — a small matter of a one-hundred-thousand-dollar bribe. A revelatory letter is delivered in the nick of time, and Mrs. Lee recognizes with a shudder the motives which have almost led her to accept Ratcliffe — "ambition, thirst for power, restless eagerness to meddle." Somewhat cluttered by melodrama and sentimentality, the ending makes its ironic moral: reform not, that ye be not reformed.

The comic intrigue of *Democracy* weakens at the end, but the historian-novelist's strength lay elsewhere than in making up a story. He peopled his tale with an abundant variety of characters who give the illusion of representing society and the human gamut, the sense of wide observation by which the satirist enforces his theme. Most of them are partial portraits from life. Best known of the sitters is James G. Blaine, the Plumed Knight of Republicanism and the unwitting model for Ratcliffe. Most of those who lent qualities to the fictive characters came from within the Adams circle, unlike Blaine, and many took on an autonomous vitality in the novel, as even their lively nomenclature suggests. There is Miss Victoria Dare, for example, who plays the chaste hussy, almost a caricature of the Daisy Miller type, or Mr. Hartbeest Schneidekoupon, the young *rentier* from Philadelphia who interests himself in Mrs. Lee's sister Sybil Ross as well as in yachting and the protective tariff. Among those who provide an international perspective is the British ambassador Lord Skye, who notes the customs of the aborigines and enjoys telling about the congressman who brought along to dinner two "very respectable constituents from Yahoo City, or some such place; nature's noblemen, he said." More amusing than British irony is the earnest eastern European decadence of Baron Jacobi, the Bulgarian minister; a "witty, cynical, broken-down Parisian *roué*," connoisseur of sin and believer in "everything that was perverse or wicked," he seems the quintessence of the villains that figure so prominently in Henry James's Europe-symbolism. When Ratcliffe protests his own political virtue by double-talk about purifying American society before trying to clean up American government, the Baron intuitively notes the assumption that America cannot be improved because, really, there is no room for improvement. Diplomats, according to Adams, being the natural enemies of senators, Jacobi lets himself be outraged by the Prairie Giant's smug certainty of American righteousness and European corruption; in a fine set speech he proclaims that he has nowhere found the elements of corruption so widespread as in America and predicts a Washington of the future that would put Rome under Caligula into the shade. What the Baron's rhetoric does not accomplish, Ratcliffe's sanctimoniousness does. On the presupposition that everything is for the best in the best of all possible countries, he rejects everything that does not fit his ideas: Darwin should not be read, for example, because "such books . . . disgrace our civilization; they degrade and stultify our divine nature; they are suited only for Asiatic despotisms where men are reduced to the level of brutes"; a Baron Jacobi might accept such a book, but never a self-respecting American senator. In the interplay of fictional characters, the historical theme of American exceptionalism is transformed into the literary theme of American innocence.

Adams freely used friends and enemies to contrive a situation and expound a theme, but in rounding out his cast he did not spare himself. The several chips off the author's block are interesting characters if only because they prove that Madeleine Lee was by no means a sufficient projection of the writer. Aspects of the novelist appear in a number of his figures. C. C. French, for one, a reform congressman from Connecticut who has failed of re-election, is a projection of the might-have-been, "the educated gentleman in politics," particularly strong in what he calls "badinaige," a Henry Adams who falls flat. Another, who seems at first glance to be a judicious blend of James Russell Lowell and John Lothrop Motley, bears a strong likeness to the image of professional success which Adams had held up to young Lodge. In his youth Nathan Gore wrote satire, but he became a "deep student" for years — "until his famous 'History of Spain in America' placed him instantly at the head of American historians, and made him minister to Madrid . . . this being the nearest approach to a patent of nobility and a government pension which the American citizen can attain." Gore's reward proves costly, since it has made him a dependent of the politicians and, with a change of administration, brought him to Washington, hat in hand, seeking office like any other member of a spoils-system society. Henry Adams never came close to experiencing that fatality, but he did not hesitate to assign the victim some of his own characteristics. Gore "knew how to hold his tongue," as Adams claimed he did himself, and "he had learned to eschew satire," — in public, that is, like his author. In the private company of friends he still talks as freely as he might once have written. Gore has given up the quest for statesmanship and with some sincerity credits Ratcliffe with being "a shrewd practical politician." Confronted by Mrs. Lee's desperate question of "whether America is right or wrong," he speaks up for prudent hopefulness:

> I believe in democracy. I accept it. I will faithfully serve and defend it. I believe in it because it appears to me the inevitable consequence of what has gone before it. Democracy asserts the fact that the masses are now raised to a higher intelligence than formerly. All our civilisation aims at this mark. We want to do what we can to help it. I myself want to see the result. I grant it is an experiment, but it is the only direction society can take that is worth its taking; the only conception of its duty large enough to satisfy its instincts; the only result that is worth an effort or a risk. Every other possible step is backward, and I do not care to repeat the past. I am glad to see society grapple with issues in which no one can afford to be neutral.

Another and a more important character elaborates Gore's advice against trying to repeat the past. Carrington, an impoverished and disenchanted Confederate veteran, a lawyer who is in the capital not for politics but for the private practice of his profession, has an external history much like Adams' friend James Lowndes and quite unlike Adams' own, but the author was obviously very much at one with this Virginian "of the old Washington school," an eighteenth-century American whose world has been destroyed by the Civil War. Having fought for the South out of loyalty, not out of enthusiasm, Carrington has come through from defeat with a sharpened moral perception. It is he who remarks that Ratcliffe, once an antislavery leader in Illinois, would not be so courageous again, now that he has become "older, more experienced, and not so wise." Although he is Ratcliffe's rival in love, he is singularly helpless in direct encounters with the American political giant; his one victory, the exposure of the senator's corrupt past, he wins by the pen, not the sword. But if he is an inarticulate suitor in the present, he is able to find words for the past. On an excursion to Mount Vernon, where historic issues have a physical presence, he gives his simple catechism:

> Mrs. Lee asked Carrington bluntly whether he regretted the destruction of this old social arrangement.
>
> "One can't help regretting," said he, "whatever it was that produced George Washington, and a crowd of other men like him. But I think we might produce the men still if we had the same field for them."
>
> "And would you bring the old society back again if you could?" asked she.
>
> "What for? It could not hold itself up. General Washington himself could not save it. Before he died he had lost his hold on Virginia, and his power was gone."

Adams could claim to have made an unsentimental acceptance of the past, not only because he could name its virtues and still reject the notion of going back, but also because he could entertain a number of other attitudes as well. He made Mount Vernon the backdrop for a stylized procession of his characters who one by one come forward to declare what the great national symbol means to them. Victoria Dare, affecting the vulgar realism of modernity, audaciously mocks the image "compounded of Stuart's portrait and Greenough's statue of Olympian Jove with Washington's features" and proposes instead that of a coarse English country

squire, "very awkward, very illiterate, and very dull; very
bad-tempered, very profane, and generally tipsy after dinner."
Ratcliffe is a more serious debunker, though he admits with
frank respect that the squire of Mount Vernon is "almost the
only Virginian I ever heard of, in public life, who did not die
insolvent"; however he may have exploited his mediocre
talents in the eighteenth century, "if Washington were President now, he would have to learn our ways or lose his next
election." Between Victoria Dare's mock vulgarity and the
genuine article, Gore the historian and Carrington the man of
the past work out a joint position. Their problem is how to
deal with the Washington of myth as well as the Washington
who really existed. Carrington testifies to the myth and, even
more important, to the possibility of regretting the pastness
of the past without delusions about a return; on behalf of New
England, Gore accepts the mythic Washington as the apotheo-
sis of old Roman virtue. Adams, who had taken down the
Father of His Country to fit the needs of scholarly history in
the *Gallatin*, put his fictive cast through a ritual of atonement
as if he were acknowledging that the historian who blinds himself to the mythic ideal ends by missing all the values in history. The argument of a character whose "strong point was
facts" did not satisfy. For years Adams came back and back
to the "moral problem which deduced George Washington
from the sum of all wickedness." In that problem his own extended past crossed and tangled with the national experience,
so that the author of the *Education* concluded that "Mount
Vernon was only Quincy in a Southern setting. No doubt it
was much more charming, but it was the same eighteenth
century, the same old furniture, the same old patriot, and the
same old President." Almost at the moment when he was
making a realistic Washington for the sake of scholarship, he
turned, in *Democracy*, to the kind of question which made his
historical writing strong in more than facts alone.

Novel-writing gave Adams the chance to go a step beyond
his old maxim on literary style, "Get rid of your tricks. What
will then come, is according to the will of God and your own
good sense." Having rid himself of journalistic bombast, he
now worked to develop a more supple prose. Despite conscious struggles with the *Gallatin*, he had loaded that biography
with thirty-line chains of semicolon clauses, all too appropriate
to the heavy weight of his scholarship. Relaxing with the
fictive medium to which he felt no professional responsibility,
he turned out to have a facility for thinking in images that
gave his style lightness and range. In the *Gallatin* he had
worked with the idea of poignancy, rather than the look of it,
and not quite brought off his intended portrait of the tired
statesman. In the novel, by contrast, he could touch in the
background of a ride to Arlington with a single phrase which
made explicit his historical reference and at the same time
evoked his sense of the past: as the national cemetery comes
into view, Sybil Ross is startled "by the long white ranks of
head-stones, stretching up and down the hill-sides by thousands, in order of battle; as though Cadmus had reversed his
myth, and had sown living men, to come up dragon's teeth."
There still were many passages of incredible flatness, for
Adams could no more sustain his new powers of style than he
could his skill at narrative. But in the play of language as in
the contrivance of dramatic scenes, Adams found that notions
embodied in his novel were different in kind from the abstract
ideas and empirical facts with which he had been intellectually
concerned.

What Adams learned from writing *Democracy*, if we look to
its effect on his later writing, was the obvious and difficult
truth that the form of history is representational and the
medium was words. At the time, he was probably aware
only that the audience he sought was changing. He wanted
to recapture the general readers for whom his journalistic

pieces had been written, but he had in mind still other readers, too. The little group composed of his wife, the John Hays, and Clarence King, who with him made up "The Five of Hearts," listened to him read chapters of his novel at their teatime meetings and were pleased to find how amusing the ten-o'clock scholar could be at five. Their approval may have come too easily and perhaps encouraged the snobbish alarm at mechanization and barbarization that lurks in so many corners of the book. Hay and King, officeholders both, no doubt enjoyed the impudent suggestion that office and integrity were incompatible — for most people. What counted most was that the standards of wit and taste in the inner circle were high since, in his serious work, Adams thought for himself and did not fall in with the fashionable attitudes of any group. Established in Washington, Adams no longer wrote only for curious students and professional colleagues, but for the friends in his drawing room and the anonymous Americans outside.

☆ ☆ ☆

When Adams sailed for Europe at the end of May 1879, he left the proofsheets of the *Gallatin* with Lippincott, the unsigned "secret" manuscript of *Democracy* with Henry Holt, and in his study at Washington a neat pile of transcribed documents for his *History*, materials he had gathered in the course of his biographical researches. In England he continued the pattern of discipline and relaxation which he had followed at home: while he labored diligently at the Public Records Office and the British Museum, he also found ample time to renew friendship with Gaskell and with Henry James and to cultivate a new friend, a brilliant Oxford historian of his own age, John Richard Green. To canvass European archives for the international history of the Jeffersonian era, he had to use all the influence he could come by through family and class and profession, but he got what he wanted from Paris and Madrid and a pleasant trip for himself and his wife, too. Back in London, he worked out the veins he had started and several others, collecting old pamphlets, reading through the files of yellowed newspapers, searching into private collections. As he consolidated his materials, confidence ran high and the pleasure of "working only for the work's sake" still higher. He enjoyed watching his bits of knowledge fall into order, especially since the shape they took provided an ironic amusement of its own. The thoroughly informed historian could see the element of the ridiculous in the half-informed statesmen who were to be actors in his story. The friend of Green could see another irony, too, perhaps at his own expense: Green's *Short History of the English People* had emphasized the last word in its title and tried to subvert "drum and trumpet history" by underplaying political events and treating them as results, not causes, of social change. Henry Adams' growing assurance as a scholar encouraged the satirical bent of the writer.

Having taken spoils somewhat different from what his fictional heroine had collected, Adams too had "exhausted" Europe. He settled into a placid round of Washington winters and summers at the seashore cottage he and his wife had built next door to her father at Beverly Farms, north of Boston. In published work, his brimming energy of these years showed itself only in its by-products. Steady application produced a draft covering the first administration of Jefferson in the spring of 1882, but Adams was not ready for a test printing of six copies until two years later, or for publication until 1889. Volume by volume, he worked through the age of Jefferson and Madison, submitting his printed draft to private critics, revising the text in his determination to make it readable, putting the parts aside until he could be sure they fitted his whole design. Meanwhile, as diversion, finger exercise, and convenience for printing materials for his own future reference, he undertook his *John Randolph* in much the same spirit as he had done his novel. In fact, his satirical biography put his "scandalous libel" on democracy in the shade, since the reputation of the Virginia statesman has never quite recovered from his assault.

The libel on Randolph did not consist in any falling off of scholarship: Adams insisted on factual accuracy as a matter of course, but for a popular audience he assumed his right to radical freedom of selection and treatment. Freedom of selection was simply liberty to economize the number of facts by which to convey his basic story, not license to distort it. He had the responsibility of showing how other opinions than his own could be arrived at, but his fully-earned responsibility as a scholar gave him the privilege of expressing his own judgment by literary means that would have been suspect in an unknown. He felt certain that he could portray Randolph as a Don Quixote of the Old Dominion without committing a debauchery on the truth.

Adams' conception was not exactly that of a good-natured spoof. He made it clear that the world of John Randolph was utterly different from the Mount Vernon he had presented in *Democracy*. He mentioned Washington but twice in the biography, once in elaborating his assertion that Randolph was "too true a Virginian" not to have opposed ratification of the Constitution, and again in giving Randolph's toast at the time of the Jay Treaty crisis, "George Washington — may he be damned!" He never mentioned at all the name of Carrington which he had given to the idealized Virginian of his novel, although the Carringtons were intricately bound to Randolph by ties of neighborly ill will and political opposition. More positively, he filled the book with innuendoes, as on his subject's courage, that apologists have only strengthened by their attempts at reply. John T. Morse, the general editor

of the American Statesmen series, came to regret his choice
for this volume, as if only sympathetic biographies should
have been included. It is true that Henry Adams did not
simply record, but perpetuated the animosity between
Randolph and his own family, but he had made a case for
taking seriously the historic conflicts within the early republic.
He did not conceal his bias, he controlled it and made antipathy a means of insight.

In describing the colonial aristocracy into which Randolph
was born, Adams did not simply repeat the abstractions about
feudal France which he had contrasted to Gallatin's Geneva.
Like his master Tocqueville, who accepted the shift from
aristocratic to democratic times as a "providential fact," he
knew that the democratic picture of the old order had another
side. He appreciated the qualities of personal force, *virtú*,
and temperament which Tocqueville said were disappearing
in the placid, prudent, practical world of equality; even
though he kept up a tone of straight burlesque, he left evidence
of more complicated feelings:

> The life of boyhood in Virginia was not well fitted for teach-
> ing self-control or mental discipline, qualities which John
> Randolph never gained; but in return for these the Virginian
> found other advantages which made up for the loss of method-
> ical training. Many a Virginian lad, especially on such a re-
> mote plantation as Bizarre, lived in a boy's paradise of indul-
> gence, fished and shot, rode like a young monkey, and had his
> memory crammed with the genealogy of every well-bred horse
> in the state, grew up among dogs and negroes, master equally
> of both, and knew all about the prices of wheat, tobacco, and
> slaves. He might pick up much that was high and noble from
> his elders and betters, or much that was bad and brutal from
> his inferiors; might, as he grew older, back his favorite bird at
> a cocking-main, or haunt stables and race-courses, or look on,
> with as much interest as an English nobleman felt at a prize-
> ring, when, after the race was over, there occurred an old-

fashioned rough-and-tumble fight, where the champions fixed their thumbs in each other's eye-sockets and bit off each other's noses and ears; he might, even more easily than in England, get habits of drinking as freely as he talked, and of talking as freely as the utmost license of the English language would allow. The climate was genial, the soil generous, the life easy, the temptations strong. Everything encouraged individuality, and if by accident any mind had a natural bent towards what was coarse or brutal, there was little to prevent it from follow-lowing its instinct.

Adams' vantage on this world was not to be defined in terms of New England discipline, piety, or temperance. In suggesting these standards he could afford a two-edged irony, for he took a position above sectional controversy. To convey his fascination with a social environment that was "in itself an education," he assumed the manner of a Darwinian naturalist. He did not press his point about monkeys (not, that is, until a bitter comment on the jungle tactics of Randolph's later career), but in the tropical profusion and primeval freedom of the Southern countryside, he studied a variant of the human species that went by the name "Virginian gentry." It was the offshoot of an older race, "the child of the English squirarchy, and reproduced the high breeding of Bolingbroke and Sir Charles Grandison side by side with the coarseness of Swift and Squire Western." Adams suggested, in his role of mock-scientist, that the race of country squires was an unstable genetic combination that covered a wide gamut of personal qualities and tended toward a mutant form:

> The contrasts were curious, in this provincial aristocracy, between old-fashioned courtesy and culture and the roughness of plantation habits. Extreme eccentricity might end in producing a man of a new type, as brutal at heart as the roughest cub that ran loose among the negro cabins of a tobacco plantation, violent, tyrannical, vicious, cruel, and licentious in

language as in morals, while at the same time trained to habits of good society, and sincerely feeling that exaggerated deference which it was usual to affect towards ladies; he might be well read, fond of intelligent conversation, consumed by ambition, or devoured by self-esteem, with manners grave, deferential, mild, and charming when at their best, and intolerable when the spirit of arrogance seized him.

Behind the mask of Darwinism, Henry Adams was seriously concerned with the problem of whether eccentricity was or was not a force that could control historical change. His biographical treatment of the specific case seems to use the same definition as was later set forth in the *Education* — "actual exuberance of force," "self-assertion, bluff, brutal, blunt." Eccentricity in the *Randolph* stood as the equivalent to chivalry in his Spanish model, not only a human but an historical type; it was the old regime which would not pass when its time was done. As in the *Education*, Adams regarded Englishmen and Southerners as equally good examples, and he pointed out the "English" ways of Randolph and his society so constantly as to fix the word as a key epithet in this earlier book. He argued that Virginia depended on the mother country "for its tastes, fashions, theories, and above all for its aristocratic status in politics and law," but that the American Revolution effected a crucial change of conditions:

The Declaration of Independence proclaimed that America was no longer to be English, but American; that is to say, democratic and popular in all its parts, — a fact equivalent to a sentence of death upon old Virginian society, and foreboding dissolution to the Randolphs with the rest, until they should learn to master the new conditions of American life.

Needless to say, John Randolph did not adapt himself to the quiet, efficient, unaristocratic, "American" ways which the new time called for. To the biographer, his erratic inefficiency was predictable from childhood: "As for the boy John Randolph, it is said that he had a warm and amiable disposition, although the only well-authenticated fact recorded about his infancy is that before his fifth year he was known to swoon in a mere fit of temper, and could with difficulty be restored." With the adult, Henry Adams was even less indulgent than with the child. He noted every evidence he could of "the impulse to contradict" and "the passion for referring every comparison to one's self." What kept the portrait from becoming wanton travesty was the historian's interest in the extreme variant of the species, the archetype of squirarchical eccentricity:

> As the character of Don Quixote was to Cervantes clearly a natural and possible product of Spanish character, so to the people of Virginia John Randolph was a representative man, with qualities exaggerated but genuine; and even these exaggerations struck a chord of popular sympathy; his very weaknesses were caricatures of Virginian failings; his genius was in some degree a caricature of Virginian genius; and thus the boy grew up to manhood, as pure a Virginian Quixote as ever an American Cervantes could have conceived.

To assert that Randolph as "representative man" bore a similarity to the knight of La Mancha was quite different from establishing that their characters were congruent. After all, how pure a Quixote could any Virginian be? Adams kept his eye on Cervantes' theme, the anachronism of social forms, but the forms were different: the illusory background of John Randolph was not a pageant of flowering chivalry; rather, it was the Southern ideal of a classical (slave-based) democracy. Adams had ideals of the same eighteenth-century vintage himself, and the retired reformer of 1882 found that the "young reformers of 1800" cast a new light on the age

from which he stemmed. If for them "every boyish scrape
was a Greek tragedy, and every stump speech a terror to the
enemies of liberty," then the word *failure* which had seemed
so pathetic with respect to Gallatin might become much less
portentous. To write burlesque without jeopardizing history
was both an intellectual and a literary problem, and its solution marked a turning point in Adams' personal development.

Adams' general treatment of Virginia society extended to
his particular subject, and the very first scene of the political
drama struck the mock-heroic note. Randolph came upon
the national scene in 1799 at the moment when Virginia was
debating action on the famous resolutions against the Alien
and Sedition Acts. "By the tavern porch of Charlotte, at the
March court," young Randolph tried his fiery oratory against
the aged Patrick Henry. The patriarch of American liberty
came forward to warn his fellow citizens not to "raise their
hand against the national government." The historian, looking before and after, linked the orator of the Revolution "with
the awful judgment which fell on this doomed region sixty-
five years afterwards," and the satirist, much less darkly, tried
to fix the sense of history at Charlotte by drawing the scene
as a parody of a Benjamin West painting. West's well-known
"Death of Pitt" had given only the hushed grandeur of a
great statesman's passing; Adams aimed to outdo the painter
by playing up the "element of contrast in the composition":

> . . . When the old man fell back, exhausted, and the great
> audience stood silent with the conviction that they had heard
> an immortal orator, who would never speak again, make an
> appeal such as defied reply, then it was that John Randolph's
> tall, lean, youthful figure climbed upon the platform and stood
> up before the crowd.

Randolph's unrecorded reply might be sketched by logical
conjecture, but "what he could not answer, and what must

become the more impressive through his own success, was the splendor of a sentiment; history, past and coming; the awe that surrounds a dying prophet threatening a new doom deserved." Following "vague tradition," Adams rounded off the incident with Patrick Henry's last words to his young opponent: "Young man, you call me father; then, my son, I have something to say unto thee: *Keep justice, keep truth,* — and you will live to think differently." The next paragraph began at once with "Randolph never did live to think differently," and with that wicked slur the tone of the political narrative was set.

The connection between Adams' satiric and theoretical arguments was established by this opening scene, for the states' rights which Randolph championed in 1799 were to be the persistent concern that gave serious meaning to his career. If "men forgot the system of opinions of which it made a part" and "isolated, degraded, defiled by an unnatural union with the slave power, the doctrine became at last a mere phrase," then Adams found all the more reason for regarding Randolph's faith in the "inspired truth" of states' rights as the Virginian Quixote's helmet of Mambrino. That the tone of the book must shift from light comedy to bitter irony was indicated by the problem which the historian's longer view suggested: "What warranted such enthusiasm in this threadbare formula of words? Why should thousands of simple-minded, honest, plain men have been willing to die for a phrase?" The answer lay in the Jeffersonians' belief that in the program they had built up in the 1790's they had found the way to shake off the burdens of the past and build a new world without the evils of the old, to restrict that "supreme, irresponsible, self-defined power called sovereignty, which held human rights, if human rights there were, at its mercy," and thereby safeguard the American continent from repeating "the miserable experiences of Europe." The Republican program raised the historical issues that meant most to Henry Adams: confederation versus consolidation, American exceptionalism as against the universal corruptibility of institutions, the principle of humanity in conflict with practical circumstances. But two particular questions, stemming from Adams' analysis, show how the ridiculous and the terrible could exist together in his subject: Would power ever be limited by men who came to power for the purpose of limiting it? If only power could limit power, could sovereign states contest the national sovereignty without resort to force? Given the old Jeffersonian program as a yardstick, human frailty could be easily measured; yet, for all that the satirist might condescend to his subject, he remained aware that its consequence was national disaster.

To place Randolph, Adams had to put the foremost of the democrats into his picture. He credited Jefferson with working out the general lines of democratic government in America, but what he insisted on was that the great Virginian had failed to develop the theory of his practice. Whatever that theory might be, it was not expressed by the earlier program. The reforms enacted by the first Congress to meet under Jefferson's Presidency and Randolph's legislative leadership were to have begun a new book of precedents, but "payment of debt, reduction of patronage, abandonment of etiquette, preference of Spanish dollars, touched only the surface of things." Nothing in the Constitution was altered. No Federalist act was officially denounced as unconstitutional. As Adams saw it, "the government was reformed, as an army may be cut down, by dismissing half the rank and file and reducing the expenses, while leaving all its latent strength ready at any moment for recalling the men and renewing the extravagance." The superficiality of the Jeffersonians was not simply miscalculation; tragic error of judgment never was just a mistake, a petty cause of immense doom. The author of

"The Anglo-Saxon Courts" had not changed his mind, but only his point of view, as he portrayed the flaw of Jefferson as a radical self-deception about human nature. Once the Republicans came to power, they saw no reason why power should be opposed; confident that change of personnel made unnecessary any change of institutions, they forgot their own far-reaching criticisms of instituted power. And Jefferson, who thought the past could be easily undone, was in this frailty the leader of his party:

> In his mind, what had gone before was monarchism; what came after was alone true republicanism. However absurdly this doctrine may have sounded to northern ears, and to men who knew the relative character of New England and Virginia, the still greater absurdities of leading federalists lent some color of truth to it; and there can be no doubt that Mr. Jefferson, by his very freedom from theological prejudices and from Calvinistic doctrines, was a sounder democrat than any orthodox New Englander could ever hope to be. Thus it was that he took into his hand the federalists' constitution, and set himself to the task of stripping away its monarchical excrescences, and restoring its true republican outlines; but its one serious excrescence, the only one which was essentially and dangerously monarchical, he could not, or would not, touch; it was his own office, — the executive power.

That the man who held the highest view of human nature should illustrate so well its fundamental weakness was an irony worthy of a Hawthorne fable. In fact, Adams like Hawthorne used the assumptions of his ancestors' Puritanism even though their religion was not his. He had gone out of his way to note the books "which made the library of every New England farm-house" but were missing from Randolph's intellectual environment, *Pilgrim's Progress* and Baxter's *Saint's Everlasting Rest*, and the reason for his doing so now became clear. If Jeffersonian faith in the perfectibility, if not

the perfection, of human nature was a necessary tenet of
democracy, Jefferson's ingenuous failure to touch the power he
held himself would seem to undermine the foundations of
democracy. Spelled out in this way, the issue reached the
height of seriousness; looked at in the event, however, the difference of appearance and reality was so obvious that the historian could not restrain a satirical exuberance. Prideful folly
wears the comic mask when men take too great a part in
creating their own delusions:

> The republicans were over-confident in their own strength
> and in the permanence of their principles; they had in fact
> hoodwinked themselves, and Mr. Jefferson and John Randolph
> were responsible for their trouble. The party had really fought
> against the danger of an overgrown governmental machine;
> but Mr. Jefferson and John Randolph had told them they were
> fighting against monarchy. Setting up, to excite themselves,
> a scarecrow with a crown upon its head, they called it King
> John I., and then, with shouts of delight, told it to go back to
> Braintree. The scarecrow vanished at their word, and they
> thought their battle won. Randolph saw from time to time that,
> so far as there had been any monarchy in question, the only
> difference was that Thomas Jefferson instead of John Adams
> wore the shadow of a crown, but even Randolph had not the
> perspicacity or the courage to face the whole truth, and to
> strike at the very tangible power which stood behind this imagi-
> nary throne. He, like all the rest, was willing to be silent now
> that his people were masters . . .

Adams had elsewhere related the intellectual inconsistencies
of the Jeffersonians to the triumph of circumstance in human
affairs; now his task was to relate them to the character of the
"aristocratic democrat" whose life he was writing. He devoted a chapter to Randolph "In Harness" for his party, showing how the Virginia congressman gave all for party discipline
when Old School Republicans still held to the privileges of in-

tegrity and voted independently of caucus and administration. He then turned to Randolph the "Centralizing Statesman," who went full distance with Jefferson in out-federalizing the Federalists: with the Louisiana Purchase, the Virginia Republicans not only altered the constitution, they also changed the fundamental conditions of American society. The piled historical associations of Adams' early scenes took on a new irony when he showed that the Virginians' expansionism made inevitable a new America "without traditions, history, and character," in which a majority of the states came into being as "the mere creatures of the general government." Success for a time concealed the inconsistency of the Jeffersonians and the defects of Randolph's congressional leadership, but a surge of false confidence led the squire of Roanoke beyond his depth: he slipped into fighting for the removal of Justice Chase and for Georgia's recovery of the Yazoo lands on grounds of technicality when technicalities were against him. A states' rights argument on the Yazoo question was undermined by the fact that Northern democrats and Southern aristocrats had voted together to effect the Louisiana Purchase and to impeach Justice Chase, that is, to increase the national power and render the Supreme Court subordinate to the legislative power of the people through Congress. Had popular government won its battle against judicial supremacy, Southern agrarians might have been counted on to support the nationalization of power for as long as they could remain the dominant influence among Republicans. But Randolph failed to see what the slightest effort toward a political theory would have made clear: "strict construction" served the purposes of judge-made law in the long run; if the Jeffersonians had accepted "loose construction" and national concentration of power in the matter of Louisiana, was it not better to deal with the judiciary problem in the same way, ignore technicalities, and fight for a national democracy under legislative rule? Republican experience since 1801 pointed in that direction, but Randolph chose instead to argue on lines where he was bound to fail. Overestimating his own technical capacity for prosecuting Chase, he led his party to the defeat which exposed its instability.

Adams regarded the impeachment of Chase as "a landmark in American history, because it was here that Jeffersonian republicans fought their last aggressive battle, and, wavering under the shock of defeat, broke into factions which slowly abandoned the field and forgot their discipline." In managing the prosecution, Randolph was for the first time in his life "compelled to follow a long and consecutive train of thought within the narrow bounds of logical method." When the Senate returned a verdict of acquittal on March 1, 1805, his "decided" failure in this one test of his reasoning capacity matched the failure of the heterogeneous Republican party to act as a coherent legislative force. Lacking the eighteenth-century virtues of reason, resoluteness, and calm, Randolph was unfit for handling power; reverting now to his old policy of resistance to centralization, he showed himself as equally incapable of serving in a constructive role of opposition. A man who "had the merit of seeing others' mistakes if not his own," he gained no credit from a position that allowed him to detract from the credit of others. He attacked from all sides at once: in refusing funds for a secret negotiation, he demanded an honest bellicosity of the administration; in fighting appropriations for defense, stood for a policy of peace. The Virginian amused the House with his wit: he could ironically delay presentation of an appropriations bill until All Fools' Day and then barb his criticisms with the sting of truth; but he could not forge a program out of his piecemeal observations or use his brilliance to affect the course of legislation. The difference between constructive opposition like Gallatin's and the factionalism of John Randolph lay in the ability to compel governmental responsibility. Unable "to play a losing game with coolness and skill," he could not stand the test of failure.

Adams argued that Randolph's second career in opposition displayed the gradual weakening of the states' rights program as a rational program for governing society. He admitted that he might have cast his story in a straighter mold and shown Randolph as his "Virginian admirers" saw him, an apostle of consistency. By such a view, Randolph would be the one statesman to give Southern history the appearance of continuity. But Adams and the hypothetical Virginian interpreter had a basic disagreement that could be put in a single sentence: "Between the slave power and states' rights there was no necessary connection." He refused to take the easy way and report a simple evolution from the Republican program of 1798 to nineteenth-century Southern politics. Looking beyond verbal professions, he found that the slavery interests had in fact been a centralizing influence in American history, responsible for "all the most considerable encroachments on states' rights." He listed a long series of measures from the Louisiana Purchase to the Dred Scott case to show that slavery "required centralization in order to maintain and protect itself, but it required to control the centralized machine; it needed despotic principles of government, but it needed them exclusively for its own use." He bent over backward to insist that the states' rights doctrine had been "sound and true," the only possible "starting point of American history and constitutional law." Events made the doctrine obsolete as a practical democratic program, but it remained for Randolph to bring dishonor on the theory, to effect its "prostitution to the base uses of the slave power." The Randolph who re-entered politics in 1815 was no longer the fit subject for a genial satire on quixotism in America. Like Ratcliffe in *Democracy*, he had grown "politically sagacious" at the cost of losing his moral sense. More experienced and less wise, he tilted at the windmill of consolidated power only when the wind blew north-northwest:

To array the whole slave-holding influence behind the banner of states' rights, and use centralization as the instrument of slavery; alternately to take the aggressive and the defensive, as circumstances should require, without seeming to quit the fortress of defence; to throw loaded dice at every cast, and call, "Heads I win, tails you lose," at every toss, — this was what Randolph aimed at, and what he actually accomplished so far as his means would allow. The administration of [J. Q.] Adams, a Puritan and an old federalist, who had the strongest love for American nationality, was precisely the influence needed to consolidate the slave-holding interest. Randolph converted Calhoun; after this conversion Clay alone divided the slave power, and Clay was to be crushed by fair means or foul. The campaign succeeded. Clay was crushed, and the slave power ruled supreme.

Adams' writing once more tended to become lurid, but the historian, unlike the novelist, tried to demonstrate the grounds of his unscreened hostility. The Randolph who was responsible for blasting the pure Jeffersonianism of 1798 with the fatal curse of slavery seemed to change in character. Slavery became his monomania. He debated every legislative measure as though Emancipation were its object, and he saw every question of national power as connected with the war-making power by which abolition might be effected. The speech of January 31, 1824, in which Randolph first prophetically linked the slavery issue with the war power, revealed to the biographer a "new fusion of terrorism with lust for power." Adams sharply observed that the effect of Randolph's violent speech "must be to create the dangers which it foretold, and to bring the slave power into the peril which it helped to create." The era of the Jeffersonian experiment was over, and the nation moved into the dull gloom of years leading up to the great American catastrophe.*

*Adams' premises about democracy, slavery, union, and the central historical importance of the Civil War seem so unexceptionable that we may overlook

To support the changes in theme and characterization which he was trying to convey, Adams had to depart from his earlier model. Subjects he had handled lightly at the beginning of the book reappeared to show the difference in his tone. He picked up the story of Randolph's English debt, which harried him through life, and embellished the story with a classical analogy such as Randolph never dreamt of. The satire was altogether changed into invective:

> This patriot would accept no tawdry honors from a corrupt and corrupting national government! He would not take a seat in the Cabinet, like Clay, to help trample on the rights of Virginia! He would not take a foreign mission, to pocket the people's money without equivalent! He owed everything to his constituents, and from them alone he would receive his reward! This speech was made in February, 1828. In September, 1829, he was offered and accepted a special mission to Russia; he sailed in June, 1830; remained ten days at his post; then passed near a year in England; and, returning home in October, 1831, drew $21,407 from the government, with which he paid off his old British debt. This act of Roman virtue, worthy of the satire of Juvenal, still stands as the most flagrant bit of diplomatic jobbery in the annals of the United States government.*

---

the fact that they are also limited. What the student of politics presented as an era of twilight, a student of culture, Lewis Mumford, renamed "The Golden Day." To regard the prewar years too much through the eyes of John Quincy Adams meant ignoring the age of Emerson.

*William Cabell Bruce, whose *John Randolph of Roanoke* (1922) is a conscientious defense of Randolph particularly from the attacks of Henry Adams, has an important rebuttal of this point. He found that Randolph stayed in St. Petersburg almost a month, 26 days to be exact; that his English debt was paid before the Russian mission; that tallying the appointment officially at thirteen months and eight days, Randolph's pay and expenses were not illicit. "In our judgment, the acceptance by Randolph of the sum allowed him for his salary, outfit, and return expenses is entirely reconcilable with the stainless probity which had marked the earlier stages of his public career; though his mind was so gravely affected, during the latter years of his life, that it would be unjust, in any view of the case, to hold him to the same measure of moral

Although Randolph's contemporaries called him mad, Henry Adams refused to say that his wild talk and inexplicable actions were more than eccentricity. The biographer brought onstage all the "furies" of Randolph's later life — drink, avarice, family pride — but he would allow no excuse. To Randolph's own plea that "vindictiveness" was a "part of his Powhatan inheritance," Adams countered: "His insulting language and manner came not from the heart, but from the head: they were part of his system, a method of controlling society as he controlled his negroes. His object was to rule, not to revenge . . ." Finally, he returned to the question of Randolph's sanity and, re-examining the case in strictest justice, found "no apparent proof that he was less sane in 1831 than in 1806, except that he was weakened by age, excesses, and disease." His last words on the subject were uncompromising:

> Neither sickness nor suffering, however, are excuses for habitual want of self-restraint. Myriads of other men have suffered as much without showing it in brutality or bitterness, and he himself never in his candid moments pretended to defend his errors: "Time misspent, and faculties misemployed, and senses jaded by labor or impaired by excess, cannot be recalled."

Uncharitably letting Randolph write his own epitaph, Adams established his rational responsibility and thereby made the Virginian statesman an object of contempt and disgust. By thus inverting the terror and pity a Virginian admirer might

---

responsibility for his conduct then as before." Adams' attack is weakened by its needless inaccuracies.

The acrimony of the debate is shown by the fillip Bruce gave to his stolid apology for Randolph by adding, "He, at least, did not charge the Federal Government, as John Quincy Adams did in 1814, when he had been one of our Peace Commissioners at Ghent, for the expenses of a return journey to his post at St. Petersburg which he had never actually made." Such a charge requires more proof than citation of the mud-slinging congressional debates of 1827–28, but neither biographer pressed for accuracy when he could settle for a congenially disagreeable contemporary view.

see in his subject, he justified his own shift from boisterous mockery to virulent innuendo. Adams even persuaded himself, or, more properly, he wrote with utter conviction. By the time he saw the biography in print, he referred to it as his "intellectual brat," the first he had ever detested.

Granted that Adams sincerely detested his *Randolph*, we may find one important reason for his feeling in the work itself. The shift of emphasis from environment and circumstance to individual character made the book teach a lesson in morals rather than in history. In this sense, he had finally been caught up in provincial controversy. His last chapters hit home at Randolph but missed his larger aim of combining history with satire. The partial failure refreshed, rather than dulled, his resolution: his manuscript was hardly dry before he had begun work on another satirical biography, in which he planned to treat Aaron Burr as an "ideal scamp." What he needed was lightness of touch, not the heavy scoring of points, and in commenting on the "Burr," he expressed his realization that political satires were excellent finger exercises for the historian but had only a secondary value in themselves. To the great project of preparing the *History*, he made his scamp defer: "He was never a safe scoundrel to deal with, and may well run away and cheat the world again; but I tote about a hundred-weight of manuscript far more valuable than his, and he must bide his time." When his publisher H. D. Houghton refused that work for the American Statesmen series on the ground that Burr was not a statesman, Adams put it aside and subsequently, it appears, destroyed it. Minor work was not allowed to divert a major purpose.

His brimming energy of the early eighties continued for Henry Adams, and he found time to write a second novel, *Esther*, which he kept secret even from his intimates. *Esther*, though it indicates the growing imaginative range of the historian, belongs to a different side of Henry Adams and, as he himself asserted, to the man he later became. The labor of his days and years mainly went into the hundredweight of manuscript he was accumulating, far more valuable than all his preparatory works combined. His learning lightly carried, the fruit of his interpretive scholarship, and his literary skill, developed by his practice as a satirist, were brought together and fused in Adams' *History of the United States*. The knowledge and ideas, the skill and imagination which made the historian an artist can best be seen in his masterwork.

Chapter IV

HISTORY

1. SUBJECT AND METHOD

WHEN IN AGE Henry Adams reflected on his youth, he recalled the passage in his guidebook to Rome through which at the age of twenty-two he made his first acquaintance with Gibbon's *Autobiography*. "The thought of posing for a Gibbon never entered his mind," he protested, but he was led "more than once to sit at sunset on the steps of the Church of Santa Maria di Ara Coeli," where the idea of writing *The Decline and Fall of the Roman Empire* had germinated. Then, and for the next fifty years, he often repeated the pilgrimage and mused with Gibbon "in the close of evening, among the ruins of the Capitol." The question he asked was simply *Why*? "Substitute the word America for the word Rome, and the question became personal." The question did become personal for him, but it also became suggestive of an importance of theme in the American subject, and it finally reappeared, after the transformation worked by continued meditation, in the *History* that was conceived a century after Gibbon's. Adams' narrative began in a period apparently as little like the age of the Antonines as could be found in the experience of the West, and he used whatever history, geography, statistics, newspapers, or travelers' accounts could offer to give the reader a clear, full sketch of American life in 1800. He moved so easily among the pertinent data of an entire society that, when he came to describe the swampy hamlet which had recently become the capital, there was nothing startling but the final image. He found the city of Washington a symbol of America on the point of trying to master a continent and create on its soil a single republican nation:

> The contrast between the immensity of the task and the paucity of means seemed to challenge suspicion that the nation itself was a magnificent scheme like the federal city, which could show only a few log-cabins and negro-quarters where the plan provided for the traffic of London and the elegance of Versailles. . . . Public efforts and lavish use of public money could alone make the place tolerable; but Congress doled out funds for this national and personal object with so sparing a hand, that their Capitol threatened to crumble in pieces and crush Senate and House under the ruins, long before the building was complete.
>
> A government capable of sketching a magnificent plan, and willing to give only a half-hearted pledge of its fulfillment; a people eager to advertise a vast undertaking beyond their present powers, which when completed would become an object of jealousy and fear, — this was the impression made upon the traveller who visited Washington in 1800, and mused among the unraised columns of the Capitol upon the destiny of the United States.

Confidently Adams challenged comparison with the greatest model in the language. By his careful inversion of the Ara Coeli image, he indicated that his subject was a rising action, not a decline and fall. The suggestions of the image can be made more definite if we apply Alfred North Whitehead's comment on Gibbon to the historian who was emulating him. Whitehead adapted the famous epigram about the rise of barbarism and Christianity to Gibbon's eighteenth century, itself about to be transformed by the new forces of steam and democracy, counterparts to the external compulsion and human aspiration which had so affected the Roman Empire. Insistence on defining modern history by both these components makes it less plausible to date the present era from the American and the French Revolutions, more plausible to date it from the beginning of the nineteenth century in the country which has been the exemplary case of industrialization and democracy. The emergence of the American nation, by this view, is not peripheral to modern European history, but central, and Adams had picked a subject which has become since his time constantly more important for an understanding of the civilization in which we live. His problem was how to handle it.

One reason the United States has been the particular scene of the technological and democratic revolutions is that so little of its history has been enacted on its own territory. The absence of a feudal past with visible monuments and institutional holdovers allowed American society to develop more freely along new lines, but this freedom from complication made difficulties for the historian. To exploit the interest of colorful materials, the temptation was to emulate a rival nearer home and look to Francis Parkman's "history of the American forest" rather than Gibbon's "greatest and most awful scene" of falling empire. Parkman's *France and England in North America*, the one American work that bears examination by the same high criteria as Adams' *History*, had been appearing volume by volume since 1865, and Adams knew he had to take it into account. A glance at the geographical entity of the United States confirmed Parkman's picture of a forest continent, and Adams admitted on his very first page that such a picture conveyed the true sum of America's past and visible future even as late as 1800:

Even after two centuries of struggle the land was still untamed; forest covered every portion, except here and there a
strip of cultivated soil; the minerals lay undisturbed in their
rocky beds, and more than two thirds of the people clung to the
seaboard within fifty miles of tide-water, where alone the wants
of civilized life could be supplied. . . . Except in political arrangement, the interior was little more civilized than in 1750,
and was not much easier to penetrate than when La Salle and
Hennepin found their way to the Mississippi more than a century before.

Parkman, in depicting Europe's struggles for power over an
almost uninhabited continent, did far more than show a
change in "political arrangement": he elaborated with greater
vision and accomplishment than any other figure in our literature the image of virgin land which drew men west and helped
fill that land with a great nation. Adams granted the validity
in this image of the American past and, without derogation of
any kind, devoted himself to quite another. What concerned
him as an historian was the men of the New World on whom
the symbol worked, "on whose shoulders fell the burden of a
continent." The great forest symbolized, among other things,
a problem in ecology: "Nature was rather man's master than
his servant, and the five million Americans struggling with the
untamed continent seemed hardly more competent to their
task than the beavers and buffalo which had for countless
generations made bridges and roads of their own."

The beaver aspect of man did not lend itself to the Parkman
approach to history. The colonial historian began his narrative by declaiming the assumptions on which he proceeded:
"The springs of American civilization, unlike those of the elder
world, lie revealed in the clear light of History. In appearance, they are feeble; in reality, copious and full of force.
Acting at the sources of life, instruments otherwise weak become mighty for good and evil, and men, lost elsewhere in the

crowd, stand forth as agents of Destiny." Parkman's capital-
ized "Destiny" conveyed to the reader, not a besetting and
difficult problem like that suggested by Henry Adams' lower-
case word, but a simple romantic grandeur. The story of the
pathfinder was conventionally more heroic than that of
bridgebuilders; and although the disparity of "physical obstacles and the material means of overcoming them" might
call for courage in societies as in individuals, the qualities
which seemed dazzling in the single man might appear
matter-of-fact in the daily intercourse of large communities.
Adams accepted his subject with all its presumptive difficulties
and, with an irony almost defiant in its refusal of inflated abstractions, began his nine-volume masterpiece with the
plainest sentence he ever wrote: "According to the census of
1800, the United States of America contained 5,308,483
persons."

Adams' irony, while it did not conceal the magnitude of his
subject, emphasized the technical question of how the historian was to treat the individual. His practice works had
been mainly biographical and he meant to focus now on the
great "democratic triumvirate" of Jefferson, Madison, and
Gallatin, but he perceived his essential story to be the rise of a
new, American nationality in the civilized society of the
Western world. As a writer he found that American history
differed from European in being unromantic and that "science" was the alternative to spectacle: "Should history ever
become a true science, it must expect to establish its laws, not
from the complicated story of rival European nationalities,
but from the economical evolution of a great democracy."
Agreeing with Tocqueville that the great modern revolution
approached its natural limits only in America, he cited by contrast the European nations which were subject to external
pressures at every turn in the course of social development.
With them lay the epic possibilities, since "whatever other

character they might possess they must always be chiefly
military":

> The intensity of the struggle gave prominence to the indi-
> vidual, until the hero seemed all, society nothing; and what
> was worse for science, the men were far more interesting than
> the societies. In the dramatic view of history, the hero de-
> served more to be studied than the community to which he be-
> longed; in truth, he was the society, which existed only to pro-
> duce him and to perish with him. . . . With all the advantages
> of European movement and color, few historians succeeded in
> enlivening or dignifying the lack of motive, intelligence, and
> morality, the helplessness characteristic of many long periods
> in the face of crushing problems, and the futility of human ef-
> forts to escape from difficulties religious, political, and social. In
> a period extending over four or five thousand years, more or
> less capable of historical treatment, historians were content to
> illustrate here and there the most dramatic moments of the most
> striking communities. The hero was their favorite. War was
> the chief field of heroic action, and even the history of England
> was chiefly the story of war.
>
> The history of the United States promised to be free from
> such disturbances. War counted for little, the hero for less;
> on the people alone the eye could permanently rest. The
> steady growth of a vast population without the social distinc-
> tions that confused other histories, — without kings, nobles,
> or armies; without church, traditions, and prejudices, —
> seemed a subject for the man of science rather than for drama-
> tists and poets.

The kind of historical writing which Adams put behind
him emphasized a catastrophic individualism. Unlike the
self-styled "New Historians" who followed him by a generation, he did not scent a literary conspiracy to play up heroes
and ignore the people. He rejected his English friend Green's
vain protest, "The only war which has profoundly affected
English society and English government is the Hundred

Years' War with France, and of that war the results were simply evil." On this one question at least he took his stand for American exceptionalism: he laid the fault on Europe and on the past that the human story should be one of endless brigandage and bloodshed. Interpreting "European movement and color" thus, he implied some corresponding virtue in what was America's "chief offence, in the eyes of Europeans," its "dulness." When, after nine volumes of inquiry, he listed the chief lacks of an American subject for the historical writer, his summary was much the same as that which Henry James had made from the point of view of the novelist.* James's list had been more specific and longer, and had added at its conclusion: "The natural remark, in the almost lurid light of such an indictment, would be that if these things are left out, everything is left out. The American knows that a good deal remains; what it is that remains — that is his secret, his joke, as one may say." To explain this joke without explaining it away, to exploit this secret without making it common was Henry Adams' task.

True to the American humor which James had invoked, Adams treated the heroic with irony. What Jefferson had set out to do bore a surprising likeness to the great event which the historian meant to record: when the Republicans came to power through the "Revolution" of 1800, they intended

---

*"The negative side of the spectacle on which Hawthorne looked out, in his contemplative saunterings and reveries, might, indeed, with a little ingenuity, be made almost ludicrous; one might enumerate the items of high civilization, as it exists in other countries, which are absent from the texture of American life, until it should become a wonder to know what was left. No State, in the European sense of the word, and indeed barely a specific national name. No sovereign, no court, no personal loyalty, no aristocracy, no church, no clergy, no army, no diplomatic service, no country gentlemen, no palaces, no castles, nor manors, nor old country houses, nor parsonages, nor thatched cottages, nor ivied ruins; no cathedrals, nor abbeys, nor little Norman churches; no great universities nor public schools — no Oxford, nor Eton, nor Harrow; no literature, no novels, no museums, no pictures, no political society, no sporting class — no Epsom nor Ascot!" *Hawthorne* (1879), Chapter II.

their revolution to be "the most radical that had occurred since the downfall of the Roman Empire." Jefferson's aims — national unity, a minimal state, and enduring peace — so nearly agree with what the *History* shows to have been brought to pass that, were the author anyone but Adams, we might expect to find in Jefferson a democratic hero after all. Adams had strong Jeffersonian leanings and a qualified readiness to concede Jefferson's greatness "according to the admitted standards of greatness," but his tone implied unbelief in the admitted standards. Agents of Destiny, he seemed to suggest, might be like men commanding a river to flow downstream. The way in which he made Jefferson an anti-hero was essential to the conceptions of the science of history and the nature of his democratic subject which he was putting forward: "The scientific interest of American history centred in national character, and in the workings of a society destined to become vast, in which individuals were important chiefly as types." Jefferson typified a basic strain in the national character which he represented rather than formed, and "American Character" defined itself, not simply in the famous last chapter which bore that title, but in an action which required nine volumes to relate. Narrative form might not be sacrificed to the demands of science, but the hero was.

Adams' irony works against hunters for science as well as seekers after heroes. His introductory analysis of American society in 1800 might deceive an unwary reader, but he made Tocqueville's dictum, "A new science of politics is needed for a new world," his theme and not his starting point of method. After his daring opening sentence, one might expect him to discuss at length the social factors in American growth which have attracted historians since his time, as if "vital" statistics were the only data of scientific social history. Adams proved himself a brilliant expositor of the knowledge which statistics can give. He was equally deft in handling the figures of American customs receipts, premium rates at Lloyd's of

London, and the census itself. In looking at the report for the year 1810, his discernment showed itself to be not one, but two generations ahead of his contemporary scholars'. At a time when Frederick Jackson Turner had not yet told his colleagues in the historical profession that, with proper questioning, the census reports revealed the significance of the frontier in American history, Adams had already laid his finger on the question and on the answer that a still later generation was to make. Commenting on the third census, which took place ten years after the Jeffersonian period began, he remarked that "perhaps the growth of New York city and Philadelphia pointed to a movement among the American people which might prove more revolutionary than any mere agricultural movement westward." Important as the western movement and western influence were in fact and in the body of his *History*, Adams took a position which challenged Parkman in one generation and Turner in another: "Great gains could be made only on the Atlantic coast under the protection of civilized life." In explaining what he meant by calling the continental explorations of Lewis and Clark and Zebulon Pike "a great feat, but nothing more," he emphasized the problem of bringing the trans-Mississippi West "within reach." After a graphic narration of the historic crossings, he concluded:

> . . . But in the city of New York men were actively engaged in doing what Lewis could not do, — bringing the headwaters of the western rivers within reach of private enterprise and industry. While Lewis slowly toiled up the Missouri River, thinking himself fortunate if he gained twenty miles a day against the stream, the engine which Robert Fulton had ordered from the works of Watt and Bolton in England had been made, and Fulton returned to New York to superintend its use.

Although Adams conveyed his sense that the technological revolution surpassed even the westward movement in importance, he devoted scarcely more space to that theme than to the other. He reported faithfully the advances in steamboat tinkering, sailing-ship design, and scientific education, but he never let this information appear more than incidental to the chief matter of the *History*. He made the main body of his work a political, diplomatic, and military narrative which, superficially at least, conformed to the traditional canons of historical writing. He seemed to be composing an historical masterpiece in precisely the form which he was proving would not do at all.

Adams knew what he was doing, even though he felt an occasional uneasiness lest he be writing in the dead language of outworn historiography. In the midst of his labors, he told Parkman:

> The more I write, the more confident I feel that before long a new school of history will rise which will leave us antiquated. Democracy is the only subject for history. I am satisfied that the purely mechanical development of the human mind in society must appear in a great democracy so clearly, for want of disturbing elements, that in another generation psychology, physiology, and history will join in proving man to have as fixed and necessary development as that of a tree; and almost as unconscious.

In moments of diffidence Adams was lured by what Tocqueville had called the "dangerous tendency" of historians in democratic ages: "When the traces of individual action upon nations are lost, it often happens that you see the world move without the impelling force being evident. As it becomes extremely difficult to discern and analyze the reasons that, acting separately on the will of each member of the community, concur in the end to produce movement in the whole mass, men are led to believe that this movement is involuntary and that societies unconsciously obey some superior force ruling over them." Adams partly confirmed this prognosis when he described in significant terminology the popular "inertia" inherited from the eighteenth century or the "rates" of growth which were fixed and calculable, and Tocqueville himself had had to contemplate what Adams saw as an ultimate "democratic ocean," in which "the atom might move, but the general equilibrium could not change." But Adams never quite deserted those fellow historians and fellow Americans who "were not disposed to make of their history a mechanical evolution." That social determinism might be morally unpalatable was not a sufficient reason to make him hang back, but he was intellectually unprepared for the task of which he saw only the dim outlines. Like his friend Oliver Wendell Holmes, whose historical studies in the law opened the way for future social sciences, he recognized the limitations of his training. It was Holmes who said that "the black-letter man may be the man of the present, but the man of the future is the man of statistics and the master of economics." Rather than force scientific concepts upon his materials, Adams used these concepts for the fruitful doubt they raised about the mode of historical writing he actually practiced.

Caught in a stage between the dramatic historian and the social scientist, Adams had consciously outgrown the slogan of his professional contemporaries, "History is past politics, politics is present history." Aware that its literal meaning was inadequate, he hoped to endow the sentence with a richer, symbolic meaning and overcome the narrowness of his training: politics might be made to symbolize social development just as individuals might stand for more than just themselves. In fact, the two went together, for no historian could deal with 5,308,483 *persons*. Even when he was most disenchanted with all his characters but Gallatin and concluded "that history is simply social development along the lines of weakest resistance, and that in most cases the line of weakest resistance is found as unconsciously by society as by water," he prefaced his gloomy statement with an all-important qualification, that "the element of individuality is the free-will dogma of the science, if it is a science." He wrote the *History* on the premise which he made explicit in his final chapter:

> Readers might judge for themselves what share the individual possessed in creating or shaping the nation; but whether it was small or great, the nation could be understood only by studying the individual. For that reason, in the story of Jefferson and Madison individuals retained their old interest as types of character, if not as sources of power.

The element of individuality did not suffer in the *History* from a meagerness of *dramatis personae*. Adams directed an immense cast with great skill. To bring on the scene characters who were commonly known, at least by name, presented problems enough for a narrator, but with those who were commonly unknown he ran the risk of making all cats gray in the dark. The slowed pace at which he brought on figures like David R. Williams, the energetic congressman from South Carolina, and General Jacob Brown, in Adams' opinion the best military leader in the War of 1812, kept them in focus for readers encountering them for the first time. The middling-famous, on the other hand, might count for single men without difficulty, but their individuality might be hard to find. To this problem Adams addressed himself with a Butlerian good humor. He nourished a fondness for Nathaniel Macon, but felt constrained to bury him in a one-inch grave: "No man in American history left a better name than Macon; but the name was all he left." He cared not at all for Senator Samuel Smith, the leader of disruptive faction who for a time "held Gallatin and Madison at his mercy. Had he been able to separate them, his influence would have had no bounds, except his want of ability." He even resorted to his readers' familiarity with the recently published *Huckleberry Finn* and captioned his portrait of Joel Barlow "a compound of Milton, Rousseau, and the Duke of Bridgewater." As to the characters who typified the constructive and destructive elements in Jeffersonianism, he had to lower his tone with Gallatin, lest Horatio steal the limelight from his Hamlet, and to elevate his tone with Randolph, so that his critical opposition would be taken seriously. Jefferson, who "could be painted only touch by touch," was to be the most complex character of them all.

As Yvor Winters has said, Adams handled Jefferson with obvious pleasure in the mastered craft of portraiture; but the chief interest of character for him was its effect on intellect and ultimately, in a political history, on the theory and practice of politics. To illuminate the essential American democracy, he quarried every source and used every detail. A diplomatic dispatch, for example, might cast light upon the personality of Jefferson, which would in turn bring out some new aspect of the nation's political life. Adams appreciated how much foreign observers might help Americans to national self-awareness: given an almost automatic acquaintance with the facts of one's own past, the native benefits from the perceptions of underlying pattern that an outsider may get just by the luck of being different. Using travelers' accounts to advance his chapters on social development, Adams also realized that, for his purpose of concentrating on politics, there were no better foreign observers of events and men than the European diplomats whose business was to know America. He found that the French minister "entertained at heart a liking for Jefferson" and felt that his sardonic comment in a note to Talleyrand did not contradict that judgment: the Mercutio-like humor as well as the truth of Turreau's "There is something voluptuous in meaning well" communicated themselves to the context in which Adams quoted it and gave momentary relief to the critical bearing-down on Jefferson's increasing difficulties. But Turreau was not cited just to prove Jefferson charming; his epigram harked back to the historian's first introduction of Jefferson into his narrative. Adams had at the outset coupled Jefferson's winning personal qualities, his "sunny and sanguine" temperament, with the fact that "he sometimes generalized without careful analysis," that "he was a theorist, prepared to risk the fate of mankind on the chance of reasoning far from certain in its details," that "he was superficial in his knowledge, and a martyr to the disease of omniscience." Turreau merely supplied one touch toward completion of the portrait.

The free-will dogma which made so much of Jefferson's individuality emphasized his responsibility, also. Adams granted Jefferson the engaging qualities of his nature and was willing to distinguish between the "Virginian ease of temper" which marked his administration and the "incompetence" of Madison's, but such concessions could not alter judgment. He was rigorous on principle and as strict with himself as with Jefferson in his demands for careful analysis and certainty in details. In his mind, the posterity to which men must refer what they do or write was not just a vague conception. The test of time which he envisaged assumed a world of complex and changing relations in which an idea is not of itself demonstrable, but, in the words of William James, "*becomes* true, is *made* true by events." Adams had had a more than casual acquaintance with the founders of pragmatism, Chauncey Wright, Charles Sanders Peirce, and James, and though he had not been a very steady or devoted member of their informal club, he had published Peirce's great seminal article on Berkeley in the *North American Review* of October 1871. He had responded with a natural affinity to the new, tough American empiricism, and its idiom passed easily into his personal vocabulary. Taking the test of time upon himself in 1899, when a shroud of silence had settled over his *History*, he wrote to an inquiring stranger, "I have let the work go without further concern, knowing that in another fifty years our point of view will have wholly changed, and that my work can only be tested when the strain is put on it." The same strain of time existed for the conduct of politics, and it was the function of the historian to establish the pragmatist proving ground in which political ideas met or missed their validation by time and the facts. Adams prepared the apparatus for his empirical tests by first setting up Jefferson's "view of governmental subjects," which he found to be "simple and clearly expressed":

> The national government, as he conceived it, was a foreign department as independent from the domestic department, which belonged to the States, as though they were governments of different nations. He intended that the general government should "be reduced to foreign concerns only;" and his theory of foreign concerns was equally simple and clear. He meant to enforce against foreign nations such principles as national objects required, not by war, but by "peaceable coercion" through commercial restrictions. "Our commerce is so valuable to them that they will be glad to purchase it, when the only price we ask is to do us justice."

He concluded the passage portentously, "The history of his Administration will show how these principles were applied, and what success attended the experiment." He then proceeded to examine in minute detail the day-to-day consistency and practical effectiveness of Jefferson's and Madison's administrations, narrating with enlarged scope and more central focus the administrative history of which his *Gallatin* had given the essence. His analyses were careful, and carefully kept from being oversubtle and legalistic. It was his express conviction that "the attempt to treat politics as a branch of the profession of the law had the disadvantage of refining issues to a point which no large society could comprehend." What he held against Jefferson was his failure to face political situations squarely and educate his public to the issues, for the consequence of that failure was resort to subterfuge and the complication of government beyond the possibility of popular control. To have dropped the political theory of 1798 without constructing another in its place thus became an offense, not simply against the demands of rationality, but against the democratic principle. By Jefferson's premises, Adams defined Jefferson's accountability.

Permitting his main characters to ask their own questions, Adams could neatly justify his writing a political history; fidelity to empirical techniques, carried to this point, was convenient, since the Jeffersonians invariably chose the test of politics. That there were other kinds of test, Adams made clear. When Jefferson resolved to liberate his "priest-ridden" opposition and "introduce science into New England by political methods, President Dwight, the head of New England Calvinism, was persuading Benjamin Silliman to devote his life to the teaching of chemistry in Yale College"; at almost the same time, Harvard "scandalized the orthodox by electing as Professor of Theology, Henry Ware, whose Unitarian sympathies were notorious. All three authorities were working in their own way for the same result; but Jefferson preferred to work through political revolution . . ." A passing comment on Gallatin, that "the revolution of 1800 was in his eyes chiefly political, because it was social," aimed at the same point. If, as Adams later wrote, the historian must deal with forces "as they had been felt," the Jeffersonians demanded treatment primarily of their political experiments. And not the leaders only, for "every one admitted that Jefferson's opinions, in one form or another, were shared by a majority of the American people"; the individual served as a type.

Adams was applying to history the pragmatist concern for consciousness which emphasized that the knower's relation to a given fact is part of our definition of what the fact is. As Noel Annan has suggested, a modern translation of Ranke's famous call for history *"wie es eigentlich gewesen"* might be not "what actually happened," but "what it was really like." But the historian is a knower, too: although he granted his subjects the chance to be tested in the way they would have chosen, Adams did not fallaciously believe he should try to picture the past simply as it pictured itself. His object was to be true to the present as well as the past. He looked at once for what was timely in its own day and significant for the future in which he himself lived. He was one day to explain this dual principle of selection in a letter to Henry Osborn Taylor in which, contrasting the purposes of *Mont-Saint-Michel and Chartres* and Taylor's *The Medieval Mind*, he defined the poles between which, in the *History*, he tried to maintain an equilibrium:

> I have no object but a superficial one, as far as history is concerned. To me, accuracy is relative. I care very little whether my details are exact, if only my *ensemble* is in scale. You need to be thorough in your study and accurate in your statements. Your middle-ages exist for their own sake, not for ours. To me . . . the middle-ages present a picture that has somehow to be brought into relation with ourselves. To you, there is no difficulty in transferring ourselves into the middle-ages. . . . Our two paths run in a manner parallel in reverse directions, but I can run and jump along mine, while you must employ a powerful engine to drag your load.

Needless to say, the strictures on *Mont-Saint-Michel and Chartres* are exaggerated, but the statement suggests that in the *History* Adams successfully attached the powerful engine of his scholarship to his extraordinarily sharp critical sense and achieved both verisimilitude to one age and expressive relevance to another.

Adams' attempt to do right by both sides of the relation between himself and the past met with difficulty, for many events fulfilled the requirements of timeliness without being obviously important to subsequent American history. Such was the conspiracy of Aaron Burr, which he made a continuing concern in three volumes and the exclusive subject of six full chapters in one.* (The episode spans Volumes II–IV, with greatest space in Volume III.) From the beginning, Adams had stressed the question of whether the western settlements of 1800 were "the germ of an independent empire," and he had focused on Burr the dark light which befitted the "loadstone" and "certain centre of corruption." The Burr conspiracy brought these two stories together and provided the thread on which to narrate both the international and the domestic intrigues that encompassed Jefferson's administration. It revealed the precocious expansionism of the West. It confirmed that, in eighteenth-century terms, the United States was overextended geographically and likely not to survive the power of centrifugal forces. It demonstrated the decline of energy, competence, and authority in the national government. Because, like the conspiracy of Pickering among the New England Federalists, it "had no deep roots in society, but was mostly confined to a circle of well-born, well-bred, and well-educated individuals," it was "one more proof" of Adams' expressed point "that the moral instinct had little to do with social distinctions." Most important, it gave the first hint that there was a positive power in the hitherto inert mass of the nation. The Burr conspiracy was even a means, some would add, of

---

*The amount of space devoted to this might be explained by Adams' having available his own research for the unpublished "Life of Burr." But the handling of Burr indicated much more than a historian's warming-over of superfluous materials from a past project; it showed, rather, what had attracted an outstanding scholar to undertake that biography.

reflecting on the characters of Jefferson and Madison — and, incidentally, Jackson, who was to displace an Adams thereafter. Given the informed and exacting mind of the historian, the Burr incident had a meaning for its own time and a serious place in the longer view of national development.

As Adams made his empirical method seem to dictate the form of political history, he used the canon of timeliness to determine not only the content, but also the proportions of his work. For example, in the fifth volume, the first on Madison's administration, fourteen of the nineteen chapters deal with diplomatic history. The three chapters on domestic affairs in the middle of the book are entitled "Executive Weakness," "Legislative Impotence," and "Incapacity of Government." Chapter XVII opens with the appropriate words: "The government of the United States reached, March 4, 1811, the lowest point of its long decline. President Madison had remained so passive before domestic faction, while so active in foreign affairs, that the functions of government promised to end in confusion." The external form conveys not only information but judgment so that when the historian simply and quickly passes his verdict, the whole structure of the volume picks up the words like a sounding board and sets them reverberating.

From this general look at the way Adams worked, it appears that a decline and fall was really his subject after all. On the surface of things, he was presenting the rise of the American democracy in terms of the passing of the rule of statesmen or, as he put it, "the reign of politics." The Burr conspiracy was defeated by the underlying health of the society, not by the officials charged with protecting the state. Under Madison, the low point in the long decline of government was reached. It is this recurrent theme which emerges from the single most important change Adams made from an earlier interpretation. In the *Gallatin*, Jefferson's bold program of 1806 calling for internal improvements and a national university signified a momentary grasp of the possibilities for positive democratic government, which Canning's accession and the increase of foreign pressures kept Jefferson from realizing. Now even the momentary glory was departed. When the historian's brother Charles criticized the glowing language of his draft, Adams stripped away the rhetoric until there was hardly anything left but an equivocal suggestion that the idea was a political scheme for diverting giddy minds from foreign quarrels.* Yet it was not Jefferson, however ambiguous his motives, who bore the responsibility when Adams shifted the blame for his disappointment in the great failure from the foreign scapegoat Canning to agents more directly concerned:

> Congress . . . never succeeded in rising to the level of Jefferson's hopes and wishes; it realized but a small part of the plan which he traced, and what it did was done with little system. . . . Not by means of government, or by virtue of wisdom in the persons trusted with government, were Jefferson's objects destined at last to be partially attained.

Adams' ideal of a democratic development, fully attained and administered with the economy of systematic planning, set the high standard which made his main story seem to be a falling action.

---

*In the 1885 version at the Massachusetts Historical Society (III, 227), Adams' original sentence, with suggested deletions in brackets, read as follows: "The Annual Message of 1806 rose above [all] these [mental] limitations, [and reached a level such as lifted its author among statesmen of the highest order, whose minds, developed with experience, have by natural good sense overcome their own innate prejudices.]" On the margin of the next page is Charles Francis Adams' caustic note: "In other words, the plan of an Augustus or a Richelieu was to be worked out through a political machinery set in motion by the average voter and resulting in the American Congress. The thought was puerile." What Charles asserted so dogmatically has much in common with the reluctant conclusion which his brother Henry had reached despite the impulse expressed in his rhetoric.

Had Adams done no more than this, he would have been the last of the political historians grimly describing the end of political history and he would have been untrue to his own richer view of his subject. If only because his ideal of statecraft might leave him antiquated, he had to make his work an ultra-political history, and he found the means of doing so without radically departing from conventional form. Jefferson's statesmanly possibilities, his free will as an individual, depended not only on his knowledge and vision but on constricting necessities, so that the historian had to show another side. Furthermore, Adams was now arguing that the defeat of Jefferson's 1806 program meant the triumph of general social forces rather than of fortuitous circumstance. If politics represented the conscious development of the human mind in society, what of the unconscious developments that seemed to have a law of their own? The political historian explicitly stated that "the wit of man often lagged behind the active movement of the world," and he purposely underemphasized events which, substantially ignored in their day, he saw as important for later times, but he did include them in a wide and discreetly picked variety. He painstakingly recorded the rise of manufactures and the invention of the factory elevator, even though he restricted the space allotted to these matters. He let timely events like the conspiracy of Burr and the conduct of foreign relations set their own proportions and did not try to redress the balance by treating bobbins and spindles extensively, too. Instead of writing at length of social, economic, and technological history, he presented it intensively through the story of significant developments like the steamboat.

To the image of the steamboat Adams gave the same fine care he lavished on the portrait of Jefferson. In 1800 it was the project of "a few visionaries." In 1805 when Pike ascended the upper Mississippi and Fulton returned home with his new engine, the explorers were immediately acclaimed, but the historian spoke up for the inventor: "The greatest steps in progress were often unconsciously taken, and Fulton's steamboat was an example of this rule. Neither in private talk nor in the newspapers did his coming experiment rouse much notice. . . . So far as concerned activity of mind, politics still engrossed public attention." In 1810 when Francis James Jackson, the British minister, had been "kicked" out of Washington, "he retired to a country-house on the North River, about eight miles above New York, where he caught a glimpse of an American invention which, as he had the good sense to suspect, was more important than all the diplomatic quarrels in which he had ever engaged." When in 1815 the United States turned its attention from Europe inward upon its own development, it could do so because "the invention of the steamboat counterbalanced ocean commerce." In the prefatory chapters, slowness of communication was established as one of the main centrifugal forces in a sprawling American society, and in the concluding chapters, the steamboat is offered as a crucial reason why New York alone of the seaboard states grew as fast as the country in the nineteenth century. The contrapuntal theme of Fulton's steamboat weaves in and out of the *History*, but even the first Mississippi steamer of 1811, duly noted in the final volume, plied its way on the periphery of Adams' political narrative. The logical reason for all this concern was that "in the application of science the steamboat was the most striking success," but its symbolic effectiveness was another matter. This depended on the presentation as well as the ordering of his materials, and Adams clinched his point only when he brought together the very different elements of his story in a climactic moment:

> The attack on the "Chesapeake," the trial of Aaron Burr, and the news from Copenhagen, Holland, and London made the summer and autumn of 1807 anxious and restless; but another event, under the eyes of the American people, made up a

thousand fold, had they but known it, for all the losses or risks incurred through Burr, Bonaparte, or Canning. . . . [On August 17,] the steamboat "Clermont," with Robert Fulton in command, started on her first voyage. A crowd of bystanders, partly sceptical, partly hostile, stood about and watched the clumsy craft slowly forge its way at the rate of four miles an hour up the river; but Fulton's success left room for little doubt or dispute, except in minds impervious to proof. The problem of steam navigation, so far as it applied to rivers and harbors was settled, and for the first time America could consider herself mistress of her vast resources. Compared with such a step in her progress, the mediæval barbarisms of Napoleon and Spencer Perceval signified little more to her than the doings of Achilles and Agamemnon. Few moments in her history were more dramatic than the weeks of 1807 which saw the shattered "Chesapeake" creep back to her anchorage at Hampton Roads, and the "Clermont" push laboriously up the waters of the Hudson; but the intellectual effort of bringing these two events together, and of settling the political and economical problems of America at once, passed the genius of the people.

Society at large and its instituted government "took no notice," but if "the reign of politics showed no sign of ending" for the Americans of 1807, the historian could still claim some of the prerogatives of dramatic history. The momentary vision of the *Clermont* and the *Chesapeake* fixed in one sharp image all the vital contrasts of the *History*: the immediately and the unconsciously felt forces in society; the eighteenth-century, medieval, Homeric beginningless past and a future full of possibilities; the dominion of nature and the mastery of man; Europe and America; war and peace.

The working out of these great antinomies can be followed through the whole large-scale composition of the narrative, but they all hinge on the rise of steam and democracy. From what we have seen so far, the technological revolution seems the more important of the general causes to which the political history ironically points, for it changes society, regardless of conscious social will, as if by the mechanical action of necessary laws. The democratic revolution, on the other hand, seems to be a negative force which frustrates statesmen and conspirators alike. The term "unconscious," applied to this force, does not mean mechanical development, but appears to be nearly synonymous with human ignorance. As a satirical novelist, Adams suggested that to find democracy one ought to look anywhere but in politics, so that we have cause to suspect that his political history of the emergent American democracy says the same thing. Yet the evidence of *Democracy* suggests that Adams would hardly call increasing mechanization a sufficient criterion of progress, and the profession of a democratic faith which he made in that book, whatever the reservations, fits in with everything he ever said or wrote. We are faced with the new version of an old question: When so much that could be said in praise of democracy is left out, what remains? And we may be relieved to find that the answer is by no means secret. When we examine the introductory chapters in which the historian established his situation and his themes, we discover the positive content of Adams' faith, subtly woven in at first but gradually becoming the essential object of concern.

Adams began his survey of "Physical and Economical Conditions" with the observation that in an international and historical perspective the American democracy of 1800 did not seem very special. The five million people, mostly wedged between the tidewater and the sea, were likely to fail in their experiment of creating a single continental republic, for the problem of conquering space would probably take centuries to solve:

> In the minds of practical men, the experience of Europe left few doubts on this point. After two thousand years of public labor and private savings, even despotic monarchs, who em-

ployed the resources of their subjects as they pleased, could in 1800 pass from one part of their European dominions to another little more quickly than they might have done in the age of the Antonines.

The glancing reference to Gibbon does not stand alone, for, as William R. Taylor has pointed out, images of time flicker through the chapter — seventeenth century, thirteenth, eighth, fifth, second. The eighteenth century, which "ruled supreme," might as well be any other for all the progress that had been made in man's relation to nature. In the placid account of economic conditions, we encounter the sweep of a Sir Thomas Browne: "The plough was rude and clumsy; the sickle as old as Tubal Cain, and even the cradle not in general use; the flail was unchanged since the Aryan exodus . . ." The whole past of humanity was shored up on the far side of 1800. By contrast, "the entire banking means of the United States in 1800 would not have answered the stock-jobbing purposes of one great operator of Wall Street in 1875." To unify the continent quickly, as they must, Americans had instruments which were known to take centuries and financial means which were negligible, although their relatively equal distribution, mentioned in passing, might be a powerful resource. Tocqueville's touchstone of democracy, "equality of condition," brought up on the last page of this chapter, and the change in political arrangement casually noted on the first provide the only clues that America might overcome the past.

When Adams proceeded to the popular characteristics which escaped censuses and surveys, he found that the help of European observers was limited. Once their varying reliability was sifted, they still could only tell how Americans ate or dressed or slept. Looking at their moral observations, the historian found a bill of charges that was not only answerable, but inconsequential. The vices of frontier society, like its virtues, were mostly impermanent, and the vices of older communities "were rather survivals of English low-life than products of a new soil." As for idleness, "no immigrant came to America for ease or idleness" and "not for love of ease did men plunge into the wilderness. Few laborers of the Old World endured a harder lot, coarser fare, or anxieties and responsibilities greater than those of the Western emigrant." The safest inference was that "the people were still simple" and "likely to be conservative." Science and learning had made little progress in the last fifty years, and innovators felt themselves smothered with apathy. The problem of steam navigation had been solved in 1789, but Philadelphians refused to use John Fitch's boat; "they did not want it, would not believe in it, and broke his heart by their contempt." The West rejected Fitch as coldly as the East, and he finally took his own life. His pathetic story was but one illustration of the "popular inertia" which was the obstacle to America's success: "Conservatism possessed the world by right," but Americans "were still required, by the nature of their problems, to become a speculating and a scientific nation." Adams thus implied that the condition of technological progress was the triumph of democracy over conservatism in society at large, though the triumph was not yet in sight.

Turning from material and social to intellectual considerations, Adams surveyed the arts and sciences, the general habits of mind, and most particularly the political culture of the country, and once again the prospects of 1800 were not encouraging. In New England, he found a social system "admirably adapted for the uses of the eighteenth century" and a conservatism basically "of the English type" which, out of place and out of date, dourly waited for the catastrophes that democracy would surely bring:

> History and their own experience supported them. They were right, so far as human knowledge could make them so;

but the old spirit of Puritan obstinacy was more evident than reason or experience in the simple-minded, overpowering conviction with which the clergy and serious citizens of Massachusetts and Connecticut, assuming that the people of America were in the same social condition as the contemporaries of Catiline and the adherents of Robespierre, sat down to bide their time until the tempest of democracy should drive the frail government so near destruction that all men with one voice should call on God and the Federalist prophets for help. The obstinacy of the race was never better shown than when, with the sunlight of the nineteenth century bursting upon them, these resolute sons of granite and ice turned their faces from the sight, and smiled in their sardonic way at the folly or wickedness of men who could pretend to believe the world improved because henceforth the ignorant and vicious were to rule the United States and govern the churches and schools of New England.

Southern resistance to the nineteenth century was different from New England's in kind, but not in degree. Despite the vision and cosmopolitan breadth of Jefferson, his "reforms crippled and impoverished the gentry, but did little for the people, and for the slaves nothing," and his program of 1798 was as much a dead end of political thought and practice as Tie-Wig Federalism: "The science of politics, if limited by the Resolutions of Virginia and Kentucky, must degenerate into an enumeration of powers reserved from exercise." As for the Middle States, New York had energy which it threw to the side of innovation and a society which, "in spite of its aristocratic admixture, was democratic by instinct." But the alliance of Jefferson with Aaron Burr and the Livingstons and the Clintons, whose ideals had so little to do with "the austerity of Cato and the simplicity of Ancus Martius," was unpromising: "The political partnership between the New York Republicans and the Virginians was from the first that of a business firm; and no more curious speculation could have been suggested to the politicians of 1800 than the question whether New York would corrupt Virginia, or Virginia would check the prosperity of New York." Although the intellectual activity of the older states warranted finer analysis than the popular habits of frontier society, it offered little reason to expect that popular inertia and the weight of the past would be overcome. That little, however, was important. New York stood for innovation; the mental attitude of New England could not long persist when evidently "the thoughts and methods of the eighteenth century held possession of men's minds only because the movement of society was delayed by political passions"; if the Virginian Jefferson "appeared ill at ease in the position of a popular leader, he seemed equally awkward in the intellectual restraints of his own political principles." And the one omission from this summary of Adams' sketch is crucial, for "had New England, New York and Virginia been swept out of existence in 1800, democracy could have better spared them all than have lost Pennsylvania."

Of all the states which came under the survey of America in 1800, Pennsylvania, the most populous, showed the most encouraging signs of progress. With over half the banking capital of the country and the flourishing beginnings of important industries, Pennsylvania could also boast the most active public spirit of any society in the Union. It contained the only sanitary, well-watered, well-lighted city in America, with a model market and a model jail; its citizens and commerce enjoyed the use of fine turnpikes, with more under construction; its enterprise was constructing canals at a faster pace than any other state; its foreign trade was second only to that of New York. But when Adams turned from material considerations to the question of political culture, he faced a major difficulty. Although he described Pennsylvania as "the only true democratic community" then existing in the

East, he had to use indefinite or negative terms: the state was "neither picturesque nor troublesome"; it "contained no hierarchy like that of New England; no great families like those of New York; no oligarchy like the planters of Virginia and South Carolina"; the people could not be said to have a Yankee smartness, even though they usually won what they set after and "never committed serious follies." The baffling simplicity of these essential democrats presented the riddle on which the whole *History* is based:

> To politics the Pennsylvanians did not take kindly. Perhaps their democracy was so deep an instinct that they knew not what to do with political power when they gained it; as though political power were aristocratic in its nature, and democratic power a contradiction in terms.

In a sense, so long as American democracy has an unfinished history, the riddle of whether democratic power is a contradiction in terms must remain unanswered. In practice, we reply to the conundrum not with an answer but with a choice. The choice which Adams made can be seen in the final chapter of his introduction, his delineation of American ideals. He had established, in accordance with the canons of the French "scientific" historian Taine, the people, the milieu, and the time, but he felt that what the record showed was somehow insufficient. To depict the economic, the social, and even the intellectual situation had been comparatively easy, since the data, subjected to scientific criticism, might yield their story. But the moral situation left no documents that helped; only the misleading survived and perhaps only the misleading had ever existed. The recorded attitude of a Wordsworth had been "poignant scorn," and only a bold historian dared say that "the unconscious poet breathed an atmosphere which the self-conscious poet could not penetrate." Worse than the fact that documentary evidence existed only

to mislead was the utter lack of evidence of any other sort.
There was good cause to observe imaginative caution:

> In the early days of colonization, every new settlement rep-
> resented an idea and proclaimed a mission. . . . No such char-
> acter belonged to the colonization of 1800. From Lake Erie to
> Florida, in long, unbroken line, pioneers were at work, cutting
> into the forests with the energy of so many beavers, and with no
> more express moral purpose than the beavers they drove away.

Whatever his misgivings, Adams felt compelled to render
the atmosphere which the unconscious poet breathed. There
was little to go on. Citing the adverse comment of Europeans made some of his reservations clearer, but did not take
him far along his course. The only statements of fact he could
put into his chapter seemed not to take him much farther:
he pointed out the birthdate of Emerson in 1803, and that
of Lincoln in 1809, "the moment when American character
stood in lowest esteem"; and he noted the lower-class origins
of some half a dozen visionary inventors, who were "the outcome of typical American society" and whose inventions
"transmuted the democratic instinct into a practical and tangible shape." Facts were scarce, and the eagle-stretching
oratory for which Americans were famous gave due warning
that rhapsody was an inadequate substitute for facts. The
only clue for one who wished to frame an answer to the
Wordsworths of the Old World came from the greatest
foreign analyst of American society. Alexis de Tocqueville
had written:

> I readily admit that the Americans have no poets; I cannot
> allow that they have no poetic ideas. In Europe people talk a
> great deal of the wilds of America, but the Americans them-
> selves never think about them; they are insensible to the won-
> ders of inanimate nature and they may be said not to perceive

the mighty forests that surround them till they fall beneath the hatchet. Their eyes are fixed upon another sight: the American people views its own march across these wilds, draining swamps, turning the course of rivers, peopling solitudes, and subduing nature. This magnificent image of themselves does not meet the gaze of the Americans at intervals only; it may be said to haunt every one of them in his least as well as his most important actions and to be always flitting before his mind.

Nothing conceivable is so petty, so insipid, so crowded with paltry interests — in one word, so anti-poetic — as the life of a man in the United States. But among the thoughts which it suggests, there is always one that is full of poetry, and this is the hidden nerve which gives vigor to the whole frame.

The high priest of Adams' faith at twenty-five still wielded power over his imagination at fifty. In transforming Tocqueville's insight into the hidden but "abundant mine of poetry" in American society, Adams made a profound commitment of his own to democracy in America:

> Only with diffidence could history attribute to such a class of men [as the American democrats] a wider range of thought or feeling than they themselves cared to proclaim. Yet the difficulty of denying or even ignoring the wider range was still greater, for no one questioned the force or the scope of an emotion which caused the poorest peasant in Europe to see what was invisible to poet and philosopher, — the dim outline of a mountain-summit across the ocean, rising high above the mist and mud of American democracy. . . .
>
> For himself [the American] cared little, but his dream was his whole existence. The men who denounced him admitted that they left him in his forest-swamp quaking with fever, but clinging in the delirium of death to the illusions of his dazzled brain. No class of men could be required to support their convictions with a steadier faith, or pay more devotedly with

their persons for the mistakes of their judgment. Whether imagination or greed led them to describe more than actually existed, they still saw no more than any inventor or discoverer must have seen in order to give him the energy of success. They said to the rich as to the poor, "Come and share our limitless riches! Come and help us bring to light these unimaginable stores of wealth and power!" The poor came, and from them were seldom heard complaints of deception or delusion. Within a moment, by the mere contact of a moral atmosphere, they saw the gold and jewels, the summer cornfields and the glowing continent.

Beneath the generalized strokes of Adams' portrait of the American after Tocqueville, a reader may think he detects the features of Colonel Beriah Sellers. The touch of Twain reminds us that in Adams' irony was an element of the American humor he regarded so highly. The democrat was in on the secret joke of what the severe political analyst and the would-be technological determinist left out. The scion of presidents, not the first of his family to be accused of blood-pride, made steerage immigrants, malarial frontiersmen, and lower-class inventors his heroes alongside the Virginia aristocrat to whom he gave his qualified allegiance. At both ends of the empirical relation between the historian and his subject were American visionaries. Even the reader least well-disposed toward Adams would have to say that the callow novelist with his empty phrase about "the true democracy of life" had been forced to articulate the imaginative conception behind the cliché, something the historian could neither deny nor ignore. But whether we refer to Adams' vision or his cold conception, its nature and quality can only be assessed as it is sustained through the nine volumes of his *History*. In his execution of the work we may judge whether his grasp of both necessity and aspiration, steam and democracy, informs the political record and whether his art, like that of the eight-

eenth-century model he was emulating, presents a view of
what exists in history besides the follies and miseries of mankind.

2. EXECUTION AND DESIGN

ADAMS' six prefatory chapters comprise a masterpiece of
analytic discourse, at the end of which college assignments
and popular acquaintance with the *History* usually stop. But
the prologue is no substitute for the drama. Adams, unlike
his master Tocqueville, had a further aim than the static
observation of American democracy. What interested him
was the American democracy *in action*, and to this he gave
more than nine-tenths of his space. If we are not put off by
the prospect of a long work, we may see why, to avoid the
faults and combine the virtues of his *Gallatin* and his *Randolph*,
Adams required more than the sum of their lengths. Am-
plitude is necessary to the historical form. Neither the
dramatic nor the scientific historian simply tells a story or
argues a thesis. What distinguishes a history from documentary fiction and from straightforward exposition is that it
requires the techniques of both and can use the economies of
neither. If an historian generalizes without adequate demonstration, he is rightly condemned by the professional scholar,
and if he presents all the relevant data with a too resolute
conciseness, he loses the general reader whose voice is also
heard in judgment. Further, in selecting "all the relevant
data," he must appear to make "all the data" relevant. No
history can present all the facts, but every historian tries to
persuade the reader not only of his specific accuracy, but of
his catholicity — both to be tested by whatever outside
knowledge his audience can bring to bear. Considering these
things, we can understand what Adams meant by saying he
had written "a dozen volumes of American history for no

other purpose than to satisfy himself whether, by the severest process of stating, with the least possible comment, such facts as seemed sure, in such order as seemed rigorously consequent, he could fix for a familiar moment a necessary sequence of human movement." His "familiar moment" suggests an event already familiar to his public and indicates his responsibility to both more and less scholarly readers; but it is a familiar moment of *fixity*, signifying the esthetic as well as the scientific achievement of his work. The "for no other purpose" seems more than a mask of modesty, since only concentration of intent could compose a history which was to serve so many functions. No doubt he did write to satisfy himself, having tried to make his standards the highest. Yet the least contestable statement to be inferred from his sentence is the paradox which links the historian's strict literary economy with the actual massiveness of literary output.

Largeness of scale and grandeur of subject connect history with a much older literary form. Although we sometimes refer to things that have happened and speak loosely of the "epic" of invention, say, or of democracy, the term applies to a narrative form and, in its proper sense, can help us make out the intrinsic design of Adams' *History*. The analogy suggests a reason why Adams did not break away from the age-old and in some respects deplorable chronicling of warfare: epic poetry relates the trials of heroes and usually the ultimate trial by combat with its life-and-death gravity; a history which narrates the similar crucial test of a whole society may show the serious import of melodramatic and spectacular events. On the other hand, the contrast between the legendary subject matter of epics and the systematically verifiable data of histories, in which the deficiency of leaders cannot be entirely glossed, makes clearer Adams' preference for the mock-heroic tone. While parody in its ironic way implies the existence of greatness, the representation of deflated heroes remains logically unassailable. Sometimes we get both effects at once: in the great parody of Spanish honor, Don Quixote is an object not only of ridicule but of affectionate respect. In Adams' *History*, the mock-heroes tend to stay deflated and the protagonists of his epical narrative seem to be democracy and invention. To see how he did it requires a close look at his execution of the work.

The shift from exposition to action is made without a break. Immediately following the chapter on American ideals, the *History* presents their foremost exponent at his inauguration. Jefferson, previously introduced in his intellectual capacity, now appears as a personality and a solid figure. The first contemporary description to be cited catches the awkwardness of the man, the "loose, shackling air" and "rambling, vacant look" which fit with the portrait of the American as comic hero. Jefferson's painstaking simplicity of costume for the solemn occasion evokes a reference to Carlyle's Teufelsdröckh, for the new President "seemed to regard his peculiar style of dress as a matter of political importance"; Adams was making light with one of America's favorite symbols of republican plainness. He could also, with more devastating effect, give his irony a Gibbonian turn: "The exaggerations or equivocations that Jefferson allowed himself, which led to the deep-rooted conviction of Marshall that he did not tell the truth and must therefore be dangerous, amounted to nothing when compared with the dishonesty of a corrupt man." The several voices of his satire accompany Adams' bringing on-stage the main participants in the inaugural ceremony — the really corrupt Aaron Burr; Madison and Gallatin, the other two aristocrats in Jefferson's "democratic triumvirate"; and John Marshall, Jefferson's greatest opponent and "of all aristocrats the most democratic in manners and appearance." (The outgoing President, John Adams, was absent from the ceremony and is likewise missing from the text; only after five hundred and fifty-six pages of circumambulation does the reader come across the name of "Washington's successor" and "Jefferson's predecessor.")

To Adams, the inauguration was important for what was said there, and he proceeded at once to the address which was America's highest expression for 1801. Using textual criticism as the means of integrating narrative and documentation, not to mention satire, he worked out a hypothetical Federalist reaction to the speech. Such an observer, conservative rhetorically as well as politically, would note Jefferson's mixed metaphors: when the "spasms" of European war became "billows" that touched even the American shore, laughter might almost drown the words of Jefferson which followed, "We are all Republicans, we are all Federalists." In the "orthodoxy" of his Federalism, the President seemed "to belittle the revolution which had taken place." But "in no party sense was it true that all were Republicans or all Federalists," and Jefferson "had no idea of harmony or affection other than that which was to spring from his own further triumph." Deeper criticism was leveled against the easy assertion that ours was "the strongest government on earth":

> Clearly, Jefferson credited government with the strength which belonged to society; and if he meant to practise upon this idea, by taking the tone of "the strongest government on earth" in the face of Bonaparte and Pitt, whose governments were strong in a different sense, he might properly have developed this idea at more length, for it was likely to prove deeply interesting.

The distinction between the strength of society and the power of government was one which the historian, at least, felt obliged to develop at length. For the moment, however, his task was to note the way in which the two became blended in political thought. Commenting on Jefferson's sketch of an agrarian commonwealth under a "wise and frugal" government, the coming of which would "close the circle of our felicities," Adams refurbished his critical vocabulary with a word to which he had already given special weight. In his opening chapter, which established a single character for all the past before 1800, he had said with deliberate ambiguity that "as yet Americans did not dream that the experience of mankind was useless to them." The chapter on ideals confirmed the practical need of dreaming in America, but the final word on Jefferson's Arcadian view of the American future emphasized a quite different meaning. Adams remarked on the Jeffersonian utopia, "The possibility of foreign war alone disturbed this dream." The dream which was a practically effective vision might also be a delusion that Americans were exempt from the historic conditions of human life.

Although Adams briefly discussed Jefferson's assumption that the automatic rule of economic interest must naturally produce a reign of justice in the world, his immediate intention was to reinforce the pattern set by the chapter on the inaugural. In the succeeding chapter on the organization of government, he continued the progression from ideals to practice. He covered the appointment of the Cabinet and the filling of lesser offices, the plans for reducing taxes and the actual reduction of military services. "Congress and the Executive appeared disposed to act as a machine for recording events, without guiding or controlling them," but "by an unlucky chance the system never became fully established." Events themselves were to be Adams' main comment: When the American consul at Tripoli refused a demand for higher tribute, war followed and taxes had to be reimposed. A few frigates dispatched to the Mediterranean did not, however, lead to a major change in policy: "That enlightened govern-

ments like those of England, France, and Spain should rob
and plunder like an Algerine pirate was in theory not to be
admitted." From this point, Adams' pattern expands in
widening concentric circles like waves from a dropped stone:
the first two-thirds of Volume I analyze the American
democracy and get the great experiment under way, but the
last third concerns itself with international affairs. In
Volume II the proportions are reversed. The last note of
Volume I, so carefully prepared for that "Peace is our passion" seems a refrain, is the citation of Jefferson's letter from
which the phrase comes. The last note of Volume II is struck
only after Jefferson's foreign entanglements have become desperately snarled with England, France, and Spain at once:
"The greatest triumph to be then hoped from Jefferson's
peace policy was the brilliant close of his only war." The last
circle of the expanding theme of war and peace is only reached
with the completed story of a nation which lost its character in
pursuing the peace policy, found it again in a war, yet survived the war with its pacific quality still the firmest trait in
that character.

In his chapter on "Organization," Adams took up other
themes from earlier suggestions. The administration that was
to have been too pure for the spoils system could not resist the
chance to equalize the Federalists in the civil service by replacing at least half with solid Republicans. In New York,
the Federalists were not the only "victims of the scandal,"
since Jefferson took sides with the Clintons against Burr in a
sordid struggle that would have corrupted a lesser man. "On
both sides the game was selfish," the historian averred, "and
belonged rather to the intrigues of Guelphs and Ghibellines in
some Italian city of the thirteenth century than to the pure atmosphere of Jefferson's republicanism." Adams followed the
presidential leadership as it ushered its program through the
legislative session, where he was most interested in the act

that founded a military academy at West Point, "for the government thus assumed the charge of introducing the first systematic study of science in the United States." Science apparently belonged to the future as corruption to the past.

As the energy of progress spent itself, the historian returned to the theme of corruption. By the sixth chapter on domestic affairs, called simply "Personalities," the meaning of "democratic triumvirate" becomes inverted and no longer refers to Jefferson, Madison, and Gallatin. The affair of the scurrilous journalist James Callender came to a head, and the "Scotch adventurer" who had once enjoyed Jefferson's favor turned on his protector with all manner of vicious slanders. The hurt President should have ignored them, but "unluckily for him, he undertook to contradict Callender's assertions." Tom Paine, notorious at least in New England as an enemy of religion and social order and a traducer of President Washington, returned to America with Jefferson's blessing and began to turn out anti-Federalist invective that embarrassed the President far more than it helped him. "The storm of recrimination raged with noisy violence amid incessant recurrence to the trio of godless ruffians, — Jefferson, Paine, and Callender" — that was the Federalist notion of what a "democratic triumvirate" must be. As bad as the partisan illusion was the actuality of unsavory alliances designed to ruin Burr, who had himself not yet given any sign that he deserved such treatment at the hands of his old friends. As the issue of democracy was settled and conflict over principle began to wane, American politics began to decline.

Adams here executed for the second time within a volume a major transition. Whereas the introductory spiral from material conditions to spiritual qualities led without a break to the expression of national ideals by Jefferson in power, the spiraling descent from high policy to low invective and lower intrigue led to the sharpest of contrasts. Immediately follow-ing the petty disputes of his American personalities, Adams in-troduced an individual who dwarfed them all. Adams' thir-teenth, like Gibbon's famous fifteenth chapter, brought into the narrative a new and essential influence, not "a pure and humble religion," but a corrupt and violent society, and the scale of discourse changed:

> Most picturesque of all figures in modern history, Napoleon Bonaparte, like Milton's Satan on his throne of state, although surrounded by a group of figures little less striking than himself, sat unapproachable on his bad eminence; or, when he moved, the dusky air felt an unusual weight. His conduct was often mysterious, and sometimes so arbitrary as to seem insane; but later years have thrown on it a lurid illumination. . . . Ambition that ground its heel into every obstacle; restlessness that often defied common-sense; selfishness that eat like a cancer into his reasoning faculties; energy such as had never before been com-bined with equal genius and resources; ignorance that would have amused a school-boy; and a moral sense which regarded truth and falsehood as equally useful modes of expression, — an unprovoked war or secret assassination as equally natural forms of activity, — such a combination of qualities as Europe had forgotten since the Middle Ages, and could realize only by reviving the Eccelinos and Alberics of the thirteenth century, had to be faced and overawed by the gentle optimism of Presi-dent Jefferson and his Secretary of State.

There had been a Ghibelline touch to Jefferson's struggle with Burr, but the object was a functionary's job in New York and not power over the temporal dominions of the Pope. Some of Jefferson's faults might parallel certain characteristics of Napoleon, but the lines could never meet. Difference of de-gree was everything: Jefferson's awkwardness at his vices called for burlesque, but Napoleon seemed to fit the language of hyperbole. Little James Madison stood at Jefferson's side, while beside Napoleon stood Talleyrand, "a figure even more sinister and almost as enigmatical." And to complete the contrast, the Spanish court could be juxtaposed to the Federalists' "trio of godless ruffians," since Napoleon and Talleyrand were to wrest Louisiana from Spain only to make America the beneficiary of their nefarious work. Paine and Callender seemed innocent as children after a look at the perfectly moral, exceedingly religious, utterly degenerate Don Carlos IV, a king too busied by his self-amusement to find time to reign, whose ministers came to power as each in turn took the queen for his mistress. In the perspective of Spanish decadence, American character seemed as simple as Adams had alleged.

As he approached the Louisiana episode, Adams put into practice a resolution taken at the early stages of writing. In 1881 he had expressed to Lodge his concern about the "extreme monotony" of his subject. He had fairly decided "not to attempt giving interest to the society of America in itself, but to try for it by way of contrast with the artificial society of Europe, as one might contrast a stripped prize-fighter with a life-guardsman in helmet and breastplate, jack-boots and a big black horse." At once he added the qualification, "The contrast may be made dramatic, but not the thing." He aimed to get dramatic contrast without taking the focus off his true subject: if Spain had over the United States "the influence of the whale over its captors," the remark pointed forward to the Louisiana Purchase and that first moment in American history when "all parties agreed in admitting that the government could govern." Beyond that was the lure of Florida by which Napoleon led American diplomacy into tortuous paths that tried the nation's sense of shame: American claims to West Florida under the Louisiana Treaty depended on the Napoleonic technique of falsehood; when American troops moved into West Florida to maintain order after a cooked-up revolution, the government used Napoleonic methods to plunder a defenseless empire. At last, indeed, Adams applied the same epithet, "force or fraud," to Napoleon's European dictatorship and to the American republic.

The story of the Louisiana Purchase carried Adams well into his second volume. To trace the story from its beginning, he showed that Napoleon obtained the retrocession of Louisiana from Spain as a first step toward a revived transatlantic empire for France, of which the plantation island of Haiti was to be the center. For the first time an American historian pointed out that the revolution of Toussaint Louverture, which cost France so heavily in funds and more heavily still in her finest troops, diverted Napoleon from his New World ambitions and shunted him back to his old plans for a Continental System. The island revolution received no aid from the liberal and interested Virginian administration and did not even later win appreciative remembrance by the Americans. As Adams saw it, "the prejudice of race alone blinded the American people to the debt they owed to the desperate courage of five hundred thousand Haytian negroes who would not be enslaved." Napoleon prepared his ultimatum to the English, and sold Louisiana to the eager Americans. The constitution was, according to Jefferson, made a "blank paper," and the Resolutions of 1798 were, according to Adams, made "waste paper." John Quincy Adams alone in Congress proposed a constitutional amendment to legitimize the treaty, and only a small minority stood up against the proconsular method of organizing the new territory, "by an act of sovereignty as despotic as the corresponding acts of France and Spain." In Jefferson's next annual message, "no hint was given that Congress stood in danger of overstepping the limits of its powers, or would do well to return within them."

Events at home took on the imperial cast as well. Jefferson suggested to his legislative managers the impeachment of

Justice Chase. He brought the idea forward by a series of
rhetorical questions which he claimed to ask his correspondent
Nicholson simply "for your consideration; for myself, it is
better that I should not interfere." Adams' comment was
simple: " 'Non-intervention,' according to Talleyrand, 'is a
word used in politics and metaphysics, which means very
nearly the same thing as intervention.' " Whatever the fall
from pristine grace, Jefferson was encouraged by a triumph
at the polls beside which even his great diplomatic victory
shrank, for in the election of 1804 he won such success as
"might have turned the head of any philosopher that ever
sat on a throne." The sun of popularity was unsteady, however, for the clouds of international complication were gathering over Washington as thickly as over Paris. While Monroe
and Talleyrand became embroiled at the scene of onetime
triumph, Madison at Washington alienated the Spanish
minister by pressing erroneous claims on the subject of
Louisiana's eastern boundary. And Great Britain finally
entered the narrative when Jefferson's republican informality
at the White House fell upon the new and unwarned British
minister as a deliberate insult arranged to humiliate him
before his French opponents and to make his wife a laughing-
stock to the world. Adams was not implying that a personal
misunderstanding could sway the fate of nations. He put the
incident of Anthony Merry's seeming slight carefully in its
context of an economic and diplomatic situation that became
more and more precarious as American competition began
to threaten English mercantile prosperity. But the debacle
of Merry's first dinner at the President's did show how ease of
temper became a carelessness of conduct leading to quasi-
Napoleonic acts of state:

> Of all American hospitality none was so justly famous as that
> of Virginia. In this State there was probably not a white man,
> or even a negro slave, but would have resented the charge that

he was capable of asking a stranger, a foreigner, a woman, under his roof, with the knowledge that he was about to inflict what the guest would feel as a humiliation. Still less would he have selected his guest's only enemy, and urged him to be present for the purpose of witnessing the slight. Reasons of state sometimes gave occasion for such practices, but under the most favorable conditions the tactics were unsafe. Napoleon in the height of his power insulted queens, browbeat ambassadors, trampled on his ministers, and made his wife and servants tremble; but although these manners could at his slightest hint be imitated by a million soldiers, until Europe, from Cadiz to Moscow, cowered under his multiplied brutality, the insults and outrages recoiled upon him in the end. Jefferson could not afford to adopt Napoleonic habits. His soldiers were three thousand in number, and his own training had not been that of a successful general; he had seven frigates, and was eager to lay them up in a single dry-dock. Peace was his passion.

In continuing the parallel characterization of Jefferson and Napoleon, Adams had to maintain a delicate control over his material. Dramatically, the interest of manners might make up for the want of outdoor spectacle, but as he remarked of Irving's *Knickerbocker History*, "few literary tasks were more difficult than to burlesque without vulgarizing, and to satirize without malignity." What kept his own satire from becoming out-and-out denigration was that he showed how ill the Napoleonic coat fit Jefferson, the exponent of ideals he himself shared. The complications of Volume II arose as Americans adopted the high tone of European diplomacy and, in the case of Spain, pursued "a quarrel which could lead only to disappointment or war." The opening of Volume III made it clear that America would not go to war, for Jefferson's Second Inaugural put all doubts to rest by declaring history to be his witness that "a just nation is taken on its word, when recourse is had to armaments and wars to

bridle others." Manners, character, and national policy were
intertwined, as Adams' comment suggested:

> The sentiments were excellent; but many of Jefferson's fol-
> lowers must have asked themselves in what history they could
> find the fact, which the President asserted, that a just nation
> was taken on its word; and they must have been still more per-
> plexed to name the nation, just or unjust, which was taken on
> its word by any other in the actual condition of the world.

The historian found fault equally with a Florida policy
that was unjust and a statesmanship that brought the government to a choice "between war and humiliation more dangerous than war," but he did not deny the national necessity
of possessing in West Florida the mouths of the rivers which
were vital highways of the Mississippi Territory. To build up
pressure on Spain, Jefferson tried by a few kind words to the
injured British minister to leave Napoleon "under apprehen-
sions." Dabbling in power politics, he casually attempted "a
task which several European governments were then employ-
ing half a million armed men to accomplish, hitherto without
success." If Jefferson was going in for power rather than
justice, why not seize Florida in the moment when Spain was
helpless in Napoleon's grasp, and when the risk of war with
France involved the compensating chance of standing "at
the head of the coming popular movement throughout the
world"? But Jefferson preferred to exercise the most monarchical function allowed under the American Constitution and
play a diplomatic game instead:

> He played a game of finesse hardly safe in the face of men
> like Godoy, Talleyrand, and Napoleon, whose finesse was
> chiefly used to cover force, and was not betrayed or derided by
> factious opposition in the press. Besides being unsafe, it was
> unfair to himself. Jefferson was an honest man, and in putting
> on the outward appearance of a Talleyrand, he resembled an

amateur imitating Talma and Garrick. Gestures and tones
alike were unnatural, awkward, and false; they exposed him to
ridicule. If President Jefferson had taken the public into his
confidence, he would have told the American people that under
no circumstances would he consent to war; but that if the great
Powers of Europe combined to injure America, she would close
her ports, abandon her commerce, shut herself within her own
continent, and let the world outside murder and rob elsewhere.
Such an avowal implied no disgrace; the policy it proclaimed
was the alternative to war; and as the radical doctrine of the
Republican party, the course was not only that which Jefferson
meant to take, but it was that which he took. The avowal might
have invited aggression, and have been followed by failure; but
he would have done better to fail on a direct issue of principle,
than to fail after evading the issue until the issue itself was lost.

In developing "the contrast," an American theme older
than the republic itself, Adams followed the difference in
manners to differences in political and social process. America's international relations, which in the second volume
reached the height of success and then sank sharply, continued
downward in Volume III. Misunderstandings multiplied,
not into war, but into confusion. As Adams suggested, there
was a continentalist tendency in Jefferson's statesmanship as
in Napoleon's; but the harder Jefferson tried to acquire
Florida, the more clearly he demonstrated that American
conditions of diplomacy differed from European. When
Florida negotiations slowed to a standstill, it became apparent
that this acquisition, a Southern interest, could be effected
only through the power of Northern votes. When Jefferson
asked for a secret appropriation, a dozen Virginia congressmen
went into opposition "and for the first time in a struggle vital
to Jefferson's credit, more than half the majority consisted of
Northern men." The defection of John Randolph dealt the
greatest blow, for erratic as he was, he was the only member

George M. Cushing, Jr.

THE ADAMS HOUSE IN QUINCY

HENRY ADAMS AS
AN UNDERGRADUATE

Harvard University Archives

Massachusetts Historical Society

HENRY ADAMS
AT HIS DESK AT
BEVERLY FARMS

FROM AN ARCHITECTURAL DRAWING for Henry Adams' house at 1603 H Street in Washington. The building, now torn down, was designed by H. H. Richardson.

Fogg Art Museum

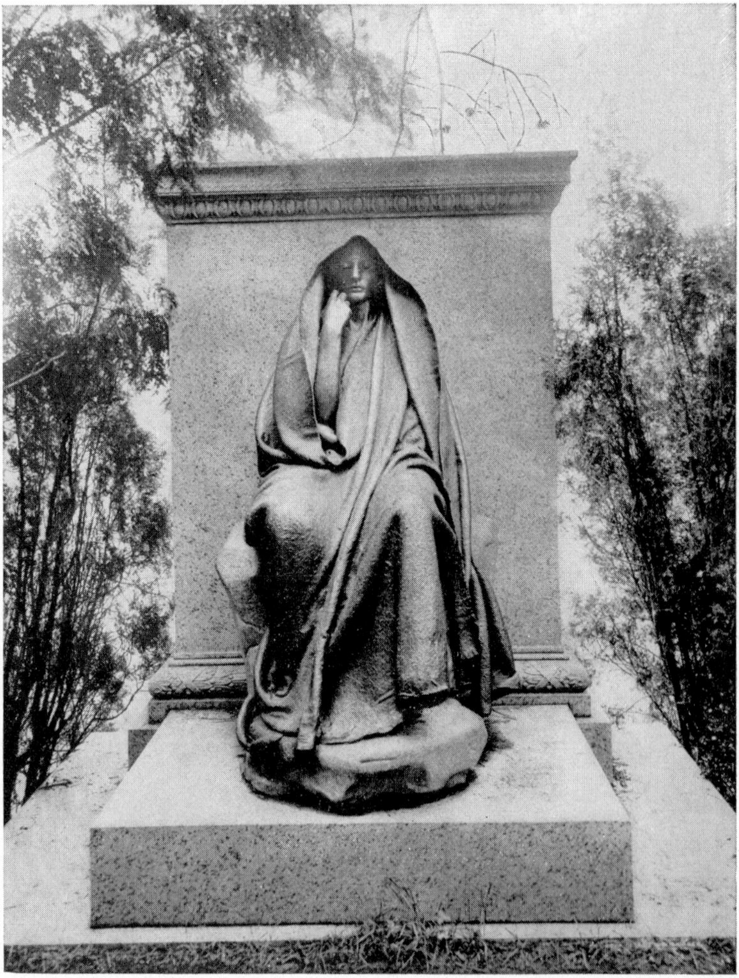

A Tahitian watercolor by Henry Adams

The Adams Memorial
by Augustus Saint-Gaudens,
Rock Creek Cemetery, Washington

COUTANCES CATHEDRAL

BROOKS ADAMS
ABOUT 1900

Mrs. Robert Homans

HENRY ADAMS
IN 1900

*Massachusetts
Historical
Society*

young women about the play. One lives in constant company with diseased hearts, livers, kidneys and lungs; one shakes hands with certain death at closer embrace every day; one sees paralysis in every feature and feels it on every muscle; all one's functions relax their action day by day; and, what is worse, one's grasp on the interests of life, relaxes with the physical relaxation; and, through it all, we improve; our manners acquire refinement; our sympathies grow wider; our youthful self consciousness disappears; very ordinary men and women are found to have charm; our appreciations have weight; we should almost get to respect ourselves if we knew of anything human to respect; so we affect to respect the conventions, and we ask only to be classed as a style.

Mrs. Robert Homans

A PAGE FROM HENRY ADAMS' LETTER TO
BROOKS ADAMS, DECEMBER 19, 1899

of the House on whom the administration could rely to conduct its business with a show of competence. The victory
left the Administration "master of the field, but strong in
numbers alone." The same Ninth Congress which almost
undermined executive conduct of foreign affairs, failed at its
next session to respond to Jefferson's program for internal
improvements, while at that very moment Napoleon was
implementing his Continental System by lawless confiscations
under the Berlin Decree, issued November 21, 1806.

Adams concentrated on the American side of the story,
devoting the first half of Volume III to the knotting of the
Florida problem and the second half mainly to the unraveling
of the Burr conspiracy. Both halves showed the country as
unconsciously and peacefully heading toward a continental
system that in Europe was the brilliant conception of a dictator
whose instruments were political machination and outright
violence. Covering a complicated series of events from
Jefferson's first determination on an internal-improvements
program to the trial of Aaron Burr, the historian built his
details into a symmetrical structure and related structure to
theme. The central paragraph of the book is the point on
which the balance rests. It begins by contrasting the quiet
progress of America with the spectacular energy of Napoleon,
shows how little the American story fitted the categories of
conventional political history, and finally asks the question
that makes the materials relevant to social history:

> Although the merchants had been robbed, the people at
> large were more prosperous and contented than ever. The
> summer of 1806 was one of quiet and rapid progress. While
> Europe tossed on her bed of pain, and while Russia built up the
> fourth coalition against Napoleon, only to drench with blood
> the battle-fields of Jena, Eylau, and Friedland, the United
> States moved steadily toward their separate objects, caring
> little for any politics except their own. . . . The American people

went to their daily tasks without much competition or mental effort, and had no more wish to wrangle about problems of the future than to turn back on their path and face Old-World issues. Every day a million men went to their work, every evening they came home with some work accomplished; but the result was matter for a census rather than for history. . . . As far as politics proved anything, the evidence seemed to show that the American tended already to become narrow in his views and timid in his methods. The great issues of 1776 and of 1787 had dwindled into disputes whether robbery and violence should be punished by refusing to buy millinery and hardware from the robbers, and whether an unsuccessful attempt to purloin foreign territory should be redeemed by bribing a more powerful nation to purloin it at second hand. The great issues of democracy and republicanism were still alive, but their very success removed these subjects for the moment from the field of politics. That a democracy could for so long a time maintain itself above Old-World miseries was a triumph; but thus far the democracy had been favored by constant good fortune, and even in these five years conservatives thought they felt a steady decline in moral tone. What would happen when society should be put to some violent test?

The great violent test of American society was to be that of war, but Burr's conspiracy came first "to try the strength of a true democracy." Burr's wild attempt to make the West his separate empire and the minor skirmishing of the War of 1812 are the microcosms in the *History* of internal and external strains on the American democracy, but they seem a little slight withal, especially from an historian who deeply realized the Civil War as his nation's crisis and who, almost alone in his time, anticipated the twentieth century of conflict. Adams' searching out of the full significance of the War of 1812 will presently be seen, but the Burr episode, which seems even less proportionate to the crisis it may be said to represent, demands a further word at once. For all the explicit significance with which Adams freighted the incidents involving Burr, he apparently felt more than his analysis could convey. What he felt can be described only in a roundabout fashion, but it may be summarily put that the merest scent of treason stank to his extremely refined national sense and that Burr reeked with treason through and through. Years after the War of the Rebellion had almost everywhere become the War Between the States, he was to entitle the first of the Civil War chapters in the *Education* simply "Treason." That word had lain behind the academic fencing between the student and master of Harvard days. The biographer of George Cabot and the editor of *New England Federalism* kept their disagreements cordial through a long friendship until, one evening during the First World War, Lodge vehemently sailed into President Wilson and Adams brusquely silenced him: "Cabot! I've never allowed treasonable conversation at this table and I don't propose to allow it now." The historic allegiance of the Adamses had been neither sectional nor partisan, but national to the core. In the nationalism of Henry Adams, distilled through three generations before it passed to him, treason became by so far the first of the cardinal sins that all the others shrank in comparison. Inefficiency, incompetence, even moral laxity were damnable by judgments of the intellect only. Adams' judgments of reason were often so strict that the historian seemed to mete justice without mercy, but his judgments from a loyalty above ordinary reason were stronger still. The nationalist criterion for social judgment has showed its terrifying limitations to our own time, but what our world is desperately trying to outgrow once had to be grown into. Adams' love for the American democracy was founded on a communal instinct deeper and more humane than his admiration for reasoned statesmanship. Because he had ends beyond the analysis of practical politics, his political analyses escaped the narrowness of legalistic reasoning while they kept the hardheaded sternness of intellectual precision. He saw that Burr led the first great attempt at secession in American history. From his point of view, when Jefferson did not take strong measures to preserve the Union, his statesmanship failed where Lincoln's later rose to the national emergency. And when Jefferson later sought Burr's conviction on less than the constitutional minimum of evidence, he was subverting institutional freedoms that Lincoln waived under his war powers only to preserve. In being hard on Jefferson, Adams made clear the seriousness of his later saying that Lincoln provided the only other major subject in America's nineteenth-century history.

Adams' gravity almost overwhelmed his sense of humor; but in its political aspect, the Burr affair had elements of farce, and the historian allowed a touch of *The Beggar's Opera* to enter his description of the trial. When James Wilkinson, commanding general of our Western forces and pensioned spy of imperial Spain, became the government's hero and star witness, Adams could not resist quoting: "That Jemmy Twitcher should peach me, I own surprised me. 'Tis a plain proof that the world is all alike, and that even our gang can no more trust one another than other people." But the main irony was at his own expense. He deplored and deplored Jefferson's not taking action on the grounds that the people could be relied on to defeat the conspiracy. Yet true as it was that the people "had instituted a government in order to provide themselves with proper machinery for such emergencies," he found himself agreeing with the neglectful President. The people who day by day went quietly to work destroyed Burr's scheme by ignoring it.

The same irony affected the political history in more direct ways. The people also appeared, though to less advantage, through their representatives in Congress — of whom none were more representative than the mediocre delegation from Pennsylvania. As the debate on ending the importation of slaves revealed, the executive interest was not the only one they frustrated. Carrying the day "against the ablest leaders of New England Federalism and the most gifted masters of Virginian oratory," their success "was partly due, not to their energy or talents, but to the contempt which their want of genius inspired. Not their own wisdom, but their antagonists' errors decided the result, and overthrew successively Church and State in New England and a slave-holding oligarchy throughout half the continent." Adams had brought up the subject of Pennsylvanian democracy in his first volume by saying emphatically, "If its soil bred little genius, it bred still less treason." And though he dwelt now upon the stolid patience and inert weight of the democratic congressmen, he was still ready to rise to their defense. When the British minister disapprovingly noticed the presence in Congress of "one tailor, one weaver, six or seven tavern-keepers, four notorious swindlers, one butcher, one grazier, one curer of hams, and several schoolmasters and Baptist preachers," Adams answered succinctly: "The most aristocratic American of the twentieth century will probably agree with the most extreme socialist in admitting that Congress, in 1808, might with advantage have doubled its proportion of tailors, butchers, and swindlers, if by doing so it could have lessened the number of its conspirators." He had his qualms about commonplace democracy, but he hewed to the line he had marked out elsewhere that it was the one experiment worth making, that every other possible step was backward. With that conviction, he did not represent the contrasting histories of America and Europe simply in the difference between Jefferson and Napoleon. Into the rapidly complicating action of the *History*, he brought his last major character, the ambiguous group personality of American democracy. This done, he could shift his narrative from internal tests of national cohesiveness like the Burr affair to the ordeal of external violence.

Adams' design now began to show itself in broader outline:

in the first volume, the Jeffersonian experiment in negative government was organized; in the second, centering on the Louisiana Purchase, an implicit decision was made to base American politics on national sovereignty; in the third, the nation demonstrated passive ability to withstand Burr's kind of decentralizing force. Adams then counterweighted his cumulative emphasis on home affairs. He opened Volume IV on the note of transition from minor to major action: "The inefficiency of the Government in doing those duties which governments had hitherto been created to perform, was shown even more strikingly in the story of the 'Chesapeake' than in the conspiracy of Burr." In this fourth volume, the Embargo provides the chief test of pacific national policy in a warring world; in the fifth, the American government, ineptly resorting to the European diplomatic weapons of threat and perfidy, stumbles toward a general dissolution; Volume VI describes the germination of popular energy which lifted the nation from the nadir of politics — at the cost of going to war. The second trilogy balances the first by emphasizing international rather than domestic problems, and it also serves as the transition from the quiet development of a nation more acted upon than acting to the story of the last three volumes. The final third of the long *History* is chiefly concerned with America's unwilling but active engagement in the War of 1812.

Adams recognized that the Embargo was Jefferson's alternative to war, and he called it "an experiment in politics well worth making," even though he judged it to have failed. He centered his fourth volume on this experiment as he took the narrative from the *Chesapeake* incident to Jefferson's unhappy retirement. The diplomatic repercussions of the *Leopard* attack led to the mutual retaliation of British Orders in Council and Napoleonic Decrees against commerce with the enemy, until there could be "No More Neutrals." Adams then followed the Embargo through the stages of legislation and enforcement, analyzed its cost to the nation and effectiveness as an instrument of international relations, and recorded the acknowledgment of failure in the fact of repeal. His three-part composition — international complication, establishment of the Embargo, failure of the experiment — is punctuated by focal contrasts in the manner of the opening volume. After the first third comes the story of Fulton's successful experiment, for Adams the clue to a more likely, if unpolitical, alternative to war. The second third ends with juxtaposed chapters on "The Cost of the Embargo" and "The Dos de Maio." The cost that Adams reckoned highest was neither financial nor constitutional but moral, for "the embargo opened the sluice-gates of social corruption" and "turned every citizen into an enemy of the laws." On May 2, 1808, in the most politically backward of countries, the Spanish *people* began the first major uprising against Bonaparte's military empire and "while all Europe, except France, joined hands in active support of Spanish freedom, America, the stronghold of free government, drew back and threw her weight on the opposite side." The difference between American vice and European corruption had narrowed until the one stronghold of democracy left after Napoleon's seizure of power gave up its moral leadership and began aligning itself with the dictator against the world and its own best principles.

Jefferson's second term ended in political confusion and personal debacle. The historian claimed that "with but one exception the remark of John Randolph was destined to remain true, that 'never has there been any Administration which went out of office and left the nation in a state so deplorable and calamitous.' " He summed up the close of Jefferson's "reign" by hinted references to Jackson, but his language also recalled the trying last days of two Adams administrations: "He who longed like a sensitive child for sympathy and love left office as strongly and almost as generally disliked as the least popular President who preceded or followed him." He did not hesitate to quote again a letter to Gallatin, used in the biography, which could hardly have appealed to a merely prejudiced observer. Gallatin's correspondent had made the unflattering comparison, "I verily believe one more year of writing, speaking, and appointing would render Mr. Jefferson a more odious President, even to the Democrats, than John Adams." The irony of Jefferson's position had become almost too great for satire, but Adams treated his retirement with the minimal decorum which could suggest the seriousness that lay behind his ironies:

> He had undertaken to create a government which should interfere in no way with private action, and he had created one which interfered directly in the concerns of every private citizen in the land. He had come into power as the champion of States-rights, and had driven States to the verge of armed resistance. He had begun by claiming credit for stern economy, and ended by exceeding the expenditure of his predecessors. He had invented a policy of peace, and his invention resulted in the necessity of fighting at once the two greatest Powers in the world.

The historian denied any intention to say that "the blame for this failure rested wholly upon Jefferson," but his free-will emphasis on individuality seemed to cross both generosity and judiciousness. The best he could do was cut all his actors down to scale. Among his own ancestors, he was as hard on the young cub as on the old bear. As Volume IV ended with Jefferson at the low point of his career, Volume V concluded with John Quincy Adams enjoying high success as American minister to Russia. In a volume devoted to diplomatic snarls, he won the only signal victory; in a volume which developed Napoleon's character as a foil, no longer for Jefferson, but for the American nationality itself, Adams attained a victory "Napoleonic in its magnitude and completeness." When the Czar refused to follow Napoleon and confiscate American shipping in the Baltic, Russia was to face the likelihood of war in order to preserve America's mercantile freedom from the Berlin and Milan Decrees. Yet, in the moment of his triumph, John Quincy Adams drew from his historian-grandson the most brilliant and perhaps the sharpest brief characterization in the whole massive work:

> The American minister felt but one drawback, — he could not wholly believe that his victory was sure. Anxious by temperament, with little confidence in his own good fortune, — fighting his battles with energy, but rather with that of despair than of hope, — the younger Adams never allowed himself to enjoy the full relish of a triumph before it staled, while he never failed to taste with its fullest flavor, as though it were a precious wine, every drop in the bitter cup of his defeats.

The direction of diplomatic history in Volume V was toward choice of England as the national opponent, not on the positive grounds which might have justified the decision, but rather because of Napoleon's straight-faced falsehood that American ships could not have been seized in Continental ports since the Berlin and Milan Decrees were not in force against America. In the last days of the Eleventh Congress, administration supporters in the House pushed through a restoration of nonintercourse with Britain by inventing the parliamentary rule of the previous question and cutting off debate. Napoleon's incredible power to deceive, at a time when ten million dollars' worth of American merchandise and two to three hundred American ships and crews were in his hands, had only slight moral significance, for "politics were to him a campaign, and if his opponents had not the sense to divine his movements and motives, the disgrace and disaster

were none of his." But what the Americans did, in making the
House "rather a court of registration than a deliberative
body," called for the historian's most vigorous denunciation
as he sought in vain for the "sufficient cause" behind their
action: "Their object was not to strengthen government, or
to prepare for war, or even to suppress popular liberties for
their own pleasure, but merely to carry out an Executive
scheme which required no haste, and was to be followed by
no strong measures. As far as human intelligence could be
called blind, the intelligence which guided the House was the
blind instinct of power." Even as it ludicrously imitated
Napoleon's arbitrary and unpredictable behavior, the Republican administration was proving itself incapable of
governing. For Adams, the "most improbable of all the
caprices of politics" was not the great Napoleonic lie which
changed American policy, but the ironic situation which
followed from that change:

> . . . At the moment when the Czar of Russia and the King of
> Sweden were about to risk their thrones and to face the certain
> death and ruin of vast numbers of their people in order to pro-
> tect American ships from the Berlin and Milan Decrees, the
> new minister of the United States appeared in Paris authorized
> to declare that the President considered those decrees to be re-
> voked and their system no longer in force!

The fifth volume closed on the wasted triumph of the
minister to Russia, and the sixth opened on the negative
success of William Pinkney, the minister to England. According to Adams, whose family for three generations had
held that post in critical times, "America never sent an abler
representative to the Court of London." With all the diplomatic virtues, Pinkney carried on his difficult work until he
was left with "no resource but to lose his temper, which he

did with proper self-control." Pinkney's taking his "inami-
cable leave" was not a continuation of the knotted and re-
knotted negotiations which had filled Volume V. It rightly
belonged at the beginning of a new volume, for the minister
spoke up to the issues, refusing the passive part usually
assigned the American on the international scene, and the
meaning of his mettle gradually became clear. There shortly
occurred, practically on "the scene of the 'Chesapeake's'
unredressed outrage," an incident which reversed that important event. The frigate *President*, Captain John Rodgers
in command, opened fire on an approaching British warship
that refused to show its colors and left it disabled after an
action of about fifteen or twenty minutes. The narrative
quickened. In the Cabinet, Madison overbore Monroe, his
new Secretary of State, and the decision to fight England and
not France was finally taken. Then two chapters on Indian
affairs in the Northwest followed, with ample justification:
"As in the year 1754 a petty fight between two French and
English scouting parties on the banks of the Youghiogheny
River, far in the American wilderness, began a war that
changed the balance of the world, so in 1811 an encounter in
the Indian country, on the banks of the Wabash, began a
fresh convulsion which ended only with the fall of Napoleon.
The battle of Tippecanoe was a premature outbreak of the
great wars of 1812." The epic simile prefigured a change in
the mode of action. Adams quickly introduced the Twelfth
Congress which met November 4, 1811, with its new blood
among the young "War Hawk" Republicans, none over forty,
none who "could remember the colonial epoch, or had taken
a share in public life except under the Constitution of 1789,
or had been old enough to feel and understand the lessons
taught by opposition to the Federalist rule." There were
debates and hesitations, but war was declared June 18, the
day after the British withdrew their Orders in Council.

Halfway through the volume, the ironic climax was reached: "War with England was about to restore commerce with her; alliance with France was a state of war with her."

When the United States, after long compounding its own half-understood difficulties and after longer being used as a pawn of European politics, makes its first show of energy in the *President*'s attack on the *Little Belt*, the effect is one of relief, almost of exhilaration. The reader may well wonder whether the bellicosity which creates this impression is Adams' or his own. For the seeming militarism of Henry Adams was far from simple; it grew from studious reflection on the nature and possibility of peace. If peace was incompatible with a morally careless expansionism such as the American quest for Florida, it was equally unlikely that a just nation be taken on its word. Again and again Adams criticized the sanguine liberal assumption of Jefferson that interest could rule the world pacifically. If, on the other hand, active moral leadership of world democracy was incompatible with peace, the apparent answer of withdrawing from the world at large was by no means easy: "So deeply were American interests founded in the affairs of Europe that even in the Baltic they were the rock on which Napoleon's destiny split; for the quarrels which in the summer of 1811 became violent between France and the two independent Baltic Powers . . . were chiefly due to those omnipresent American ships, which throve under pillage and challenged confiscation." Peace was the natural aim of a great democracy, and the particular experiment of American democracy was the peaceful organization of an entire continent; but Adams insisted that more than good intentions were necessary to bring about a new age of man:

> The unfailing mark of a primitive society was to regard war as the most natural pursuit of man; and history with reason began as a record of war, because, in fact, all other human occupations were secondary to this. The chief sign that Americans

had other qualities than the races from which they sprang, was shown by their dislike for war as a profession, and their obstinate attempts to invent other methods for obtaining their ends; but in the actual state of mankind, safety and civilization could still be secured only through the power of self-defence. Desperate physical courage was the common quality on which all great races had founded their greatness; and the people of the United States, in discarding military qualities, without devoting themselves to science, were trying an experiment which could succeed only in a world of their own.

In the actual state of the world, the nature of war, too, had to be considered. It had to be said that the effect of sustained violence was the creation of nationality. The response to the *Chesapeake* affair had been recorded as the first truly national emotion ever felt by the American people, although "a single blow, however violent, could not weld a nation." Before the reign of politics ended, the politicians would have to behold their nemesis when the British foray set fire to Washington and "from the distant hills of Maryland and Virginia the flying President and Cabinet caught glimpses of the ruin their incompetence had caused." Less passive effects were more obvious: Madison's Annual Messsage of 1813, "which seemed written in a spirit of panegyric upon war," signified more than his own reversal of character. The peace policy had misconceived the human nature of the Americans themselves. After their first taste of victory, they craved more battles, more victories, more military glory. Just after the dismaying news that General Hull had been forced to surrender Detroit and his entire army, came word that the general's nephew Captain Isaac Hull of the frigate *Constitution* had met the *Guerrière* at sea, cut her to pieces in a half-hour battle, and, after making prisoners of her crew, sunk her. The people found in this ample compensation for the whole lost province in the West:

With the shock of new life, they awoke to the consciousness that after all the peace teachings of Pennsylvania and Virginia, the sneers of Federalists and foreigners; after the disgrace of the "Chesapeake" and the surrender of Detroit, — Americans could still fight. The public had been taught, and had actually learned, to doubt its own physical courage; and the reaction of delight in satisfying itself that it still possessed the commonest and most brutal of human qualities was the natural result of a system that ignored the possibility of war.

When William James later searched for a "moral equivalent of war," he was willing, for the sake of argument at least, to "consider only the higher aspects of militaristic sentiment." Starting from that point, he proposed as a substitute for the honorific military emotion, "civic passion" and "civic honor." James looked to the future and to the best qualities in man; Adams dealt with the past and the particular experiments which the American democracy had made. In his comment on the Embargo, he noted that the policy of peaceable coercion eliminated the military virtues of courage, discipline, sense of duty, and self-sacrifice while bringing forth no substitute; it made "many smugglers and traitors, but not a single hero." And in his treatment of the war, he reminded his readers that moral equivalents had to be sought not only for noble devotion, but also for the dark brutality which lurked beneath the pervasive militaristic sentiment.

As a military conflict, the War of 1812 may appear to our more callous time as a trifling episode, but Adams did not write military history because of the great glory in it. The American character emerged from its unformed simplicity in the trials of war, and heroes were interesting as types. Once again the historian used a conventional form to serve an unconventional breadth of purpose: "Decatur and Hull were engaged in a social rather than a political contest, and were aware that the serious work on their hands had little to do

with England's power, but much to do with her manners."
From the people came a new generation of capable and courageous leaders. Even Jackson, consistently drubbed whenever
he had appeared in the narrative, was redeemed in his
greatest test. His preparations for the defense of New Orleans
were as haphazard as the politically directed preparations at
Washington, but the resemblance held only "until the moment
when in each case the British expedition came within sight. . . .
Jackson needed to see his enemy in order to act; he thought
rightly only at the moment when he struck."

Generalship like diplomacy was to remain a field for individual action, and Adams looked for a better test of social
characteristics than the making of a few national heroes in the
essentially antiheroic American democracy. He picked his
cases scientifically, pursued his inquiry disinterestedly, and
reported his findings with the coolness of logical demonstration. To him, the battles of Chippewa and Lundy's Lane
proved that the American common soldiers were more than
equal to the British, even though the British had been schooled
by centuries of military exploit. At New Orleans, Americans
faced regiments which, having fought under Wellington, came
overseas directly from their victorious Peninsular campaign.
Furthermore, it was the British who chose not to fight an infantry battle, but to challenge a contest of artillery. With the
same exciting precision that he used in describing every important battle of the war, Adams analyzed the artillery duel to
show exactly the remarkable superiority of the Americans. The
nub of his argument was that American excellence over Europeans in the handling of heavy ordnance was not a simple sign
of military instinct: "Critics constantly said that every American had learned from his childhood the use of the rifle, but he
certainly had not learned to use cannon in shooting birds or
hunting deer, and he knew less than the Englishman about the
handling of artillery and muskets." In the matter of gunnery,

the historian could show both dramatically and statistically a technical aptitude which was the popular equivalent of turning to science. It was technology which differentiated the new man of the Western world from the European common man.

The great test of American character took place on the ocean, "the only open field for competition among nations" and the field on which Americans were to turn their backs during a century of internal development. In the fourth volume, as England pressed the situation which brought Jefferson's administration to its wretched end, British policy appeared to stem from disrespect for a nation that would not fight back when injured. The historian, though he gave full value to this belief in American cowardice, added that "beneath the disdain lurked an uneasy doubt which gave to contempt the virulence of fear":

> Already the American ship was far in advance of the British model, — a swifter and more economical sailer, more heavily sparred and more daringly handled. In peace competition had become difficult, until the British ship-owner cried for war; yet he already felt, without acknowledging it even to himself, that in war he was likely to enjoy little profit or pleasure on the day when the long, low, black hull of the Yankee privateer, with her tapering, bending spars, her long-range gun, and her sharp-faced captain, should appear on the western horizon, and suddenly, at sight of the heavy lumbering British merchantman, should fling out her white wings of canvas and fly down on her prey.

The one sectional pride which Henry Adams let survive in his nationalized patriotism was his love of the Yankee ship. In Volume V, when American destiny seemed to hang on the chances of foreign complication, the "omnipresent American ships" in the Baltic brought European affairs to a crisis. In Volume VI, the *President*, under Captain Rodgers, gave the long awaited first sign of American energy; and when, in the second half of that volume, the sorry conduct of the war proved to be the harvest of accumulated incompetence, Hull's victory with the *Constitution* was the needed stimulus for morale which kept the nation alive. In Volume VII, all but one of the land campaigns came to nothing because they could not be sustained, and in that one, against the Creeks, Jackson could not find his defeated enemy and so imposed a confiscatory treaty on his Creek *allies!* As for the war at sea, the government did not capitalize its one great advantage and, neglecting to build more sloops, relied on the strategically less effective privateers. Privateering was poor business since, "like every other form of gambling," it attracted "more adventurers than it could support"; and it hurt the navy since "seamen commonly preferred the harder but more profitable and shorter cruise in a privateer, where fighting was not expected or wished, to the strict discipline and murderous battles of government ships, where wages were low and prize-money scarce." Nevertheless, in the private warfare, development of the schooner matched that of the sloop, and Americans, for the first time in open competition with the world, "proved their capacity to excel, and produced a creation as beautiful as it was practical":

> All great nations had fought, and at one time or another every great nation in Europe had been victorious over every other; but no people, in the course of a thousand years of rivalry on the ocean, had invented or had known how to sail a Yankee schooner.

The British could not rig or man the American vessels they captured so that they would sail with the qualities which Americans proved them to have. In Volume VIII, American victories outweigh the counter story of New England disaffection. The narrative extends from the show of brute courage in

infantry battles at the beginning to the technological feat of
the artillerists at New Orleans, but it is the theme of popular
intelligence, as developed from the common stock of nautical
knowledge, which takes the central position in the book. The
sloops-of-war and the privateers showed what Americans
might have done rather than what the English really had to
fear. Yet between them they enforced a practical blockade of
all British coasts, raised Lloyd's rates in a time of European
peace to twice what they had been at the height of European
conflict, and gradually "repaid every item of the debt of insult" compiled during the previous years. By the conclusion
of the entire work, the American sailing ship has become the
symbol of the American divergence from European pattern,
the quickness of mind that made the past history of naval
progress seem incredibly meager, the ingenuity which "excited a mixture of irritation and respect in the English service,
until Yankee smartness became a national misdemeanor."

As the denouement of the narrative shows, Adams did not
overplay the note of celebration or forget the problem of
peace. He showed how the nation could muster energy for
victories but not for victory. At the heart of Volume VIII, he
coupled with the chapter on sloops and privateers one called
"Exhaustion," in which the limits of national energy were defined by Federalist dissidence, the success of the British blockade, and the lack of popular rallying to the cause of war even
after the stinging humiliation of the sack of Washington.
Peace became the only solution, the reiterated watchword of
the historian of war as much as it had ever been Jefferson's
watchword in the anxious years before. The search for peace
was expressed not only in his rhetoric, but in his composition.
The external form of the *History*, with its significant ordering
of chapters and volumes, made clear the historian's interpretation and at the same time served his conscious intention of
being true to his subject. Adams had another technique be-

sides dramatic contrast for treating simultaneous episodes in different theaters of action — the technique of viewing his materials consistently from a single observation point. Earlier, he had told the reader of the declaration of war and only then let him learn, as Madison himself learned, that the Orders in Council had been withdrawn the day before. Now he told of the dwindling of military energy and described the last stage of governmental breakdown, depressed his reader further with the story of the Hartford Convention and of the threat to New Orleans, and at last revealed (following the order in which the news reached Washington) that Jackson's victory at New Orleans and Gallatin's brilliant negotiations at Ghent had retrieved the country from the brink of collapse. Henry Adams' point of view, appropriate to both historian and subject, was Washington; his dramatic composition, by its very nature, reflected his national outlook.

In this respect, the external structure of the *History* is congruent with the intrinsic form of the action. The international theme implied in Henry Adams, as in his friend Henry James, a national theme which only the broader perspective could make clear. In using foreign relations to define his American subject, he did not lose the parts in the whole. Sectional differentiation could be noted in both causes and consequences: continental expansion brought America into the web of Talleyrand's and Napoleon's duplicities, but Florida had been a particular issue for the South, sea commerce for the North, Canada for the West; and the result of foreign involvement was that Virginia "drained the poison which her own President held obstinately to her lips" while New England, "under the pressure of Virginia legislation," abandoned commerce, turned to manufacturing, and lived to relish "the contrast between her own prosperity and the sufferings of her neighbors." But the international scene in which sectional interest shrank in relative importance gave him his best chance for presenting the nation and its leaders. He held that "the story of diplomatic adventure, which has so often an interest beyond what could be supposed possible from the contact of three or four quiet and elderly gentlemen meeting about a green table, or writing letters inordinately long, owes that interest in most cases to a hope or a despair." He was referring to the difficulty of fathoming the arbitrary will of a Napoleon and the contrived policies of a Talleyrand, and the greater difficulty of fathoming the foreign relations of Jefferson and Madison which so often showed neither energy nor careful contrivance; but the phrase may be applied to his own accomplishment in international history and the subtle rendering he gave to the mystery of human behavior and the elucidation of shaping interests. He put Jefferson and Madison on the same stage with Napoleon, Talleyrand, Canning, Wellington, and all the leadership of Europe. These Americans, like those of Henry James's international fiction, behaved with sublime innocence on their first contact with Europe, but they did not fare so well as their fictional counterparts thereafter. First, they became enmeshed in the game of power until their political behavior sank to the moral level of "Europe." Second, they learned nothing from experience, so that Madison's last official act, vetoing an Internal Improvements bill, served to complete a pattern of retrogression:

> As Jefferson lost the habits of power and became once more a Virginia planter, he reverted to the opinions and prejudices of his earlier life and of the society in which he lived. As Monroe grew accustomed to the exercise and the necessities of power, he threw aside Virginian ideas and accepted the responsibilities of government.

Even in this pattern, however, they perhaps shared a typicality with Jackson at New Orleans who "thought rightly" only under the pressures of action.

Adams could not stop with the story of individual statesmen who, if the age of politics was drawing to a close, did not sufficiently represent the nation. He not only drew the general character toward which his typical individuals seemed to point, but he put this character at the center of the action. He first showed the American democrat dreaming, like Jefferson, of peace and plenty. The American had a continent to subdue and no time to waste in looking back to Europe. But the time came when "England required America to prove by acts what virtue existed in her conduct or character which should exempt her from the common lot of humanity, or should entitle her to escape the tests of manhood, — the trials, miseries, and martyrdoms through which the character of mankind had thus far in human history taken, for good or bad, its vigorous development." Confronted with the failure of peaceable coercion,

> America began slowly to struggle, under the consciousness of pain, toward a conviction that she must bear the common burdens of humanity, and fight with the weapons of other races in the same bloody arena; that she could not much longer delude herself with hopes of evading laws of Nature and instincts of life; and that her new statesmanship which made peace a passion could lead to no better result than had been reached by the barbarous system which made war a duty.

America not only faced trial by combat successfully, but came from it with moral integrity. At the end, the nation retained its chief trait, antipathy to war, and it had proved its superiority in "international tests of popular intelligence." Adams' American won as signal a triumph on the international scene as any hero of a James novel.

Adams kept the symbolic action within the bounds of rational design to the very end. He began the ninth and final book by relating in detail the negotiation of the Treaty of

Ghent, turning the narrative from arms to diplomacy. The detail had a double purpose: he satisfied his "haunting" dismay that no general historian had ever done the same justice to the making of peace as to the making of war, and he also established his foundation for recapitulating the spiral structure of his opening chapters in Volume I. The first three chapters bristle with facts about the war's end. The next three, compressing the last two years of Madison's administration, proceed on a more generalized level. The following three survey the results of sixteen years in the national economy, in religious and political thought, and in literature and art. Finally, there is the most generalized chapter of all, to which the whole massive work had been leading, Adams' coda on "American Character."

Rational composition was linked in Adams' mind with the systems of science, and for the rhetoric of his concluding chapters he drew heavily on the language of dynamics, Darwinian biology, and Comtean sociology. Although he let the word "physics" appear only once in the body of the text, social formulae framed in the vocabulary of that science were already a part of his thinking equipment. The peculiar idiom of his later years revealed itself in his description of the "inertia" of eighteenth-century society, in the attempt to calculate the effectiveness of the Embargo as an "engine" of power politics, in his working out "rates of increase" for wealth and population, and in his unremitting concern for national "energy." Development from fixity to motion, from multiple possibilities to a settled direction, he referred not only to physics but to the popular idea of evolution. Once again, the text of the narrative is noncommittal: in the passage that equates war and violence with "laws of Nature" (quoted here on the preceding page), we cannot tell who is speaking, the moralist or the Darwinist. The one occasion when Adams explicitly used a jungle image of natural selection is his description of Indian culture ruined by contact with American frontier settlement, and even in that instance he carefully shifted his scientific metaphor: Governor Harrison's "account of Indian affairs offered an illustration of the law accepted by all historians in theory, but adopted by none in practice; which former ages called 'fate,' and metaphysicians called 'necessity,' but which modern science has refined into the 'survival of the fittest.' No acid ever worked more mechanically on a vegetable fibre than the white man acted on the Indian." In the concluding chapters, the transition from the simple society of 1800 with its impermanent characteristics to the nation of 1817, when "the traits of American character were fixed," became a story of emergent evolution as well as mechanical necessity. One thing seemed sure in either case: the development of the American nation after 1817 would lack the complicated interest which the beginnings of American democracy, seen in European perspective, had offered. The only complication thereafter would be that of the social science which democratic uniformity made possible, though Adams ironically put his thesis in an unanalytic figure of speech, the elaborate image of an Old World landscape:

> Travellers in Switzerland who stepped across the Rhine where it flowed from its glacier could follow its course among mediæval towns and feudal ruins, until it became a highway for modern industry, and at last arrived at a permanent equilibrium in the ocean. American history followed the same course. With prehistoric glaciers and mediæval feudalism it had little to do; but from the moment it came within sight of the ocean it acquired interest almost painful. A child could find his way in a river-valley, and a boy could float on the waters of Holland; but science alone could sound the depths of the ocean, measure its currents, foretell its storms, or fix its relations to the system of Nature. In a democratic ocean science could see something ultimate. Man could go no further. The

atom might move, but the general equilibrium could not change.

Adams claimed that he, no more than any other historian, "cared to hasten the coming of an epoch when man should study his own history in the same spirit and by the same methods with which he studied the formation of a crystal," and yet "the interest of such a subject exceeded that of any other branch of science, for it brought mankind within sight of its own end." Neither statement excluded the other. He conceded that the democratic and industrial revolutions had already taken place. Like Tocqueville, he thought that men must understand not only what is wanted of society and of government, but also what is possible. And the "democratic ocean" did not mean to him the worst of all possible worlds. He thought that it ought not to be expected of the era after 1817 that the individual rise to such heights as he might have reached in older and smaller societies, but that "the chief function of the American Union was to raise the average standard of popular intelligence and well-being." Did it not perform this function? The results which the *History* reported seemed to confirm Tocqueville's observation that as the eminence in American culture receded, the mean rose. But the historian did not therefore relax his own intellectual standards. His criticism was clearest when, in the final survey, he commented on the popular religious movements which "might testify to intellectual stagnation as well as to religious or social earnestness." The rising sectarian leaders and the staid founders of Unitarianism were at one not only in mildness, but in the suggestion "that the Church should ignore what it could not comprehend. . . . They founded new churches on what seemed to resemble an argument that the intellectual difficulties in their path must be unessential because they were insuperable." In political as in religious thought, Adams saw an apparent agreement "not to press principles to a conclusion." In the arts he found no sign of great originality or a pervasive love of beauty more notable than "the swift-sailing schooner, the triumph of naval architecture. If the artistic instinct weakened, the quickness of intelligence increased." As for the noble art of government, popular inertia overcame the pressure which almost turned the country to European methods, "and no sooner did foreign dangers disappear than the system began to revert to American practices; the national government tried to lay aside its assumed powers."

All these comments answered questions the historian had put before the beginning of the narrative. In stating the problems to which the *History* would be devoted, Adams promised an inquiry into the direction progress would take in a democracy, a unified continental society, a technological and scientific age. Now he could put Q.E.D. to every item in his list but one, "What will you do for moral progress?" Unanswerable by science, this question was the clue to the historian's art, and unanswered by history, it gave rise to a whole new list of questions about the American people on the last page of his work:

> They were intelligent, but what paths would their intelligence select? They were quick, but what solution of insoluble problems would quickness hurry? They were scientific, and what control would their science exercise over their destiny? They were mild, but what corruptions would their relaxations bring? They were peaceful, but by what machinery were their corruptions to be purged? What interests were to vivify a society so vast and uniform? What ideals were to ennoble it? What object, besides physical content, must a democratic continent aspire to attain? For the treatment of such questions, history required another century of experience.

A hundred years after Madison's retirement, Henry Adams was an old man with a year to live, still devoted to his essential and unanswerable questions. Nineteen-seventeen was the year of the dinner-table incident with Lodge which closed the long debate between the historian and his most challenging student, the one who most of all "betrayed the consciousness that he and his people had a past, if they dared but avow it, and might have a future, if they could but divine it." In that year of the Russian Revolution, when America was turning again from new departures in democratic self-development to involvement in the violent history of Europe, Adams' questions took on an added urgency for his countrymen, and his subject, the rise of American democracy, assumed a radical importance for the world. The stern patriot who abruptly silenced Lodge was not quitting the discussion — and could not without withdrawing his *History* from circulation. Though he liked to claim with arch self-deprecation that not ten persons had ever read his masterpiece, he knew that through it he was speaking to the future. Now that science, more literally than Adams intended in 1890, has brought mankind within sight of its own end, his work reminds us that man must have other ends in sight besides catastrophe.

But a history does not simply deal with problems, it represents an action. Henry Adams' father, in his biography of John Adams, put a good case misleadingly when he stated that "if rigid moral analysis be not the purpose of historical writing, there is no more value in it than in the fictions of mythological antiquity." In our own time, the literary competition between historical writing and mythological fictions has emphasized the dichotomy and not favored the historian. But between the isolated human being of modern society and the generic Man of myth is an area of public life which finds its classic expression, as Burckhardt phrased it, when men are citizens who write for citizens. History is about the public past which the men of a society inevitably share, and though its subject is neither the private life of the individual nor the submerged unity of the race, it looks in both directions. Thus Adams' *History* rigidly analyzes the acts of particular characters and also presents the American democrat in whose mock-heroic figure we glimpse the shape of greatness. Like other masterpieces of historical art, it shows how much too sharply the lines may be drawn in the ancient dispute between poetry and history.

Chapter V

THE LAST LESSON OF EDUCATION

WITH THE COMPLETION of his *History*, Henry Adams' debt to his fathers was paid. Using empiricist methods which stemmed from their intellectual tradition and insights which in large part derived from their political experience, he had provided an intelligent citizen's guide to American democracy. The benefits he drew from his extended biography, however, had not come without limitations. The most obvious defect of the *History* is its dearth of pictorial interest. A glimpse of Jefferson's shackling presence at his inauguration or of Napoleon's imperial conduct of global affairs from his bath did not endow the figures of his political equation with flesh and blood; the low black hull and white wings of the schooner became a dominant image partly because there was so little competition. This deficiency in the realm of sense, as well as the extraordinary symmetries of composition, can be connected with a view of life which regarded being and feeling as less important than thinking and doing, satisfaction as less important than duty. In a word, the Puritan character survived Puritan belief. We may follow Henry Adams in admitting the Puritan's "thought higher and his moral standards better than those of his successors," but if we are to find the human link between the classic monumentality of the *History* and the baroque richness of *Mont-*

Saint-Michel and Chartres, we must concern ourselves with what the ancestral Adams view left out.

The professional scholar who dealt with the public and its problems kept his personal sensibility subordinate to his historical career, but the other side of the man existed all along. Indeed, it can be traced almost as far back as his bent for politics: Adams' New England stock had been crossed with an exotic strain. John Quincy Adams, a rising diplomat of thirty, had married in London at a safe three thousand miles from the matriarchal disapproval of Abigail Adams, who would have preferred demonstrable qualities of Quincy granite in her daughter-in-law. The bride of his choice was Louisa Catherine Johnson, whose father was an American Southerner. Henry Adams' "quarter taint of Maryland blood" may be an unrewarding datum of biology, but it is a fruitful metaphor. Louisa Johnson's grandchild did not have to invoke the laws of heredity to prove her influence on himself. He had in boyhood known his un-Bostonian grandmother as the Madam and had been charmed by her Louis Seize manners and tastes. The charm was so great that hers was the ancestral biography he came closest to writing despite a whole range of more formidable choices. He actually undertook to do her memoir, appropriately when he himself reached thirty and broke from the restraints of Quincy to the relative Bohemianism of Washington. By the spring of 1869, he could report himself well begun on the story of this "ancient lady of our house," though he predicted that long and patient labor would be required for the job. It is appropriate, too, that the future historian's project should have ended in an unfinished collection of preliminary materials, the symbol of his own incomplete rebellion against parental discipline. It was not until he wrote the *Education* that he finally interpreted what he found in his grandmother's diaries: the requirements of John Quincy Adams' austere politics made her life, "as the venerable Abigail, long since at peace, foresaw, one of severe stress and little pure satisfaction." In her chafing against the constraints of her husband's New England conscience, she became for her grandson the peculiar intimate sign of his own emotional nature. Her recollected image disclosed to him the antinomies of easy Southern ways at odds with the Northern necessity of unremitting work, and of feminine sensibility in ultimate opposition to a masculine sense of duty. In his later years, Henry Adams more and more reflected on these basic contradictions in human destiny and his own life.

What Louisa Johnson stood for in Henry Adams' mind was not just contradiction, but complication. As the *Education* argues, Quincy and Boston could by themselves explain his seeing twofold distinctions everywhere in life; the contrasts of winter and summer, town and country, constraint in society and freedom in nature were ingrained in his experience. The problem lay elsewhere: "After a January blizzard, the boy who could look with pleasure into the violent snow-glare of the cold white sunshine, with its intense light and shade, scarcely knew what was meant by tone." The New England temperament, unsettled by its double vision, might hesitate in judgment of the facts, but it was seldom uncertain about seeking the course of conscience among the ambiguities of this world. Absence of tone nurtured a confidence that morally, if not intellectually, choices were as clear-cut as black and white. Starting from his doctrinaire assumption, the moral agent could make some simple observations and act upon them with assurance, whereas, if he started with an open sensibility, he might become aware of complications that subverted the whole system. Conscience — that is, a New England conscience — taught that pain was the first instrument of human education. Yet the self-analyst's conscientious memory began the order of childhood impressions with the pleasures of color and taste.

Conscience induced in the twelve-year-old boy, making his first trip into the slave-ridden South, a violent sensation of evil; but his feeling of revulsion had "another side," strong enough to charge the memory for life:

> The May sunshine and shadow had something to do with it; the thickness of foliage and the heavy smells had more; the sense of atmosphere, almost new, had perhaps as much again; and the brooding indolence of a warm climate and a negro population hung in the atmosphere heavier than the catalpas. The impression was not simple, but the boy liked it: distinctly it remained on his mind as an attraction, almost obscuring Quincy itself. The want of barriers, of pavements, of forms; the looseness, the laziness; the indolent Southern drawl; the pigs in the streets; the negro babies and their mothers with bandanas; the freedom, openness, swagger, of nature and man, soothed his Johnson blood. Most boys would have felt it in the same way, but with him the feeling caught on to an inheritance.

Louisa Johnson meant his capacity to be educated in tone. Thanks to her, the contrarieties he loved to ponder existed in lively tension rather than lifeless dichotomies.

It is not necessary to attribute to the twelve-year-old boy the brimming consciousness of the reminiscent sexagenarian in order to profit from this autobiographical suggestion. Indeed, the experience of the child could not have been very acutely felt, since Adams was able to conceal its meaning from himself for over half his life. Throughout his earlier career, he resolutely acted on the assumption that public duty and private sensibility were as far apart as Massachusetts and Virginia, as different as male and female, and his active preoccupation with history and the public world forestalled his reopening the question. Nevertheless, the complexity of his other side left its traces in his work. In the brief preface to his volume of Federalist documents, he had noted in unpolitical terms the pathos of John Quincy Adams' political isolation. In *Democracy*, his satire on the debasement of public duty was enriched by his private vision, never more pointedly than when, from the lush hills of the green Virginia spring, an eye sensitized to color saw the government buildings of the distant capital as "whited sepulchres." The *History* solemnly recorded the close of the reign of politics and the unconscious development of national power, but it also presented a Jamesian fable of innocence and experience. There is evidence all along that Adams had other imaginative resources besides high moral standards and intellectual rigor.

The boy's first trip south, however dimly it may have been felt at the time, set a pattern of travel into exotic country and discovery in oneself of unmasculine reponsiveness to un-New-Englandly solicitations. To a Boston youth on his grand tour, Europe was sufficiently exotic and the sense of art was hardly less strange than the sense of atmosphere. At twenty, Henry Adams could not respond without embarrassment to the things which compelled the imagination of his later years: the would-be student of the civil law felt the delights of music to be a "temptation," and his extravagant praise of stained-glass windows brought forth an awkward "If I go on I shall be silly." When his truant excursions from Berlin mounted up, he finally took the tone of the culture-hunting young American and denied to his brother Charles the guilt of his impracticality. His callowness was in many ways more attractive than the snobbishness of a decade later. The London years had made him an amateur of drawings, dilettantish rather than enthusiastic, and a self-styled connoisseur of manners. The fastidious journalist who covered the sordid politics of Washington looked forward to another European trip as to a "moral bath" in civilized society. He said nothing about renewed immersion in the arts. Nature shattered the illusory order of civilization with the cruel blow of his sister's death. Despite his mannered assumptions, a primary fact of sense broke through. But he did not have long to reflect on this last lesson of education before he arrived home and had thrust on him the burdens of professorship. In the activity which left his assumptions intact, he pursued a Middle Ages which conformed more nearly to his legal studies at Berlin than to his vision of the cathedral windows at Nürnberg. The dutiful professor tried to give his students a view of Gothic architecture as well as of the development of legal institutions; the happiest discovery of his researches was Viollet-le-Duc's great work on medieval archeology; but concern for the arts was just a scholarly parenthesis. As he later said, "the text of a charter of Edward the Confessor was uncommonly remote from a twelfth-century window." Well past the first exposure of youth, the mature Henry Adams could take art in his stride as a scholar and gentleman, which is almost to say that he could take it or leave it alone. The Salic law of his masculine inheritance led him to the hundred court and the constitutional crisis of Anglo-Saxon England.

While Adams' notion of nineteenth-century civilization expanded beyond the horizons of Quincy and Boston to include Washington, England, Europe, he kept in occasional touch with parts of the world that lay outside the pale of Victorian respectability. He did so from various motives — the enjoyment in nature of relief from responsible activity, the pleasure of testing physical endurance which the genteel world left out of the question, curiosity about cultures different from his own. The diplomatic private secretary who was passing the crisis of his adolescence marked the phase with a brief vacation trip to the Scottish Highlands in August 1863; as Elizabeth Stevenson has pointed out, it was on the long evening row to the Isle of Skye that he first felt anxiety and egotism fall away. After his first year of teaching at Harvard,

Adams took up an invitation to go west and rough it with the expedition of the Fortieth Parallel Survey; from that summer he could date his lifelong intimacy with Clarence King. In the following summer of 1872, after his quiet wedding to Marian Hooper, he crossed the Atlantic again, but his goal was not simply Europe: the Adamses planned to spend the winter of their honeymoon year in Egypt. The bridegroom was a strenuous sightseer and camera-hunter whose interest ran more than snapshot deep. On the trip up the Nile, he worked his daily stint at the ancient law of the Germans, but he soon began to study that of the Egyptians, too. The whole mind was becoming engaged.

For a vigorous young scholar in a strange new country, the normal response was intellectual activity rather than spiritual rest or physical exertion; but he set too hard a pace for his wife. Marian Adams was not delighted by the dusty walks and amateur photography to which her husband introduced her. Though she liked seeing pyramids in the remote distance, she was humiliated by her apathy to a closer view. "I must confess," she wrote, "I hate the process of seeing things which I am hopelessly ignorant of, and am disgusted at my want of curiosity." Self-reproach and boredom were compounded by a devastating homesickness for her father, with whom she had been secure among familiar things. Her high spirits faltered, then collapsed. The bewildered husband who tended her gave no word of the event, but a two-and-a-half week gap in Mrs. Adams' letters was followed by a return of equanimity and — once they were back in Europe — of liveliness. The Adamses never again left the paths of the conventional tourist, though they traveled in a style much higher than that set by Cook's. For the couple the spring season, passed in London, was more successful than winter in Egypt. The discretion of the husband and the duty of the scholar prescribed the itinerary of their later trips.

After the great move of 1877, the Adamses set their roots deep. "Every now and then," the historian admitted, "in my bourgeois ease and uniformity, my soul rebels against it all, and I want to be on my wanderings again, in the Rocky Mountains, on the Nile, the Lord knows where"; but he caught himself up at once, "It is ludicrous to play Ulysses." He played Darby to his Joan instead, and with great success. On his next European journey, that of 1879–80, he could claim to miss Washington with a positive hunger. There at home, their social life was a joint enterprise. It was through Henry that they knew the Hays and King, but Mrs. Adams could be pleased at the list of her old friends whom she brought into the circle — H. H. Richardson, John La Farge, Augustus Saint-Gaudens, Henry James. The happy couple commissioned Richardson to build them a house in Washington adjacent to the Hays', and they passed their summers at Beverly Farms next door to Dr. Hooper. The cycle of their seasons was no better arranged than their daily round with its afternoon rides — usually toward Rock Creek and the semi-wilderness of Washington's outlying area — and the equal satisfaction of domestic privacy or select company. Amid this calm regularity, Henry Adams worked away at the *History* "without looking backwards."

During his wife's lifetime, Adams' major digression from routine came through imagination rather than through travel. Novel-writing was itself a departure from propriety. To some extent Adams shared the feeling of Hawthorne, a generation earlier, that his New England forebears would writhe to know that a descendant of theirs had become a mere teller of stories. At least he did not sign the family name to *Democracy*. He carried concealment a good deal farther with his second novel by using a pseudonym, Frances Snow Compton, and by having it published in 1884 without any advertising to make its name known to the public. From a professional or a personal point of view, the secrecy was appropriate, since the book could in no way be justified as a preparatory exercise for the *History*. And the pseudonym was also right, combining as it did the female version of a recurrent Adams name with ironic suggestion of the New England Comtean's bleak scientific outlook: Frances Snow Compton was protesting against the rational, masculine, publicly committed historian and the well-adjusted, self-assured man of the world. *Esther* declares the emotional bankruptcy of both religion and science, the great contesting forces in the nineteenth-century struggle of belief. In the midst of personal happiness, halfway through his greatest sustained literary effort, Henry Adams surveyed the life of his time and reported the drying-up of instinctual resources under the chill wind of intellectual necessity.

As in his earlier novel, Adams developed his plot around the prospective marriage of a female protagonist, but this time the affair is as much of the heart as of the head. Esther Dudley can passionately love the man of religion but cannot share his faith. She cannot love the man of science although intellectually they agree on fundamentals. The side of the triangle which links her with the Reverend Stephen Hazard gets the most attention. The heroine's amateur talent and the rush to complete the murals of St. John's Church make it plausible that she should help paint one of the minor figures. Her involvement with the elegant new church leads logically to her engagement to St. John's accomplished young rector, but the parishioner's love for her pastor is complicated by her gradual recognition of their incompatibility. No honest effort can revive primitive belief in her modern mind, and without belief the capacity for passion is made barren. She resolutely breaks with Hazard before either of them sacrifices integrity and turns love to hatred. The absolute personal honesty which prompts her action is the only quality

she possesses complete. In painting, she has a fine "trick of
the imagination" but lacks the patience to acquire technical
merit; in her attempt to become religious, she has the patience
for theological study but lacks the mysterious endowment
of faith. Her father had perhaps been right in whimsically
naming her after Hawthorne's Esther Dudley, the spinster
defender of an integrity passing out of fashion, but she also
reminds the reader of another namesake and of Hawthorne's
insistent contrast between Hester Prynne, with her almost
medieval resources of passionate energy, and the pallid nineteenth-century American woman. Looking at this decline
from the point of view of the unlucky woman, Adams seemed
to argue that for private life as for public, the time was out of
joint; that in an age when heroic action had become impossible, heroic dimensions could be made out only in failure.

Adams lavished his best material on the characterization
of Esther Dudley. He had used life models before, but now
he made his heroine a partial portrait of Marian Adams. As
though he were rifling his letterbook of a dozen years back,
he described Esther in terms he had used for his new fiancée:
she made an imperfect face and figure serve so smartly as to
appear handsome; she knew nothing well but covered the
fact by her quick intelligence. He meant the affectionate
ironies to imply other womanly powers, less easily named
and not very convincingly suggested by his meager command
of expressive language. What he tried with only partial success was to represent a woman caught in a spiritual turmoil
that takes her far beyond her depth and yet possessing a
feminine self-sufficiency that brings her through. He came
closest when he compared his heroine to "a lightly sparred
yacht in mid-ocean," a figure curiously like the image for
quickness of intelligence which he put into his *History*. Unfortunately, the novelist made Esther's security in her inner
resources less apparent than her inability to find something

outside herself which could force a personal submission and give her life a purpose. She is caught between a world of science which is lifeless and a world of religion which is powerless to be reborn. She is as essentially undramatic as her model was lively.

In the heroine of *Esther*, it is hard to distinguish clairvoyance from introspection and decide whether Adams had greater insight into his wife's personality or his own, but the author's other projection in his novel is much less tantalizing. George Strong, like Nathan Gore in *Democracy*, embodies the Adams who warily but positively accepted the prevailing conditions of his time. Since Strong is a composite portrait of the novelist and of Clarence King, the friend he most admired, we can hardly mistake the sympathetic light in which he is presented. He is like Adams in having a forehead "so bald as to give his face a look of strong character, which a dark beard rather helped to increase," but unlike Adams, who struck observers as slight, quiet, and saturnine, he has a figure made for action, a restless eye, and a naturally ingratiating manner. Strong is a professor of geology. Like his creator, he is wealthy enough so that "his professorship was little more to him than a way of spending money." Like King, he is equally popular among the rough miners of Nevada and the brilliant society of three continents. He is, incidentally, a connoisseur of oriental art and, we infer, of such oriental religions as give a perspective to the Christianity which his cousin Esther Dudley tries to accept. As the spokesman for unromantic liberalism, he occupies the far point of the lovers' triangle and, in his relation to Esther, he makes possible a dialogue between personifications of two aspects of Henry Adams.

Strong is at first a curious but disinterested observer of Esther's complications. He is, however, an entirely human scientist, capable of losing his detachment. Handicapped though he is by a late start and too long familiarity, he becomes a suitor. To Esther, he remains "an old glove that fits well enough but will not cling," someone she turns to for knowledge but not for love. Although he declines to answer her troubled question "Is religion true?" he lets her put him through the pragmatist catechism which is his alternative to a religious credo:

> "Is science true?"
> "No!"
> "Then why do you believe in it?"
> "I don't believe in it."
> "Then why do you belong to it?"
> "Because I want to help in making it truer."

Empirically, he equates the hypothetical status of Christian dogma and Euclidian axiom, but his will to share in making scientific truth is strong enough for him to dispense with the satisfactions of the other hypothesis. On the other hand, he is capable of recognizing Esther's spiritual thirst. He thinks it requires something stronger than Fifth Avenue Episcopalianism and recommends the Roman Church, experienced as it is in handling the unsubmissive will. At the climax of the book, he hands her an ivory crucifix, an *objet d'art* picked up from the mantelpiece, and exclaims, "There! How many people do you think, have come to this Christ of yours that has no meaning to you, and in their struggle with doubt, have pressed it against their hearts till it drew blood?" When Esther takes him at his word and silently presses the crucifix harder and harder against her breast, Strong intervenes and pulls it away in alarm. If Esther could marry religion as an act of will rather than of faith, he would readily bluff her intellect into submission. But when the action threatens to become desperately — and unseemly — physical, he breaks in on behalf of propriety, liberal thought, and the common sense of his time. Even more interesting than the incompatibility of Esther and Hazard is the struggle between Esther and Strong, for this projects the elements of Henry Adams' imagination which made him a citizen of his age and an alien in it.

The plot of *Esther* leads to an insoluble dilemma, and the novel dimly suggests a way around it other than distraction in science. The heroine with her nineteenth-century doubts can love but cannot marry the man of thirteenth-century ideas. Wharton, the professional artist in a world of amateurs and connoisseurs, is the one figure in the book who can mediate between the centuries. He designs windows and murals in the medieval tradition, though he is aware of his limiting conditions. In his view, the building he decorates is more a theater than a church, for without a Madonna at its heart, it has no heart. In part, at least, he speaks for the author, since it is he who describes Esther Dudley by plagiarizing from Henry Adams. At the beginning of the novel he recognizes Esther as an ideal woman of the present or even of a future world in which pagan naturalism has come again, but he insists that there is nothing medieval about her. He notes her as an American type and admires the gay courage with which she sails into the unknown ocean. He can also name her defect with unhesitating candor. "A soul is like a bird," he tells her, "and needs a sharp tap on its shell to open it." He does not foresee the impossible situation in which her soul will be enmeshed when grief at her father's death begins the complicating action, but his business is perception, not prediction. Adams gave to Wharton a fineness of judgment, as accurate for men and women as for pictures, such as he sensed in his friend La Farge. His respect for the artist's purity of vision, not to be put off the mark by circumstance of place or time, was to become deeper as their intimacy grew. In his novel he portrayed almost by guesswork the quality of mind which in a few years he would studiously cultivate.

The thinness of *Esther* as a novel accounts for its interest as a

biographical document. When Adams later said that the book
was written in his heart's blood, he no doubt referred to the
frighteningly accurate portraiture of his wife more than to his
own painful introspections, but the coincidence of fiction and
fatality became true after the fact. At the time of his writing
the book, he had very humanly adjusted himself to limited
satisfactions for the unlimited desires he was expressing: the
equilibrium between science and art in his work allowed him
to deny exclusive allegiance to either; his twelfth-century
longings soon settled for the neo-Romanesque house which
Richardson would build in La Fayette Square; the relished
happiness of his middle years attested that sheer vitality had a
genuine spiritual value. *Esther* recorded Adams' awareness
that more things existed in heaven and earth than were
dreamt of in his political philosophy. He shared in the widespread Victorian doubt that an impeccably arranged existence
could rule out every insoluble problem.

The relation of art and life became topsy-turvy when
Marian Adams, a year after the fictional counterpart had appeared in print, was called to Boston to attend her father's
deathbed. Dr. Hooper's lingering death was more like that of
Esther Dudley's father in the novel than it was like Adams'
actual experience, the brief melodramatic struggle of his sister
against the stronger forces of nature. There was no grim
gaiety, no clear-cut diagnosis, no relieving certainty that the
end would follow quickly. Days stretched into weeks; after
March came April. Henry Adams commuted between the
lonely restlessness of Washington and the equally lonely use-
lessness of Boston, helpless by letter or by presence to ease his
wife's ordeal. When the vigil came to its necessary end, he
brought her back to Washington enervated and depressed.
He arranged a summer holiday at Virginia Springs and came
back with a false sense that her depression had been lifted by
the change. By fall he had become the watcher. A silent

tearless melancholy settled permanently on Marian Adams, the effect of her father's long agony and the half-recognized symptom of her own. Love could merely look on and learn that dying was as mysterious as living. One Sunday afternoon Marian Adams went upstairs to rest, selected the potassium cyanide from her photographic supplies, and quietly took her life.

December 6, 1885, Henry Adams' life was "cut in halves." Religion was not in his make-up, science offered no consolation, vitality itself seemed to have failed. All that remained was the passionate memory of what he had lost. "I admit that fate at last has smashed the life out of me," he wrote; "but for twelve years I had everything I most wanted on earth." Accepting the isolation of absolute bereavement, he rarely tried, then or ever, to communicate the grief he felt. In a silence through which the hands of friends could not reach, he gradually picked up the torn threads of his existence. The world would not wait for the heart to recover, and the surviving part of the man had commitments which kept him moving along lines already taken up. As the Washington winter drew to a close, Adams moved into his new home at 1603 H Street, where he could contemplate the equestrian statue of Andrew Jackson in the square outside and the empty house within. During the spring he applied himself regularly to Madison's military complications, and only in June, with the *History* well in hand, did he yield to the Ulysses in himself and depart for the Orient. Involvement with the world and the requirements of his calling helped condition the reflexive impulse of his grief, but it was an inner mastery of self which imposed a unity on the roles that Adams continued to act and those he took up in the latter half of his life.

Flight to Japan, that summer of 1886, made clear the limits of escape. He traveled with John La Farge, whose acute sensuous responsiveness taught a lesson which the author of

Esther might have anticipated. Though he went half seriously in search of Nirvana, Adams witnessed in himself its very opposite, not the destruction but the reawakening of sense. Unlike his old friend Sturgis Bigelow, the guide and supervisor of his Japanese tour, he could not convert himself from Bostonian to Buddhist. His occidental perspective would not be abolished. His honest search led Adams, like the Western pilgrim of *A Passage to India*, to find only a travesty of Nirvana, an identity in all experience that offers no relief to the crowded consciousness which cannot become a part of what it apprehends:

> Positively everything in Japan laughs. The jinrickshaw men laugh while running at full speed five miles with a sun that visibly sizzles their drenched clothes. The women all laugh, but they are obviously wooden dolls, badly made, and can only cackle, clatter in pattens over asphalt pavements in railway stations, and hop or slide in heelless straw sandals across floors. I have not yet seen a woman with any better mechanism than that of a five-dollar wax doll; but the amount of oil used in fixing and oiling and arranging their hair is worth the money alone. They can all laugh, so far. The shop-keepers laugh to excess when you say that their goods are forgeries and worthless. I believe the Mikado laughs when his ministers have a cabinet council. The gilt dragon-heads on the temples are in a broad grin. Everything laughs, until I expect to see even the severe bronze doors of the tombs, the finest serious work I know, open themselves with the same eternal and meaningless laughter, as though death were the pleasantest jest of all.

He could not merge himself in the general laughter. The closest he came to Nirvana was to regard the world as show, and the best use he could make of this attitude was to sharpen his skill as a spectator.

After his wife's death, travel was the chief new element in Adams' yearly cycles. Hardly arrived home from Japan, he determined to do more. He wrote Gaskell, "The only practical result of the trip has been to make me earnest to close up everything here, finish history, cut society, foreswear strong drink and politics, and start in about three years for China, never to return." He never did get to China. In his next journeys, he headed for the semisavage rather than the supercivilized areas of the world. During the years when he was finishing the *History*, he wandered off to Cuba, the Rocky Mountain West, and the receding Carolina wilderness, and when his work was done, he made his climactic voyage to the South Seas. In other respects, his note to Gaskell was fairly accurate. He closed out history, following his brother Charles's advice to "suppress the patriotic glow" but essentially completing his original design. He cut society, neither accepting nor sending invitations, but keeping a highly sociable seclusion among intimates for whom invitations were superfluous. He even foreswore politics to the extent of passing an election day in Yosemite, content to cast his vote "among the big trees, indifferent to what political party they belong." The bonds of work and duty slowly relaxed, but the old regularity of his life was still discernible. Niece-companions and close friends relieved the isolation in his big stone house as he worked through the Washington winters. In summer, he did not return to Beverly Farms, but went instead to Quincy, taking over from his brother Brooks the responsibility of watching over his old widowed and unwell mother. At the end of the second summer, he wrote the last sheet of his manuscript. Although Gibbon was in his mind at the deliverance as at the beginning of his work, the rainy Quincy autumn kept him for a week from imitating Gibbon's commemorative walk through his garden, long enough for the glow to fade. A hard winter's work went into preparation for printing, and the next spring he went back to stay by his dying mother and then close the house of his ancestors. In the fall the first volumes of the

History at last came out, and by the spring of 1890 Adams was ready to leave for foreign parts. He hung on in Washington into the summer, however, "detained by the last sheet of Index, and by hopes of taking La Farge with me again." The cycle seemed to be running down as he diagnosed his fitful state:

> My disease is ennui, probably the result of prolonged labor on one work, and of nervous strain. The reaction of having nothing to do after steady labor without change for so many years, is severe. Probably it will rapidly disappear with travel. It has hitherto always done so.

At fifty-two, Henry Adams might easily have given in to his world-weariness. He had conquered his streak of morbid ennui when he entered manhood, but he never quite annihilated it. The young dandy had his attacks of nerves despite assiduous activity as a reformer and a wit. The assistant professor did better, but he had to live with the frightening memory of his wife's breakdown on the Nile. The historian wrote two novels about heroines unmoored by grief and used up by one great love. The widower knew moments when personal relations came down to shuffling the cards for solitaire, vitality to aging senses "cut down to a kind of dull consciousness," work to a matter of tinkering with an index. He set his affairs in order in anticipation of the voyage out. Acting as his own literary executor, he went through his papers and burned whatever he thought too trivial or too personal to keep, including, possibly, a diary. He saved a thin sheaf of sonnets which promised less for his future career than they expressed dissatisfaction with the one he was ending. One of these, the second of a pair entitled "Illusion," achieves a few lines of genuine poignancy. It lists a number of conventionally poetical beauties which —

Shine by illusion, and whoso, among
Their beauties, grasps at secrets to be wrung
From love alone, shall their enchantment lose. . . .
Only man's ignorance avails to save
Divine perfection from a human grave.

Intelligence was no substitute for love or knowledge for immortality. But if sometimes he thought he had lost everything except intelligence and knowledge and doubted the value of these, he erred. He had shrewdly predicted that travel would relieve his ennui, and he had wisely chosen to take La Farge as his companion again.

Adams no sooner boarded the train with La Farge than he brought out his watercolors. On the way west he wrote to his niece, "All yesterday I labored to attain sage green for the sage-brush. Of course I do not try yet to draw; all my ambition is limited to finding out what the colors are." He had neglected his senses and disciplined his mind long enough. Freed equally from inhibition and duty, he started at the beginning — with the first sense he could remember. Riding out from Honolulu, he vied with La Farge at the new game of how to see a palm tree, what to make of a new world "full of life and color." He resorted again and again to his paintbox. When he looked at the results, he saw that they had little in common with La Farge's "wild daubs of brown and purple," but were rather "like young ladies' embroidery of the last generation." Nevertheless, with the enthusiasm of a boy he kept on fishing in the hope of a bite tomorrow. Before he left Hawaii, he could report, "I enjoy myself, and the sense of living, more than I have done in five years. I am glad to be dead to the old existence, which was a torture, and to forget it, in a change as complete as that of another planet." To get the good of travel, he had not remained passive. The first step toward recovering the sense of living was to cultivate the sense of sight.

In making watercolors the instrument of his sensuous education, Adams introduced himself to what he later called tone. As an abstraction at least, he had known it as long ago as his sneer at Emerson's dictum that "photographs give more pleasure than paintings." To him, the remark argued "extreme sublimation or tenuity of intelligence. . . . If Mr. Emerson was in some respects more than human, he paid for it by being in other respects proportionately less." He still took snapshots himself, but by the time he got to Samoa he was ready to warn, "Remember that the photograph takes all the color, life and charm out of the tropics, and leaves nothing but a conventional hardness that might as well be Scotch or Yankee for all the truth it has." The Yankee traveler was referring to Robert Louis Stevenson, whose inability to see the primitive world in any terms but those of his Scottish youth seemed to leave him farther from the artistic vision of a La Farge than even Henry Adams was. Still later, from Tahiti, Adams was to declare, "I hate photographs abstractly, because they have given me more ideas perversely and immoveably wrong, than I ever should get by imagination." As he learned more and more the inadequacy of the medium he knew how to use, he kept on studying the medium he was too old to master. Undeceived about his own talent, he still thought that the amateur painter could get something which the collector of drawings and maker of photographs had missed. He wrote without embarrassment, "I go on, trying every day to make pictures, and every day learning, as one does in a new language, a word or two more, just to show that the thing is laughable. Still, I have learned enough, from La Farge's instruction, to make me look at painting rather from the inside, and see a good many things about a picture that I only felt before." With the investment of work and the willingness to work imperfectly in order to learn, he gained a sensuous responsiveness to both art and nature.

Adams' casual reference to painting as a kind of language indicated the medium through which he could best express his new sensitivity. Henry James, when Hay showed him some of Adams' travel letters, commented on the power of self-revelation "hitherto unsuspected in H. A.," but qualified his interest by saying that he wanted "more account of the *look* of things — places — people." Adams began to render precisely this, and to do so he, like James, employed the language of painting, as when he described the Samoan landscape at midnight: "Sky, sea and land are all judicious water-colors, toned with one general purplish wash with the most exquisitely delicate gradations, but never running into violent contrasts. Even the whites have an infinite gradation of violets, when contrasted with the dead white of a ship or a house." Out of context, these sentences are scarcely luminous, but they do show Adams' growing ability to rid himself of literary preconceptions when he wanted to see with the eyes alone. What is more, he knew how to find his way back from pictorial expressiveness to verbal wit. Evoking the qualities of light, motion, moisture that the camera left out, he denounced the photograph, "which simply gives one conventional character to New England and Samoa alike," and dryly added, "Now New England is not alike." If Adams' paintings showed the same inescapable meticulousness as his handwriting, his letters had the spontaneity which continuous daily practice in his craft made possible. They, like La Farge's watercolors of the same time, display the release of imagination which occurred when a finely trained talent expressed in the free medium of the sketch its response to the South Sea openness of experience. Previous discipline of craftsmanship allowed each of the companions now to use his technique so readily as to be barely conscious of it. Given that condition, each could find the other's way of seeing a stimulus to his own.

Although Adams could use the vocabulary of his painting-

master to help describe the mobile colors of the tropic landscape, he faced a more difficult task as an observer of native
dance and song. To find terms for this, he got no hint from
anything in his own native culture except through some
shrewd guesses about primitive Greece. So slight a hint was
enough. Witnessing his first Siva, he began to understand
the Polynesian cult of physical beauty and his own and
La Farge's enthusiasm for the physique and movement of the
glistening dancers who seemed to have stepped from the sea.
"No future experience," he wrote, "short of being eaten, will
make us feel so new again." A total change had taken place in
what his New England eyes could see. In Japan, he had
declared against his inhibitions and taken notice of the monuments of phallic worship, "One cannot quite ignore the foundations of society." In Samoa, he could record immediate
delight in "the sensation of seeing extremely fine women, with
superb forms, perfectly unconscious of undress, and yet evidently aware of their beauty and dignity. . . . A handsome
girl, unmarried, of sixteen years old, tall and strong, is as superb a creature here as the world has to offer, unless the young
giant of a chief is still handsomer. Crowned with their usual
garland of green leaves, they are Greek fauns and Apollos to
a man." His own ignorance of the art he watched and his correspondents' lack of usable reference severely limited his
ability to describe the dance, but he did convey what the performance led him to see. If he protested too much that he
could detect no slightest trace of indecency, he also asserted
unequivocally, "I never had fully understood how little mere
beauty of face had to do with beauty itself." Learning to use
and trust his senses, he came to a new understanding of the
foundations of society.

Adams, in seeking out the concrete qualities of his new experience, extended his curiosity to the ancient song and legend
of the islanders. "My only object," he said, "is to find out

what they have done." In this, the continuity with his old life was more apparent. The scholar had canvassed the Library of Congress for all the available Western records of Polynesian lore, so that the historian could shift his interest from institutional records to heroic narratives, from what happened to the artistic product of the past. Once again, however, the lessons of the mind became fruitful only after direct personal involvement. Samoa did not provide the occasion for that, and Tahiti, the next stage of Adams' journey, almost did not. There, Adams found the pervasive melancholy of a primitive culture much further disintegrated than any he had yet seen. The town of Papeete had, for him, an aspect of "lost beatitude quite symbolic of Paradise," and the shanty-dwelling people, a "half-castitude that permeates everything." He went on:

> Yet even when I forget the half-breeds and the cottages, and go swimming, so to speak, in the blue and purple light, I never lose consciousness of a sort of restless melancholy that will not explain why it should want to haunt a spot that by rights ought to be as gay as a comic opera. . . . If I could only paint it, or express it in poetry or prose, or do anything with it, or even shake it out of its exasperating repose, the feeling would be a pleasant one, and I should fall in love with the very wrinkles of my venerable and spiritual Tahitian grandmother; but when one has nothing else to look at, one rebels at being forever smiled upon by a grandmother whose complexion is absolutely divine, and whose attitude indicates the highest breeding, while she suggests no end of charm in conversation, yet refuses to do anything but smile in a sort of sad way that may mean much or mean nothing.

The baffling atmosphere provoked him less than the curious social situation whereby he found himself on close terms with the legitimate but displaced branch of the royal line. In his host Tati Salmon he discovered a corpulence and jollity like his friend Richardson's; in Tati's European-educated sister he saw an exotic strength and fading beauty that put him in mind of Hawthorne's Miriam in *The Marble Faun*; in their mother, whom he claimed as his spiritual Tahitian grandmother, he noted the pure unexotic dignity of a matriarch who possessed in her stored memory the entire unwritten history of her race. The transition from friendliness to something closer was marked by the formal adoption of the American visitors into the Teva family, and the matriarch regally conferred on them names, titles, lands, and privileges pertaining to the island nobility. The lost-Eden sense of decay and the tranquil condescension of his native friends were congenial to Adams, a personal relation to Tahiti could hardly go much further, and yet the tropical paradise became as boring to him as it seemingly was to the permanent inhabitants. Like the Melville of *Typee*, who was often in his thoughts, he could turn his mind to nothing but escape. While he waited for the steamer that would take him on to Fiji, his old ennui reasserted itself. He complained of boredom such as he had never known before, "even in the worst wilds of Beacon Street or at the dreariest dinner-tables of Belgravia," and he could think of just one remedy for his chronic restlessness: "Motion alone amuses, and I see only the desert of Gobi that offers room for even a moderate exercise of the horse." To relieve the stranded feeling, he suggested to Marau Taaroa, the queen-pretender, that she let him take down her memoirs. She agreed and, more important, her mother Arii Taimai joined the pastime and offered Adams knowledge of Tahiti tradition beyond what she had imparted even to her own children. What he then found out about himself was that ancient legend might be as good a field for exercise as the Gobi Desert, that when spectatorship by itself did not satisfy, imaginative labor was an alternative to the anodyne of motion.

The project which Adams began in order to divert his last

weeks in Papeete took more than a decade to reach its final form and even then was less important for itself than for the light it sheds on him. In the book now known as *Tahiti*, Adams quit playing Humpty Dumpty and tried to fit together his new sensibility and his old discipline of scholarship. At first he had deprecated, in his letters home, the "knowledge that would have made a great Professor of me twenty years ago, but now has no other value than to amuse me for the moment, and perhaps to amuse you some day when my wanderings end." Work made a difference. It not only distracted his thoughts, but reminded him of the pleasure to be taken in "a little more, or at least a little more exact knowledge of the island than I should ever have got from books or conversation." The historian who was reappearing in Henry Adams could take satisfaction in what he did as well as what he learned. He had mastered a method well enough to try a new way of handling it. Instead of using documents to illuminate social development, he used what he could learn of social development to throw light on his "documents." Although knowledge of the past became a means rather than an end, it was a necessary means and Adams took time to work it up. His literary materials had to be strung upon a narrative and his narrative had to be based on facts if he was to avoid a hopelessly tangled obscurity. On the eve of his departure, he proudly claimed to have worked as hard as ever he did at home and to have come up with two thoroughly rewritten chapters which made "a very learned disquisition on Tahitian genealogy, mixed up with legends and love-songs."

Adams' comment on his first two chapters describes the entire book he finally produced, the *Memoirs of Marau Taaroa*, which he printed in 1893, and the revised version of 1901 in which he shifted the point of view to the queen-mother Arii Taimai, the main source of his information. The book cannot interest a Western audience as much as the Polynesian family for whom Adams wrote it, if only because so many new names and facts are bound to overwhelm an uninitiated reader. The translated materials have a simple authenticity and properly command the center of attention, but apart from Adams' few sharp notes on the effect of Western imperialism, too little of the historical context of his story was conveniently transmissible. Primitive Tahiti was too alien a world for Adams to bring into relation to his occidental readers; the medieval culture from which his modern world was alienated but not historically separate would prove a more tractable subject. Subject, however, was less of a difficulty than method. Adams handled his subject well in his freely dashed-off sketches, but when he came to the infinitely less casual task of writing a full-length book, all his ease evaporated. He ruefully observed: "I am not the man to write Polynesian. My methods are all intellectual, analytic and modern." His monographic accuracy, like his camera, left out color and life. He could not yet, except in letters, apply what he learned from La Farge's painting, which might not be "an exact rendering of the actual things he paints, though often it is near enough to surprise me by its faithfulness; but whether exact or not, it always suggests the emotion of the moment." As a result, *Tahiti* is the most esoteric book he ever wrote.

Trying to distract his impatience for departure, Adams found that engagement of the mind led to commitment of the heart. The daily interviews which made his wait pass quickly brought him to an intimate knowledge of the old chiefess who was the last possessor of so many island traditions. His rapport with Arii Taimai transcended the need for an interpreter. In her farewell speech, made with the dignity and feeling of natural royalty, he recognized what he had found that was beyond history. "Though it was in native," he wrote, "and I did not understand a word of it, I quite broke down. I shall never see her again, but I have learned from her what the

archaic woman was." The desire to commemorate this archaic woman, his spiritual ancestress, as he said, gave him a
project which was to span the decade between his two careers.
Working on the memoir during the nineties, he claimed to get
more pleasure from it than from "my dreary American history,
which is to me what Emma Bovary was to Gustave Flaubert."
He was expressing much the same mood as he had felt in
Tahiti when he got news of how the *History* was being received
at home:

> Really I think I do not much care, for I feel that the history
> is not what I care now to write, or want to say, if I say anything.
> It belongs to the *me* of 1870; a strangely different being from
> the *me* of 1890. There are not nine pages in the nine volumes
> that now express anything of my interests or feelings; unless per-
> haps some of my disillusionments. . . . I care more for one chap-
> ter, or any dozen pages of *Esther* than for the whole history, in-
> cluding maps and indexes . . .

Unfortunately, what Adams cared for he did not know how to
do. The old historian knew something about commemorating
ancestors, and the *me* of 1890 needed to come to terms with
that other self. The South Sea letters and the volume of
memoirs, taken together, point the way to Adams' extremely
personal expression of an historical subject in *Mont-Saint-Michel
and Chartres*; but as they stand, they mark the disparity between his epistolary and his formal writing, between his vision
and his capacity for rendering it, during the interval of his
two careers. Yet Adams' relation with Arii Taimai did more
than clarify for him his new interests and feelings. In having
something to miss, he had something to take away. His last
few weeks in Tahiti began with "My life here has ceased to
be more than mere waiting for departure" and ended with
his resolve to complete the literary labor he had undertaken
almost by chance. He left knowing not only what he cared
for, but that he cared to say it.

Renewal of purpose marked the end of Adams' voyage out.
The stages of his long journey back were many, but they led
in their various ways toward his later career. At Fiji, the next
stop after Tahiti, he suffered a return of the insomnia which
had tormented him in the anxiety of his wife's last months and
in the loneliness of the years thereafter. Insomnia was part of
the cost of starting homeward, but with it came wakefulness of
the imagination. His letters from Fiji contain the first sentences which are minted in the later style of Henry Adams. In
them wit juxtaposes the distant and the near, the abstract and
the personal, reflecting on the values of Adams' own society
and on the enduring profligacy of nature in one easy stretch:

> I had a fair taste of the tropical forest. Flowers were rare and
> not much worth noticing, but like a true Yankee I consoled
> myself by reflecting that at every step I trampled on plants
> worth at least five dollars apiece in New York or London, and
> that no emperor tossed so much possible wealth about, as I
> did. The forest had a charm of its own, not of color or of scent
> or of any of the qualities that we like most in our woods, but for
> depth of verdure, richness of parasitic growth, with lines and
> masses quite strange to our notions, and a certain waste and ex-
> travagance quite profligate and reprehensible, but not wicked.
> The missionaries would stop it if they could, but the rains fall,
> and the ferns and creepers still cling high on the tree trunks.

From his elementary lessons in painting Adams was proceed-
ing to a school of all the senses. In his prose, he matched an
increased range of sensuous appeal with lively play of mind
and devised the literary attitude by which he could make his
varied observations hang together. He had used the device
of point of view before, but now he extended that principle of
composition to his very choice of words and made it literally
mean a point of perception. Sometimes it weaved back and
forth between the letter writer and the object of his description: "Curiously enough," he told Mrs. Cameron, "I have

always found the cannibal a most insinuating fellow, remarkable for his open and sympathetic expression. His impression of human nature is evidently favorable. He regards men as I regard snipe." Sometimes the point of view was interesting because it was so fixedly placed: "In the middle of the Pacific Ocean," he reported to Lodge after he had traveled to Sydney, "all things assume a curiously level grade of interest. The political and social status of a few half-naked Samoans, Tahitians and Fijians, seems just as important as the doings of Australia, the card-play of the Prince of Wales, or the speeches of Benjamin Harrison." Adams' sense of humor and his sense of irony often blended as he converted his restless consciousness into the fine intellectual alertness that he took with him into old age.

The most important stopping place after Tahiti was Ceylon, for it put an end to old illusions about escape. First, at Kandy, he failed to find contentment in the lush tropic landscape: "Another Paradise opens its arms to another son of Adam, but the devil of restlessness, who led my ancestor to the loss of his estate, leads me." Then Adams went inland by oxcart to see Anuradhpura, the ruined holy city where Buddhism had flourished two thousand years before. Among the brick domes that had lost their architectural decoration and even their plaster sheathing, he found nothing to admire but bigness and the family of monkeys that scampered overhead at dusk. Ceylon was an anticlimax. Visually, it let Adams know that the life of pure sensation could pall as much as that of pure thought or pure practical will, and spiritually, it offered no alternative. Adams sat for half an hour under the sacred bo tree, a shoot of the original tree beneath which Buddha had attained Nirvana, and as he simply reported, he left "without attaining Buddhaship." Meditating the experience during the long, calm shipboard days that took him across the Indian Ocean, the Red Sea, and the Mediterranean, he

wrote the first of his longer poems, "Buddha and Brahma."
Like the figures in Adams' novels, those in his verse narrative
resemble their creator. First there is the young man who
fails to attain Buddhaship even though he is a sincere disciple:
unable to forget the world's questions or to accept Gautama's
enigmatic answer, he returns to his Brahman father and asks
him to interpret where the Buddha had remained silent.
The father, in a speech that takes up over two-thirds of the
poem, gives a double answer. The clear alternative to re-
nunciation and the simplest course for youth is "*Think not!
Strike!*" For those who, like the father, have found that they
can neither renounce the world nor reform it, there is the
more intricate path of acceptance and detachment. The
detached self behind its veil of silence preserves a discipline
as strict as that of either piety or action:

> *Never can we attain the Perfect Life.*
> *Yet in this world of selfishness and striving*
> *The wise man lives as deeply sunk in silence,*
> *As conscious of the Perfect Life he covets,*
> *As any recluse in his forest shadows*
> *As any Yogi in his mystic trances.*

Admittedly "content to tolerate what I cannot mend," the
father neither prizes nor undervalues his state of mind, he
accepts it: "Gautama's way is best, but all are good."
Adams' poem was the justification of the third way which he
would try to make his own. For one who could not get rid of
self in Gautama's way or in the strenuous life, he commended
the disciplined withdrawal of self to an inner realm of silence
where, apart from what the man might say or do or see, an
essential integrity could be preserved.

Adams' verse reflections on the incident at Anuradhpura
defined the point of view he was working toward in his prose
— the Brahman pose of spiritual calm and wise silence, the

role of an old man contriving words behind which he remained half concealed. Both the incident and the poem were early episodes in what was to be a slow development. Before Adams started on his long Pacific journey, he had already indicated, at least in negative terms, what these episodes would mean. He had commented on the Buddhism of Sturgis Bigelow: "Thousands and millions of men have taken his road before, with more or less satisfaction, but the mass of mankind have settled to the conviction that the only Paradise possible in this world is concentrated in the three little words which the ewig man says to the ewige woman."* This conviction, as much as anything else, carried him past the road to Nirvana and back to a world where he expected that "all the old perplexities, with plenty of new ones, are going to revive." Revive they did, particularly after he bade goodbye to La Farge in Paris and then to Mrs. Cameron, the confidant of his almost daily letters and the strongest tie to home of his wanderings. Left alone, he often found good reason to dread "the solitude of hotels and the weariness of self — self — self." On the other hand, his "going on for a new avatar" often proved to do wonders. When he joined his London friends, the would-be Brahman noted with satisfaction that his own patience amid the *fin-de-siècle* gloom was greater than theirs. He arrived back in Washington in February 1892, and went at once to see the monument which he had commissioned to be done in his absence, the stone setting by Stanford White and the statue by Saint-Gaudens that was

*Adams was not so summary with Bigelow as this single sentence by itself might imply. His letter went on: "Sturgis calls this the Fireside, and thinks he knows better. He looks for Paradise in absorption in the Infinite. Probably the result will be the same. Sooner or later, fate commonly gets bored by the restless man who requires Paradise, and sets its foot on him with so much energy that he curls up and never wriggles again. When Sturgis can't squirm any longer, and suddenly realizes that Paradise is a dream, and the dream over, I fear that he is too sensitive a nature to stand the shock, and perhaps it wouldn't be worth his while to try."

to express "the acceptance, intellectually, of the inevitable."
He returned often to look at the bronze figure in every detail,
to check the artist's subtlety and taste and capacity to speak
through his medium, but, as he said, "St. Gaudens held up
the mirror." He was testing himself as well as the sculptor
— his own capacity to respond to the work of art and accept
its meaning.

Adams was as far removed from the professional satisfaction
as from the personal happiness of a decade before. On his
arrival in Europe from the East, he looked into the Paris and
London archives where he had burrowed so vigorously in the
days of his marriage. Now he was hunting errors that apparently no critic but himself would look for in the *History*. He
continued for the next ten years to make corrections and revi-
sions for a second edition that would never be called for, but
he could not channel much of his energy into that. Nor did
the private man of 1892 take much pleasure in the embarrassment of honors that came to the historian. Adams put so
many conditions on accepting an honorary degree from
Harvard that President Eliot testily reminded him he was
not conferring the degree upon himself. A minor riding-
accident gave him his excuse for avoiding an honor which he
oversensitively thought might look like favoritism.* He accepted the honorary doctorate of Western Reserve University,
where the governing board were not his "old friends, relations
or connections," but he took the degree *in absentia*. Declining
to be a prophet in his own country, he dodged other kinds of
professional recognition, too, or half dodged awkwardly.
The American Historical Association had elected him vice-
president in his absence abroad; the meeting which heard
Turner read his famous essay in 1893 elected Adams presi-

---

*The sprained ankle which prevented his attending the Harvard Commence-
ment on June 29, 1892, did not keep him from maneuvering the Washington
baseball park a week earlier.

dent even though he was not there to receive the honor; the annual session of 1894 listened to its presidential address in the form of a letter, read on behalf of an historian who had discovered urgent business in Mexico. In that same year of 1894, Adams tried, on grounds of having laid aside the career of historian and withdrawn himself as a "candidate for honors," to decline the Loubat Prize of Columbia University. He yielded only with the understanding that he did not condone the choice of the judges. Neither his preference for critical readers over formal ceremony nor his excessive shyness and affectation of shyness explained the gyrations which he went through. There was also a kind of benumbed dismissal of the past, as in his refusal to attend weddings, even that of his brother Brooks.* These incidents of the nineties passed from his conscious memory with the quality of dreams, for he wrote altogether ingenuously in 1902 that "curiously enough, now first, after a dozen years of apparent indifference, I receive rather numerous compliments on my poor old History, which might reasonably have been forgotten. I like the compliments. Indeed I like flattery very much; — more than anyone I know; but I wish it had come earlier or in some form that would have made me work." By that time, when he was once again the fully committed writer, Adams was able to speak as affectionately of his "poor old History" as ever he had of his "melancholy little *Esther*." It was not for lack of encouraging recognition that the historian was at loose ends.

The malaise that characterized the historian entered the correspondence of the private individual, also. It cropped up only occasionally, but when it did, the Brahman role he had invented in his poem collapsed. The witty observer of past and present could see George M. Pullman and Andrew Carnegie and Grover Cleveland as "our Crassus and Pompey and

---

*Adams made no exception to the latter rule until 1906, and then only for his fatherless niece Dorothy Quincy, who asked him to give her away.

Caesar, — our proud American triumvirate, the types of our national mind and ideals"; but a much less sanguine Adams could belabor President Cleveland as "our fat-headed sculpin who thinks he rules us." In Paris, the cultivated man of the world might spoof the closing strain of *Lakmé* — " *'Dieu protège nos amours!'* As far as I can see, this is all God has to do in Paris anyhow"; but the Philistine snob could dismiss "Verlaine's expiring gnashings of rotten teeth" and "the other refuse" of current literature. Adams read widely in the naturalists, decadents, and symbolists, all of whom were exploring literary paths his own imagination was to follow, but he expressed an equally strident dislike for them all. He was more at home with the staider forms of serious writing, history, criticism, and social analysis, but even with them he showed a curious imbalance: he blushed to admit himself fascinated by the "anti-semitic ravings," to use his words, of Edouard Drumont. Deploring the new poetry as a "reflection of its own decay," he made the primary error of taking the subject matter of a work of art for the work itself; rejecting what seemed tormented and unhealthy, he fell in with the deceptive vigor and actual morbidity of the antisemitic movement of the nineties.

Adams' antisemitism, which showed most often when his pose of calm detachment was least in evidence, provides a gloomy index of the difficulties through which he was passing. Antisemitic stereotypes and clichés were current among Victorians on both sides of the Atlantic and the younger Adams sometimes used them, but the disciple of Tocqueville and Mill had a genuine liberal's distaste for either scorn or pride of race. The historian was quick to catch Jefferson for a scornful reference to Jews, and the author of *Democracy* had his heroine deplore a Jewish friend's pride of blood as if he were ironically cautioning himself. It was after his wife's death, when nervous strain became a fact of daily existence, that a change occurred. He began combining images of the Jew as he had glimpsed him in little art shops and big hotels with concepts of the Jew as, alternatively, a financial tycoon or a typical bourgeois. Sometimes the word "Jew" expressed snobbery that went hand in hand with brilliant social comment; sometimes the epithet was charged with an inchoate desire to abuse "goldbugs," his other term for bankers. He talked of Jews most often in his letters to Brooks Adams. Henry suddenly became much closer to Brooks when, in the summer of 1893, he was called home to Quincy to help see his family through the great Panic. Their common interest in fiscal developments as a clue to history was for a while a common obsession, and their mood fell in with the widespread populist antisemitism during an era of "Cross of Gold" rhetoric. Since the bond of interest with Brooks did not change when Henry's mind had turned to other fields, his letters to his brother continued to be full of cant about "the Jews" after his other correspondence pretty much dropped the subject. His antisemitism was not simply a home-grown product, however, as his fascination with Drumont testified: his intelligence was as cosmopolitan in its vices as in its virtues.

Adams showed at his worst in his letters on the Dreyfus case to Mrs. Cameron, the person to whom he wrote with least conscious contrivance of his language and thought; the freedom of relation that called forth some of his wittiest sketches also brought to the surface his feelings on "the Jew scandal," his contempt for Anglo-American indignation at Zola's imprisonment, his indifference to the fact that the "howling Jew" was innocent. He not so ironically took sides as an anti-Dreyfusard at one time, because he would rather support the nationalism of the French in France than that of the British in South Africa. He had no trouble identifying the military campaigns against the Boers and the legal campaigns on behalf of Dreyfus: "Both of them are Jew wars, and

I don't believe in Jew wars." His more temperate letters to
Hay showed Adams' perplexity in more reasonable form.
"I can't find out whether I am Dreyfusard or Anti," he wrote.
His fear of demoralizing the army and therefore the state
worked against his desire for individual justice, and his reaction to the messy handling of the case was that "the army,
the navy and the civil government have all admitted and
proclaimed their incapacity to maintain France as one of the
great powers." His virulence began to taper off after the
Dreyfus affair, partly because it had run its course, partly
because he was harnessing his intellectual energies to hard
constructive work. The latter explanation is the one hopeful
aspect of a story which is disagreeable in itself and necessarily
alarming to a world that has witnessed antisemitism as a catastrophic social event rather than as, in Adams' case, a datum of
personal psychology like insomnia or addiction to privacy. One
consequence of the episode is the occasional obscure use of
the word "Jew" which disfigures, albeit inessentially, his late
masterpieces — pockmarks of a disease that can be fatal.

Despite confusions of spirit and purpose, an order gradually
emerged in Adams' life during the nineties. He traveled
more and more restlessly, but Washington and Paris were his
bases. The Old World and the New, in his *History*, had stood
for the sense of the past and the possession of the present and
possibly the future, and they came to have the same meaning
in his life. When he stayed at his American home, he studied
such authors as Karl Marx and Karl Pearson, vied with his
brother Brooks in trying to chart statistically the tendencies
of history, and watched politics as though it were a performance run specially for him. In new ways, he bent his
mind to his old interest in politics, economy, and science. At
his Paris apartment, he began to submerge himself deeper
and deeper in the art, literature, and philosophy of the Middle
Ages. The nieces who banished loneliness from the house in

La Fayette Square flocked to Paris, also, where their uncle presided over their initiation to the refinements of Gothic architecture and the Théâtre Français. The cycle of the year became regularized for Adams, as it had in the days of his marriage, only now it was a case of "half the year burrowing in twelfth-century art and religion; the other half, seated . . . in the very centre of the web, with every whisper of the world coming instantly to my ear." The two halves were never wholly distinct. During the late summer of 1899, when he was denouncing Dreyfus most violently and reporting the imminent collapse of society, he could claim in the same breath that his plunge into architectural study was bringing him genuine peace: "Hardly once have I felt irritable or irritated or depressed." The anxiety he did not recognize was that of reaching a momentous decision. "I am happy with my twelfth-century churches and literature, and look with dread to winter and Washington," he wrote toward the end of September. "I am a sexagenarian Hamlet with architectural fancies, and content 'were it not that I have bad dreams' — and mosquitoes." A few weeks later, he came to the sticking-point: he determined to organize his various and seemingly random studies toward the object to which he had unconsciously been heading. Once he wrote to Mrs. Cameron, and admitted to himself, that he was working on a "guidebook," a quiet elation set in. He stayed on in France till the very end of the year, setting his photographs and notes in order and adding to them as fast as he could. Writing from Paris in December, he took a new tone with his younger brother. Instead of answering one of Brooks's dismal letters in kind, Henry spoke with the detachment he had envisioned in his poem:

> What one really wants is youth, and what one really loses is years. Life becomes at last a mere piece of acting. One goes on by habit, playing more or less clumsily that one is still alive. It is ludicrous and at times humiliating, but there is a certain style

in it which youth has not. We become all, more or less, gentlemen; we are *ancien régime*; we learn to smile while gout racks
us. . . . We get out of bed in the morning all broken up, without nerves, color or temper, and by noon we are joking with
young women about the play. One lives in constant company
with diseased hearts, livers, kidneys and lungs; one shakes hands
with certain death at closer embrace every day; one sees paralysis in every feature and feels it in every muscle; all one's
functions relax their action day by day; and, what is worse,
one's grasp on the interests of life relaxes with the physical relaxation; and, through it all, we improve; our manners acquire
refinement; our sympathies grow wider; our youthful self-
consciousness disappears; very ordinary men and women are
found to have charm; our appreciations have weight; we
should almost get to respect ourselves if we knew of anything
human to respect; so we affect to respect the conventions, and
we ask only to be classed as a style.

Having passed through a decade of tension, Adams arrived
imaginatively at the destination he had marked out during
his long journey round the world. The personal motive of
reducing self-consciousness had become the artist's motive —
unself-conscious conversion of experience into language. In
making the principle of his style into a rule of self-discipline,
he finally connected his "two separate lives; one, in the world
Which we must ever seem to treat as real; The other in ourselves behind a veil Not to be raised without disturbing both."
His prose, with its color and life as well as clarity and dignity,
now so far outstripped his verse that his role is best defined in
the words of a poet who much admired his later work.
Yeats's "Sailing to Byzantium" portrays with surprising accuracy the sixty-one-year-old Henry Adams:

> *An aged man is but a paltry thing,*
> *A tattered coat upon a stick, unless*
> *Soul clap its hands and sing, and louder sing*
> *For every tatter in its mortal dress . . .*

Studying "monuments of unageing intellect" overbalanced for Adams not only the sensual world of the young that Yeats contrasted with the magnificence of art, but also a realm of abstraction where the mind gazed darkly at scientific or economic data and presented no check to irresponsible emotions. Besides helping us see Adams' mask and motive more distinctly, Yeats's poem indicates the way in which the writer and the historian came to terms. Study, a means to ascertain the past, could also be pursued in order to project oneself into history. Although the professional scholar could make no use of the observation, a younger Henry Adams had marked the debunking passage in his Michelet in which the Normans, made by legend into Viking giants, turned out to be little men afraid of seasickness like himself; his projections into the past started from political theory, not physical reality. The middle-aged traveler, who learned from his "venerable and spiritual Tahitian grandmother" the difference between straightforward history and vital memory, was not so inhibited. His last letter from Tahiti disclosed a freer imagination bidding good-bye to the scene of its own former greatness in war and love. "I wrote poetry then," Adams remarked. "That was a century — or two — or three — ago." Tahiti, though, was too far from Adams' other world for him really to possess it. Back from the Pacific, the onetime editor of John Quincy Adams became the filial grandson of a president who sometimes departed from New England ways, and he piously attended the revival of Grétry's *Coeur-de-Lion*. Richard and the Crusades were close, but he still had to come back to the Normans. Normandy was to be his Byzantium. Midway through his troubled years, in August 1895, the voyager who had sailed past the tropic Eden that was no country for old men and the silent Nirvana that was too distant for his ordinary humanity crossed the threshold into a "Norman paradise," where he moved at his ease amid the sensuous con-

creteness of art and the imaginative remoteness of time. He
had gone with the Lodges to escape the Paris heat and to help
himself somehow endure another month of "this muck-heap
life of Europe." He came back with what he had not looked
for, release and self-possession and a memory which would
carry him into his own future:

> Not for several days or more have I enjoyed happier mo-
> ments than among my respectable Norman ancestors, looking
> over the fields they ploughed and the stones they carved and
> piled up. . . . With true Norman work, the sensation is that of
> personal creation. No doubt Amiens and Chartres are greatly
> superior architecture, but I was not there. I was a vassal of the
> Church; I held farms — for I was many — in the Cotentin
> and around Caen, but the thing I did by a great majority of
> ancestors was to help in building the Cathedral of Coutances,
> and my soul is still built into it. I can almost remember the
> faith that gave me energy, and the scared boldness that made
> my towers seem to me so daring, with the bits of gracefulness
> that I hasarded with some doubts whether the divine grace could
> properly be shown outside. Within I had no doubts. There the
> contrite sinner was welcomed with such tenderness as makes
> me still wish I were one. There is not a stone in the whole in-
> terior which I did not treat as though it were my own child. I
> was not clever, and I made some mistakes which the great men
> of Amiens corrected. I was simple-minded, somewhat stiff and
> cold, almost repellent to the warmer natures of the south, and
> I had lived always where one fought handily and needed to de-
> fend one's wives and children; but I was at my best. Nearly
> eight hundred years have passed since I made the fatal mistake
> of going to England, and since then I have never done anything
> in the world that can begin to compare in the perfection of its
> spirit and art with my cathedral of Coutances. I am as sure of
> it as I am of death.

The driven wanderer, fleeing more than self, had at last found
something he could believe to be as sure as death. Before the

carved and piled stones of his ancestors, he could recognize in
the mirror every impulse of his spirit. It was as if soul clapped
its hands and sang,

> *Consume my heart away; sick with desire*
> *And fastened to a dying animal*
> *It knows not what it is; and gather me*
> *Into the artifice of eternity.*

The Adams who was at his best in Coutances existed in a
biographical as well as a broader historical continuum. He
can be identified in the private secretary who, struggling to
find himself in London, first differentiated himself from his
older brother Charles. The boyish dream of a medieval
cloister fulfilled itself when the old man became "a twelfth-
century monk in a nineteenth-century attic, in Paris." The
resisted call to profess medieval history took on another meaning for one who returned to the Middle Ages "because I was
tired, and wanted quiet and solitude and absorption." And
year by year after 1895, the self-discovery at Coutances became more central to Adams' life. A "scholar" once again,
only "without consciousness of a mission as teacher," he moved
from architectural monuments to literary, bagging cathedrals
and battling subjunctives, heaping up photographs and books.
In 1899, as the hobby was becoming a definite project, he
entered a hermit-like seclusion, his monastic rule — "I must
not be agitated!" Within two years thereafter he had a manuscript which he tried out on La Farge. The twelfth-century
monk turned to his onetime model for a medieval character,
the one man, as he had written from his attic cloister, who
could be of value to him: "He alone sees." But La Farge
could only help after the fact, as a listener. The writer had to
work by himself, face isolation without agitation, and have the
courage to say finally, "In art, it is one's self that one must
please."

Adams called the guidebook from which he read to La Farge his "Miracles of the Virgin," and one of the arguments he developed in it was that the art of the twelfth century had aimed to please the Virgin, not the artist. He counted himself an adorer of the Virgin, a role he always distinguished from being a worshiper in the Church. What he adored was the eternal feminine source of life and color; his twelfth-century Notre Dame summed up for him everything that went into the education of the artist in himself. When he later said "The mind resorts to reason for want of training," he simply put elliptically what that education had been. He made the same point more elaborately when, in a pause between drafts of *Mont-Saint-Michel and Chartres*, he felt in twentieth-century America the ennui which he never experienced in twelfth-century Normandy. "By way of relief from boredom," he wrote Mrs. Cameron in 1901, "I have returned to verse, and have written a long prayer to the Virgin of Chartres." The "Prayer" was his best poem. In it, he spoke as one who humbly remembered the days of his worship, his cathedral-building, and his singing with Saint Bernard of the Virgin's hymn. He confessed to have deserted the Mother to seek the Father's world and to have arrived in the kingdom of power without glory, where man worshiped himself and recognized no other god but the dynamo. He made clear his actual position by interjecting a "Prayer to the Dynamo," such as would be chanted by the "lords of space," the "Atom-Kings" of a world without emotion. But he returned to the Virgin with the prayer that, even in his modern predicament, he still could utter: "Help me to see! . . . Help me to know! . . . Help me to feel! . . . Help me to bear! . . ." The light, the strength, the sense, and the power to endure that Adams sought in prayer, he had already found in life: his wife's tragedy gave him awful knowledge, La Farge's friendship quickened his eye, Arii Taimai lent a primeval dimension to what he could feel, his twelfth-century

"Byzantium" steadied him in his capacity to bear. With his "Prayer to the Virgin of Chartres," he took leave of the nineteenth century, not simply to fly back in time, but to enter the twentieth and, as an artist, become a contemporary to posterity.

The decade in which Henry Adams arrived at old age began with "Buddha and Brahma," in which he first projected himself as an old man. He is the father who speaks his wisdom to a son even more than the son who returns to the way of his father. Ten years later, "Prayer to the Virgin" expressed his relation to the Mother and his recognition of religious strength in a society to which he claimed kinship. The poem presents his claim at the same time that it admits the remoteness of his world from the Virgin's. In the intervening years, as life arranged itself between the twelfth-century house at 1603 H Street and the nineteenth-century attic on Avenue de Bois de Boulogne, the aging Henry Adams played his role less and less clumsily. In December 1897, when the Middle Ages were an interest just one degree stronger than a hobby, and return to Washington did not seem worth the transatlantic crossing, Adams' thoughts were with his wife and he sent his quiet thanks to the friend who paid an anniversary visit to the Rock Creek grave. He wrote of his own prospect of going there once for all: "When one has eaten one's dinner, one is bored at having to sit at table. Do you know that I am sixty in six weeks, and that I was only forty-seven when I finished my dinner?" Adams did not rise from table to join his lady. Rather, he found the courage to revisit Egypt, traveling with the Hays, and to relive the memories of twenty-five years and the pain of twelve years before. At the next anniversary, he defied a little better the emotional bleakness of surviving with only the memory of his wife's intimate presence. On the sixth of December, he wrote: "Once more I come back to this day, my low-water mark of life. Singular, how one goes on, with-

out caring to, or anything to go on for, or anyone to go on with!
Poor Mrs. Hay doesn't like to have me say that my only
present activity in this world is to prepare myself for a better;
she thinks it bad taste for a joke, and bad morals if serious;
religious people never approve of abandoning America except
for Europe." Gradually, however, he was summoning the
will and strength for a new literary career. The next year, he
took up as a writer the themes of art, science, and religion
which he had dealt with before. He was ready to face the
problems of *Esther* in the world of fact, not fiction, though if
the subject matter of his late works was historical, the method
was personal. In *Mont-Saint-Michel and Chartres* and the *Education*, the solution to Adams' problem of unity was to be art,
and the solution to his problem of progress was to be imagination. In 1901, fully launched on his second career, he came
back to Washington, and to the house he had built for his wife,
with a sceptical detachment. "The semi-annual miracle is
once more complete," he wrote. "The operation of coming
to life again in an old incarnation is more or less weird. . . .
My secret conviction is that I'm buried out at Rock Creek, but
my double certainly seems to be swearing as usual at 1603."
The profane vigor of the double masked a fine creative vitality
at the still center of his being.

Chapter VI

THE UNITY OF THE IMAGINATION

"MY NOTION of Travels is a sort of ragbag of every-thing; scenery, psychology, history, literature, poetry, art; anything in short, that is worth throwing in . . ." When Henry Adams got back to Paris after his Pacific journey, he was so much impressed with the literary journalism of Jules Lemaître and Anatole France that he thought of joining their game. He did not want to play alone, however. What he wished was to get Hay and King to collaborate in his project, as if the Five of Hearts were still five and the calendar could be turned back to the summer-like repose of a decade before. His friends' obligations were not the only reason why his proposal could not be realized. Al-though he had learned the value of the special personal im-pression which was the basis of the criticism he admired, he had not unlearned his discipline in scholarly responsibility; and although he had, for the time, passed beyond the desire to write for the sake of scientific or civic advancement, he could not so readily shift to another mode of writing. Still, the no-tion of travels persisted. The Norman tour of 1895 gave him a subject; solitary work eventuated in a book; and *Mont-Saint-Michel and Chartres* contains something of all the subjects he listed in his definition, though nothing is simply thrown in. The ragbag proved to be a silk purse and the casual project turned into a labor of infinite patience. After the trial reading of 1901, Adams put almost as much time into finishing the manuscript as he had given to writing the first version. Instead of performing for the general public, he printed one hundred copies and distributed them at the end of 1904 as New Year's gifts to particular friends. Hardly anything remained of the critical causeries he had thought of emulating except his conception of the book as a talk, "a running chatter with my nieces." The idea of writing travels was so transmuted in the ripe imagination of Henry Adams that the term helps readers not just to recognize the genre of his book, but to apprehend its vivifying form.

Mont-Saint-Michel and Chartres is in three ways a travel book. As the title announces, it is a guidebook to two places which tourists frequent, but in presenting his tourist-guide as the narrative of a guided tour, Adams crossed the well-scuffed threshold between the Baedeker manual and the literature of travel. La Farge had instructed him in the use of eyes *and* feet, and he put the lesson to good use in his simulated sightseeing at Mont-Saint-Michel, at Chartres, and on the trip from one to the other. The narrated physical movement of the tourist is the fundamental drama of the book, but this concrete action is only presented in order to lend substance to an imaginative journey. The solid church door of the abbey of Mont-Saint-Michel is also the "*pons seclorum*, the bridge of ages, between us and our ancestors." To travel across this bridge and enter the world of medieval thought and emotion is an object which requires the informed responsiveness of the historical imagination. The honest statement of personal response, which takes precedence over the historian's professional responsibility to get in "all the facts," leads to a third and still more intimate story of travel. Crossing to the Middle Ages imaginatively can only occur with the recognition that the road to Chartres is a pilgrimage way. The tour of uncle and niece and the imaginative journey of writer and reader are modulations of the spiritual progress of Henry Adams, a pilgrim of art who knew the difference between his own reverence and actual belief. The bridge of ages could not be crossed on foot, and although the farther side could be seen by the eye of the mind, the medieval past could be finally recaptured only by going to one's knees. When the metaphor of the bridge changes at last to " 'Pons Sanctorum' — over which only children and saints can pass," the formal achievement of *Mont-Saint-Michel and Chartres* completes its self-definition. In this precarious three-fold unity of imaginative form, Adams devised the principle of order to which his restless years of travel had been leading.

Adams began by establishing the relation of writer to reader and the fiction by which the physical journey is presented. In the opening lines of his preface, he quoted an unidentified Elizabethan verse, "Who reads me, when I am ashes, Is my son in wishes," and then immediately disclaimed that relation as too close for his own time. The shift in artistic convention betokens a centrifugal development in society, and so the opening note of the personal narration prefigures the closing note of the historical narrative. To find a usable substitute for the filial relation that once prevailed, Adams sought to transcend his mortality by writing not for nephews, who, "as a social class, no longer read at all," but for nieces, with whom there might be an easy, convenient connection, "capable of being anything or nothing, like a Mohammedan or Polynesian or American marriage." However easy and flexible, there must, for the sake of communication, be some tie between writer and reader closer than that between authors in general and the abstract public. Adams addressed his written text to those who would consent "for the time, to be nieces in wish," prepared, if the experience warranted, to suspend detachment for intimacy. To meet the difficulty of travel and the greater difficulty of an attentive hearing, the writer postulates just a single niece as companion to her uncle. The isolated silent reader of the long prose work, unsocial symbol of our atomized culture, is represented by this niece in a hopeful aspect: "One niece is much more likely than two to listen" and, even in default of listening, "to carry a kodak." The only quality assumed of the audience is susceptibility to things seen. However complex the feelings he expressed, Adams saw the need to found feeling on precise visual response, even a camera exactness that is the apparent opposite of his emotional objective. The rapid series of light ironies in the preface define the point of view from which Adams made his own painterly selection of materials: the sense of a receding past, recalled with affection, and of an actual present, accepted without rancor; consciousness of a personal need for kinship in a society where, as Adams later put it, "the family was extinct like chivalry"; the seeking out of a feminine sensibility, capable of emotion, and the soliciting of perceptive rather than emotive responses. This done, the preface quickly takes uncle and niece on a June voyage from New York to Cherbourg to Mont-Saint-Michel, where, in a pause at Madam Poulard's, the uncle's talk begins.

The uncle's monologue may be divided in two parts. For ten out of sixteen chapters he talks about architecture, following the shortest possible way (which is not always the straightest route) to the medieval world which the historian was trying to evoke. The stones of architecture are the foundation on which the discourse on manners, poetry, piety, and philosophy is built. Starting from their monumental solidity, the dialectical progression is somewhat like that in the analytic chapters of Adams' *History*, although the old terms — economy, political theory, social character — have been transformed. The pattern is perhaps even closer to Henry James' conception of his narrative art, in which the first half of a work supplies the stage for the drama of the second. The most obvious way in which *Mont-Saint-Michel and Chartres* conforms to this is in style, for the architectural journey provides a vocabulary of metaphor to be used later in the book. The linguistic organization is a fair clue to the narrative structure. En route between the main points of the physical journey, the uncle tells his niece that they "have set out to go from Mont-Saint-Michel to Chartres in three centuries" — the aim is to convert the tour in space to a journey in time. Then, when the pilgrimage is achieved, the travelers rest from conscious effort to cross the centuries and simply watch the drama of the medieval imagination present itself. The difference may be easily noted. In the second chapter poetic texts are used to deduce the pristine society of Mont-Saint-Michel, and a story of William the Conqueror visiting the abbey is constructed with open artifice. By Chapter XI, the tables are turned and the historical acts of "The Three Queens" are related only as they aid immediate response to the presented poetry of courtly love: "For us the poetry is history, and the facts are false." The authority with which Adams could write *"for us"* invites the reader to ask how the uncle has translated his niece with a kodak into the realm of imagination.

The avuncular talk begins with an imaginative leap: "The Archangel loved heights." The symbolic meaning of Saint Michael's statue atop the church tower precedes description of the sculpture, and the past tense warns us that the speaker is recovering a meaning that has been lost — Church and State, "both militant," protected by the conqueror of Satan and the mightiest of all created spirits. The tourist who climbs to the summit of the rock can feel, like the pilgrims of old, the infinity of sky and immensity of sea over which Michael keeps his vigil. There is no difficulty with nature, "but when we turn from the western view, and look at the church door, thirty or forty yards from the parapet where we stand, one needs to be eight centuries old to know what this mass of encrusted architecture meant to its builders, and even then one must still learn to feel it." Looking, understanding, and feeling, although they are functions one of another, are treated separately at this first stage of the journey, for the presence of the niece constantly reminds the uncle how slow are the steps to a unified sensibility. Every time the narrator is swept along by his feeling for the past, he is pulled back to the actual as soon as he recalls his listener. After proposing the idea of two hundred and fifty million arithmetical ancestors and slipping into identification with the Norman farmers who quarried granite for the Abbey Church, made their annual pilgrimage to the Mount, awaited orders to turn out for Duke William's English campaign, suddenly the uncle comes back to dates and measurements, the evolution of ground plans and the problems of construction, the history of Romanesque and the qualities of its style. The shift from what was once felt to what can now be seen repeats itself until the niece can hold the two attitudes of the uncle almost at once. She thus serves to dramatize the multiplicity of Adams' initial assumptions and to register within the narrative a developing unity of tone. Before that unity is achieved, she will also witness how gruff an uncle may be when his feeling for color and life is checked by the presence of a companion with a camera.

The narrowing difference in sympathy between uncle and niece reduces the imaginative distance between the reader and Adams' subject. The first chapter ends as the uncle argues his case for supposing that Duke William might have stayed at the abbey and that the *Chanson de Roland* would often have been sung there, and the next chapter presents the conjunction of these two events as if it were real. At this stage of the book, we are conscious that the picturesque possibility defies historical probability and we see the scaffold of suppositions which the author needs in order to construct an occasion for poetry. In the ten chapters on architecture, cathedral ground plans and details of chronology are often in-

serted in the text, but verse only once more: the great twelfth-
century Latin hymns are set into the chapter on the Virgin
as "documentary proof of her majesty at Chartres." The
eleventh chapter begins with the last of the genealogical tables
and ends with the poetry of Thibaut of Champagne. A page
of verse is followed by the comment, "Does Thibaut's verse
sound simple? It is the simplicity of thirteenth-century glass —
so refined and complicated that sensible people are mostly
satisfied to feel, and not to understand." After the two-
sentence invitation simply to read, two pages of poetry con-
clude the chapter. The scaffolding of artifice and scholarship
is dispensed with and the verse carries its own weight.

The pull from tourist geography to poetic history, which
we have been noticing, is constant because Adams' subject
matter was not simply the two places named in his title, but
the whole of French medieval culture. His first excuse for
departing from a straightforward architectural guide was a
good one. Since the Abbey Church retained from the eleventh
century only four arches of the nave, the transepts, and the
piers of the central tower, he had to turn elsewhere to fill out
his analysis of Romanesque. Rather than lose the fixed setting
of his tourists' journey, he chose to keep uncle and niece at
Mont-Saint-Michel and gather his evidence from another art.
His method implied an organic unity of culture whereby
"the 'Chanson' is in poetry what the Mount is in architecture."
To bring the two together, he set his scene amid the oldest
surviving Romanesque work on the Mount, the eleventh-
century refectory, and he drew from romance, chronicle, and
tapestry the authority for his *dramatis personae* — Duke
William at the Archangel's shrine, the jongleur Taillefer
entertaining the company with song. He interpolated stage
directions from the text or, as he pointedly called it, the
libretto, and he added his own comment on the reactions of
the ducal and the monastic audience. What the Duke or the

Abbot responded to in the poem, he argued, was the same as what tourists could see in the older building: dignified simplicity, strength, and solidity; intensity of purpose and absence of self-consciousness; masculine power and martial religion. The terms might seem vague and permissive, but Adams defined them by his close examination of detail: that there were no women in the *Chanson* fitted with the virtual exclusion of the Virgin from the abbey; the "laisse" of assonances, the linked series of near rhymes, gave a weighty emphasis to the poem comparable to the iterative effect of Roman arches down the nave; the relics in the hilt of Roland's Durendal could be said to serve the sword — "the sword is not in service of the relics" — just as Michael stood guard against the perils of the sea. He read carefully Roland's dying prayer and his last gesture of proffering his right-hand gauntlet to God, and his interpretation argued the naïveté of both the poetry and the society: "God the Father, as feudal seigneur, absorbs the Trinity, and, what is more significant, absorbs or excludes also the Virgin, who is not mentioned in the prayer. . . . Death was an act of homage." The uncle who digressed into criticism at the Mount was not trying to make his niece a scholar any more than Adams at Tahiti had tried to make himself a professional painter, but he did require a niece who wanted "to learn the alphabet of art in France" to undergo a discipline of technical exercise like his own under La Farge. The goal in either case was to attain the practical understanding on which a trustworthy taste might be founded. Although a feeling for the *Chanson* would at once make clear the analogy to Romanesque, the congruence of imagination in poetry and architecture had to be worked out painstakingly. Adams wanted his subject, an organic culture, to exist for dispassionate reason as well as feminine intuition.

Adams concerned himself not only with the relation of

poems to buildings, but with the relation of both to time. To understand the plans and discriminate the styles of Mont-Saint-Michel required careful attention to temporal change. The reward of scrutiny would be an enlarged conception of organic culture, for the similarity of the arts in a single epoch of the Middle Ages was matched by the compatibility of works from different periods. When uncle and niece looked down the Romanesque nave of the Abbey Church to the Late Gothic choir, Adams underplayed the contrast between the naïve assertiveness and the self-conscious rhetoric of the two styles. Then, after the eleventh century had been sounded and the tourists were ready to move on to the twelfth-century work of the Transition, Adams picked up the metaphor which had tempered the earlier description, that of masculine naïveté and womanly charm, and pointed to "the quiet, restrained strength of the Romanesque married to the graceful curves and vaulting imagination of the Gothic." The church showed strength and grace joined in perpetual concord, the Transition halls showed the two styles in a stunning union. He dated this work about 1115 and tried to fix it in his reader's mind that the promenoir at the Mount, the famous crypt at Saint-Denis, and the western portal of Chartres were built at the same time. Still arguing the coherence of medieval culture horizontally, so to speak, he went on to name Suger, architect and abbot of Saint-Denis, Bernard, the domineering figure of French mysticism, and Abélard, the rationalistic innovator in philosophy, as the historical counterparts to his architectural trinity. These three abbés, who personify the book's dialectical progress through the stages of building, feeling, and thought, were the Transition as Duke William, his host the abbot, and his minstrel had been the Romanesque. Having established the middle term of his chronology, Adams moved his tourists through the great Gothic halls, where the evident object of the planner had been to capture and work with light, to the exquisitely ornamented cloister which crowned the whole Mount, where the architect meant "to reassert, with all the art and grace he could command, the mastery of love, of thought and poetry, in religion, over the masculine military energy of the great hall below." The uncle dates the cloister with its moral that "love is law" in relation to Saint Francis' preaching to the birds at Assisi. He continues to read poetry out of "the shell — the dead art — and silence" of the stones as he and his niece descend from the Mount and view the magnificent exterior construction of the Merveille, built out from the original jutting rock: "The sum of this impossible wall, and its exaggerated vertical lines, is strength and intelligence at rest." But the poem in which time unfolds ends in a dissonance, for the uncle finally turns his eye from the Merveille to the fifteenth-century battlements:

> The world is an evident, obvious, sacred harmony. Even the discord of war is a detail on which the Abbey refuses to insist. Not till two centuries afterwards did the Mount take on the modern expression of war as a discord in God's providence. Then, in the early years of the fifteenth century, Abbot Pierre le Roy plastered the gate of the châtelet, as you now see it, over the sunny thirteenth-century entrance called Belle Chaise, which had treated mere military construction with a sort of quiet contempt. . . . It frowns in a spirit quite alien to the twelfth century; it jars on the religion of the place; it forebodes wars of religion; dissolution of society; loss of unity; the end of a world.

Both the harmony and the dissonance which Adams perceived in Mont-Saint-Michel were essential to his presentation of his historical subject matter. The continuity of styles repeated itself at Chartres. The relation of narrator and listener is a faded example of the filial piety there expressed by the easy movement from the twelfth-century portal to the leaping Gothic of the nave: "The new artist drops unwillingly the hand of his father or his grandfather; he looks back, from every corner of his own work, to see whether it goes with the old." Adams himself knew what it meant to render homage to a father or grandfather, and the search for an historical continuum was the one motive that transcended the break between his civic and his cultural concerns. His own experience also taught him that histories must deal with endings as well as origins, that the rise of new societies out of old is not a phoenix-like recapitulation of identical form, that what is lost may be decently lamented without a sentimental grief. His feeling for the eighteenth-century republic which gave way to the American democracy was more complex than the single somber sentence that concludes the visit to the Mount: "Nothing is sadder than the catastrophe of Gothic art, religion, and hope." But the idea that values pass out of history as well as accrue is the same in both works. In the *History*, it provides the irony that statecraft declined as democracy rose. In *Mont-Saint-Michel and Chartres*, it is the assumption from which Adams could deduce a drama of the mind and a tragic view of history. To read poetry out of the dead stones of architecture, Adams had first to conceive of history as tragedy. But the scholar in him insisted that the history be authentic.

☆   ☆   ☆

In the same way that the guided tour becomes first an historical journey and then a spiritual pilgrimage, the book of travels approaches the form of a history and only thereafter becomes a tragic poem. The narrative deals with materials that fortuitously belong to Adams' personal and imaginative experience, but categorically belong to the objective order with which the cultural historian is concerned. Although

Adams came to cultural history as if he were its first practitioner, the genre in fact evolved within the bounds of professional historiography. Boasting a formidable name, *Kulturgeschichte*, and honorable forebears that went back to Voltaire's *Essai sur les Moeurs*, it came to maturity halfway through the nineteenth century in the work of Jacob Burckhardt. The Swiss scholar converted to the foreground of his work those elements of civilized activity that political historians summarily treat as background. The emergence of the genre was one result of a general tendency among nineteenth-century intellectuals to see culture, rather than the state, as man's bulwark against anarchy. The new genre reflected not only a general broadening of taste, but a despair of political action. Although its scholarly discipline supplies men who face cultural confusion in their own time with the steadying knowledge of more coherent epochs, it suggests no solution to political problems. Considering works of art to be more valuable social products than legal institutions, Burckhardt dealt with social and political behavior only as it was stylized by the prevailing imaginative habits of an era. But if his treatment of "the state as a work of art" has continued to bother and baffle conventional historians, it should not have troubled Adams, had he been aware of it. In writing of America under the "reign of politics," he had treated political activity as virtually coextensive with the young nation's imaginative life. Adams' independent "invention" of cultural history did not involve a change of method so much as a change of premise; he was simply adjusting the formula of his friend Holmes and arguing that art, not law, "is the witness and external deposit of our moral life."

The genre Adams chose to work in presents two great difficulties, a paucity of dramatic interest and an excess of demands for knowledge. Since cultural history forgoes the simplification of political narrative and aims instead for what

Burckhardt called "a well-rounded picture," the form has an attenuated dramatic appeal. Burckhardt's *Age of Constantine* depicts basic changes in the way men thought and his *Civilization of the Renaissance in Italy* celebrates the imaginative qualities of a unique historical moment, but intellectual seriousness is an imperfect substitute for basic physical action as an organizing principle in his books. In *Mont-Saint-Michel and Chartres*, Adams used the same two devices for capturing his reader's interest. He dealt with a great change that he conceived in tragic terms and he celebrated his three changing centuries with an enthusiasm that approached veneration. He also refused the limitations of cultural history by containing his subject in the dramatic medium of a personal narrative and went beyond them, as we shall see, in the pictorial form which he gave his book. But if he transcended one difficulty, he seemed to evade another. Whereas Burckhardt the trained student of art could be said to slight political history, Adams the scholar of legal institutions as much as said he was slighting other disciplines. Traveling from Mont-Saint-Michel to Chartres "in three centuries," Adams' narrator declared his object to be "not technical knowledge; not accurate information; not correct views either on history, art, or religion; not anything that can possibly be useful or instructive; but only a sense of what those centuries had to say, and a sympathy with their ways of saying it." Such a statement, however, should deceive only the gullible. Adams did not dispense with technical knowledge, accurate information, or correct views; he used them as means to his esthetic end. In the chapter that ends with the seeming dismissal of scholarly instruments, uncle and niece have taken the long road to Chartres in order to study on their way the churches of Normandy and the Ile de France. They have inspected towers, apses, and windows with utmost diligence and studiously labored to distinguish the French and Norman styles, the stages of evolving Gothic, and the nice shifts from the Church of Michael the Archangel to the Church of Mary Queen. Adams did not confuse the study of facts with the sense and sympathy which were his eventual goal; but in having the uncle explain his roundabout journey, he was himself explaining the only methods possible to the cultural historian:

> While conscientiously trying to keep as far away as we can from technique, about which we know nothing and should care if possible still less if only ignorance would help us to feel what we do not understand, still the conscience is happier if it gains a little conviction, founded on what it thinks a fact. Even theologians — even the great theologians of the thirteenth century — even Saint Thomas Aquinas himself — did not trust to faith alone, or assume the existence of God; and what Saint Thomas found necessary in philosophy may also be a sure source of consolation in the difficulties of art.

The one alternative to the rational instruments of discourse would have been abandonment to self-expression. The choice was to communicate the unverifiable estheticist reaction to Mona Lisa's smile or the perceptible form and content of the esthetic object. Adams restrained himself from indulging in the impressionism of a Pater because experience taught him that self was suspect and conscience demanded that he found conviction on what looked like fact. His casual remark — "If only ignorance would help us to feel what we do not understand" — makes it clear that he respected the limitations of his genre even though he went elsewhere for his form.

The methods of cultural history come down to a scholarly discipline and intellectual responsibility that immunize a writer against folly when he has to deal with fields which he cannot approach as a professional expert. Since Adams, as his ironies so often imply, took a perverse delight in the amateur pose, he was lucky that a deeper instinct protected him from falling into amateurishness. As a tough-minded professional, in the *History* and even in the early effort on Anglo-Saxon courts, he had resisted popular clichés about progress and race and tried to generalize only from the political data with which he worked. As an amateur of the arts he needed an uncommon sense of hard fact to avoid the current formulas of the medieval revival. For with *Mont-Saint-Michel and Chartres*, Adams joined a movement that had been growing more vast and vague ever since Walter Scott first redeemed the Middle Ages from outer darkness. His academic experience, based as it was on rationalist criticism and institutional analysis, had not exposed him to the tides of emotion that produced an Oxford Movement, a Pre-Raphaelite Movement, a Crafts Movement, and an infinity of Gothic railway stations. Although the cult of the Middle Ages flourished most in England, it was an international phenomenon, inspiring keen interest and sometimes acute research in a dozen aspects of the medieval past. The harvest of new knowledge rarely interfered with men's talent for seeing the reflection of their own desires, so that a hitherto approving public was shocked when Newman's study of the Middle Ages led him to the Catholic Church and Ruskin's led him to socialism. Matthew Arnold, who saw life steadily and saw it undazzled by the special light that makes converts or radicals, gave the medievalist sentiment its highest expression. In "Stanzas from the Grande Chartreuse," the poet meditated on the silent discontent which took him to the Carthusian monastery in hopes that rest among the monks might give him repossession of his soul at no cost to his rationalist beliefs. But Arnold's intellect and feelings were too subtle to typify the general state of mind in which he shared. Closer to the norm was Adams' friend and college teacher James Russell Lowell, whose poem "A Day at Chartres" (later simply renamed "The Cathedral") recorded the medievalist nostalgia for pre-scientific worship, pre-industrial simplicity, and pre-democratic social order — for the antithesis, in a word, of the society which Adams' *History* portrayed as modern and American. At the level of vaporous opinion, Adams no doubt sympathized with his old teacher, but he constitutionally could not subsist on Lowell's ethereal plane. Rather, he used his master's metaphor as a method, labored to "read Bethel on a pile of stones," and chose to let the objective materials of history speak for what he felt. The humility of the scholar controlled the sentiment of the medievalist in Adams. He did not think his experience of the Middle Ages could be important if it were merely subjective.

Adams' scholarly conscientiousness was reinforced by his historical consciousness. He read Newman and Ruskin and Arnold and took them seriously, but he also understood their sequential relation to an eighteenth-century temper with which he was even more familiar. As an historian, he detached himself from both traditions. He confessed a humorous addiction to "the supreme phrase of his idol Gibbon, before the Gothic cathedrals: 'I darted a contemptuous look on the stately monuments of superstition.'" But when he quoted that phrase in the *Education*, he added, "Gibbon brought the French Revolution. Ruskin brought reaction against the Revolution."* In culture as in politics, Adams was even less

---

*Adams' epigrammatic formula necessarily left out a lot. He knew the prevailing tepidity of the medievalist movement and dimly saw that his Gargantuan friend Richardson, who used Romanesque forms creatively to invent a new architectural style, was an exception of international proportions. He was also aware that American adherents to the revival tended to come from the pedigreed upper middle class who felt themselves being displaced by the new plutocracy, and that the American pattern was not very different from the English.

The classic formula for the English brand of medievalism is Thomas Love Peacock's caricature of Coleridge: "He had been in his youth an enthusiast for liberty, and had hailed the dawn of the French Revolution as the promise of a day that was to banish war and slavery, and every form of vice and misery, from the face of the earth. Because all this was not done, he deduced that nothing was done: that the overthrow of the feudal fortresses of tyranny and

comfortable with reaction than with revolution. Although it was easier for a medievalist to keep free of the complacent Gibbon than of the great English evangelist of Gothic, Ruskin's name is not mentioned in *Mont-Saint-Michel and Chartres* and his descriptive terms like "savage," "changeful," and "grotesque" do not appear there. Adams saw that love of the savage and grotesque, like contempt for superstition, threw more light on the reflexes of modern sensibility than on the architecture he was trying to see. In getting at the nature of Gothic, he may have derived from Ruskin something more than edification, but he characteristically resorted to Viollet-le-Duc's *Dictionnaire Raisonnée* of French medieval architecture for the data of construction.

Although Adams recognized Viollet's supremacy as an archeologist and the consequent high authority of his taste, he did not make over to Viollet the *raisonneur* his right of private judgment. He cited because he approved the Frenchman's praise of the old tower and flèche of Chartres — "the greatest and surely the most beautiful monument of this kind that we possess in France" — but he used his own critical and historical intelligence to arrive at Viollet's conclusion. "Although an ignorant spectator must accept the architect's decision on a point of relative merit," his comment ran, "no one is compelled to accept his reasons, as final." He took issue with his authority's using the word *adresse* (dexterity) where he himself would have chosen the term *droiture* (simple rightness). In his twofold criticism, he argued analytically by quoting Viollet

superstition was the greatest calamity that had ever befallen mankind; and that their only hope now was to rake the rubbish together, and rebuild it without any of those loopholes by which light had originally crept in." (*Nightmare Abbey*, Chapter I.) Peacock, writing in 1818, reminds us that English and European medievalism was literally connected to the political reaction after the Peace of Vienna and has continued to have political connections that, often happily, make American medievalism look even farther removed from ordinary reality.

himself on the frankness with which the builders proceeded from the bottom of the tower to the top of the flèche with no marked break at any point, and he argued historically by noting that the thirteenth-century master builder Villard de Honnecourt had passed by the old tower of Chartres without interest and lavished his attention on the intricate cleverness of Laon. Weak spots were harder to find in Viollet than in Ruskin, but the detection of faulty reasoning led to the investigation of fact. Yet, on investigating, Adams found that his thirteenth-century authority offered as little help as his contemporary. Villard de Honnecourt's judgments on his art demanded respect, but as an expert in Gothic building, he wrote with a technician's interest in the problems of *adresse*. What Adams wanted to discover were the values, over and above technical qualities, which made the *droiture* of the south tower pre-eminent. Having come to the point where technical, systematized information availed him no further, he was forced to turn from concentrated analysis to comparative evaluation. Since the twelfth-century rivals of the Chartres flèche had not survived, the most feasible comparison was with the sixteenth-century tower at the north side of the same façade. He stated simply the difference in construction between the classic and the ornate towers, came quickly to the point where he had to account for his preference of taste, and made his case against the north tower in the language not of Ruskin or of Viollet, but of the historian Adams: "Its chief fault is to be where it is. As a companion to the crusades and to Saint Bernard, it lacks austerity. As a companion to the Virgin of Chartres, it recalls Diane de Poitiers." The amateur critic and archeologist yielded to the historian in the attempt to understand, beyond the personal organization of impressions and the technical organization of materials, the vital pattern of expressed values embodied in the work of art.

The need to deal with ultratechnical meaning in art became

more urgent as Adams proceeded from the flèche, which symbolized aspiration, to the western portal, which symbolized "the Way to Eternal Life as it was seen by the Church and Art of the first crusade." The sculptured doorways, whose survival of the perils of fire and destruction was itself "the best attested Miracle de la Vierge in the long list of the Virgin's miracles," required a perceptive reading of their iconography. But if it was important to know what the figures stood for, the historian also trained his reader's eye upon the evidence of things unseen: "Among all the imagery of these three doorways, there is no hint of fear, punishment, or damnation." As Mont-Saint-Michel showed the masculine energy of the eleventh-century Church Militant, the twelfth-century portal of Notre-Dame-de-Chartres displayed the spirit of love and accessibility of grace by which Christ was identified with His Mother in the Church Triumphant:

> Not only is fear absent; there is not even a suggestion of pain; there is not a martyr with the symbol of his martyrdom; and what is still more striking, in the sculptured life of Christ, from the Nativity to the Ascension, which adorns the capitals of the columns, the single scene that has been omitted is the Crucifixion. There, as everywhere in this portal, the artists seem actually to have gone out of their way in order to avoid a suggestion of suffering. They have pictured Christ and His Mother in all the other events of their lives; they have represented evangelists; apostles; the twenty-four old men of the Apocalypse; saints, prophets, kings, queens, and princes, by the score; the signs of the zodiac, and even the seven liberal arts: grammar, rhetoric, dialectics, arithmetic, geometry, astronomy, and music; everything is there except misery.

From all three portals, at the cathedral front and at the two transepts, he drew evidence of an imaginative shift from God the Father as feudal seigneur toward the Virgin as Queen of Heaven. At the Virgin's door of the west façade,

Mary appeared in the costume of a Byzantine Empress — not
a feudal queen merely, but a symbolic representation of
universal peace. Adams made clear that art here expressed
the ideals of society, "an authority which the people wanted,
and the fiefs feared," rather than the literal state of affairs:
"In all Europe, at that time, there was no power able to enforce justice or to maintain order, and no symbol of such a
power except Christ and His Mother and the Imperial
Crown." Religious ideals and social disorder were both facts
about the medieval world, but in the realm of art, where the
organizing power of the symbol effected a unity of concrete
expression, the relevant facts about Chartres all led to the
Virgin. The lessons of the western porch were repeated more
emphatically in the women's porch of the north transept,
where the sculpture transformed Mary from an oriental
empress to a French queen. Its iconography asserted the
divine birth of the Virgin, her divine resurrection, and her en-
thronement in heaven as an equal of her Son, in short, her
divine right as Queen. The statuary revealed that the touchstone of Mary's glory was grace and love: even the representation of Abraham and Isaac suppressed the note of harshness
and stressed the poignancy of tender affection and perfect faith.
Appropriately, the chief donor of the north porch was Blanche
of Castile, who, as regent and queen-mother during the reign
of Saint Louis, had political pretensions and practical power
comparable to that which the sculpture proclaimed for the
Virgin. The south porch, on the other hand, was given by
Pierre de Dreux, who openly resisted Blanche's royal authority. Its sculpture reduced the Mother's status to more
orthodox proportions and celebrated Christ, not as Saviour
but as Judge: "The whole melodrama of Church terrors appears after the manner of the thirteenth century, on this
church door, without regard to Mary's feelings"; yet even in
the Porche de Dreux, in the gable over the archway, and above

it in the higher gable of the transept, figures of the crowned Virgin symbolized the ultimate obeisance which the rebellious noble conceded to the otherworldly queen.

In discussing the interior of the church, the historian showed himself true to character, for he undertook the scholar's task of dislodging the intellectual errors of his time. Ruskin was not his primary target as he went after the savage and grotesque popular notion of Gothic which identified the style with darkness, hoary age, and mystery (and by "mystery" usually meant "fear"). Rather, it was as though the niece of his text had been reading her Uncle Brooks and needed a corrective: for Brooks Adams, the most vehement of nineteenth-century medievalists, had divided all history into ages of Fear and ages of Greed and portrayed a fear-ridden medieval era, dominated by military and priestly types, in contrast to modern times, exploited by the commercial personality. Henry Adams presented the soldiers and priests of the eleventh century as motivated by pristine energy and joy, and the citizens and artists of the twelfth century as transforming the older emotions by the spirit of love and grace. For him, failure of nerve and the beginnings of fear came later, in the Châtelet of Mont-Saint-Michel and the Doomsday sculpture of the Porche de Dreux. And when he had his narrator, inside the church, invite his niece to accustom her eyes "to the light" rather than the darkness, he took account of the view which Brooks Adams had distilled from current preconceptions. Brooks's *Law of Civilization and Decay* had said:

> The gloom of the lofty vaults, dimly lighted by the subdued splendour of the coloured windows, made the interior of the Gothic cathedral the most mysterious and exciting sanctuary for the celebration of the miracle which has ever been conceived by man; while without, the doors and windows, the pinnacles and buttresses, were covered with the terrific shapes of demons and the majestic figures of saints, admonishing the

laity of the danger lurking abroad, and warning them to take refuge within.

Denying such a picture, Henry would counterpose the image of "a toy-house to please the Queen of Heaven," but to make headway against an attitude the opposite of his own, he had to support his vision with discursive argument.

Against his own brother, Adams marshaled evidence to show that the shadows of Gothic were a function of its sculptured quality, that the Gothic building was architecture in the round which used shade to play against light, and that the history of Gothic interiors was first of all the continuous replacing of walls by windows. As for mysticism, he held that a generation which accepted Wagnerian music-drama had no right to find esoteric or private meaning in work where "even the symbols that seem most mysterious were clear to every old peasant-woman." Nor could he attribute hoary age to the generation of the first and second Crusades, that "took ideas wherever it found them; — from Germany, Italy, Spain, Constantinople, Palestine, or from the source which has always attracted the French mind like a magnet — from ancient Greece"; that handled them with taste and developed them with such quickness that history seemed to speed up and the planet to revolve faster than at any time until the present. The knack of seizing new and old ideas from other cultures and putting them to original use was a sign of youth which he had celebrated in his own country during the Jeffersonian era. Whereas the American revolutionized his world with the steamboat, the pivot-gun, and the clipper ship, the medieval Frenchman turned the pointed arch into a new system of architecture, jumped from his Byzantine models to a new system of color decoration in glass, and developed stone carving to a level that had not been reached since Athens.

Disposing of one error after another, Adams clearly refused

to limit the opposition of the ages to a simple contrast of dominant vices, fear and greed. Adjusting his vision to the light of
aspiration rather than the gloom of depravity, he took his
pleasure "not in seeing the death, but in feeling the life." He
read in the works of man "the struggle of his own littleness to
grasp the infinite" and reflected that the differing centuries
expressed this one motive in different ways: "a miracle or a
dynamo; a dome or a coal-pit; a cathedral or a world's fair."
For him, the speed of intellectual commerce in the Middle
Ages, "without the aid of steam," and the swift transport of
his own age hastened to a common end, although "one does
not now carry freight of philosophy, poetry, or art." To recognize the contrast of joy and power, one must first perceive a
basis for comparison: if it proved hard to see aspiration in a
coal-pit, the same kind of paradox existed in the *greed* for
novelty and *gluttony* for ideas which "produced the western
portal of Chartres, with its statuary, its glass, and its flèche,
as a by-play." The twelfth-century motive, underscored by
irony, was not a low appetite, but zest for "the fun of life"; its
product was not an engine for exciting fear, to be tested, like
American handiness at gunnery and steamships or dynamos
and world's fairs, by statistical analysis, but was the handiwork of joy and required the judgment of esthetic pleasure.

In the neatness of his rebuttal, Henry Adams was tacitly accepting one positive idea from his brother's version of the
Middle Ages. The contrast of joy and power, as much as that
of fear and greed, implied the division of history into imaginative and materialist ages. The older brother discerned no relation to himself, or to the twelfth-century Frenchmen he admired, in the propositions set forth by Brooks's *Law*: that the
money value of the miracle went up with the influx of bar-
barians into the Roman world; that the ruling power, as well
as two-thirds of the real property, of Europe gradually passed
to the medicine men who monopolized the fearful means of

supernatural intervention; that the triumph of Gothic imaginativeness was eclipsed after the Crusades when the return of precious metals to the West drove down the value of fetishes and, as a social consequence of Gresham's Law, the materialist supplanted the "emotionalist." What Henry did was to construe as irony what he could not swallow as history. More imaginative than Brooks, he modified the language of materialism to fit his needs and thereby reinforced his contrast of past and present with implicit satire. He could let his narrator, caught up in the beauty of Chartres, wax lyrical, and then have him suddenly stop, abashed at his "waste of words," and say: "One no longer adopts an idea unless it is driven in with hammers of statistics and columns of figures." It was to satisfy the demand for literal exactness "which lights up every truly American eye" that he traced the cult of the Virgin from its Byzantine beginnings to the building of Chartres. Giving "the measure of this devotion, which proves to any religious American mind, beyond possible cavil, its serious and practical reality," he put the cost of Mary's churches in dollars and cents — a billion dollars in France alone between 1170 and 1270. A measure of devotion he more strongly felt was in the great hymns to the Virgin, but he retrieved himself from the poetry of faith to analyze the lurking scepticism that lay behind it, turning from Saint Bernard and Adam de Saint-Victor to the bourgeois capitalist who "watched the Virgin with anxious interest":

> The bourgeois had put an enormous share of his capital into what was in fact an economical speculation, not unlike the South Sea Scheme, or the railway system of our own time; except that in one case the energy was devoted to shortening the road to Heaven; in the other, to shortening the road to Paris . . .

Having the uncle speak a language for his twentieth-century niece to understand, Adams reminded his readers that to understand the Middle Ages they had better become bilingual.

The manner of the satire discloses the method by which Adams tried to relate knowledge and insight. Despite his irony of tone, he was demonstrating what William James straightfacedly called the "cash-value" of ideas. As he had with Jeffersonian political theory, so with thirteen-century religious faith Adams assessed the credit and credibility of a hypothesis by its power to get things done. Having once proposed the American character as a working hypothesis to account for the rise of a democratic, technological society, he now proposed the supernatural power of the Virgin as the key to the problem of medieval French achievement: "The restless appetite that snatched at the pointed arch, the stone flèche, the coloured glass, the illuminated missal, the chanson and roman and pastorelle, the fragments of Aristotle, the glosses of Avicenne, was nothing compared with the genius which instantly gave form and flower to them all." The historian was still using his old techniques, but this time he was passing beyond history. In *Mont-Saint-Michel and Chartres* he showed the pragmatist method for what it was — a modern empiricist version of the classical argument from design which weights measurable concrete evidence more heavily than the verbal testimony to which it gives only a secondary authority. Adams cited contemporary accounts in the manner of an orthodox historian and argued that "of all Mary's miracles, the best attested, next to the preservation of her church, is the building of it"; in particular, he translated a letter describing the pious labor of those who "bent their proud and haughty necks to the harness of carts," the silence among the Virgin's toilers as if there were "hardly a person present," the love which established a "unity of hearts." Despite the meaning of such words for him, he accepted the discipline of scholastic theology and empiricist history and founded his thesis on what could be presently observed: "Without the conviction of her personal presence, men would not have been inspired; but, to us, it is rather the inspiration of the art which proves the Virgin's presence, and we can better see the conviction of it in the work than in the words." This was the special sense of his presenting the hymns which Bernard and Adam de Saint-Victor chanted as "documentary proof" of Mary's majesty at Chartres, and added, "If you are to get the full enjoyment of Chartres, you must, for the time, believe in Mary as Bernard and Adam did, and feel her presence as the architects did, in every stone they placed, and every touch they chiselled." The historian helped effect a willing suspension of disbelief, but for anything more positive than that, we must see how the artist worked.

☆   ☆   ☆

In terms of narrative, Adams' chapter on "Towers and Portals" concludes with the entry of uncle and niece into the cathedral, and in terms of argument it ends with the clear necessity of establishing at least a functional definition of the Virgin as organizing symbol. The second five chapters, during which the tourists remain within the church edifice, are devoted equally to examining specific art objects and to demonstrating that the only way to feel or even understand the art is to take the Virgin as real. The argument began by exhausting the processes of technical analysis, so that one came round, in a phrase of Pascal that had impressed itself on Adams, to the ignorance from which he started — now transformed into a philosophic ignorance that was aware of itself. In contrast to not knowing the sensibility of the Middle Ages because of indifference, an _ignorance savante_ was the proper instrument for establishing a rapport between nineteenth-century intelligence and twelfth-century instinct. Unless it became conscious of its limits, the systematizing mind would come to a dead end in the

face of Norman naïveté, or the *droiture* of the old tower, or the
empirical fact that the great medieval monuments were built
by a supra-logical quality of imagination that gradually disappeared as church architecture "became a pure matter of
mechanism and mathematics." The ignorant tourist who
questioned the reasoning of technical criticism dramatized the
principle that "true ignorance approaches the infinite more
nearly than any amount of knowledge can do," while the
abundant information on roses, apses, stained glass, and
church design reminds us that Adams wanted to transcend
ordinary knowledge rather than dismiss the reason altogether.
The interplay of empirical toughmindedness and transcendental impulse drives both argument and narrative toward a
climax at the end of Chapter X. Only when the reality of the
Virgin has been sufficiently demonstrated does the text depart
from the solid monuments of architecture to focus on the less
obviously substantial products of medieval culture.

Although, for the narrator, conscious ignorance was the beginning of wisdom, he could not pursue his goal single-
mindedly. He was not traveling alone. While his niece ac-
customed her eyes to the light, he tried bringing her to his
point of view by resuming a tone he had taken at the outset.
He had then suggested that "the man who wanders into the
twelfth century is lost, unless he can grow prematurely young,"
and had advised the study of Wordsworth "whose practical
sense equalled his imaginative genius." Only after his entering Chartres did the advice have a context which revealed its
full intent. Inside the church, he invoked the image of
Wordsworth's eternal child with greater urgency and clearer
purpose. He could no longer call upon the Norman ancestors
who helped build the abbey on the Mount, especially since he
argued that the cathedral was built not by men but by the
Virgin. To go this greater imaginative distance across the ages
required a state of mind that might be reached slowly by the

exhaustion of scientific knowledge or, quicker and more easily, by recovering childhood intimations of immortal things. The romantic image for communion with nature became the old man's artifice for translation out of nature to a Yeatsian perspective on the Byzantine splendors of the Virgin's church: "To us, it is a child's fancy; a toy-house to please the Queen of Heaven — to please her so much that she would be happy in it — to charm her till she smiled." The shift from historical exposition to lyric evocation was the shortest way to make historical tourists into pilgrims of art, and although the main freight of the book could not be transported over such a shortcut, travelers on foot might sometimes use the path.

The lyrical digressions were necessary to the argument, for esthetic contemplation of Chartres cathedral required of tourists a lively apprehension of the divine force that built it. This was different from an understanding of its purpose, and by virtue of the difference, the uncle of the narrative hoped to avoid the delicate subject of belief:

> If you want to know what churches were made for, come down here on some great festival of the Virgin, and give yourself up to it; but come alone! That kind of knowledge cannot be taught and can seldom be shared. We are not now seeking religion; indeed, true religion generally comes unsought. We are only trying to feel Gothic art.

But when he tried to explain why the architects imperceptibly raised the vaulting of the nave in order to accommodate the gigantic western rose and why they rejected the "mathematically and technically perfect" model of Paris to build an irregular but brighter and bigger apse at Chartres, he came very close to the overwhelming question. Although the professional language of Viollet-le-Duc might sound more reasonable to tourists, he chose to paraphrase the archeologist in a less scientific idiom. It was not enough to note that

Chartres was unique in being built "not for its nave or even for its choir, but for its apse"; he felt compelled to add: "It was planned not for the people or the court, but for the Queen; not a church but a shrine; and the shrine is the apse where the Queen arranged her light to please herself and not her architect, who had already been sacrificed at the western portal and who had a free hand only in the nave and transepts where the Queen never went, and which, from her own apartment, she did not even see."

The uncle never spoke for long in the lyric mode. In departing from his usual style, he gave his niece an exercise of imagination which he dared not ask her to sustain. The power to enter the mood of the "prematurely young" was limited and sporadic, totally unlike his companion's dependability with her kodak. Inside the church, where visitors must close their cameras and depend on their own sensuous responsiveness, he faced what he thought was a nearly insuperable problem: ignorance, whether childlike or philosophic, was the clue to feeling the naïveté of the eleventh century and the instinctive intelligence of the twelfth; but if the naïveté had yielded to self-consciousness and instinctive intelligence had devolved into mechanism and mathematics, how, after seven centuries' further progress in the same direction, should the imaginative faculty be recoverable? At the Mount, he had casually stated, "Our age has lost much of its ear for poetry, as it has its eye for colour and line, and its taste for war and worship, wine and women." Now the need for feeling brought the uncle to this theme again. Between attempts to conjure his niece with poetry, he fell almost to scolding her into belief that the Virgin's was the designing hand. From reckless lyricism he went to the opposite extreme of harsh invective:

> You may, if you really have no imagination whatever, reject the idea that the Virgin herself made the plan; the feebleness

of our fancy is now congenital, organic, beyond stimulant or strychnine, and we shrink like sensitive-plants from the touch of a vision or spirit . . .

He was soon contrite about his loss of temper, but he softened his attack only by making it more general:

> Society has no right to feel it as a moral reproach to be told that it has reached an age when it can no longer depend, as in childhood, on its taste, or smell, or sight, or hearing, or memory; the fact seems likely enough, and in no way sinful; yet society always denies it, and is invariably angry about it; and, therefore, one had better not say it.

The difference between lyrical evocation and rhetorical intimidation was the measure of his plight. As his own vision became more intense, the uncle sensed a growing discrepancy between what he could see and what his listener could. He gave ambiguous encouragement by reducing the odds for feeling from "not one man in a hundred thousand" to "not one tourist in a hundred — perhaps not one in a thousand of the English-speaking race," and he tried with indifferent success to restrain himself from mentioning the atrophied imagination; but his impatience with taking the long route for his pilgrimage never broke loose again. Willing to "plod on, laboriously proving God, although, even to Saint Bernard and Pascal, God was incapable of proof," he was able to change the function of his invective from expression of his own tense feelings to creation in his niece of an anxiety such as may precede a new sense of reality.

Adams' narrator had another reason for slipping back from figurative speech to scholastic proofs. The metaphors of the toy-house and the Queen's apartment cast an obviously artificial light, even for eyes still narrowed by the outdoor sun. Thereafter he returned from argument to poetry again, but, because he wanted his niece to see Chartres in its original glory, he conscientiously avoided personal fancy and built his metaphor of more plausible material. Having done with his general introduction to "The Virgin of Chartres" and his detailed analysis of "Roses and Apses," he turned in the eighth chapter to "The Twelfth-Century Glass" and, in particular, to the inside wall of the western front. The uncle cautiously noted the gemlike colors of the twelfth-century lancet windows and the jeweled brilliance of the thirteenth-century rose-window above them; he called attention to their blending like clustered stones and to the harmony of effect as of "a single large ornament; a round breastpin, or what is now called a sunburst, of jewels, with three large pendants beneath"; then he transformed the sharp image of his similes into a metaphorical evocation of Mary, who "placed upon the breast of her Church — which symbolized herself — a jewel so gorgeous that no earthly majesty could bear comparison with it, and which no other heavenly majesty has rivalled." In trying to make his poetry conform to history, the tourist-guide gave a new turn to the pragmatist method. To justify his sunburst image, he suggested an ultramodern predictive theory of art: "An artist, if good for anything, foresees what his public will see; and what his public will see is what he ought to have intended — the measure of his genius." The modern audience ought at least to observe in the Virgin's jeweled rose with its three gemmed pendants "a little of the effect she meant it to produce even on infidels." Argument and image fitted in close detail, for the binoculars revealed that her rose with "all the hues of Paradise contains or hides a Last Judgment," but one conveying neither fear nor threat:

> The rudest ruffian of the Middle Ages, when he looked at this Last Judgment, laughed; for what was the Last Judgment to her! An ornament, a plaything, a pleasure! a jewelled decoration which she wore on her breast! Her chief joy was to pardon; her eternal instinct was to love; her deepest passion was

pity! On her imperial heart the flames of hell showed only the
opaline colours of heaven.

Though he shifted his talk from the work of art to the faith it
represented, he fell back again before he pressed his niece too
far. But he gave the last word to faith, ending his chapter with
the quiet portrayal of Notre-Dame-de-la-Belle-Verrière, who
calmly accepted without quite demanding the instinctive love
of all mankind: "She will accept ours, and we have not the
heart to refuse it; we have not even the right, for we are her
guests." Not by argument or anger, but by the appeal of love,
he patiently cultivated his niece's will to believe; and taking
his metaphors more and more from history, he began transforming the guided tour into an historical drama.

The next chapter, the ninth, moves around the church by
examining the thirteenth-century legendary windows. In the
stained-glass narratives with divine subject matter, the narrator pled the need to by-pass questions of historical accuracy
and arrive at the testimony of religious feeling for which the
windows were "original documents." As for the secular representations of the Charlemagne Window, they were "never intended to teach religion or instruct the ignorant, but to please
the Queen of Heaven as they pleased the queens of earth with
a roman, not in verse but in colour." Only one hypothesis
could explain how "the taste of the royal family, and of their
tailors, furriers, carpenters, and coopers, should fit so mar-
vellously, one with another, and with that of the Virgin." The
harmony of the donors and their gifts brought the uncle once
more to his argument from design, which he put parabolically
by imagining the architect of Chartres, who consulted the
Virgin with prayer on his daily questions. He returned from
his imaginary architect to himself with a statement in which
poetry and argument converged and both pointed toward an
approaching climax:

That the Virgin answered the questions is my firm belief, just as it is my conviction that she did not answer them elsewhere. One sees her personal presence on every side. Any one can feel it who will only consent to feel like a child. Sitting here any Sunday afternoon, while the voices of the children of the mâitrise are chanting in the choir — your mind held in the grasp of the strong lines and shadows of the architecture; your eyes flooded with the autumn tones of the glass; your ears drowned with the purity of the voices; one sense reacting upon another until sensation reaches the limit of its range — you, or any other lost soul, could, if you cared to look and listen, feel a sense beyond the human ready to reveal a sense divine that would make that world once more intelligible, and would bring the Virgin to life again, in all the depths of feeling which she shows here — in lines, vaults, chapels, colours, legends, chants — more eloquent than the prayer-book, and more beautiful than the autumn sunlight; and any one willing to try could feel it like the child, reading new thought without end into the art he has studied a hundred times; but what is still more convincing, he could, at will, in an instant, shatter the whole art by calling into it a single motive of his own.

The summer is over: the architectural tour which began with the pleasant June arrival at the Mount ends at Chartres on a Sunday afternoon shortly after the singing of the choirboys has faded. As the church empties, uncle and niece walk freely to the *croisée* and look more closely at the seven great windows in the clerestory above the sanctuary. The uncle now assumes a shared consciousness that the Virgin, enthroned in the central window, provides the single dominating relation that unifies the whole. With the church to themselves, they stand where worshipers would have been most thickly crowded in the time when the monumental figures "represented the real world, and the people below were the unreal and ephemeral pageant." Looking down the transepts to his left and right, the narrator can project himself anew into the rivalry of Queen Blanche of France and the rebellious Duke Pierre de Dreux, still witnessed in the competing roses of the north and south as vividly as in the year 1230. The language of past and present intermingles as he turns toward the altar again for a last look at the Virgin of Grace, presiding unassertively over all. Fact seems to rule over figure when, about to leave the church, he pauses — to *kneel* with the thirteenth century and feel "the little one still can feel of what it felt." The narrator's vision and his perception become one and make up his whole experience:

> We see, and the artists meant that we should see, only the great lines, the colours, and the Virgin. The mass of suppliants before the choir look up to the light, clear blues and reds of this great space, and feel there the celestial peace and beauty of Mary's nature and abode. There is heaven! and Mary looks down from it, into her church, where she sees us on our knees, and knows each one of us by name. There she actually is — not in symbol or in fancy, but in person, descending on her errands of mercy and listening to each one of us, as her miracles prove, or satisfying our prayers merely by her presence which calms our excitement as that of a mother calms her child.

The narrator can go no farther on the pilgrimage way, and he has no wish to test whether his niece has come with him as far as he has gone. Believing that what comes unsought can seldom be shared, he tries to conceal his intensity of emotion by passing it off upon the supposed pilgrims of the thirteenth century. But he cannot keep his words from sounding personal when, moving away at last, he reflects, "It was very childlike, very foolish, very beautiful, and very true — as art, at least." He will not claim more for his experience than he can rationally justify, but as the satirist of bourgeois investment in cathedrals, he has insisted that "illusion for illusion — granting for the moment that Mary was an illusion — the

Virgin Mother in this instance repaid to her worshippers a larger return for their money than the capitalist has ever been able to get, at least in this world"; as a "pilgrim of art," he cannot settle for less than the memory of that illusion. Like the stoical Henry Adams who composed an ambiguous "Prayer to the Virgin," the uncle of the text treats his emotional experience as a paradox of historic consciousness, not as a sign of religious calling. He undercuts his statement of direct vision more severely than he has any of his figurative images:

> We have done with Chartres. For seven hundred years Chartres has seen pilgrims, coming and going more or less like us, and will perhaps see them for another seven hundred years; but we shall see it no more, and can safely leave the Virgin in her majesty, with her three great prophets on either hand, as calm and confident in their own strength and in God's providence as they were when Saint Louis was born, but looking down from a deserted heaven, into an empty church, on a dead faith.

The art might seem more durable than the faith that gave it being, but the wisely ignorant tourist knows better than to dismiss as unreal the experience which has filled for him the empty church. However it might be valued for other purposes, it must be judged the indispensable means for comprehending the medieval world into which it has transported him. That assumption is written into his very next words, in which he leaves the story of his spiritual journey to resume at a higher point his historical discourse: "After *worshipping* at the shrines of Saint Michael on his Mount and of the Virgin at Chartres, one may wander far and wide over France, and seldom feel lost; all later Gothic art comes naturally, and no new thought disturbs the perfected form."*

*My italics.

Since the vision at Chartres was not an end, but a means of access to the world of Gothic art, Henry Adams dropped the story of his narrator's spiritual progress in the moment when it might have to be considered in other relations. He was writing a tourist guide, not a devotional handbook, and he held firm to the intellectual distinction between the two. He had no desire to teach faith, which he thought was unteachable and knew he had not learned.* He was trying to lead his

---

*It would be highly dangerous to take the narrator's vision of the Virgin as Adams' spiritual autobiography in a broader sense than that suggested here. The model for the narrator's experience seems to exist in another life than the author's. The sentence "If you want to know what churches were made for, come down here on some great festival of the Virgin, and give yourself up to it; but come alone!" points to Brooks Adams' overwhelming sense of religious presence at Le Mans Cathedral, probably in 1890. On September 21, 1895, Brooks wrote:

> I am delighted to hear that you have been making a Gothic pilgrimage. On the whole, the parts of my life which I look back to with the greatest delight are those I have spent among the churches and castles of the middle-ages. If I have a particularly weak spot it is for Le Mans, I suppose because it was there I first came to understand what the great poem meant. I remember the day well. I came to Le Mans largely by accident, and on strolling up to the cathedral I found some great function was at hand. I asked what was on foot, and they told me they were to sing the mass of the Fête-Dieu. I had never heard a great mass in a Gothic Church, and I sat down in the nave to listen. The people came in and sat down about me; the peasantry. The bishop and chapter came in and the service began. The light was blazing through those thirteenth century windows of the choir, and lighting up that marvellous glass of the twelfth century of the nave, the arches were misty with incense, and the mass was sung by a choir of boys, under the lead of one of the canons with a simplicity and feeling that I had never imagined, and with an execution that is impossible out of France. As it went on and they sang their hymns, I confess I disgraced myself. I felt for half an hour as I know the men must have felt who stained those windows, and built those arches, I really and truly did believe the miracle, and as I sat and blubbered in the nave, and knelt at the elevation, I did receive the body of God. That was years ago now, but it was the day on which I first conceived the meaning of it all . . .

Henry Adams was always wary of Brooks's passionate intensity, and his cool reply to this letter underscores the difference between what he felt at Coutances (see page 230 above) and what his brother had earlier felt at Le Mans. Evidence of a similar experience in the older brother's life exists only in the "Prayer to the Virgin" and *Mont-Saint-Michel and Chartres*, that is to say, in original literary

audience to esthetic contemplation, not personal salvation. By sticking to his purpose, he avoided opposite dangers to which a break in method would have exposed him: what Ruskin denounced as the base fatuity "of being lured into the Romanist Church by the glitter of it, like larks into a trap by broken glass," and what Eliot has called in Arnold "a counsel to get all the emotional kick out of Christianity one can, without the bother of believing it." With his pragmatist method, he "proved" religion by its power to get things done, in particular, by the power of the Virgin to organize the multifold esthetic experience of Chartres Cathedral. He proved his point by story as well as argument, but he never lost sight of the crucial assumption which he shared with Pascal: "Faith is different from proof; the one is human, the other is a gift of God." Regarding even an effective will to believe as merely human, he made the narrator's sensation of seeing the Virgin as real occur for the sake of its function in the book. Moving toward the climactic moment of the personal narrative, the uncle declares the premise of his journey: "For us, the world is not a schoolroom or a pulpit, but a stage." After the climax, the personal narrative becomes secondary to another, larger action. The moment of vision lifts the curtain that kept

---

compositions, not in the testimony of letters; the event occurred at the writing desk and not in a church, and the consequence was literature, not submission of will, acceptance of dogma, or entry into a communion.

Adams never saw a way to get beyond Pascal's category of reasonable and unhappy men, who seek God not having found him. Despite the hopes of his Catholic friends, he became increasingly adjusted to that state, and some years later, when the advent of world war crystallized his perennial attitude, he wrote of a clerical acquaintance: "Father Fay is no bore — far from it, but I think he has an idea that I want conversion, for he directs his talk much to me, and instructs me. Bless the genial sinner! He had best look out that I don't convert him, for his old church is really too childish for a hell like this year of grace." Except as his historical imagination carried him back to the High Middle Ages, he remained a stoic: God existed for him in the realms of essence and historical existence, perhaps, but not in the realm of present reality.

twentieth-century eyes from seeing beyond the surfaces of architecture and reveals the platform on which an historical drama plays itself out.

☆　　　☆　　　☆

Adams' dramatic subject was that of the book's first architectural excursion into Normandy, the shift from the masculine power of the eleventh century to the feminine power of the twelfth, and the reversion of the thirteenth. Masculine energy built Mont-Saint-Michel; the Virgin built Chartres; but after the exhausting effort of faith and imagination, it was left to the discursive reason to find ways of holding together a culture which intelligence by itself never could have built.* Behind this pattern lay the writer's own experience — the energy which the historian dedicated to the problems of his fathers was transformed in the scribe of Arii Taimai and the devotee of the Virgin's work, but to make good what he then found Adams had turned to the study of Viollet-le-Duc and Thomas Aquinas. The art which he served by intellectual methods was itself methodical, with proportions as neatly measured as in the scientific art of architecture. In the first part of his book he gave half his space to what men did, half to the Virgin. Dividing his last six chapters with the same

---

*Adams' view of the relation of the reason to imagination corresponds to the theological view of the relation of reason to faith. The source of his own formulation was Pascal on the heart's reasons that the reason does not know. In his copy of the *Pensées*, he underscored the following passage: "Would to God we never needed reason, but could apprehend all things by instinct and feeling. But nature has refused us this good and, quite the contrary, given us very few intuitions of this kind; all other knowledge can only be got by reasoning." (My translation. The original is given in *The French Education of Henry Adams*, p. 196, where this and the other underscored passages brought together by Professor Max Baym give the extrinsic evidence of Pascal's importance to *Mont-Saint-Michel and Chartres*.) Adams recognized, when Bergson's *Evolution Créatrice* (1907) came into his hands, that his own thought had been moving in the same direction.

even hand, he presented the triumph of feminine imagination and the subsequent return to masculine dominance.

In the second part of *Mont-Saint-Michel and Chartres*, the relation of the narrator to his audience and his materials is fixed, and the action occurs only within the area of the historical subject. The change in the locus of action is immediately evident. The subjective account of the architectural tour culminates in a personal vision of divine love within the physical reality of the cathedral. The historical account of medieval culture begins with the human actors who actually performed their play of courteous love upon the artificial stage of the medieval imagination. Yet the two parts fit so neatly that attention is not strained in shifting from "The Court of the Queen of Heaven" to the French courts where in the twelfth and thirteenth centuries the queenly line of Eleanor of Guienne held sway. What holds the book together at this point is "the coincidence that while the Virgin was miraculously using the power of spiritual love to elevate and purify the people, Eleanor and her daughters were using the power of earthly love to discipline and refine the courts." The conventions of romance were secular and heterodox and they existed in a world of crude realities, but they gave great women strength to teach and enforce "an ideal that contradicted the realities, and had no value for them or for us except in the contradiction." The ideal prevailed in the Courts of Love which arbitrated the conduct of high society and in the literature of love which that society commissioned. Among people who "looked on life as a drama — and on drama as a phase of life, — " the same canon of interpretation applied to the "Romance of Tristan and Isolde" and the obscure affair of state whereby Queen Blanche won support for her regency from Thibaut of Champagne. Adams did not ask his readers to decide whether Thibaut's love poetry was actually written to Queen Blanche, but only to notice "how

Thibaut kept the same tone of courteous love in addressing
the Queen of Heaven." The work of the historical dramatist
was relatively easy so long as he could summarize, paraphrase,
and translate texts that were inherently dramatic. Letting
the twelfth and thirteenth centuries speak for themselves,
Adams proceeded from the effect of the courtly ideal in
society to the power of woman in secular literature and the
power of the Virgin in the golden legends of her miracles.

The chapter on "The Three Queens," as it moves from the
language of social behavior to the language in which the
Virgin was addressed, recapitulates the order of perceptions
which the narrator experienced on his architectural tour, and
the whole sequence of the feminine chapters repeats this
pattern in an elaborate variation on the theme "The proper
study of mankind is woman." Balanced against the review
of the courtly ideal in society is Adams' examination of the
ideal in literature. The secular poets "showed as little interest
in religion as the poets of the eleventh century had shown for
it in their poems of war," but the poetry of love is as relevant
to the action as the *Chanson de Roland* was earlier: the elegant
"chante-fable" of *Aucassins et Nicolette* and the thoroughly
unaristocratic mock-romance of *Robin et Marion* both display
the calm, frank civilizing power of heroines endued with the
power of love. But the chapter on "Nicolette and Marion"
moves on to the end of medieval poetry in the *Roman de la
Rose* and suggests, in Adams' interpretation of the poem, not
the climactic vision in Chartres, but the moment after: "An
undertone of sadness runs through it, felt already in the picture
of Time which foreshadows the end of Love — the Rose —
and her court, and with it the end of hope. . . . For the first
time since Constantine proclaimed the reign of Christ, a
thousand years, or so, before Philip the Fair dethroned Him,
the deepest expression of social feeling ended with the word:
Despair." The rising note of Thibaut's prayer to the Virgin

and the poignant fall with which the following chapter ends creates a tension that is resolved by the presentation of Mary as "the mother of pity and the only hope of despair." To Adams, hers was the highest synthesis of man's knowledge and his aspirations. What distinguished the Church of Mary Queen from the Church of the Trinity that followed was that the later theology offered a God of Justice, Order, Unity, Perfection, whereas "strict justice, either on earth or in heaven, was the last thing that society cared to face":

> If the Trinity was in its essence Unity, the Mother alone could represent whatever was not Unity; whatever was irregular, exceptional, outlawed; and this was the whole human race. . . .
> Mary concentrated in herself the whole rebellion of man against fate; the whole protest against divine law; the whole contempt for human law as its outcome; the whole unutterable fury of human nature beating itself against the walls of its prison-house, and suddenly seized by a hope that in the Virgin man had found a door of escape.

By the miracles of the Virgin, mercy relieved despair and "filled heaven with a sort of persons little to the taste of any respectable middle-class society, which has trouble enough in making this world decent and pay its bills, without having to continue the effort in another." It was not rational to dispense such favor to outlaws, no-goods, and riff-raff, and the devils laughed, "We get the grain and God the chaff." But Mary, with "her arbitrary acts of mercy" and her woman's will, offered a unity which exceeded reason and which the world pronounced beautiful and good.

In relation to his dramatic subject matter, Adams gave his narrator a revised function which followed logically from the earlier action. Among literary monuments, he could scarcely project a tourist moving physically from one esthetic encounter to the next. He could not disguise the author's selection from so wide a range of material as the narrator's necessary progress through a given scene. Obliged to do without the literal action by which he had organized the first part of his book, he trusted that he had established the imaginative setting of his drama by his insistence that "half the interest of architecture consists in the sincerity of its reflection of the society that builds." He hoped that by his story of the tourist's spiritual pilgrimage, he had established a point of view from which the action made sense. That story fixed the character of the speaking uncle so that his further comments appear to come, not simply from an obtrusive author, but from a traditional choric figure — one who can comprehend glory without being able to play the role of hero or saint. The uncle stays in the role he has conventionalized and, like a chorus, finds that his emotions are best articulated by the action which he registers with sympathy and understanding. The more his consciousness is defined by the main action, the less he is explicitly aware of his listener. So he mentions Wagner's *Tristan*, not as a touchstone of his niece's modern sensibility, but as an element of the historical setting. He uses it as a marker, like the stone-age original of the medieval romance, to show the centrality of his twelfth-century subject. Witness to the whole span of time, he freely brings Lord Bacon on his stage to state a modern version of the case against Abélard's syllogistic reasoning, and he uses Pascal to define the recoil of spirit from the mind's struggle to prove God to the heart's struggle to know God directly. He no longer does battle against his listener's naturalistic premises, but singles out the historical figures of Faraday and Clerk-Maxwell and endows with their views a "mechanic" interlocutor of Aquinas. Interpreting the historical action to his half-forgotten companion, he echoes propositions that he has already advanced at length: "The twelfth and thirteenth centuries, studied in the pure light of political economy, are insane"; the ideals of courtly love were a form of religion, but "the religion is dead as Demeter"; "illusion for illusion, courteous love . . . was as substantial as any other convention; — the balance of trade, the rights of man, or the Athanasian Creed"; the varied and even radically contradictory motives of medieval culture were embraced by a Church that was "more liberal than any modern State can afford to be." The ironies of historical perspective are less barbed as they are no longer aimed at a specific target. Stated without rancor, they contribute to the cosmic irony that underlies the dramatic action. Operating like the Fate of classical drama, a tragic necessity propels the action from its twelfth-century climax toward the catastrophe of Gothic art, and the narrator is fully aware of it. He prizes what is lost: "Not even the collapse of the Roman Empire compared with a calamity so serious; for that had created, not destroyed, a faith." He accepts the loss without bitterness, because he accepts the world. The burden of his choric testimony is that the universe, since the time of Aquinas and his great philosophic synthesis, "has steadily become more complex and less reducible to a central control. With as much obstinacy as though it were human, it has insisted on expanding its parts; with as much elusiveness as though it were feminine, it has evaded the attempt to impose on it a single will." The abstract necessity in terms of which he holds no one to blame requires acceptance, not of a theory of history, but only of the primary assumption of any historian that the constant change in human affairs deserves a serious account. The assumption of movement in history implies the tragic denouement of the historical drama at hand, whereby "the trouble was not in the art or the method or the structure, but in the universe itself which presented different aspects as man moved." The choric comment links the world of art where medieval values survive and the world of flux in which time has its seeming victory. The narrator may not know or be able to tell the state of his spirit, but knowing and telling whatever is relevant to the book in which he exists, he focuses the vision of his audience on an historical action that he thinks more important, more interesting, and more worthy of pity and terror than his private story.

The denouement was Adams' greatest difficulty. In the feminine triad of chapters, he had shown the medieval imagination defying fact and transcending reason through the active idea of love and its embodiment in the Virgin, and this he could do mostly in words that were already set down for him. In the masculine chapters, he had to present the paths of thought and act as they radically diverged, only to be brought together at the end in the precarious unity of the scholastic synthesis; and for the most part, he had to make his action out of the meager dramatic possibilities of philosophic texts. To suit his purpose, he did not hesitate to contrive an imaginary debate like the one that might have taken place between the doctor of the schools, who represented official resistance to new dialectical techniques, and Peter Abélard, the reckless innovator. In seven pages of invented dialogue, he exploited the theatrical interest of intellectual conflict without paying heed to the professional scruple that puts verifiability of incident ahead of verisimilitude. When he could remain within the bounds of historical discipline, he did so willingly, but he gave first consideration to the requirements of his own special literary form. With the mystics, whose drama of the mind could be made known through their poetry of faith, he could give his characters authentic speeches and not break the rules of historical exposition. But when he came to treat Thomas Aquinas, he once again avoided the undramatic method of formal analysis and chose instead to develop an extended metaphor, presenting Thomas in the figurative act of building a philosophic edifice, a Church Intellectual designed on the plan of the Church Architectural. Adams the dramatist could not always use the subject that the historian would have chosen, but when he departed from the craft he had so eminently practiced, he went in the direction, not of falsehood, but of imagination. In his historical drama, he told no untruth about the facts of the past, but rather devised fictions — when he had to — to bring out the lively aspect of his materials, to show them as signs of human commitment in dramatic terms.

Adams used the logician's world of Abélard to introduce the Church of the Trinity which succeeded those of God the Father and of Mary Queen. It was the philosophers who transferred the Mother's attributes of Love, Charity, and Grace from the human symbol of the Virgin to the abstract concept of the Holy Ghost. In philosophy, however, as in architecture, the sophistication of technique had to wait for its proper time: to the twelfth century, Abélard's world of abstract reason seemed a necessitarian order that allowed no room for God, or Church, or man, and his theology was condemned. But Adams did not stop his chapter with the humiliation of Abélard's intellectual pride. He had treated the Prodigal Son window at Chartres as prefiguring Abélard's story, and he acted on that insight. He gave the final word to the Abbot Peter the Venerable, shelterer of Abélard's last years, who dared rebuke Saint Bernard himself in his great victory over the dialectician with a warning against spiritual pride and who reassured Héloise on her lover's death of the ultimate triumph of love after life's long history of calamities. Abbot Peter reaffirmed the spirit of the Transition, as defined by Adams, "the equilibrium between the love of God — which is faith — and the logic of God — which is reason"; yet the situation which brings him on stage shows that what piety and imagination joined men were putting asunder.

Not just reasoners, but doubters of reason made the equilibrium of the Transition unstable. As Adams presented "The Mystics," their war on intellect was no more anti-intellectual than that of any other sceptics. Conscious that the evidences of logic and nature were too contradictory and unreliable to lead to God, they deemed intellectual pride to be the worst form of the primary sin. Aware of their pitiable state of ignorance they, "like Pascal, touched God behind the veil of scepticism," by making love their starting point. In twelfth-century France, the so-called mystics stayed within the bounds of the Virgin's imaginative synthesis, as defined by Adam of Saint-Victor:

Salve, Mater Pietatis,	Hail, Mother of Divinity!
Et totius Trinitatis	Hail, Temple of the Trinity!
Nobile Triclinium!	Home of the Triune God!*

The significance of chronology remained what it had been, and the contrast between the poetry of hope, in which terror, when it appeared at all, was utterly conventionalized and controlled, and another kind of hymn was familiar: "The 'Dies Irae' does not belong, in spirit, to the twelfth century; it is sombre and gloomy like the Last Judgments on the thirteenth-century portals; it does not love. Adam loved." In making poetic expression rather than books of instruction in religious exercises his subject matter, Adams seemed to ignore the practical substance of the contemplative way. But his criticism of the *Dies Irae* was the same as Peter the Venerable's criticism of Bernard: it named the simplest of religious duties and the essential. Moreover, he maintained the parallel to his previous chapter by refusing to end on a note of discord. Since the French with their *mesure* could

---

*Adams' translation. He had put his translation of the hymn "Salve, Mater Salvatoris!" in his chapter on the Virgin of Chartres, so that in his chapter on the mystics he could let the Latin stand by itself.

not furnish the norm for intuitive religion, he looked beyond the Alps to Assisi. There Saint Francis dedicated his visionary knighthood to his mistress Poverty and sought to annihilate pride by absorbing himself in love of God's natural creation. Accepting the illogicalities of the world and insisting on "practices and ideas that no Church could possibly permit or avow," Francis represented a heterodoxy that was tolerated by the Church which condemned the heresy of Abélard. The synthesis of love still prevailed:

> Nothing in twelfth-century art is so fine as the air and gesture of sympathetic majesty with which the Church drew aside to let the Virgin and Saint Francis pass and take the lead — for a time. Both were human ideals too intensely realized to be resisted merely because they were illogical. The Church bowed and was silent.

In the Church of the Transition that accepted the enormous complexity of its membership and in Saint Francis' "Cantico del Sole" which embraced the whole world, including finally even death, Adams found a single clear meaning. Only love, not reason, could encompass the whole of life in its unity. But with the passing of time and of the few gifted individuals who made Franciscan piety seem a possibility for everyman, men inevitably turned from intuitive submission to the forces of nature to the intellectual effort of seeking the order of the world through reason. Even though reasoning might be destroyed by what it left out of the unity it made, still man's intellect was the force for organization in the world while absorption in nature's multiplicity was a force for anarchy. Adams interpreted the change as a fundamental defensive reflex on the part of society, since "unless it asserts law, it can only assert force." He claimed that "Saint Thomas was working for the Church and the State, not for the salvation of souls, and his chief object was to repress anarchy." But if social necessity required that men fall back to the method of reasoning that had been rejected in the time of Abélard, the aim of the thirteenth century was to preserve as much as it could of the ideals of Saint Francis. The juxtaposition of Abélard and the mystics posed the antinomy that really mattered: in Adams' view, Thomas Aquinas achieved the synthesis not only of earlier philosophic development, but of the two opposing forces which eventually tore medieval culture apart.

By examining Saint Thomas' work as an individual and social act in history, Adams avoided going beyond his depth in philosophic exposition. When his argument required that he explain particular doctrines, he did so with care, often adding his own translation into the modern language of the scientist. The primary language, however, for getting at philosophy as a human product in history was that of the architect. Aquinas on the Creation is presented thus not only as an authoritative statement of medieval metaphysics, but metaphorically as the erection of the main body of the Church Intellectual. Adams thought the figure justified because in his eyes the *Summa Theologiae*, like the High Gothic architecture of Beauvais Cathedral, marked the extreme point of modernity, of excessive scientific and technical development that medieval culture ever reached, and because both monuments survived "practically unchanged" despite the vicissitudes of centuries. Adams never worked so hard to sustain poetry and argument at once as he did in elaborating this metaphor. For him, the Thomist doctrine of the Trinity, with the Holy Ghost as the power of love and grace, crowned the scholastic design of a world structure, "a restless weight on the Church piers, which, like the central tower, constantly tended to fall." He left implicit his running analogy to Beauvais, since the fall of the cathedral's crossing tower in the sixteenth century would have made direct comparison too obvious. What he did emphasize was that, unlike the Church of the

Transition, which required the presence of the Virgin to be esthetically complete, the thirteenth-century church needed men to fill it and keep it from seeming empty and cold. To bring God and man into the same church demanded the harmonization of divine omnipotence and human freedom of choice, and philosophy must solve the logical paradox by frailer means than logic. Divine omnipotence could be built into the system only by accounting for evil on the principle of negation, only by constructing a "philosophical apse" which went beyond the laws of plain experience and ignored the tragic perception on which the Virgin's church had been built:

> The student of the Latin Quarter was then harder to con-
> vince than now that God was Infinite Love and His world a
> perfect harmony, when perfect love and harmony showed them,
> even in the Latin Quarter, and still more in revealed truth, a
> picture of suffering, sorrow, and death; plague, pestilence, and
> famine; inundations, droughts, and frosts; catastrophes world-
> wide and accidents in corners; cruelty, perversity, stupidity,
> uncertainty, insanity; virtue begetting vice; vice working for
> good; happiness without sense, selfishness without gain, misery
> without cause, and horrors undefined. The students in public
> dared not ask, as Voltaire did, 'avec son hideux sourire,'
> whether the Lisbon earthquake was the final proof of God's
> infinite goodness, but in private they used the *argumentum ad
> personam divinam* freely enough, and when the Church told them
> that evil did not exist, the ribalds laughed.

This laughter was altogether different from that of the ruffians who saw the Virgin transform the flames of hell into the heavenly colors of her western rose at Chartres; but Adams admired the structure which set its philosophical apse on the insubstantial ground beyond tragedy, because the other great component of Thomas' edifice was so remarkably built in. Man's free will, the force for multiplicity in the unity of God's world, harmonized with the rest when free will meant aspiration to God and became the flèche that reached above Aquinas' church into the heavens. Adams commented simply, "The spire justifies the church."

Mont-Saint-Michel and Chartres ends with the difficult chapter on Saint Thomas, in which Adams insisted on treating the *Summa Theologiae* as a work of art. His refusal to deal with theology in terms of discursive argument has laid him open to charges of heterodoxy and obscurantism, the very charges that he was most concerned to avoid. In private, he protested in all seriousness that he would be "much mortified if detected in an error about Thomas Aquinas, or the doctrine of universals. Even to the freest of free-thinkers, an error on the doctrine of Grace should be infinitely more disgraceful than one on a question of dates." What his adverse critics are forced to leave out of their case is the curious fact that the unbelieving amateur Adams sketched an historical view of the scholastic synthesis which agrees, to a remarkable extent, with that of an orthodox, professionally eminent philosopher like Etienne Gilson. Gilson, like Adams, finally comments on his modern re-examination of the medieval experience, "It is a sad old age that loses all its memories. If it were true, as some have said, that St. Thomas was a child and Descartes a man, we, for our part, must be very near decrepitude." Also like Adams, and in a more important respect, Gilson sees the intellectual product of the High Middle Ages as the result of an historical equilibrium as well as an intellectual synthesis: "Failing to maintain the organic unity of a philosophy at once truly rational and truly Christian, Scholasticism and Christendom crumbled together under their own weight." Reading back from the vantage point of modern scholarship, we can attend with renewed seriousness the assertion of Adams' book about scholastic science, that "the essence of it — the despotic central idea — was that of organic unity both in the thought and the building." The historian stopped with the chapter on Aquinas because he wanted to show the stage when reason began to preponderate in the work of the medieval imagination, but when the work was still the labor of love which the mind took up from the simple piety of the mystics. His further observation that "modern science, like modern art, tends, in practice, to drop the dogma of organic unity," is an historical comment from which — despite the misinterpretation of some critics — he did not derive the principles of his own practice. For him, historical writing as much as theological reasoning "turns always into art at last," and the common analogue of both these disciplines was architecture.

As Aquinas, in his view, treated the aspiration of medieval man, Adams himself treated the achievement of medieval men. He used the method that the earlier architect of Chartres had employed on the old tower and spire: in ten weighted chapters he built with the stones of Mont-Saint-Michel and Chartres, and then he imposed on that solid foundation tower the lighter structure of his cultural analysis. The shift from heavier to lighter construction occurs, to use his words for Thomas, "suddenly, without show of effort, without break, without logical violence," when the vision at Chartres enables him to move easily to the next higher level. His design follows the Norman scheme of equal stories, so that three chapters of the first part bring us to "The Merveille," the man-made wonder of stonework at Mont-Saint-Michel, and three chapters of the second part bring us to "Les Miracles de Notre Dame," the miracles of the spirit worked by the Virgin. This chapter culminates in a simple verse-tale of the ignorant tumbler who could offer Mary no other gift than to dance for her in the crypt of his abbey. The abbot who detects him is shocked first to see what he takes for blasphemy, and then to see the Virgin appear with her handmaids and fan the brow of her lowly servant who has danced until he fainted. Like the visit to the Virgin's church, the chapter on the Virgin's miracles concludes with our being prepared for the next higher stage: "If you cannot feel the colour and quality — the union of naïveté and art, the refinement, the infinite delicacy and tenderness — of this little poem, then nothing will matter much to you; and if you can feel it, you can feel, without more assistance, the majesty of Chartres." At the utmost point of attenuation, where masculine mind has resumed domination over feminine imagination, such simplicity is gone, but the idea of unity still holds complexity together in the prose of Henry Adams and in the complex craftsmanship of his thirteenth-century subjects:

> Knowing by an enormous experience precisely where the strains were to come, they enlarged their scale to the utmost point of material endurance, lightening the load and distributing the burden until the gutters and the gargoyles that seem mere ornament, and the grotesques that seem rude absurdities, all do work either for the arch or for the eye; and every inch of material, up and down, from crypt to vault, from man to God, from the universe to the atom, had its task, giving support where support was needed, or weight where concentration was felt, but always with the condition of showing conspicuously to the eye the great lines which led to unity and the curves which controlled divergence; so that, from the cross on the flèche and the keystone of the vault, down through the ribbed nervures, the columns, the windows, to the foundation of the flying buttresses far beyond the walls, one idea controlled every line; and this is true of Saint Thomas's Church as it is of Amiens Cathedral. The method was the same for both, and the result was an art marked by singular unity, which endured and served its purpose until man changed his attitude toward the universe. . . . Granted a Church, Saint Thomas's Church was the most expressive that man has made, and the great Gothic cathedrals were its most complete expression.

Adams' architectural rhetoric at the end is intricate, but not confused. It was impossible to have a naïve response to the

Gothic edifice he was describing. He knew what the cross on the flèche and the keystone of the vault symbolized, but he also knew in himself the limitation of a merely symbolic comprehension. And although he compared the Church of Aquinas here to the cathedral of Amiens, he had Beauvais on his mind, too, as he went on with his comment. He defined his personal position, not to express self-pity that the time was out of joint, but to make clear the human situation which determined what the historical scholar could see. Unable to stop with what the High Gothic symbolized in theological terms, he continued on to its meaning in history. By getting back to history, he brought the work of Aquinas and his contemporaries back into the realm of tragic life:

> Of all the elaborate symbolism which has been suggested for the Gothic cathedral, the most vital and most perfect may be that the slender nervure, the springing motion of the broken arch, the leap downwards of the flying buttress — the visible effort to throw off a visible strain — never let us forget that Faith alone supports it, and that, if Faith fails, Heaven is lost. The equilibrium is visibly delicate beyond the line of safety; danger lurks in every stone. The peril of the heavy tower, of the restless vault, of the vagrant buttress; the uncertainty of logic, the inequalities of the syllogism, the irregularities of the mental mirror — all these haunting nightmares of the Church are expressed as strongly by the Gothic cathedral as though it had been the cry of human suffering, and as no emotion had ever been expressed before or is likely to find expression again. The delight of its aspirations is flung up to the sky. The pathos of its self-distrust and anguish of doubt is buried in the earth as its last secret. You can read out of it whatever else pleases your youth and confidence; to me, this is all.

The last lines of the book bring us back to the narrator, the tourist-uncle who shows his niece the historic monuments of medieval France, the wayfarer who is led by the spirit of woman and the intervention of Mary to a paradisiacal vision, the pilgrim whose road does not stop where the view is best but continues on, with the inexorability of history, to the present world of the living where he tells his experience. Scenery, psychology, history, literature, poetry, art — all these are materials for the story he relates. But the controlling purpose of the narrative is to show, in its own form as in its subject, how vast a world can be found by the senses and how great a work the intellect may do when it serves the highest vision of the imagination and defies, knowingly, the terrors of fact which always beset that vision. Because the pilgrim-artist has discovered the realm of tragedy, the tourist-historian of *Mont-Saint-Michel and Chartres* works in a realm beyond that which can be marked out by any particular theory of history. The naïveté of the Romanesque, the refinement of the Transition, the scientific modernity of the Gothic all had their appeal to him because he saw them as phases of life which he had experienced in his role as a human being as well as in his capacity as a scholar. His aspiration expressed itself in the very shape of his composition, but the anguish of his doubt was also there, almost buried out of sight, in the continual presence of time that foreshadowed the end of love.

Chapter VII

MODERN MAN IN A MULTIVERSE

THE EDUCATION OF HENRY ADAMS, which deals with the
world of power as *Mont-Saint-Michel and Chartres* with
the world of joy, was not a book that the author expected to write. The older Henry Adams differed enough
from the *me* of the 1870's so that he no longer cared to try re-
forming the world. He dedicated himself, publicly at least, to
the ideal of silence which the Brahman of his poem had recommended. Lacking any desire to imitate prophets and pro-
testers like Carlyle or Ruskin, he saw but one alternative: if he
declined to make a career of "abusing the society of my time,
nothing remains but to quit it, and seek another." Without
knowing it, he was predicting the effort of imagination by
which he came to "lead a hermit's life, intellectually in the
twelfth century, and corporeally in no recognised division of
time." What he did not count on was the double who constantly went back on the Brahman's farewells to politics.
After 1893 his brother Brooks's speculations on the movement
of modern society became his intimate concern. During the
next few years his friend Lodge emerged as a leading figure in
the United States Senate. In 1898 Hay returned from the
London embassy to take office as Secretary of State. In 1901
Roosevelt succeeded to the Presidency. He found himself on
the outskirts of importance, closer to men of power than he had

ever been before, and he became the obscure man behind the scenes whose personal detachment has made him more irritating to posterity than the overt protesting philosophers whose model he eschewed. But his position was not an accident wasted on indifference; rather, it was an involvement which confirmed his alienation. At the death of McKinley, Brooks dashed down to Washington to set up headquarters at 1603 H Street, and Henry in Paris revised his old Roman analogy to speak of "my triumvirate friends — Roosevelt, Hay and Lodge — who are now running our foreign affairs and have a way of running them in my house at the cost of my comfort." The discomfort was not just a cheerful irony, for Henry Adams in 1901 sensed that Crassus and Pompey and Caesar had been replaced by Antony, Lepidus, and Augustus. He agreed with his powerful friends on very little.

Before Adams understood his disagreement with his brother and with the Second Triumvirate, he spent a long time trying to understand just what he did believe. Until he could reestablish the coherence of his political ideas, he could have nothing worthwhile to say about the world his friends were trying to run. One aspect of his personal troubles in the nineties was the political confusion which stemmed from the conflict between what he wanted as a liberal and what he saw as an analyst. The Panic of 1893, which set his several brothers' fortunes tottering and led to his recall from Europe to help, meant more to him than just a conspiracy of goldbugs. In institutional terms, he regarded it as the failure of American capitalism, of an economy run by trusts and a government run by the incompetent agents of big business. He reacted in social terms, also, for he felt that mass unemployment in a healthy young country was a grim absurdity that could only lead to total breakdown. Recognizing that the issues of class conflict were befogged by both sides and holding in equal contempt the purveyors of free silver and the goldbugs, he doubted that anything could be done to change the course of events and he saw little wisdom in trying. One side of him looked forward to the climax of a general collapse out of which a new order might come. In this mood, he wrote: "Although I — very doubtfully — hold that on the whole the election of McKinley will do more mischief than that of Bryan, and, as a conservative anarchist, am therefore inclined to hope for McKinley's success, while I help Bryan all I can, certainly I cannot make so very complicated a program intelligible to any party." What was intelligible in his conduct in 1896 can easily be overstated, but it provides the clue to his later politics. As a detached observer, he foresaw anarchy. As a conservative, he would throw no bombs but let the future anarchy come from those responsible for the breakdown without any help from him. As an incorrigible liberal, he quietly supported Good-Government Republicans and Reform Democrats and even put five hundred dollars into Bryan's campaign chest. The veteran opponent of consolidated government and concentrated power found that his diffidence was soundly based. Having backed an agrarian uprising, he watched the forces of Mark Hanna turn it back; and having at the same time worked anonymously and hard for Cuban freedom, he saw that question of principle resolve itself into a minor problem of American expansionism. His brother and Lodge and Roosevelt, with their imperialist and warlike policies, apparently had a better cinch on the future than he did. Before long, he was reporting to an English friend:

> The reaction of fashionable society against our old-fashioned liberalism is extreme, and wants only power to make it violent. I am waiting with curiosity to see whether the power will come — with the violence — in my time. As I view it, the collapse of our nineteenth century J. S. Mill, Manchester, Chicago formulas, will be displayed — if at all — by the collapse of Parliamentarianism, and the reversion to centralised govern-

ment. . . . The despot, the gold-bug and the anarchist are the
real partners in the Trusts of our political future. To which
class should one profess allegiance? I am in a tight place.

Feeling more and more like Rip Van Winkle, who also woke
to a world utterly changed by twenty years, for a while he tried
to align himself with the rising generation. As an historian, he
had discerned that only an international scale provided a significant measure of what was happening to a nation, and as a
private citizen with a unique vantage for watching the conduct
of foreign affairs, he could readily apply his own version of
socialist and anarchist theory to the world at large: "It is running a race to nowhere, only to beggar its neighbors. It must
either abolish its nationalities, concentrate its governments and
confiscate its monopolies for social economics, or it must
steadily bump from rock to rock, and founder at last, eco-
nomically; while it will founder socially if it does concentrate
and economise." On the travels by which he escaped the
present, he began to look in on the future as well as the past.
In the spring of 1898 he made careful observation of socialized
Hungary, where "the forests, the mines, the banks, the very
street-cars, and, for all I know, the babies and the pug-dogs,
are, or might be, in principle, made, bred and educated solely
by and for the governing commissions or committees. What
is more curious, the result seems to be reasonably consistent
with a degree of individual energy and character." His conclusion was that "one need not love Socialism in order to
point out the logical necessity for Society to march that way;
and the wisdom of doing it intelligently if it is to do it at all."
Adams momentarily envisioned an ideal socialism which
transcended nationality and was consistent with individual
energy, but a mere glimpse could not revive youthful hope or
generate a practical belief in a utopia he might help to build.
Rather, he felt himself "an old man of ninety who wants to
outlive one or two other old men, to see how their estates cut
up." His self-characterization was an honest one, for in-

tellectual curiosity was more important than humane sentiment in determining the meaning of this vision. What lasted
from this phase of his peregrinations was the insistence that a
real choice could be made between intelligence and drift.

Adams, like the Marxists, argued for a "scientific" socialism, and in true Marxian fashion his detached science was
that of a very much involved observer. As he recognized the
extent to which Karl Marx lay behind his brother's historical
theories, we must recognize that he himself came to study
Marx through the influence of his brother Brooks. The inveterate liberal was also the anti-Dreyfusard to whom patriotism was energy and the energy of the state a good which
probably outweighed the disruptive force of individual justice.
Like the passion of antisemitism, the passion of war was an
evidence of directed energy which he found deceptively attractive at first. He had scarcely left Hungary, when he was
speaking of the hostilities between America and Spain as "a
God-send to all the young men in America." The forces of
centralization had attained power and become violent in his
own time after all, and he was content to point out that in the
imperialist and nationalistic struggle for survival intelligent
efficiency was no longer a matter of choice: "The only possible political party must stand on a well-defined platform of
State Socialism." The growth of monopolies under governmental protection led him to assert that the capitalists "have
abandoned their old teachers and principles, and have
adopted socialistic practices." The paradox convinced him
that the possibilities of history were narrowing down to a
single inevitability. The social-democratic theory of Eduard
Bernstein taught him that even Marxists were dropping the
old notion of class conflict ending in revolution, and the inference of his firsthand observations on French politics confirmed that the old oppositions were fading practically as well
as theoretically. He took the ineffectual playing of parliamentary politics by Jaurès and the trade unions to mean that

they had "sold out to the *bourgeoisie*, expecting to swallow the government in the end, and without calculating the chance that the government might swallow them. We are now one great economic machine with no opposition but the anarchists." Every analytic effort led to the same conclusion, and yet Adams the state socialist proved to be every bit as complicated as Adams the populist of a few years earlier. He could not quite consent to the conclusions that science and passion reached. By his calculations, for example, the Boers ought to be forced into the expanding system of concentrated power, but he could not bring himself to support the South African war. His attitude on this question can of course be deduced from conflicting calculations: antisemitism, anticapitalism, anti-British feeling, thirst for an unshared American hegemony among imperial powers — all these were parts of the equation. But one other factor entered in. In June of 1900, he stepped out of his twelfth-century cloister and wrote his friend Hay a comprehensive treatise on the explosive potential of every corner of the globe. He set up the intricate problem from which "the mathematical formula for the world" had to be derived. Then he paused for a brief reflection:

> As one who belongs wholly to the past, and whose traditional sympathies are with all the forces that resist concentration, and love what used to be called liberty but has now become anarchy, or resistance to civilisation; I who am a worm — and trodden upon, at that — am quite Chinese, Asiatic, Boer, and anarchist; but, if I ran the present machine, and saw that anyway I had got to run into the gutter, would I shut down, or put on steam?
>
> I am a coward and should shut down, but the next man would put on all the more, and the result would depend on the forces, as before; so we come back to study the forces, and there we stick.

In the confused series of his political allegiances, there was a consistent Henry Adams. The man who voted with the populists even in a losing game, who preached intelligence as against mindlessness, who would shut down sooner than steam ahead along the path he saw before him, had one constant trait — his detached curiosity. In 1896 he declined to resume his place as a professional historian on the ground that he could not understand the field, but he added to his elaborate statement of disaffection the simple postscript: "I am glad to hear other men, if they think they have something worth saying; but it is as a scholar, and not as a teacher, that I have taken my seat." A couple of years later, he began dissociating himself from his brother's political urgency. "My business is to look ahead," he argued; "it's for the practical man to run the machine and save the pieces." He thought of himself as having really retired from the world of power, even if he had not completely withdrawn. The return of John Hay to the house next door led to a still clearer notion of his retirement. He began taking daily walks with the friend who needed diversion from the strains of office, and he carefully worked at the technique of silent listening. His usefulness depended on the delicacy with which he played the confidant, but he saw the irony of the role: "I never advise. I only diagnose, but it comes to the same thing." It did not entirely come to the same thing, however. From Hay's frank conversation he recognized that the diplomatist, although not given to the weapons of war with which his more strenuous friends liked to exercise, was part of the machine of empire to which he was "dead opposed." The advice Adams withheld was advice he knew would not be taken. What was left when the historian, the reformer, and the adviser were gone was the deeply informed private citizen who trembled in his little shoes, he said, "at the sight of these enormous masses of hostile peoples running at fearful speed on roads that run across each other so often." The detachment of this little man was lonely, his intellectual vigor was great, what he saw was frightening. Yet these characteristics in combination did not produce a helpless confusion. He discovered one principle which could express both his timidity and his thirst for efficiency, both his humanity and his intelligence: "Violence is always waste."

As Adams outgrew the various political programs which he tried during the nineties, he began to call himself more and more frequently a "Conservative Christian Anarchist." In some respects, "C.C.A." was a term for his confusion and meant the same thing as "conservative anarchist" had meant in 1896, someone who resists centralization but anticipates (often with morbid glee) his own defeat with a general cataclysm to follow. In this frivolous sense, he talked of establishing a party of two, the other member admitted for the purpose of contradicting anything Henry Adams might say. But it was the twelfth-century monk who revised the epithet, and in *Mont-Saint-Michel and Chartres* he tried to work out an unconfused definition: "Absolute liberty is absence of restraint; responsibility is restraint; therefore, the ideally free individual is responsible only to himself. This principle is the philosophical foundation of anarchism, and, for anything that science has yet proved, may be the philosophical foundation of the universe . . ." Adams accepted a world in which religion and society no longer provided sanctions for individual conduct. Within that world he chose, on his own responsibility, to conserve the liberal values among which he had lived for as long as he could remember and, ultimately, the Christian values of which he had acquired a personal memory after great pains. Not always, not even consistently perhaps, but at his best he adhered to this position. What he believed was summed up by a sentence he marked in his Pascal: "The empire founded on opinion and imagination reigns for a while and is sweet and unconstrained, but the empire of force reigns forever."* Sharing Pascal's scepticism and his profound religious fear

*My translation of "L'empire fondé sur l'opinion et l'imagination règne quelque temps, et cet empire est doux et volontaire; celui de la force règne toujours."

but not his faith, Adams took a position just one step away from desperation, and he sometimes lost his footing. The main thing that saved him from despair was his responsiveness to other forces than that of concentrating power. His human multiplicity kept him from submitting altogether to the fabricated unity of an historical theory. Sometimes the anarchist with his open sensibility gave in to the rigorous intellectual who wanted to see all problems solved on a systematic basis, and then Adams looked upon the certainty of doomsday with a more than thirteenth-century relish: "To me, the new economical law brings or ought to bring us back to the same state of mind as resulted from the old religious law, — that of profound helplessness and dependence on an infinite force that is to us incomprehensible and omnipotent." But having found out the sweetness of twelfth-century unity under the Virgin, he could not long rejoice his soul at the prospective twentieth-century synthesis under totalitarian power. He followed Saint Francis as an example of anarchism and accepted as real a whole variety of things besides the apparent historical inevitability of his world. For this reason, his definition of where he stood philosophically affected the politics of Henry Adams. He had found the classic escape from the trap of ideology.

In the role of Conservative Christian Anarchist, the student of power came to terms with the whole experience of Henry Adams, just as the devotee of the Virgin had earlier. It was not easy to work free from the compelling economic necessitarianism of his brother Brooks, but Henry came to see that the game of following paths of trade left out too much. Fiscal analysis simply did not take into account the two primary forces which he had made the subject of his *History*, the technological and the human. The historian doubted that to understand the empire of force one need only know Lombard Street or Wall Street. Eventually, he revised Pascal to cover the hollowness of Brooks's theories as well as the empty church at Chartres. "Please," he wrote his brother, "give up that profoundly unscientific jabber of the newspapers about *MONEY* in capital letters. What I see is *POWER* in capitals also. You may abolish money and all its machinery, the Power will still be there, and you will have to trapeze after it in the future just as the world has always done in the past." This statement, by which Henry Adams finally declared his independent line of thought, was hardly more interesting than the process of his arriving at it. For if the actual formulation derived from the theologian whom the C.C.A. read and pondered, its immediate causes were the multiplicity of his intellectual interests and the acuteness of his trained perception.

As with the twelfth century, so with the twentieth, discursive knowledge came before the immediate perceptions around which the later Henry Adams then organized his experience. All during the nineties, he kept alive his interest in science as well as public affairs. Although the grim series of financial, physical, and mental breakdowns which beset his friend Clarence King made him deeply aware of the scientist's human fragility, he cultivated rising leaders of the profession to see what he could learn from their personal authority. He paid his way as a curious amateur by devouring volume after volume, until he felt himself at last to have become "a dilution of Lord Kelvin and St. Thomas Aquinas." Well enough informed to be a good listener, he conversed with Frank Emmons about the latest geology or with Samuel Langley about the new physics, and he gradually recognized through them that the Darwinian and Newtonian formulas were breaking down as much as those of Tocqueville and Mill. The ideas he tried out scientifically were often no less confused than his political programs. On the other hand, when instead of trying to solve the problems of science he tried to understand its relation to his present world, he did better.

His clue to the relation came not from the books he studied, but from the visible product of scientific advance. The journey from his Parisian hermitage to the Washington of 1900 made him rub his eyes:

> It is not easy, after a year of lying in bed, to get up, and jump onto a railway train going at full speed. . . . From the moment of landing in New York, I was conscious of a change of scale. Our people seemed to sling at least twice the weight, twice as rapidly, and with only half the display of effort. There is now almost no sense of effort, for instance, about our great railways; but the sense of energy is overpowering.

Although the image of the steamboat was replaced by that of the railroad, the symbol of the machine still provided the common denominator of social, economic, and scientific history and the key term "energy" remained as useful as it had been in the *History*. But change of scale made an enormous difference. As soon as Adams began putting his calculations on this new basis, he sounded like the future author of the *Education*. Within a few weeks, he wrote Gaskell:

> My country in 1900 is something totally different from my own country of 1860. I am wholly a stranger in it. Neither I, nor anyone else, understands it. The turning of a nebula into a star may somewhat resemble the change. All I can see is that it is one of compression, concentration, and consequent development of terrific energy, represented not by souls, but by coal and iron and steam. What I cannot see is the last term of the equation. As I figure it: — 1830 : 1860 :: 1890 : x, and x always comes out, not 1920, but infinity.

Modulating from a Rip Van Winkle-ism to an astronomical image, contrasting the energy of souls and steam, laying out an equation for its suggestiveness without pretending that he had counted the years till doomsday, Adams wrote with the ease of a man who had learned to live with several views at once of the same subject. Suddenly he was handling his ideas on power with the facility of the traveler to the far Pacific or the guide to the Middle Ages. Scholarship reinforced discovery, and Adams' reading now had a direction. Geology was the means of "carrying my field a little back of T. Jefferson." Physics taught the mysteriousness of the new forces, so that at the Paris Exposition of 1900 he gave a fascinated respect to the dynamos. He said he kept going back to pray to them, and when he made his figure good in his poem on the Virgin, he showed that the symbol that brought together his thoughts on the modern age also furnished an ironic connection with his twelfth century. The several worlds of Henry Adams were coming into a single focus.

In a couple of years he confidently announced having "worked out my anarchistic doctrines on a philosophico-historico-scientific basis, which frees my mind from care and cant," but instead of arguing for his views as a philosopher or historian or scientist, he expressed them as an artist in the intricate form of the *Education*. Just because that book is so intricate, it may help us to see as well as we can from the external evidence what his views were. First of all, there is the flat statement to Brooks: "As I understand it, the whole social, political and economical problem is the resultant of the mechanical development of power." It is no accident that this conclusion should sound so much like what the historian once wrote to Francis Parkman about the Age of Jefferson, and we should therefore not be surprised that Adams' remark to his brother is qualified by what he wrote to others. The optimistic strain of Jeffersonianism in him had not totally disappeared. The man who had found other realities in the past besides mechanical development saw other possibilities in the future besides catastrophe. Along with the measurable factor of machine power, there was the incalculable element of the American democrat: "As yet nothing is broken. Our people are quick and practical, and have not yet lost their heads." For this reason, there was more wit than desperation in his comment on the individual leaders who constituted the apparent free-will element of his historical science. Having doubted that America, "under amiable McKinley's or Napoleonic Bryans," could deal with " a united Europe bent on mastering Asia which means the world," he gazed in perplexity at the international scene where America was coming into a leading role. The advent of Theodore Roosevelt cleared things up considerably. As far as he could see, the twentieth-century world looked like "a boys' school run wild," and the retired schoolmaster asked with feigned pathos, "What is one to do? Play Seneca to Theodonero?" Instead of opening his veins like the stoic philosopher, he held his tongue like the historian Tacitus, who, as Gibbon observed, had been educated for the republic only to live in the time of empire. The historian he was most like, however, was himself, as he watched the leader of the American democracy adopt the premises and behavior of European monarchs. He feared that Roosevelt, "playing the king," would "fetch us up somewhere with our heads against a stone wall. He and the Tsar and the Kaiser are a gay Trinity to run the machinery of an incomprehensible future. What would induce you to hire either one of the three to drive you in your, or my, automobile?" When Roosevelt's ambassador closeted himself with the Czar to arrange a Far Eastern peace, Adams remembered who was missing from the conference: "About five hundred million people were waiting with their lives and money at stake, to hear what those two jackasses said, and nobody ever suggested that the 500,000,000 should be anyhow consulted." Much further cut off from his friends in power than from the anonymous unconsulted millions, he was no longer satisfied to think of his country as speeding toward "the Russian millennium of a centralised, despotic socialism," and he conceived an alternative to the aimless careering of the titans. His devotion to the idea of "an Atlantic system" reflected something deeper than the desire of an analyst that the play of global forces be rationalized. The cause of rationality and the cause of democracy were one. "The course of concentration must be decided by force, — whether military or industrial matters not much to the end," he wrote, "but to us it is the whole game, for we are industrial." If the present offered no positive choices and thereby occasioned his equivocal resistance to centralization, the will to choose led Adams to see a future with more than one possibility, and on this his position was neither ambiguous nor indifferent.

The author of the *History* affirmed the values of a society that would be both peaceful and scientific, and his successor the C.C.A. likewise found that his political views jibed neatly with his ideas on science. The main difference was that Adams in the twentieth century no longer tried to justify America's sanguine neglect of the traditional modes of organizing power. The forces abroad in the world were too great and too dangerous, so that just letting things happen was an unsafe policy. Given the new scale of science and technology, the detached observer of the future admitted a fascination that contained more fear than hope. He wrote to Gaskell that the world

> is vastly more exciting and entertaining than it was sixty years ago as I first remember it. It interests me almost too much, but its logic is startling. It is the logic of a bicycle; an equilibrium maintained only by violating gravitation. One force annihilates another for the time, and man does nothing but upset what little equilibrium the forces had reached by habit. The fabric of human society we have long seen to be upset, but we can remodel that, on lines of force sufficiently safe. What ex-

cites me is that we have upset the equilibrium of nature, and that nature has got to turn on us, as it does in every explosion, combustion or disease. Logically the planet should at last explode or burn up.

To find the hope that existed with the fear, we may legitimately take the word *equilibrium* as a clue. The man who was recollecting the impressions of sixty years earlier for his *Education* had just written *Mont-Saint-Michel and Chartres* and was still very much involved in the job of getting it safely through the printer's. When we ask what made the scholar "without consciousness of a mission as a teacher" become the writer who labored on his "closing lectures to undergraduates in the instruction abandoned and broken off in 1877," the simplest answer is that one exertion of imagination begets another. Although Adams did not plan the first of his late masterpieces as a prologue to the second, he definitely conceived the latter as a sequel. The three centuries of *Mont-Saint-Michel and Chartres* affected the way he saw the three centuries of his own extended biography: his forefathers, with the eighteenth-century ideals they were to bequeath to him, set in motion forces which they naïvely thought they could control; in the nineteenth century, the forces maintained a certain equilibrium — "by habit," so to speak; in the twentieth century, intelligence must undertake to hold together an equilibrium which intelligence had not originally made. Obviously the great synthesis had not yet occurred, so that his view of the social machine could hardly be cheerful. "My brother Brooks," he wrote, "says it must be made to run; I reply that he had better first make his own, and the public's, mind run, for the trouble is there. The power we develope is too great for our minds to direct. A *pneu* busts, and we go into a wall." Still, there was more than indomitable curiosity in his desire to wait and see the next development in man. If he often doubted that the age of the dynamo would go very long without an explosion, he could not preach his moral as an educator without offering a desperate hope: "Can our society double up its mind-capacity? It must do it or die," he declared, "and I see no reason why it may not widen its consciousness of complex conditions far enough to escape wreck; but it must hurry." In his insistence that, at this late hour, human reason might yet save the human race, he was reaffirming his eighteenth-century heritage. And in bringing Pascal's wager up to date for the world of power, he was hoping for a modern re-enactment of the historic pattern which, in his view of the Middle Ages, had led to Aquinas. With his own mind free from care and cant, the author of a travel-guide for nieces who wished to enter the thirteenth century turned his attention to strangers entering the twentieth century and prepared a volume "to fit young men, in universities and elsewhere, to be men of the world."

☆   ☆   ☆

Referring to *Mont-Saint-Michel and Chartres* as "a study of thirteenth-century unity," Adams called his *Education* "a study of twentieth-century multiplicity" and presented in it his own journey through the world of power. In this world one travels alone. Unlike the "nieces in wish" whose avuncular guide leads them to the already organized experience of art, the "active-minded young men" who enroll under the crotchety lecturer move vicariously among the welter of facts which are encountered in life. Where the earlier audience might miss its object because of an atrophy of sense, students of the *Education* are kept aware (sometimes to the point of exasperation) that the possible failure of the modern mind is not only general, but personal. But Adams was not beguiling his readers to eternal frustration in a world of bewildering variety, he was inviting them to participate in the creative act by which one man set his world in order. What he asked was that they share with the protagonist of the narrative his task of "running order through chaos, direction through space, discipline through freedom, unity through multiplicity." The difference from *Mont-Saint-Michel and Chartres* arose from the contrast between the finished past with its unaging monuments and the uncompleted present with its urgent duties. Adams was not changing his metaphysical assumptions. The "task of education" was the same thing, after all, as "the moral of religion, philosophy, science, art, politics, and economy," only instead of looking back, it looked to the future.

In taking Adams as "a model of self-teaching," we have to start by granting that any version of the past depends on the questions asked and the materials examined. Viewed in terms of power and violence, the thirteenth century could stand as the nadir of the past, and seen from the historical stage of the medieval imagination, the eighteenth century with its leering Voltaire could seem an all-time low point; but by switching his questions, the later Henry Adams could make both these periods appear glorious. Valuation and perception were indeed functions one of the other. Adams, however, did not stop with an easy relativism. He was not satisfied to treat his books as independent answers to different questions, and he declined to exclude from either facts which were primarily relevant to the other. He took into account not only discrepancies of fact, but also discrepancies of historical time. The tourist-guide used the dynamo, the coal pit, and the world's fair to furnish a perspective on the Virgin's world, and the student of multiplicity resolved not only to examine the workings of power, but to establish if he could the relation between the dynamo and the Virgin. Hard as it might be for a man engaged in one of these worlds to take cognizance of the other, the writer's insistence that he was one person, not two or several, required it. His problem therefore was not wholly objective. As the past had "somehow to be brought into relation with ourselves," so, too, the present. And because the question thus included the human individual, he went beyond history, in the *Education* as in *Mont-Saint-Michel and Chartres*, and asked what kind of self was necessary if there was to be a comprehensive relation between a man and his world.

The complicated personal drama was so essential to his study of twentieth-century multiplicity that he called his book *The Education of Henry Adams*. Despite the appearance of his name in the title, however, he meant it when he sent his corrected copy to Henry Cabot Lodge for posthumous publication and asked that it be printed "as I leave it." He would have deplored the innocent addition of *An Autobiography* on the title-page. He had no desire to leave a complete record of his life, and although he took his own experience for subject matter, he used only as much as suited his purpose. In the "Editor's Preface," which he wrote for Lodge's signature, he invited comparison with the *Confessions* of Saint Augustine, who, as he once put it in a letter, "alone has an idea of literary form, — a notion of writing a story with an end and object, not for the sake of the object, but for the form, like a romance." In his own avowed preface, he made the same point in an opposite way. He quoted the two opening sentences of Rousseau's *Confessions*, in which the first personal pronoun appeared more than a dozen times, and dryly observed that Jean-Jacques had "erected a monument of warning against the Ego." In short, art took precedence over autobiography in his personal narrative. If Rousseau was an admitted model of his form, he was also the anti-model of his didactic content.

Adams established the protagonist of his story as "a manikin on which the toilet of education is to be draped in order to show the fit or misfit of the clothes." He cautioned anyone

looking for a simple memoir: "The object of study is the gar-
ment, not the figure. The tailor adapts the manikin as well
as the clothes to his patron's wants." By selection and adaptation, he did somewhat alter the history of Henry Adams as
it actually occurred, but in bringing the clothes-philosophy of
Sartor Resartus up to date, he like Carlyle used the metaphor
of clothing to distinguish superficial appearance from essential reality. At first glance, Carlyle's irony seems to have
turned into an almost overbearing archness, since the manikin
suggests a lifeless construct on which the author may arbi-
trarily hang the diverse lessons that he picked up here and
there in life; but this interpretation only represents the
side of Adams which perversely enjoyed antagonizing his
readers. Once we get past the clothes-professor's irritating
gestures of defense and concealment, we may see that the
manikin is not only a tailor's dummy, but — as the etymology
makes clear — the Little Man who seems to be the Everyman of the twentieth century. Such a protagonist may be
far from the old heroic ideal, but he is still man "the only
measure of motion, of proportion, of human condition."
In this classical sense, the manikin truly represents Henry
Adams *homunculus scriptor*, the self-consciously little writer
who by means of a seemingly passive perception found the
organic unity in his multiform experience.

The first sentence of the narrative presents Henry Brooks
Adams, born "under the shadow of Boston State House" and
christened by his uncle "the minister of the First Church
after the tenets of Boston Unitarianism." If we recall the
opening image of *Mont-Saint-Michel and Chartres* — that of
the Archangel Michael standing for Church and State "both
militant" — we may quickly reckon the difference in proportion between the pinnacle of the Archangel's Mount and
the summit of Beacon Hill. Underlying the contrast, there
is a usable analogy of another sort. As a measure of motion,

the diminutive Bostonian starts his travels in an eighteenth
century which is in its way as simple as the eleventh. By the
traditional polity which lasted into Adams' youth, New
England produced "statesmen, not politicians." These men
who "guided public opinion, but were little guided by it,"
the old social system endowed with certain clear beliefs:

> Politics offered no difficulties, for there the moral law was a
> sure guide. Social perfection was also sure, because human na-
> ture worked for Good, and three instruments were all she asked
> — Suffrage, Common Schools, and Press. On these points
> doubt was forbidden. Education was divine, and man needed
> only a correct knowledge of facts to reach perfection . . .

In its unmilitant way, church as well as state encouraged
self-assurance. To the little boy who attended the Old Stone
Church in Quincy, it seemed as though every parish must
have former Presidents and leading citizens "who sat on the
main aisle in the best pews, and had sat there, or in some equivalent dignity, since the time of St. Augustine, if not since the
glacial epoch." Apparently, the eighteenth century was
founded on rock as solidly as the Abbey on the Mount.

The historical journey that starts from such simplicity
is actually complicated even at the beginning. Each of the
three chapters which fix the eighteenth-century norm has its
discordant notes: even the little citizen encountered facts
which should have riddled his inherited faith. In idyllic
Quincy, the would-be child of nature learned the limit of
natural freedom when his grandfather, "contrary to the in-
alienable rights of boys, and nullifying the social compact,"
quietly and firmly led the Rousseau-ish rebel to school. That
incident disclosed the internal contradictions in the liberal
system, but John Quincy Adams, by doing the disreputable
work of tyranny without a show of irritation or a word of cant,
also taught a way of accepting contradictions. If the boy

took in that lesson simply by being overawed, he more consciously learned from the same teacher the principle of resistance to "Boston," which was itself a part of the eighteenth-
century landscape. The Adams children got their Bibles
from the old President "while their grandfather Brooks
supplied the silver mugs," and the gifts of love spelled the
difference between the utopian ideal of Quincy and the State
Street ideology of pecuniary enterprise, indoor plumbing, and
progress. In theory, the leaders of the metropolis "chose men
to represent them because they wanted to be well represented,
and they chose the best they had." In fact, Daniel Webster,
the choice of these Boston idealists, "took, not as pay, but as
honorarium, the cheques raised for him by Peter Harvey from
the Appletons, Perkinses, Amorys, Searses, Brookses, Law-
rences, and so on, who begged him to represent them."
From each such contradiction, the boy went on to one more
difficult. The most striking that he met came during his trip
to Washington at the age of twelve. Antislavery was the
single clearest moral stand to be taken in politics, and yet
at the end of the wicked road of slavery "and product of the
crime stood Mount Vernon and George Washington," the
fountainhead of the eighteenth-century ideal. If he, like
his elders, ignored "the moral problem that deduced George
Washington from the sum of all wickedness," he had a harder
time evading the fact that the moral agents of antislavery,
who scorned Daniel Webster and all political machines,
deduced a senate seat for Charles Sumner from a deviously
clean-handed bargain with machine politicians: "On that
line, too, education could go no further. Tammany Hall
stood at the end of the vista." The boy did not recognize it,
and no one told him, but the eighteenth century was dead.

The ironies of history are partly dramatized in the difference between expectation and event, idea and actuality. Even
this requires the ironic style of the *Education* in which we may

distinguish several voices of Henry Adams. The obvious need
for a distinction of narrator from character lies in the fact that
"ten pounds of unconscious babyhood" could scarcely describe
its own start in life, but technical necessity is transformed into
an instrument for presenting major themes. Had the little
citizen really understood the contradictions he met, he would
have been paralyzed from further action. The sixty-year-old
man stood at the elbow of the boy who represented church
and state, and observed: "That the most intelligent society,
led by the most intelligent clergy, in the most moral conditions
he ever knew, should have solved all the problems of the universe so thoroughly as to have quite ceased making itself anxious about past or future, and should have persuaded itself
that all the problems which had convulsed human thought
from earliest recorded time, were not worth discussing, seemed
to him the most curious phenomenon he had to account for in
a long life." Similarly, it was the retired historian who fixed
the close of the eighteenth century at 1848. Since it was then
that John Quincy Adams collapsed on the floor of Congress in
the midst of battle against Southern expansionism, and the
boy's father Charles Francis Adams helped found the Free
Soil Party and ran as its candidate for Vice-President, the
young scion of moral statesmanship thought the year closely
resembled 1776. But the narrator made clear that 1848
pointed to the future as well as the past and did so by looking
beyond the Adams family:

> No one, except Karl Marx, foresaw radical change. What
> announced it? The world was producing sixty or seventy mil-
> lion tons of coal, and might be using nearly a million steam-
> horsepower, just beginning to make itself felt. All experience
> since the creation of man, all divine revelation or human
> science, conspired to deceive and betray a . . . boy who took for
> granted that his ideas, which were alone respectable, would be
> alone respected.

By hindsight, the historian arranged facts and recorded the mechanical development by which his subject was unconsciously affected, but the contrast of perspectives cannot be summed up in the difference between the youthful citizen and the analytic historian. From the very beginning, the artist provides sensuous images by which we see the boy's historic situation and the boy of the narrative has other responses than those of the civic or economic man:

> He and his eighteenth-century, troglodytic Boston were suddenly cut apart — separated forever — in act if not in sentiment, by the opening of the Boston and Albany Railroad; the appearance of the first Cunard steamers in the bay; and the telegraphic messages which carried from Baltimore to Washington the news that Henry Clay and James K. Polk were nominated for the Presidency. This was in May, 1844; he was six years old; his new world was ready for use, and only fragments of the old met his eyes.
> Of all this that was being done to complicate his education, he knew only the color of yellow.

The child that lives first within the range of immediate sensation fits the overt argument no better than the old man who suggests that the book deals with how to "bear" the universe rather than carry it off. As the difference in age between narrator and subject gets smaller, the gap between the passive, private Henry Adams and the public, active character is also reduced; but at the outset, the sensibility with its unpredictable access to fresh experience constantly subverts the civic personality. To notice that color and taste begin to educate before the sense of pain goes against the teachings of the New England conscience and the psychology of a behaviorist historical theory.

The boy's instinctive senses failed to respond to Boston's progressive plumbing and succeeded in finding the attractive

subtropical luxuriance in the morally horrifying vision of the
slave states, but education of sensibility had not yet really begun. Like the citizen whose old world was dead and whose
new world was ready for use, the man of feeling waited for the
boy to pass through further stages of growth. The crucial stage
was the negative experience of college, which taught little but
left the mind open. It cut down the boy's political bias and re-
leased somewhat his literary bent. A successful Harvard education, according to Adams, "resulted in an autobiographical
blank, a mind on which only a water-mark had been
stamped." If "education had not begun," it was on the point
of beginning for the *tabula rasa* that Harvard made. A university could offer no more useful instruction at Berlin than at
Cambridge, but the boy on his grand tour recognized at least
"that a great many impressions were needed to make a very
little education." One such impression was the hellish railroad
journey through the Black Country from Liverpool to London,
but this was a "practical education" which the youth tried to
put out of his mind. On the other hand, sensibility redeemed
his failure to attain practical power through the civil law.
Sitting in a Berlin beergarden "mentally impassive" and enduring Beethoven for the sake of his friends' company, Adams
was amazed to discover himself following the music: "A
prison-wall that barred his senses on one great side of life, suddenly fell, of its own accord, without so much as his knowing
when it happened." If the older man valued the event as "the
student's only clear gain" from his German year, the young
man with a career to make regarded his astonishing new sense
as "something apart, accidental, and not to be trusted."
Willy-nilly, something had happened, however, and although
the youth who distrusted his impressions had a long way to go
before joining the old man whose trust was so firm, he at least
had a sensation far more complicated than the color of yellow.
In the chapter called "Rome," the distance might seem as

great as ever between the narrator, now using phrases like "coal-power and railways" and "steam and electricity" almost as a refrain, and the tourist of 1860 who thought his emotions on seeing Rome "must be hurtful, else they could not have been so intense." But they were finding a common ground at last, and for a moment the voices were hard to tell apart:

> Rome was actual; it was England; it was going to be America. Rome could not be fitted into an orderly, middle-class, Bostonian, systematic scheme of evolution. No law of progress applied to it. Not even time-sequences — the last refuge of helpless historians — had value for it. The Forum no more led to the Vatican than the Vatican to the Forum. Rienzi, Garibaldi, Tiberius Gracchus, Aurelian might be mixed up in any relation of time, along with a thousand more, and never lead to a sequence.

Sensibility and analysis were equally helpless before the chaos of impressions and data, and in their incapacity to find a meaning, they were one. When the boy climbed the steps of Ara Coeli and framed the historian's question *Why?* he was ready to enter the nineteenth century, the transitional period between being sure of old answers and understanding the need for new ones.

In facing the question of what ideas fitted a man for political life in the nineteenth century, the historian was sure of only one partial answer: "The generation that lived from 1840 to 1870 could do very well with the old forms of education; that which had its work to do between 1870 and 1900 needed something quite new." If the father's victorious balance in the conduct of Civil War diplomacy thus contrasted with the son's shocked ingenuousness at having expected Grant to lead a Reform administration, nevertheless statesmanship triumphed because of a fortuitous coincidence of policy and historical necessity. At least so far as a private secretary could judge, the practical value of eighteenth-century ideas had to be called in doubt, and the historian agreed. In the chapters on diplomacy, every principle on which judgments might be based and actions predicated is anatomized and left in pieces: the young man's search for motives, or even unconscious consistencies, in the behavior of presumably responsible British statesmen becomes an elaborately documented farce. The tourist who met Garibaldi had mistaken as "knowledge of men" what might have been "knowledge of one's ignorance of men," so now the apprentice-diplomat learned the hard way. Gladstone, whose words were Napoleonic in their defiance of truth, represented the highest ideals of the British conscience. Russell, who seemed friendly and strong, proved to be hostile but weak. Palmerston looked like the virulent enemy of the Union and turned out to be hesitant and moderate. The student noted the confusing appearances and the scholar dug out the realities, but the irony did not stop with the reversals of judgment that time required of one who had witnessed the event. Neither appearance nor reality in the study of men had any consistent bearing on the way the American Minister had to act toward the British leaders if he was to prevent their recognizing the Confederacy. There was simply no way of estimating the human forces with which one had to deal. In all England, there was no individual or group whom one could try to bring into line except the stolid middle classes, satirized and attacked from every side but at least reachable by an appeal to interest. If by contrast "a university man, like Gladstone, stood outside of argument," apparently an educated leadership was an obstacle to effective statecraft. In the tangle of what seemed to be a conspiracy, though in fact there was none, Minister Adams won through. But his victory was due to his intelligence less than his coolness of temper, his capacity for action less than his capacity for patience. Was this, then, an example of vigorous intelligence controlling power?

The answer was yes, although an eighteenth-century mind might not think so. The young secretary who studied the problem of handling a determined opposition found no answer that could satisfy his belief in the rationality of human affairs: "The old-fashioned logical drama required unity and sense; the actual drama is a pointless puzzle, without even an intrigue." Assuming that rationality depended on reasonable opponents rather than intelligible forces, he did not recognize that his father had inherited not only principles but temperament from the John Quincy Adams who had once overcome the determined opposition of a reluctant schoolboy. However, he did notice a subordinate detail in the picture, one that proved to be a clue to the future. The lesson was nearly lost on the New England moralist who deplored that statesmen now "depended on others for machine work and money — on Peter Harveys and Thurlow Weeds, who spent their lives in it, took most of the abuse, and asked no reward. Almost without knowing it, the subordinates ousted their employers and created a machine which no one but themselves could run." Thurlow Weed turned up in London, sent by the Secretary of State to lend unofficial help with the press. Watching the New York politician take the threads of management into his hands, young Adams obtained "a complete American education" that confounded his prejudices. Weed proved to have the kind of personal equilibrium that was Minister Adams' greatest asset, and something more besides: "His mind was naturally strong and beautifully balanced; his temper never seemed ruffled; his manners were carefully perfect in the style of benevolent simplicity, the tradition of Benjamin Franklin. He was the model of political management and patient address; but the trait that excited enthusiasm in a private secretary was his faculty of irresistibly conquering confidence." In the phrase "patient address," which came from his researches in medieval architecture, the author of *Mont-Saint-*

Michel and Chartres told how highly he regarded the skilled dexterity that was succeeding the old, simple, right-mindedness in statecraft. What interested him beyond clever management and attractive manners was the essential nature of the person who showed these qualities:

> Never, in any man who wielded such power, did Adams meet anything like it. The effect of power and publicity on all men is the aggravation of self, a sort of tumor that ends by killing the victim's sympathies; a diseased appetite, like a passion for drink or perverted tastes; one can scarcely use expressions too strong to describe the violence of egotism it stimulates; and Thurlow Weed was one of the exceptions; a rare immune. He thought apparently not of himself, but of the person he was talking with. He held himself naturally in the background. He was not jealous. He grasped power, but not office. He distributed offices by handfuls without caring to take them. He had the instinct of empire: he gave, but he did not receive.

Thurlow Weed meant much to the old historian, but he had also got through to the boy with one elementary lesson. Fascinated and shocked by Weed's political stories, the private secretary asked: " 'Then, Mr. Weed, do you think that no politican can be trusted?' Mr. Weed hesitated for a moment; then said in his mild manner: 'I never advise a young man to begin by thinking so.' " Taught thus to beware of cynicism, young Henry Adams ventured to trust. If eighteenth-century principles failed to solve the pointless puzzle of diplomacy, there were other lines to follow. Credulous of the statement that London was "the perfection of human society," he conducted an experiment so dismal in its results that not even the narrator could make it interesting. A novice in art but a would-be connoisseur, he purchased a drawing in order to test himself. He then found that the acknowledged experts were in total disagreement as to whether it was by Rafael or not and, more significantly, whether it was a masterpiece or an inconsequential sketch. As a student of Darwinism, he learned that "all he could prove was change": through the whole of evolutionary time, the *Terebratula* remained unaccountably uniform; and beyond *Pteraspis*, the oldest vertebrate and therefore "one's earliest ancestor," there lay a void through which no one could trace an evolution. The young man's course through the nineteenth century began to take shape as a series of pragmatic experiments, though he found nothing like the Virgin's pragmatically effective presence at Chartres. He made trial of ideas which his contemporaries believed in and discovered no intellectual hypothesis which did not break down.

During the London years, young Adams made no more important experiment than his venture into Darwinism: that stood to his diplomatic experience as the Old Stone Church to the Quincy Homestead of his statesmen-ancestors. The tourist in Rome had only understood how his impressions undermined the old religious teachings, for "the great word Evolution had not yet, in 1860, made a new religion of history." A few years later, he moved with his time and tried the most striking intellectual synthesis his century offered: "Unbroken Evolution under uniform conditions pleased every one — except curates and bishops; it was the very best substitute for religion; a safe, conservative, practical, thoroughly Common-Law deity." Unfortunately, the endless continuance of *Terebratula* and the dead-end of the vertebrate sequence in *Pteraspis* belied an orderly, unified development. He could not see how the Darwinist's inference of uniformity differed from the Deist's inference of a celestial mechanic: "Coal-power alone asserted evolution — of power — and only by violence could be forced to assert selection of type." What it came down to was that the new synthesis rested on something different from empirical argument:

> To other Darwinians — except Darwin — Natural Selec-
> tion seemed a dogma to be put in the place of the Athanasian
> creed; it was a form of religious hope; a promise of ultimate
> perfection. Adams wished no better; he warmly sympathized
> in the object; but when he came to ask himself what he truly
> thought, he felt that he had no Faith . . .

At this point, then, the habit of doubt reasserted itself. The
diplomatic private secretary made a final excursion to Rome
and Ara Coeli, but he returned home having "learned nothing
whatever that made Rome more intelligible to him."

The next phase of Adams' education led him from disappointment to disaster. He returned home and entered the life
of the generation "mortgaged to the railways," but "his first
struggle with a sleeping-car made him doubt the value — to
him — of a Pullman civilization." On the scene of postwar
Washington, the moral law and the Constitution seemed both
to be dead. Further, the time when eighteenth-century types
might still hold their own was past. The clue lay with a minor
figure, like Thurlow Weed in London but teaching an opposite lesson. Charles Sumner was a doctrinaire statesman, not
a poker player in the subtle game of politics, and he was no
exception to "the rule that a friend in power is a friend lost."
The poison of power had made this long-time friend into a
living monument of warning against the ego: "Sumner's
mind had reached the calm of water which receives and reflects
images without absorbing them; it contained nothing but
itself. The images from without, the objects mechanically perceived by the senses, existed by courtesy until the mental
surface was ruffled, but never became a part of thought." But
if Sumner's mind took in no new images, a changing vocabulary indicates that the young man's education was going on
apace. Observing the new mechanical forces that were ignored by the American congressmen at their daily oratory and
the American people at their daily work, he could be said to

understand that "the mere suggestion that a sun existed above him would outrage the self-respect of a deep-sea fish that carried a lantern on the end of its nose." Instead of having to deduce George Washington from the sum of all wickedness or Charles Sumner from a corrupt political bargain, he now faced the up-to-date, inductive question of explaining "the progress of evolution from President Washington to President Grant," which "was alone evidence enough to upset Darwin." If the Darwinian term "Free Fight" defined both the political scene and the lavishly beautiful Maryland spring just beyond the capital, he knew which he preferred. He might not fathom the contrast between Weed's self-effacement and Sumner's unchecked egoism, but the language of the text implied that he had in Darwinism an instrument of perception that he would learn to use.

As the chapter "Free Fight" juxtaposes the life-breeding chaos of nature and the ineffectual disorder of man, the climactic chapter "Chaos" puts side by side the naked sensual terror of nature and the fantastically artificial violence of man. The language rightly indicates that the distance between narrator and protagonist is narrowing, but they are still apart. Despite the knowledge that in America his services are unwanted, the young reformer can still be shocked when the great quarterly magazines of British liberalism will not touch his article on the New York Gold Conspiracy: respectability dares not oppose corruption. The ingenuous protagonist has not yet understood the meaning of "Free Fight." He needs further schooling before intellect can catch up with sensibility and events begin to look the same in experience as they do by hindsight. The crucial moment is the summer of 1870, when "the last lesson — the sum and term of education" occurs with the death of Adams' sister. For the young man the casual horror of his sister's accident was made more striking by the sensuous beauty of the Apennine landscape and the courageous gaiety with which the victim endured the racking tetanus. He felt no gaiety himself; "the shell of custom broken" after thirty years of protective confidence, he saw his private world turn into a nightmare:

> For the first time, the stage-scenery of the senses collapsed; the human mind felt itself stripped naked, vibrating in a void of shapeless energies, with resistless mass, colliding, crushing, wasting, and destroying what these same energies had created and labored from eternity to perfect. Society became fantastic, a vision of pantomime with a mechanical motion . . .*

The private sensation gave insight into both nature and man. When the deathwatch was over, he made his way to Switzerland in hopes that he might "recover his balance in a new world; for the fantastic mystery of coincidences had made the world, which he thought real, mimic and reproduce the distorted nightmare of his personal horror." As it turned out, the man of sensibility, were he only in the hands of nature, had to suffer and yet might also recover. His first stop after Bagni di Lucca was Ouchy:

> For the first time in his life, Mont Blanc for a moment looked to him what it was — a chaos of anarchic and purposeless forces — and he needed days of repose to see it clothe itself again with the illusions of his senses, the white purity of its snows, the splendor of its light, and the infinity of its heavenly peace. Nature was kind; Lake Geneva was beautiful beyond

---

*R. P. Blackmur has finely demonstrated the enrichment of Adams' language between the 1870 letters on his sister's death and this section of the *Education*. One linguistic resource which he does not note, however, is this reworking of phrases which Adams had used in *Democracy* and *Esther*. These echoes from books he closely associated with memories of his wife help explain not why Marian Adams is never explicitly mentioned in the *Education*, but why that omission does not distort the book. Adams' profound grief at his wife's death was too private to be literary material in any simple sense, but it lent force to his concentrated expression here of how he felt when intimately struck by death. A lifetime of writing and a lifetime of feeling both came to bear on this part of the narrative.

itself, and the Alps put on charms real as terrors; but man became chaotic, and before the illusions of Nature were wholly restored, the illusions of Europe suddenly vanished, leaving a new
world to learn.

When he continued his journey north, he encountered the
public equivalent of the lesson which death taught to the
private man, except that the political man could not find a
stage of rest beyond Napoleon III and the Franco-Prussian
War:

> In Paris, in July, 1870, the war was brought out like an opera
> of Meyerbeer. One felt one's self a supernumerary hired to fill
> the scene. Every evening at the theatre the comedy was inter-
> rupted by order, and one stood up by order, to join in singing
> the *Marseillaise* to order. For nearly twenty years one had been
> forbidden to sing the *Marseillaise* under any circumstances, but
> at last regiment after regiment marched through the streets
> shouting "Marchons!" while the bystanders cared not enough
> to join. Patriotism seemed to have been brought out of the
> Government stores, and distributed by grammes *per capita.*

The chaos of American political life proved to have been
the prelude to a full initiation that made the term applicable
at once to private life, external nature, and the whole of Western society. In the chapters leading to the climax, the word
"drift" had described the policy of Grant and the behavior of
the reformers, the course of American development and of the
young man who was trying to find his place in his own country,
and now the destination of drift was revealed. The discontinuities of experience, which made Adams repeat so often
that he had a new world to learn, attained their ultimate
form. Given this lesson in discontinuity, we can see why the
chapter "Chaos" leads at once to "Failure," the chapter
which sums up Adams' attempt to teach history as though
logical sequences really exist. But the climactic vision of mul-

tiplicity has a coherence, not of logic but of language, which also shows why "failure" is not the last word of the book. The vision occurs in three different places, Bagni di Lucca, Ouchy, and Paris, and its content is made up of three different objects, but the parts are interrelated: behind the stage scenery of the senses, the illusive attributes of Mont Blanc, and the operatic unreality of France marching toward the abyss, behind the whole *show* is the reality of shapeless energies, anarchic forces, war. In the progress from the child who knows of his complicated world only the brightness of a primary color to the young man who beholds the fearful symmetry of chaos, we have gone halfway to the older Henry Adams who declares: "Unity is vision; it must have been part of the process of learning to see." From years of accidental education, the sixty-year-old Adams learned to bridge the gulf between intellect and sensibility, so that when in 1898, far up the Nile, the traveler received word of the blowing-up of the *Maine*, the account can bring together the weight of the past and the urgency of the present and put at once the personal impression, the moral evaluation, and the analytic question: "This was the greatest stride in education since 1865, but what did it teach? One leant on a fragment of column in the great hall at Karnak and watched a jackal creep down the débris of ruin. The jackal's ancestors had surely crept up the same wall when it was building." But long before we come to the old man contemplating the eternal jackal at Karnak, we have met the young man who keeps going back to the steps of Ara Coeli and, half unconsciously perhaps, has found a unifying image for nearly the same feeling and thought. By the time we reach the climax, the action that co-ordinates the several aspects of Henry Adams and the language that has gradually harmonized his several voices have furnished a clue to running unity through multiplicity and order through chaos.

The three-part vision the chapter "Chaos" presents is not

only central, but climactic, for it is a vision of multiplicity. Compositionally, the *Education* is organized roughly on the pattern of *Mont-Saint-Michel and Chartres*. As aspiration describes the action and, symbolically, the form of the earlier book, drift describes the action and all too nearly shapes the form of the later one. The former teaches that the ultimate meaning of aspiration is love; the latter that the ultimate meaning of drift is death. The vision at Chartres carries the tourist-pilgrim into the unified world of the medieval imagination, the vision at Bagni di Lucca-Ouchy-Paris thrusts the protagonist of the *Education* into the realities of the modern multiverse. Whereas the earlier action confirmed in experience the reality of the Virgin, the other confirmed doubt:

> ... The idea that any personal deity could find pleasure or profit in torturing a poor woman, by accident, with a fiendish cruelty known to man only in perverted and insane temperaments, could not be held for a moment. For pure blasphemy, it made pure atheism a comfort. God might be, as the Church said, a Substance, but He could not be a Person.

Instead of being about the works of love which defy reality, the *Education* is concerned with the ultimate reality of the material world. Yet the terrifying negation in this climax, it must be emphasized, is a turning point and not an end.

To find out what remains when Time has brought about the end of Love in the material, historical world which Adams took to be real, we get our best help from *Mont-Saint-Michel and Chartres*. The historian without belief in a personal God followed Saint Francis in opening his sensibility to the immediately perceptible realities of his world, but he did not follow all the way. He commented on the "Cantico del Sole" in which Francis thanked God for his brother sun, his sister moon, and all the realities of nature: "Only on his death-bed he added the lines of gratitude for 'our sister death,' the long-sought, never-found sister of the schoolmen, who solved all philosophy and merged multiplicity in unity." He meant what he said about death as the irreducible factor with which every theological equation tried to cope and the absolute reality by which all experience came to the same end, but he did not, like Francis, embrace this last sister. Instead, he went on: "The solution was at least simple; one must decide for one's self, according to one's personal standards, whether or not it is more sympathetic than that with which we have got lastly to grapple in the works of Saint Thomas Aquinas." These words were the closest Adams ever came to saying, to use the words of Dylan Thomas' fine elegy, "Do not go gentle into that good night." He himself, fully conscious of how fragile were all the works of man, chose the less simple solution.

Adams' solution was not a choice of intellect over sensibility. He was forced by his own incapacity for belief to revise Pascal's radical distinction between the intuitions of the heart and the knowledge of the head. In his own way, he was approaching the distinction which Henri Bergson derived from naturalistic assumptions that instinct moves in a world of things with an intuitive sense of organic wholeness, whereas "of the discontinuous alone does the intellect form a clear idea."* In his book about intellectual discontinuities he argued the basic difference between intuition and the reasoning faculties: because of that difference, the untrained mind resisted the lessons of the senses. So long as the assumptions of intellect were

---

*It was fitting, thus, that he gave the first of his late masterpieces its title from the names of two actual places, while he called its sequel in abstract terms an "education" and a "study." Referred to in the *Education*, *Mont-Saint-Michel and Chartres* was itself turned into "A Study of Thirteenth-Century Unity." That change, however, depended on the special context. Five years after the *Education*, a second private edition of *Mont-Saint-Michel and Chartres* kept the half-title *Travels — France* which the first printing had used. Similarly, Adams' other tribute to the works of imagination, his *Memoirs of Marau Taaroa*, had for its half-title *Travels — Tahiti*.

unquestioned, sensibility appeared to be a hindrance to practical education. On the other hand, it did manage to organize
what the intellect could not. This was in essence what the
French philosopher meant when he later said: "There are
things that intelligence alone is able to seek, but which, by
itself, it will never find. These things instinct alone could find;
but it will never seek them." For Adams, life resolved this
duality by having the senses find for the intellect the object
which it sought; and this object was attained not by seeking
but by passive receptivity, not by plan but by accidental education. The narrative leads to the unification of sense and intellect in art — the one choice Adams saw as somehow opposed to death.

The old man of the latter part of the *Education* could admit
that he "knew only what accident had taught him," but first
Adams had to complete the story of the young man with a
career to make. The active man, working by means of un-
aided intelligence, ended in failure. In using that word to
describe his second experience of Harvard College, Adams for
once insisted that he meant it without false modesty. If the
professor tried to impose an order on the facts of history, he
would make his scholars "either priests or atheists, plutocrats
or socialists, judges or anarchists, almost in spite of himself.
In essence incoherent and immoral, history had either to be
taught as such — or falsified." If he chose not to teach history
as either romance or evolution, there was but one way of
organizing his materials. He could assume for his students
an end, like the Law School, and a relevant subject, like the
development of medieval law. The assumption of a purpose
gave a principle for selection among chaotic materials, but
the teacher without an overriding idea of order could only
offer a method of inquiry that led to no practical career and a
series of improvised devices for stimulating intellectual reaction. Responsive students might make failure look like success,

but the serious teacher was wary of the deception: "A parent gives life, but as parent, gives no more. A murderer takes life, but his deed stops there. A teacher affects eternity; he can never tell where his influence stops. A teacher is expected to teach truth, and may perhaps flatter himself that he does so, if he stops with the alphabet or the multiplication table, as a mother teaches truth by making her child eat with a spoon; but morals are quite another truth and philosophy is more complex still." The practical man, making his career in the neutral ground between creativity and chaos, could not judge his work by the simple canons of life-giving or life-taking. Moreover, he could not use the simple tests of instrumental value. As long as the questions raised by Ara Coeli were still unsolved, Adams declared — without intending to be either self-deprecatory or obscurantist — that the fate of morally responsible action could be known only as failure.

☆　　　☆　　　☆

Henry Adams once described the *Education* as a "centipede" that crawled twenty sections downhill and fifteen sections up a little for the view. For twenty chapters the narrative offers a literal model of a young man's attempt to become a man of the world and then, skipping the period which was devoted to action rather than preparation, it continues with the retired historian's quest to understand his chaotic world. The upswing begins with a redefinition of the aim of education. For the young man it had been "to control power in some form"; in "Twenty Years After," the object is "to react with vigor and economy . . . not at haphazard, but by choice," to the forces that give his world its shape. Despite the recognition of chaos, the protagonist has acted purposefully within his given situation, undertaken a career, and "worked in the dark." Joseph Conrad, whose own fictive journey into darkness conveyed a similar metaphysical and moral purport, expressed it as "Principles won't do. . . . No; you want a deliberate belief." But once a career is over and willed belief is no longer necessary, the mind can resume its desperate task. The young Adams had to believe Thurlow Weed's "Youth needs illusions!" if he was to avoid a premature distrust of partial knowledge. The older Adams could set himself apart from his active political friends by refusing to shut his eyes or deny evident facts: "Practical politics consists in ignoring facts, but education and politics are two different and often contradictory things." The contradiction is not absolute by any means. If action demands that we ignore unanswerable questions and dissolving doubts, it ultimately must come to terms with the same reality that unblinking observation tries to know; when purposive action is marked by good-tempered patience and freedom from cant, it shows the same negative virtues as Adams required for education. The continuity as well as the breach between theory and action defines the relation between the second part of the book and what has gone before.

Much of the difficulty in the later chapters arises from the fact that two central terms, *ignorance* and *drift*, become equivocal. In the favorable sense, a knowing ignorance is the beginning of wisdom and conscious drift is a method of learning. The old Henry Adams could report of himself:

> After so many years of effort to find one's drift, the drift found the seeker, and slowly swept him forward and back, with a steady progress oceanwards. Such lessons as summer taught, winter tested, and one had only to watch the apparent movement of the stars in order to guess one's declination. The process is possible only for men who have exhausted auto-motion.

Adams' exhausted auto-motion, like the political virtues of patience and good temper, was a negative capability whereby the mature man let sense and reason come into harmony. By cutting down the self, he caught a unified vision of the world around him. Unawareness, on the other hand, determined the bad sense of the words: the ego that contained nothing but itself (Charles Sumner's, for example) might duplicate itself until it produced a society of men "ignorant that there is a thing called ignorance"; put men in power (Grant, for example) "whose energies were the greater, the less they wasted on thought," and the purposeless drift of forces simply ensured disaster. For Adams the problem of evil and the problem of progress were one, even though he knew no solution to either. The historian's every attempt to trace a sequence led into a blind alley where he met *Pteraspis* "grinning horribly from the closed entrance," and his awareness of his own time led him to note the persistent human impulse to butchery as the "trait of *Pteraspis*, or shark, which seemed to have survived every moral improvement of society." Confronting a society which was credulous of progress and ignorant of evil, he stated that in 1892 neither he nor his friends King and Hay "knew whether they had attained success, or how to estimate it, or what to call it" —

> . . . and the American people seemed to have no clearer idea than they. Indeed, the American people had no idea at all; they were wandering in a wilderness much more sandy than the Hebrews had ever trodden about Sinai; they had neither serpents nor golden calves to worship. They had lost the sense of worship; for the idea that they worshipped money seemed a delusion. Worship of money was an old-world trait; a healthy appetite akin to worship of the Gods, or to worship of power in any concrete shape; but the American wasted money more recklessly than any one ever did before; he spent more to less purpose than any extravagant court aristocracy; he had no sense of relative values, and knew not what to do with his money when he got it, except use it to make more, or throw it away. Probably, since human society began, it had seen no

such curious spectacle as the houses of the San Francisco mil-
lionaires on Nob Hill. Except for the railway system, the
enormous wealth taken out of the ground since 1840 had disappeared. West of the Alleghanies, the whole country might
have been swept clean, and could have been replaced in better
form within one or two years. The American mind had less
respect for money than the European or Asiatic mind, and bore
its loss more easily; but it had been deflected by its pursuit till
it could turn in no other direction. It shunned, distrusted, disliked, the dangerous attraction of ideals, and stood alone in
history for its ignorance of the past.

Another difficulty in the latter part of the *Education* comes
from what is left out. Although systematic oppositions go far
to organize the multiplicity of materials — summer and winter, chaos and intelligence, blind power and purposeful awareness — death stands by itself and its alternative, love, is made
known only indirectly. Looking on a world where faith, hope,
and love seemed all but lost while the traits of *Pteraspis* could
be seen on every side, Adams made the word "death" rever-
berate with increasing frequency and emphasis to the end of
the book, as if he had a double motive — to make the social
man start using his intelligence to stave off global catastrophe,
and to make the private man begin to live, in Yeats's phrase,
by conceiving of life as tragedy. The Henry Adams of the
story, for whom there is no longer a gap in time between narrator and protagonist or a split in understanding between
sense and intellect, moves easily with this double purpose. His
general comment on modern mass society is immediately confirmed by personal observation of the sightseers at Rock Creek
who are puzzled by the Adams monument. Worship was not
the only Old World trait that appeared to be lost:

> Most took it for a portrait-statue, and the remnant were
> vacant-minded in the absence of a personal guide. None felt

what would have been a nursery-instinct to a Hindu baby or a Japanese jinricksha-runner. The only exceptions were the clergy, who taught a lesson even deeper. One after another brought companions there, and, apparently fascinated by their own reflection, broke out passionately against the expression they felt in the figure of despair, of atheism, of denial. . . . The American layman had lost sight of ideals; the American priest had lost sight of faith.

In an age when massacres, wars, and assassinations occurred so often that they were hardly noticed, Adams insisted that death was a public fact and that the ultimate intellectual crime was ignorance of mortality.

The social landscape in which the railroad was the one durable artifact, and the ignorance of mortality which suggested that faith was not only lost but out of sight, provide the basic categories through which the argument of the *Education* proceeds to its second climax in "The Dynamo and the Virgin." In three transitional chapters, new terms for the problem of unity rapidly emerge. At the Chicago Exposition of 1893, where Adams first encountered the dynamo, the historian mused upon the steps beneath Richard Hunt's great white dome as to whether this American effort at unified and classic expression meant a "sharp and conscious twist towards ideals." If it did, the ideals included neither the aristocratic nor the agrarian republic to which he had once given his allegiance. For congressional enactment of the single gold standard was finally settling the issue "between two forces, one simply industrial, the other capitalistic, centralizing, and mechanical." Political observation in Washington explained the visual experience at Chicago, where the essential thing to contemplate had not been the classic façade but the new machines behind it. His travels in America gave the first clue, and his travels abroad, the second. With the Lodges in 1895 he suddenly found himself in "the Normandy of 1200," from

which he returned with "a new sense of history." Then there
was the task of "bringing the two periods into a common relation." Symbolically, at least, he did so at the Paris Exposition of 1900 when he came to see the dynamo and the Virgin
each in terms of the other.

The extreme foreshortening of the narrative at this point
almost conceals the fact that the two realities which lie behind
the appearance of history, power and spirit, have been
blended. In the world to which Adams returned after his
career, the railroad seemed the "one active interest, to which
all others were subservient, and which absorbed the energies
of some sixty million people to the exclusion of every other
force, real or imaginary." The conjunction of the Chicago fair
and the political triumph of consolidating capitalism turned
his mind to "the new energies that America adored." If the
old gods appeared to be imaginary and conscious faith to be
lost, the old habits of observation led Adams to see blind
obedience to power in terms of worship. There was a change
in himself, too. He claimed that by 1895 he knew enough of
tropical islands, mountain solitudes, and the primitive "edges
of life," for "they educated only artists, and, as one's sixtieth
year approached, the artist began to die; only a certain intense cerebral restlessness survived which no longer responded
to sensual stimulants." The accidental education of his trip
to Normandy might suggest that the artist was by no means
dead; but the conscientious intellectual of the narrative,
acutely aware that his senses were dying, assumed that "the
alternative to art was arithmetic" and took the plunge into
statistics. He "very gravely doubted, from his aching consciousness of the religious void, whether any large fraction of
society cared for a future life, or even for the present one, thirty
years hence." He himself would at least make the effort to
calculate the earthly life one generation ahead. What "ignorance required" he undertook — despite the warnings of

his fellow historians and the knowledge that he had "not enough mathematics even to figure a formula beyond the schoolboy $s = \frac{gt^2}{2}$."

Not by arithmetic alone, but by what his trained sensibility brought to the Paris Exposition, "he began to feel the forty-foot dynamos as a moral force, much as the early Christians felt the Cross." The compelling thrum of the great machines worked on his senses until he attained a new perception of ignorance. Since he could see no more relation "between the steam and the electric current than between the Cross and the cathedral," he began to think of these forces as "interchangeable if not reversible," each an absolute in its own way — "occult, supersensual, irrational." Even the simple Newtonian formula for computing attraction through time had a symbolic as well as a mathematical value. Since every objective sequence the historian had traced led into chaos, he was ready to make one final effort: "Clearly if he was bound to reduce all these forces to a common value, this common value could have no measure but that of their attraction on his own mind. He must treat them as they had been felt . . ." Because the word "attraction" fitted both the formula and the feeling, the manikin might still be the measure of his world. Sensibility and intellect agreed to treat the symbol as a force and to "risk translating rays into faith." As forces of attraction, the dynamo and the Virgin could be brought together, provided that he remember distinctly all the while that "they were as different as a magnet is from gravitation, supposing one knew what a magnet was, or gravitation, or love."

Parallel to the action of *Mont-Saint-Michel and Chartres*, initiation into chaos let the protagonist enter the world of multiplicity he had been so long approaching. Thereafter, he moved among the symbolic artifacts of society to the ultimate vision of "The Dynamo and the Virgin." Adams would have liked to say at that point, as he did after presenting "Les Miracles de Notre Dame," that if you feel this you can feel without further assistance the whole meaning of his story. Aware that "all the steam in the world could not, like the Virgin, build Chartres," he found, nevertheless, that the Virgin of Chartres could help him understand the dynamo at the world's fair. He meant to have intellect take over as imagination began to falter so that his narrative would proceed past its second climax until it reached not the Thomist synthesis of scholastic science but a synthetic theory of history couched in a more modern scientific language. However, as he warned in his "Editor's Preface," "the scheme became unmanageable as he approached his end." Unfortunately, when the imagination faltered, the mind was tired. There were half a dozen ways to get to his conclusion, but Adams, brim full of things to say and hopeful that his intuition would organize all, tried one way after another. Each of them was interesting, but the series became an intricate confusion. His faith in the organic nature of art was too great, so that his profession took on an ironic significance: "The pen works for itself, and acts like a hand, modelling the plastic material over and over again to the form that suits it best." It was justified only at the end when the experience, dramatically presented in "Chaos" and symbolized in "The Dynamo and the Virgin," took on its discursive form in "The Dynamic Theory of History."

After the clarity attained at the Exposition, Adams entered the twentieth-century twilight. The most obvious multiplicity of the new world was in the realm of politics, where the breakup of China gave John Hay his great chance in diplomacy. Acting quickly on the first news of the Boxer Rebellion, Hay arranged a limited, collective intervention at Peking, prevented a general looting of China by the forces of imperialism, and gave reality for a time to the paper policy of the Open Door. In the volume which Adams once remarked was "wholly due to piety on account of my father and John Hay," a crucial change in the language of diplomatic history distinguished the two generations of statesmanship. Adams portrayed his friend and contemporary, not as an eighteenth-century figure like his father, but as an "artist" whose sensitivity to lines of force resulted in a virtuoso performance. The piety was extravagant which said that Hay's action "put Europe aside and set the Washington Government at the head of civilization," rendered obsolete "the diplomacy of the nineteenth century, with all its painful scuffles and struggles," broke history "in halves"; and yet the incident still carries for diplomatic historians its symbolic value as an example of American action on principles beyond short-run interest. Adams himself made clear that Hay's triumph in China was merely temporary and that the hopes it raised must serve as the object of effort rather than a cheery interpretation of prospects. The view to which the latter half of the *Education* climbed was of a land, not promised, but to be striven for.

Adams knew from his personal sense that time was running out for his friends and himself, even more than from his social observation of ignorance and clashing armies, that he had come out of the labyrinth onto "the darkening prairie" of education. In affairs of state and on every side, increasing complexity obscured what he had thought was clear, so that the sandy plain turned out to be the old maze spread wide. Geology had split the glacial epoch into "half-a-dozen intermittent chills." Lord Kelvin, "the Pontiff of Physical Religion," taught scientists to say *Ignorabimus* where they had only said *Ignoramus* before. And yet, as in *Mont-Saint-Michel and Chartres*, "no one was to blame" for the changes in the world that were taking it beyond the reach of imagination.

In one chapter, "Teufelsdröckh," the same figurative quest that had organized Adams' crossing the bridge of ages into the past gave coherence to his attempt to see the future: he dramatized his bewildered journey among dim complexities in the literal wanderings of his restless travel and the sustained metaphor of pilgrimage. Passing over the Russian plains, he saw, in contrast to the dynamic anarchy of the new America, the changeless anarchy of inertia: "From the car window one seemed to float past undulations of nomad life — herders deserted by their leaders and herds — wandering waves stopped in their wanderings — waiting for their winds or warriors to return and lead them westward; tribes that camped, like Khirgis, for the season, and had lost the means of motion without acquiring the habit of permanence." Men like de Witte and de Plehve were trying to impose direction and order on this primeval chaos, much as a Hay or an Adams worked on the problem in its American form, but this circumstance only suggested the question whether likeness or difference were more important in the two forms of anarchy. The traveler circled north and west toward the actual twilight of Hammerfest, where the silent infinite of Carlyle's Teufelsdröckh seemed to have become loquacious. All along his way into the arctic gloom, he read the cabled news reports of McKinley's shooting and his day-by-day condition, and at the utmost point of his journey he read of the President's death. The cable conquered distance as the electric light corrected the fault of nature's darkness: "The electro-dynamo-social universe worked better than the sun."

From the top of the world, Adams could look north to "the nightmare of the glacial ice-cap," east to "the ice-cap of Russian inertia," and west to the dominion of coal and steam and mechanical energy where "the power and the empire were one." So long as the kingdom and the glory appeared only as faint echoes from the past, the pattern which had

once meant "Chaos" could be felt as "The Height of Knowledge." In thirty years the content of knowledge had not
changed, even though the Washington of Theodore Roosevelt
was less operatic and better illuminated than the Paris of
Napoleon III. Blindness to reality was the common denominator:

> America has always taken tragedy lightly. Too busy to stop
> the activity of their twenty-million-horse-power society, Ameri-
> cans ignore tragic motives that would have overshadowed the
> Middle Ages; and the world learns to regard assassination as a
> form of hysteria, and death as neurosis, to be treated by a rest-
> cure. Three hideous political murders, that would have fat-
> tened the Eumenides with horror, have thrown scarcely a
> shadow on the White House.

On this scene, Hay emerges as the leading actor. It was he
who now felt death invade his private world with the loss in
quick succession of his only son, his chief in administration,
his former collaborator Nicolay, and his and Adams' intimate
friend Clarence King; and it was he who had to deal with
the chaos of politics. The chance fell to the Secretary of State
because "in domestic politics, every one works for an immediate object, commonly for some private job, and invariably
in a near horizon, while in foreign affairs the outlook is far
ahead, over a field as wide as the world." At home, progress
was determined by masses of power, and the task of government was to control the score or two of individuals who
controlled the power. These managers, who mostly "are
forces as dumb as their dynamos," serve as public trustees,
and "whenever society assumes the property, it must confer
on them that title; but the power will remain as before, whoever manages it, and will then control society without appeal,
as it controls its stokers and pit-men." Foreign affairs simply
enlarged the scale. The future belonged to neither the liberal

capitalism which the eighteenth century had envisioned nor the humanitarian socialism which the nineteenth century hoped for, though it might appear to synthesize the two: Hay's "capitalistic scheme of combining governments, like railways or furnaces, was in effect precisely the socialist scene of Jaurès and Bebel." It is hard to tell whether the height of knowledge stems from Adams' attribution to Hay of his own interest in pooling Coal-powers, as against Gun-powers, in an Atlantic System, or in the uniform view of McKinleyism at home and abroad. Clearly, however, Adams slipped in suggesting without apparent irony that a Gun-power, in this case Germany, would be transformed into a Coal-power automatically by virtue of joining his side.

Adams digressed at this point to the history of his own meditations. Even at the peak from which he surveyed the wide horizons of the world, he had the sensation of "falling forever in space." Return to Paris plunged him into "The Abyss of Ignorance," since there his eternal mystery of force compelled him to track the energy, not only of the dynamo, but of the Virgin. Reckoning his own drift as a clue to history, he noted that love of God once had been the great attractive power. When that waned, "philosophers fell back on some *vis a tergo* — instinct of danger from behind," witness Pascal's view of human restlessness and Herbert's

> *If goodness lead him not, yet weariness*
> *May toss him to my breast.*

But the "weary pilgrim" of the *Education* continued his way. The Virgin offered Love, but what the mind sought was answers. Unable to accept the Unity of the Church, he nevertheless took it as a fact in his world of multiplicity. If the latest psychology told him that the mind balanced pre-cariously over the yawning chaos of the unconscious, the loss in human self-esteem since the thirteenth century gave him a way to use man as a measure of motion. As he reported it here, he sat down at once to write *Mont-Saint-Michel and Chartres*, not in order to celebrate the Virgin by means of imagination, but merely to fix a point of relation by means of intellect.

The situation of state and church fairly well settled in his mind, Adams went on to two more categories which he thought had to be explored before he could make his final synthesis. These were the two which had been so important to his *History*, human resources and scientific advance. As for the human question, inertia of race studied in Russia looked simple compared to inertia of sex studied in America. He had long since commented on the lost religious instinct of his eighteenth-century background, wondering how "the most powerful emotion of man, next to the sexual, should disappear." In twentieth-century America, both seemed to have disappeared, and "the family was extinct like chivalry":

> The typical American man had his hand on a lever and his eye on a curve in his road; his living depended on keeping up an average speed of forty miles an hour, tending always to become sixty, eighty, or a hundred, and he could not admit emotions or anxieties or subconscious distractions, more than he could admit whiskey or drugs, without breaking his neck. He could not run his machine and a woman too; he must leave her, even though his wife, to find her own way, and all the world saw her trying to find her way by imitating him.

This was a strange revision of Bunyan's pilgrim and the wife who followed him — toward "the future reserved for machine-made, collectivist females." Adams went on to animadversions on the New Woman that were even stronger than what he had to say of the new man. But he began with the assumption that "sex is a vital condition, and race only a local one," and he concluded with the consoling notion that American ignorance of sex, like American ignorance of mortality, might not change the facts of life.

Trying as a layman to learn the grammar of modern physics, Adams inferred the metaphysical significance of current science from the kinetic theory of gas: nothing which looked like order could be called necessary — "Chaos was the law of nature; Order was the dream of man." When he translated his lessons in science into the language of morals, he brought up to date what he had said of the problem of evil in his discussion of Saint Thomas:

> He could not deny that the law of the new multiverse explained much that had been most obscure, especially the persistently fiendish treatment of man by man; the perpetual effort of society to establish law, and the perpetual revolt of society against the law it had established; the perpetual building up of authority by force, and the perpetual appeal to force to overthrow it; the perpetual symbolism of a higher law, and the perpetual relapse to a lower one; the perpetual victory of the principles of freedom, and their perpetual conversion into principles of power; but the staggering problem was the outlook ahead into the despotism of artificial order which nature abhorred. The physicists had a phrase for it, unintelligible to the vulgar: "All that we win is a battle — lost in advance — with the irreversible phenomena in the background of nature."

While every effort at unity went down before the onset of power, the human mind adjusted to more and more frequent alternations of phase "until at last, in 1900, a new avalanche of unknown forces had fallen on it, which required new mental powers to control. If this view was correct, the mind could gain nothing by flight or fight; it must merge in its supersensual multiverse, or succumb to it."

Once the terms of Adams' final synthesis were ready, all that was needed to thrust him into making it was a new force

(Chapter XXXII, "Vis Nova") pressing from behind, the "*vis a tergo* commonly called Death." The synthesis itself was to be as inclusive as his broad outlook on international politics: modern science was by its nature cosmopolitan, and so too were the human characteristics of criminal silence and willful blindness. In 1903, "from Yokohama to Irkutsk, the whole East was under war conditions; but Europe knew nothing. The banks would allow no disturbance; the press said not a word, and even the embassies were silent. Every anarchist in Europe buzzed excitement and began to collect in groups, but the Hotel Ritz was calm ... After nearly fifty years of experience, he could not understand how the comedy could be so well acted." Since the climax of young Adams' education, the failure of human energy had lost the gallant, feminine quality of his sister's death, and the anarchic forces of nature no longer veiled themselves for him in Alpine beauty. Only the Parisian show taught the same lesson in the same way.

Meanwhile, his own life so merged with multiplicity that he seemed almost to oscillate between Washington and Paris. Professing "the religion of World's Fairs," Adams traveled to St. Louis to see what the twentieth-century American, "the child of steam and the brother of the dynamo," could show him. And since the *pilgrim of power* was the *Virgin's pilgrim*, too, he traveled over France to the "World's Fairs of thirteenth-century force that turned Chicago and St. Louis pale." The *historical tramp*, as he now called himself, reached his limit of free kinetic vibration one day at Troyes, when he turned from Thibaut, Joinville, and stained-glass windows and caught the news that de Plehve had been assassinated in St. Petersburg: "Martyrs, murderers, Caesars, saints and assassins — half in glass and half in telegram; chaos of time, place, morals, forces and motive — gave him vertigo. Had one sat all one's life on the steps of Ara Coeli for this? Was assassination forever to be the last word of Progress?" Merging with the multiverse could not be distinguished from succumbing to it, for "which was he — the murderer or the murdered?" The old vision recurred and this time forced him to devise his answer. Overwhelmed by the new sciences of multiplicity, he had consented to the proposition that "the historian must not try to know what is truth, if he values his honesty; for, if he cares for his truths, he is certain to falsify his facts." Yet even then he had added that "though his will be iron, he cannot help now and then resuming his humanity or his simianity in face of a fear." The fear had come, and with the experience at Troyes, Adams committed himself to the humanity of the modern manikin:

> As long as he could whisper, he would go on as he had begun, bluntly refusing to meet his creator with the admission that the creation had taught him nothing except that the square of the hypothenuse of a right-angled triangle might for convenience be taken as equal to something else. Every man with self-respect enough to become effective, if only as a machine, has had to account to himself for himself somehow, and to invent a formula of his own for his universe, if the standard formulas failed. There, whether finished or not, education stopped.

By contriving a formula, reason could convert his multiverse into a universe — for himself at least. Determined "to shape after his own needs the values of a Dynamic Theory of History," he took into account his most deeply felt need. A lifetime on the steps of Ara Coeli had compounded the eighteenth-century question with which he started. For Gibbon it was the stately and magnificent slow collapse of Rome that demanded explanation; for Adams, "the stupendous failure of Christianity tortured history." The Fall for him was more than just the fall of Rome, and the Empire with which his dynamic theory had to deal was — as the name implied — the empire of the dynamo.

The man who tried the standard formulas and found them

wanting did not exactly invent a new one. With a pragmatic definition of force as "anything that does, or helps to do work," he continued to use the Newtonian law of attraction to describe the relation of man to the forces outside himself. Furthermore, his chart of the past was an adaptation, as he freely admitted, of the Comtean idea that individual men and human history as a whole pass through a religious and a metaphysical to a positive stage, explaining phenomena by reference first to the supernatural, then to natural laws, and finally to their own experimentally verifiable conditions. He made such ideas his own in the richly specified application of his theory. Perhaps it was because he assumed of man only the love of power that he shifted the fulcrum of history back from the thirteenth century to the fourth, but his emphasis on the age of Constantine made it clear that he was solving Gibbon's problem as well as his own. He marked Constantine's admission of Christianity "into the Trust of State Religions" as the first radical introduction of new force since the Pyramids. How to account for the breakdown of a society which, with the Pax Romana, the Civil Law, and Free Trade, "had solved the problems of Europe more completely than they have ever been solved since"? The economy of gods introduced so much new force that it shattered old institutions, and in a century the *Civitas Dei* had replaced the *Civitas Romae* in human interest. The symbol of the Cross, so understood, had to be compared in its uses and effects with those other landmarks in the history of energy, the gunpowder of the Renaissance and the rays of modern science, for "the emperors used it like gunpowder in politics; the physicians used it like rays in medicine; the dying clung to it as the quintessence of force, to protect them from the forces of evil on their road to the next life." The next great change showed how little could be credited to a conscious purpose in society. The social mind was directed less by the aim of self-

education than by the insistent teachings of the new inventions:
"The telescope held it rigidly standing on its head; the micro-
scope revealed a universe that defied the senses; gunpowder
killed whole races that lagged behind; the compass coerced
the most imbruted mariner to act on the impossible idea that
the earth was round; the press drenched Europe with anarchism." Despite almost universal resistance, "the Baconian law
held good; thought did not evolve nature, but nature evolved
thought." Steam and electricity were resisted in their turn,
but mankind seemed to be "dragged on by an attractive
power in advance, which even the leaders obeyed without
understanding, as the planets obeyed gravity, or the trees
obeyed heat and light." Unconscious history had come into
its own, but the hidden energies which nature revealed more
and more often proved destructive. They came on apace
until "the stupendous acceleration after 1800 ended in 1900
with the appearance of the new class of supersensual forces,
before which the man of science stood at first as bewildered
and helpless as, in the fourth century, a priest of Isis before
the Cross of Christ."

Thus far Adams' dynamic theory was shaped to fit the needs
of one who was, with part of his being, the Virgin's pilgrim;
but as a child of the enlightened eighteenth century, too, he
had an education to give as well as to get. For the would-be
men of the world whom he addressed, his chart was to be
merely an example of how the mind may make a unifying
formula, and "any serious student would need to invent another, to compare or correct its errors." Turning to his function as a teacher, he emphasized another aspect of his $s = \dfrac{gt^2}{2}$,
the law of acceleration rather than that of individual attraction,
the progress of power rather than the occultness of science.
The vocabulary of religion tended to disappear: he mentioned thirteenth-century theology only as a stimulant to mind

and churches as data in an architectural sequence; he cited
John Stuart Mill's *faith* that the advent of new powers would
be followed by a stationary period; he wished he could be the
pupil of the twentieth-century American who "must be a
sort of God compared with any former creation of nature,"
for by the year 2000, given the present rate of progress, he
"would know how to control unlimited power." Unable to
take lessons from the future, he recognized that all he could
hope to do was teach the mind to react. Using coal power
as his "dynamometer," he calculated the doubling of energy
in every decade since 1840 until "the force evolved seemed
more like explosion than gravitation." Progress was real, even
if it was only progress in power; and the idea that it would
stop was the illusion of mental inertia, though "nothing short
of radium fairly wakened men to the fact, long since evident,
that force was inexhaustible." He repeated that images were
not arguments, that his figures would have to be corrected,
that any other formula would do as well as his. But he was
determined to teach reaction (ambiguous word!) to the
greatest revolution since the year 300: "Power leaped from
every atom, and enough of it to supply the stellar universe
showed itself running to waste at every pore of matter. Man
could no longer hold it off. Forces grasped his wrists and
flung him about as though he had hold of a live wire or a runaway automobile ..." His science, with its "toss-up between
anarchy and order," might well be incorrect, but he was
sure of his theory in politics: "Bombs educate vigorously,
and even wireless telegraphy or airships might require the
reconstruction of society."

As an instructor to posterity, Adams chose his most telling
image from science rather than religion. Consciously ignorant
of the language of radiation, he stuck to the simplest figure
he could find, "that of a perfect comet — say that of 1843 —
which drops from space, in a straight line, at the regular

acceleration of speed, directly into the sun, and after wheeling sharply about it, in heat that ought to dissipate any known substance, turns back unharmed, in defiance of law, by the path on which it came. The mind, by analogy, may figure as such a comet, the better because it also defies law." Having presented his picture of the era that began in 1900, he elaborated his figure by asserting that if his analogy held good at all, "the mind had already entered a field of attraction so violent that it must immediately pass beyond, into new equilibrium, like the Comet of Newton, or suffer dissipation altogether, like meteoroids in the earth's atmosphere."* In his own terms, Adams might be foolhardy enough to stimulate and foolish enough to resist, but he hoped he was also intelligent enough to balance between his two attitudes toward power. If his historical theory was understood as metaphor, it could teach a moral without falsifying facts. Education, for himself and for his students, could not consist of simple literalness. As he finally explained his metaphor, he offered neither an easy solution nor a general lamentation:

No scheme could be suggested to the new American, and no fault needed to be found, or complaint made; but the next great influx of new forces seemed near at hand, and its style of education promised to be violently coercive. The movement from unity into multiplicity, between 1200 and 1900, was unbroken in sequence, and rapid in acceleration. Prolonged one generation longer, it would require a new social mind. As though thought were common salt in indefinite solution it must enter a new phase subject to new laws. Thus far, since five or ten thousand years, the mind had successfully reacted, and nothing yet proved that it would fail to react — but it would need to jump.

*The standard editions (other than the first private printing) misprint "to" for "or" in this sentence, thereby making a difficult but clear exposition into nonsense.

With his moral thus explicitly made at last, Adams briefly drew his narrative to a close. His last presented glimpse of New York conveyed the energy of a Marin painting: "The cylinder had exploded, and thrown great masses of stone and steam against the sky." But despite the frantic outlines and the movement of hysteria, the old man who had fulfilled his intellectual responsibility could face the chaos without vertigo: "A traveller in the highways of history looked out of the club window on the turmoil of Fifth Avenue, and felt himself in Rome, under Diocletian, witnessing the anarchy, conscious of the compulsion, eager for the solution, but unable to conceive whence the next impulse was to come or how it was to act. The two-thousand-years failure of Christianity roared upward from Broadway, and no Constantine the Great was in sight." In scientific language, he simply observed that "the head of the meteor-stream must very soon pass perihelion." He did not, however, leave his prophetic vision embedded in the metaphors of either religion or science. Instead, he went on to sketch Hay's unfinished business of statesmanship, focusing on the Secretary of State both Roosevelt's efforts to settle the Russo-Japanese War and his own notion of "intelligent equilibrium based on an intelligent allotment of activities." Against the repetition of the word "intelligent," he set a reminder of its opposite, and with his last comment on Hay's politics, he returned to his imperial theme:

> For the first time in fifteen hundred years a true Roman *pax* was in sight, and would, if it succeeded, owe its virtues to him. Except for making peace in Manchuria, he could do no more; and if the worst should happen, setting continent against continent in arms — the only apparent alternative to his scheme — he need not repine at missing the catastrophe.

The alternative so casually mentioned was confirmed by the equally casual notation of the Kaiser's moves in the Algeciras Incident, which even in 1905 could be seen as the prelude to general war. As for what his own generation could do, he simply recorded the death of Hay, worn out by the burdens of office. For himself, the end of education was virtually the end of life, although, as he had said earlier, "the affectation of readiness for death is a stage rôle." Having played Horatio to Hay's Hamlet and lived on to tell the story of the dead, he claimed an "assent to dismissal." He too was ready to defy augury: the future that King and Hay and he himself would not live to see might bring catastrophe, but also —

> Perhaps some day — say 1938, their centenary — they might be allowed to return together for a holiday, to see the mistakes of their own lives made clear in the light of the mistakes of their successors; and perhaps then, for the first time since man began his education among the carnivores, they would find a world that sensitive and timid natures could regard without a shudder.

That final sentence of the *Education*, with its overt, lush appeal to sentimentality, is curious. In a long book that often cuts close to self-pity without going out of control, there is no such other lapse of tone. It is hard to believe that Adams became maudlin on page 505. But there are indications that this too is an intended effect. The shift of focus to Hay, the modulation from narrative to discursive exposition, the ironic self-portrait of "an elderly and timid single gentleman in Paris, who never drove down the Champs Élysées without expecting an accident, and commonly witnessing one; or found himself in the neighborhood of an official without calculating the chances of a bomb" — these things contribute to what Joyce described a few years later as purified dramatic form, in which the artist "remains within or behind or beyond or above his handiwork, invisible, refined out of existence, indifferent, paring his fingernails." The young Joyce was writing a *Portrait of the Artist* and had his hero take over the narrative at the last; the old Henry Adams was writing an *Education* and wanted to leave nothing standing but his argument. He used the same unpalatable device as he had in *Mont-Saint-Michel and Chartres*, that of cozening the reader by antagonizing him. He assumed the attitude of an umpire who infuriates the spectators. He did not mind seeming crusty, and he had motive for killing off his self-projection in sympathy as well as in story. The title of the last chapter is "Nunc Age." The teacher tells his pupil, "Now go make your career." As he explained at the beginning of the work, the manikin's function was to be a means to education: "Once acquired, the tools and models may be thrown away." If the student is to make his way in the world, he must let go the hand of his guide and proceed alone.

The relation of teacher and pupil dramatizes the paradoxical view of history for which Adams argued. We must know how to discard the past, be free of dead men's errors, and see the startling novelty of the present, but we can do these things intelligently only if we know the past. What we would be free from can itself free us from the narrow limits of the individual ego and the mortal life span. By analysis of history, we can begin to triangulate the future; through recapture of other men's experience, we can widen the choice of values and begin to decide what we want the future to be. Adams' final exhortation to the student looks ahead, but it conveys meaning only to one who knows at least a little of the forgotten tongue of the Romans. Indeed, the incidence of Latin terminology toward the end of the book otherwise simply impresses us that the man who tried the formulas naïvely, perceived the pattern in the chaos, and finally accounted for himself to himself, is through. He consigns himself to irrevocable pastness along with the language which he uses.

In the dimness of the dead past, the looming form of the *Education* takes its place beside the ancients as well as the moderns. Its measure can be partly taken if we substitute the word Rome for the word America and compare Adams with another writer who did his work as a "climax of empire" was approaching. The *Education* twice quotes Lucretius' invocation to the increase-giving Goddess of Love, the sole mistress of the organic world without whom nothing rises to the shores of light. Lucretius remembered the traditional powers of his Goddess: Alma Venus alone could triumph over Mars, lull the savage works of war, and bless mankind with peace; but, for Lucretius too, the stupendous failure of religion tortured history — "*Tantum religio potuit suadere malorum*" — and he went on to expound a materialist theory of his atomic universe as the one knowledge through which rational men could aspire to dignity. Adams no doubt looked to the poet whom he regarded as the greatest of masculine philosophers for guidance in his own exposition of the nature of things; but he had devoted a whole volume, not just an invocation, to the feminine works of love, and he could not examine so single-mindedly the workings of power. He was acutely conscious of another model and a higher standard of judgment. In his "Editor's Preface," he quoted himself as saying, "half in jest, that his great ambition was to complete St. Augustine's 'Confessions,' but that St. Augustine, like a great artist, had worked from multiplicity to unity, while he, like a small one, had to reverse the method." He knew that Augustine's movement through the stages of wrong belief had culminated in a perception of order, precipitated by the reading of scripture rather than by the experience of death, and that Augustine could thereby conceive of memory as transcending history and solve the problem of time by positing the eternity of God. Augustine's conversion enabled him to deny the Manicheism which Adams' initiation into chaos confirmed for him.* Religious

*In his copy of the *Confessions*, at Book VII, Adams wrote: "One is sometimes almost inclined to think that Augustin stated the Manichean doctrine more forcibly than the orthodox." The spelling of Augustine's name, in this self-revealing comment, is accounted for by the fact that Adams used a Latin-French bilingual text; although an excellent Latinist, Adams obviously read the French, too, for he often questioned the translator as well as the original author.

emotion, merely remembered, did not allow Adams to envision the goodness of all things, even though it did teach him that to control power in some form was not the only, or even the primary duty of man. Writing from his twelfth-century attic in Paris, he was to deprecate, more than half in seriousness, a friend's praise for the *Education*. He would have aspired to be bound up with Augustine, he explained, "if it were artistically possible to build another fourth-century church. It cannot be. The *Leit motif* is flat." Unabashed and unconverted, he tried to do what was artistically possible with the world of his experience, and he understood from his knowledge of the past the limit of his art.

Chapter VIII

THE DARKENING PRAIRIE

AFTER THE REMARKABLE SURGE of imaginative vitality which Henry Adams experienced in his sixties, he moved beyond the point where science and art were one. It was his fate to live out his vision of the human cycle and to recognize that the force of personality was waning with age. Though he still believed that the stage which followed art must be arithmetic, he never became entirely an arithmetician. Rather, the two sides of his personality underwent a kind of shrinkage which allowed room for crankiness to seep in. Although he could not satisfy himself that the *Education* was really finished, he found neither the imaginative clues nor the physical strength to revise it. But if the artist and even the teacher in him began to die, neither ceased altogether until the man himself gave out. He remained the constant letter writer, and while the flashes of wit and profundity came more rarely, they were as brilliant as ever and looked perhaps the brighter as they stood out in the darkening prairie of his final years. He not only extended his correspondence in new directions, but he became more actively sociable than he had been since the death of his wife. In the struggle against ennui and an overburdened consciousness of death and disaster, his best weapon remained the habit of work: though large tasks were beyond his now diminished powers, he nevertheless was able to write an important post-script to the *Education*, "The Rule of Phase Applied to History," and he completed two minor works which reflected his scientific and artistic centers of interest. His *Letter to American Teachers of History*, which he sent out in 1910, and his memoir of the poet George Cabot Lodge, published in the following year, reveal an intellectual vigor which counts as a falling off only because we have the two late masterpieces as a standard of measure.

The high point of Adams' imaginative energy came at the turn of the century when he was most deeply immersed in his rediscovered Middle Ages and, at the same moment, became thoroughly re-engaged in his own time. Spending at least four hours a day on his study of spires and scholastic philosophers and working out in letters the doctrine of conservative Christian anarchy that ratified his detachment from his present age, he nevertheless found time to visit the Paris Exposition over and over again until he could extort from it some clue to the world he wanted to abandon. He came to conceive of the world's fair as a temple of modernity and "what we used to call electricity" as its God. Early in 1901, he sent his confidante Elizabeth Cameron the poem in which the germ of the *Education* appeared, the "Prayer to the Virgin of Chartres" in which he first elaborated the two sides of his vision simultaneously. In his verse, he identified himself with the historical movement away from the Virgin's world of faith and art:

> *If then I left you, it was not my crime,*
>   *Or if a crime, it was not mine alone.*
> *All children wander with the truant Time.*
>   *Pardon me too! You pardoned once your Son!*
>
> *For he said to you: — "Wist ye not that I*
>   *Must be about my Father's business?"* *So,*
> *Seeking his father he pursued his way*
>   *Straight to the Cross towards which we all must go.*

> *So I too wandered off among the host*
>   *That racked the earth to find the father's clue.*
> *I did not find the Father, but I lost*
>   *What now I value more, the Mother, — You!*

Awareness of just how far he had wandered with the host led him to include in his "Prayer to the Virgin" his statement of what modern worship had become, the "Prayer to the Dynamo," which ends:

> *Seize, then, the Atom! rack his joints!*
>   *Tear out of him his secret spring!*
> *Grind him to nothing! — though he points*
> *To us, and his life-blood anoints*
> *Me — the dead Atom-King!*

The "Prayer," addressed to a Virgin whom the speaker in the poem takes as real, is similar to the incident in *Mont-Saint-Michel and Chartres* when the narrator drops to his knees — if only for a minute. Together, they mark the point in Adams' writing when his sense of himself as a creature of history was most delicately balanced with his will to believe. This balance meant, in literary terms, the fruitful co-ordination of reason and imagination, science and love, the masculine and the feminine principles of his personality. Adams' own metaphors, as useful for describing his career as for understanding what he wrote, show how thoroughly he had merged thinking and being. The equilibrium was as unstable in his life as in his representations of life, and even when it seemed most certain, it showed traces of movement toward another phase. In April 1902, when he was sixty-four years old and at the height of his powers, he wrote Mrs. Cameron that he was "perfectly square" with the Virgin Mary, that he had dispatched his revised *Tahiti* to half a dozen public libraries, and that he was starting "a historical romance of the year 1200."

This enigmatic hint is the first sign of his turning from the travel books which mark his late access to imaginative experience to a study of political actualities in the modern multiverse. Since he referred to himself as a "twelfth-centurian" and professed to regard politics, like poetry and faith, as a medieval survival in the economical society of the present, his book about himself would seem to fit the cryptic reference to a historical romance.* For the first two years of sporadic work on the *Education,* his conception of the book in relation to *Mont-Saint-Michel and Chartres* was reinforced by the constant attention he had to give to getting the earlier manuscript properly set up in print. It was nearly five years after the germination of the work when he wrote to his brother Charles, "I am sending you a volume which contains a certain number of personal allusions which you can identify from the index. Will you oblige me by glancing over them, and in case you object to any phrase or expression, will you please draw your pen through it, and, at the end, return me the volume." The two letters between which we may date the writing of the *Education* show something more than Adams' characteristic self-concealment. As he had sent a private printing of his *History* to his brother for correction, so now with his study of twentieth-century multiplicity. The shift back from Mrs. Cameron to his earliest confidant and critic, the difference between a historical romance and a history in need of being checked, help define the change in attitude that took place during the years between. Once his book was out, Adams made up for previous reticence by talking about it often and in many ways. He never forgot that it had been for him an ex-

---

*There is no way of establishing with greater certainty the start of Adams' work on the *Education.* Although his letters help us trace his specific concerns for data and his trying out of language which recurs in that volume, he made no explicit mention of his work until he was nearly ready to print. During the process of composition he practiced, with remarkable fidelity, what he called the pursuit of ignorance in silence.

periment in literary form, but he came more and more to speak of it as a prediction of things now being confirmed or as a vehicle for the dynamic theory by which the final chapters of *Mont-Saint-Michel and Chartres* were argued to their Q.E.D.* After the printing of 1907, in time reserved for his habit of revision, Adams tended to forget the un-modern vision of his twelfth-century imagination and to regard the book as scientific exposition.

To describe the late change in Henry Adams at all is almost necessarily to overstate the case, but the writing of the *Education* did use up resources which had seemed to exist in plenitude at the start. The direction, if not the degree, of change may be seen in the reasons he privately offered for not publishing the two major works of his second career. He distributed *Mont-Saint-Michel and Chartres* to his friends as a New Year's gift in 1905, and when Mrs. Cameron wrote him in high praise, he answered gratefully:

> Vanity is a danger I can hardly fear now; on the contrary, self-depreciation has always been my vice, and morbid self-contempt my moral weakness, as it was that of the 12th-century mystics, which is the bond of sympathy between us; but we each recoup ourselves by feeling a calm, unruffled, instinctive, unfathomed scepticism about the existence of a world at all. We are mighty mean shucks, as we are well aware, but we are all that is; we know no other world, and if there is one, we know nothing about its opinions of us. . . . Among the two or three hundreds of millions of people about us in Europe and America, our public could hardly be five hundred. These five hundred count as one, for census purposes. For my own practical life, the number has certainly never exceeded a score. Anything

*Adams' letter of January 17, 1905, to Henry Osborn Taylor, first elaborates the thesis that *Mont-Saint-Michel and Chartres* exists to provide a baseline of unity by which to measure the multiplicity of its sequel. Yet even in this letter he came back to insist that the book was to be thought of only as "a sketch-study intended for my own and my nieces' amusement."

which has helped to bring that score into closer understanding and sympathy, has been worth doing. Any expression which makes on me the illusion of having done anything towards sympathy, — apart from the effect of making me hopeless, — is as near positive satisfaction as St. Francis or Pascal or I could reach.

Two and a half years later, he had to tell William James why he had skipped him in the first sending out of the *Education*:

> If I did not send it to you at once, as I did to Charles Eliot, it was because I feared your judgment more than his, but since, now, I must, let me explain.
>
> Weary of my own imbecility, I tried to clean off a bit of the surface of my mind, in 1904, by printing a volume on the twelfth century, where I could hide, in the last hundred pages, a sort of anchor in history. I knew that not a hundred people in America would understand what I meant, and these were all taught in Jesuit schools, where I should be a hell-born scorpion. I need not publish when no one would read or understand.
>
> Then I undertook, — always to clean my own mind, — a companion study of the twentieth century, where I could hide — in a stack of rubbish meant only to feed the foolish — a hundred more pages meant to complete the first hundred of 1904. No one would take the smallest interest in these. I knew they were safe. So was I.
>
> Unless, indeed, you got hold of them! . . .

Granted that James's hearty philosophic optimism always brought out the most sardonic aspect of his old friend Adams, still the thought once expressed with modesty and affection had taken on a tone of smugness and affectation. The unruffled calm of the artist was giving way to intellectual pride.

As during his youth in England, Adams' unattractive posturings in old age reflected an anxiety which has literary relevance. He came to make the idea of failure, which he had

once carefully used to define the limitations of intellect, the
solace of a flagging imagination. Though he thought for a
while of publishing both his late works, he shortly found himself convinced by his avowals that the *Education* was somehow
unfinished. "I can see where the form fails, but I cannot see
how to correct the failures," he wrote. "If you are curious to
study the literary problem, send for the *Confessions* of St.
Augustine, my literary model, and ask him why he failed too,
as artist." He masked his troubles from himself by thinking
too much and too generally about his model. He served himself ill in thinking of Augustine as a failure or dwelling on the
comparative flatness of his own leitmotif, for the faults of the
Education lay less with the conception than with the workman-
ship. He could send his book around on the idea of consulting
friends and scholars — "My notion of work is that of work
among workers" — but the correction of historical details was
not what he most needed. He came unconsciously close to his
own problem when he commented on a severe criticism to
which the historian Taine had just been subjected: "No man's
mind and memory are comprehensive enough to carry the
relations of a long story." Coming from a family of extreme
longevity and scared that he might become senile, he watched
for the breakdown, as he put it with clinical niceness, of the
Broca's convolution of his brain. Looking in this direction, he
could hardly see that the defects of his work sprang not from
failure of memory, but from something much closer to total
recall. He had made the autobiographical figure in the
Education the representative man for an age which, as the author of *Representative Men* foretold, was an age of variety; but
having perceived the major lines of significance in his life, he
made the mistake of thinking that almost anything which happened to him must have symbolic value. A major difficulty of
the *Education* arises from the anecdotal impulse which obtrudes
on the narrative, the aberrant attempt to bury and praise as

many friends as possible, the driving need to record so many ideas about modern multiplicity that the idea of multiplicity itself is obscured. These faults do not destroy the work, by any means, but they do reveal the wisdom of the advice he had dispensed when the manuscript of the *Education* was still in its earliest stages:

> Any one who means to be an artist has got to study his defects, and the only way of studying one's own defects is to lay one's work aside until it is forgotten, and then to go over it again with no other thought than to see where it is wrong. As a rule one finds that it is mostly wrong. A man is generally artistic in proportion as he sees what is wrong, and most work is good in proportion not so much to what one leaves in it as to what one strikes out. Hardly anyone who has any faculty of perception can write a volume without saying something worth keeping, but generally he swamps it in a mass of stuff that prevents the reader from noticing it.

Adams did put the *Education* aside after a fashion: lacking the strength and will to take the scissors to the *Education* and cut the text by one-fourth, as he said he ought to, he gave himself up to the faults of his qualities and began writing more. The first formal effort of his late theorizing took shape as "The Rule of Phase Applied to History," a kind of supplementary chapter to the *Education* in which he tried to restate its final argument in a scientific vocabulary more up to date than Newton's. He believed his formulation of the intellectual crisis of modern society ought to be convertible into modern terminology, and setting out to do the job of translation, Adams hoped to discover whether in fact the new terms of science were useful or even, possibly, necessary. He contrived to have his manuscript sent out for professional criticism as though it were an article submitted to the *American Historical Review*, but claiming to be as wary of scientific as he was of theological heresy, he dropped the notion of printing the essay before he ever got the report of his scientific reader. The "Rule" turned out to be the effort of Henry Adams which most nearly fitted his profession that he wrote only to educate himself. He sent the manuscript to his brother Brooks, the chief consultant of his historical speculations, but he sent it as "a mere intellectual plaything," he said, "not meant to be taken too seriously." His irony was in part at least the disguise of literal truth: he still believed that one great defect of the American character was incapacity to play, and telling Brooks of his search for a tutor in the language of physics, he wrote, "The technologists cannot go beyond their laboratory materials. The American mind refuses even to amuse itself." Significantly, he gave a second copy of the "Rule" not to a fellow seeker of historical laws but to George Cabot Lodge, the protégé in literature to whom he had confided his serious advice on the art of writing. To the poet-son of his friend the senator, he declared that he seemed to learn line from his scientific piece as he had learned color from his work in narrative. He meant to be taken at his word when he said of his late works, "The form of presenting all this, from the 12th Century till today, (in the *Chartres*, the *Education*, and the supplementary chapter) was invented in order to make it literary and not technical. I trust you will not let yourself be beguiled by the form." He was still seeking a self-education in art as well as science.

"The Rule of Phase Applied to History" starts in the manner of scholastic philosophy by attempting to found metaphysics on physics. For the Aristotelian realms of animal, vegetable, and mineral, Adams substituted Willard Gibbs's less animistic phases of matter — solid, fluid, and gas. Where the next scholastic series comprised men, angels, and God, Adams put the electron, the ether, space, and "Hyper-space, knowable only as Hyper-thought, or pure mathematics." He had turned his back on what he called the schoolboy simplicity of his Newtonian $s = \frac{gt^2}{2}$ in the *Education*, but his attempt to reproduce the complexity of the schoolmen had even greater defects: although one can follow ice through water and vapor to free electrons, the next terms of Adams' series (ether, space, and thought) give progressive degrees of abstraction without being phases to which matter is reducible. Readers of the "Rule" may feel safe in just trying to follow the analogy and forgetting the science. As Adams might have put it, his structure rests on imaginative faith. If the reader grants a willing suspension of logical incredulity, he may notice that Adams' highest order of pure mathematics corresponded neatly with the Pure Being of medieval philosophy. Whether it were a subjective idea or an objective reality, he contended that this was the one phase which granted absolute certainty to man. How far it might be known or how to approach this phase, Adams left to the "mathematicians," to whom he was assigning the function once performed by theologians. He even got in an allusion to the scholastic (though not Thomistic) doctrine that the divine attributes can only be apprehended in negative terms: ". . . Even after reducing it to pure negation, it must still possess, in the abstractions of ultimate and infinite equilibrium, the capacity for self-disturbance; it cannot be absolutely dead." The ambiguous description of creative plenitude and ultimate vitality seems to indicate that the twelfth-century Henry Adams had really ridden his hobby to a city of thought laid out on the lines of twentieth-century physics.

Adams' ironic lesson in scholastic philosophy was byplay to his translation of his basic argument. He converted his old terms of attraction, acceleration, and mass into new ones — pressure, temperature, and volume — which were the proper variables of physical chemistry. The job of the historian would still be, with much the same data as he had used before, to calculate the degree of instability of the social equilibrium and the point at which it would shift to the next phase. He should not be daunted by the difficulty of finding historical units, for it was, after all, in his own field of history that phase rules had first been invented by Turgot and Comte. Before undertaking the job himself, Adams warned the reader that Comte's critics had tacitly accepted his principles even when they fell to disputing the succession of phases he had elaborated: "Comte's idea of applying the rule had nothing to do with the validity of the rule itself." In short, convinced that there could no more be an alternative between chance and direction in history than there was in physics, Adams was deliberately trying to engage his reader in speculation on the long-term sequences of the human, and even the prehuman, past. When he put his challenge on a personal level, he suggested that the historian could learn from the physicist without accepting a particular interpretation of the phase rule:

> We live in a world of phases, so much more astonishing than the explosion of rockets, that we cannot, unless we are Gibbs or Watts, stop every moment to ask what becomes of the salt we put in our soup, or the water we boil in our teapot, and we are apt to remain stupidly stolid when a bulb bursts into a tulip, or a worm turns into a butterfly. No phase compares in wonder with the mere fact of our own existence, and this wonder has so completely exhausted the powers of Thought that mankind, except in a few laboratories, has ceased to wonder, or even to think.

Appealing to wonder rather than to catastrophic terror, Adams recurred to his argument for humility by insisting that Instinct had "overcome obstacles that Intellect has been helpless to affect. . . . The quality that developed the eye and the wing of the bee and the condor has no known equivalent in man." The insoluble problem of finding an ancestry for the *Pteraspis* was transformed to an affirmation of wonder when Adams declared that "geology itself breaks off abruptly in the middle of the story, when the fishes and crustaceans astonish by their modern airs." He played the role of a Sir Thomas Browne with gusto when he suggested that a crucial phase had occurred when, "long before the first man was sketched, the monkeys and their companions in instinct had peopled every continent, and civilized — according to their standards — the whole world." If his wit taught intellect to be humble before the past, it also taught the recognition of historical necessity: he illustrated his thesis that resistance to change of phase implies a motive power outside the changing subject with a poignant and hilarious description of the anthropoid ape desperately fighting off the cosmic obligation to become a man.

The cult of pure thought drove Adams back to the modern dogma that "nature loves the logarithm" and to the quest for a mathematical application of the rule of phase in history: "The reflection or projection of the mind in nature was the earliest and will no doubt be the last motive of man's mind, whether as religion or as science . . ." He once more used his astronomic figure of the comet's parabolic movement through perihelion in order to convey his sense of crisis, but his new graph for history was properly a hyperbola which allowed an infinitude of brute prehistory, some 90,000 years for the religious phase in man, and three or four hundred years from Bacon and Galileo onward for a mechanical phase. Since the three hundred years between 1600 and 1900 could be squared to equal the religious span, Adams was tempted to seize upon the pattern in his arbitrary figures. Using his favorite mathematical progression of inverse squares, he calculated that the human race might be pushed through the electrical and ethereal phases to the limit of thought by 1921 or, at the latest (using slightly altered measurements), 2025. That phase of

ultimate solution might be indistinguishable from utter dissolution; if the last stage proved to be "an indefinitely long stationary period, such as John Stuart Mill foresaw," then the
current of thought "would merely cease to flow." That was
not the only possibility, however, for the point of prophecy remained the same as it had been in the *Education* — to drive
home the conviction that an alternative existed and a choice
had to be made. Adams appealed to hope as he forced the will
toward a choice. The substance of his faith became clear
when he went on after depicting the static ocean of potential
thought to which the historical process might lead:

> But if, in the prodigiously rapid vibration of its last phases,
> Thought should continue to act as the universal solvent which
> it is, and should reduce the forces of the molecule, the atom, and
> the electron to that costless servitude to which it has reduced
> the old elements of earth and air, fire and water; if man should
> continue to set free the infinite forces of nature, and attain the
> control of cosmic forces on a cosmic scale, the consequences may
> be as surprising as the change of water to vapor, of the worm
> to the butterfly, of radium to electrons.

The "Rule" has that quality of art which Yeats defined
as "gaiety transfiguring all that dread." Adams was still
able to achieve a fable in formulas which, instead of referring
to the animal stories of early man, used metaphors from
modern science to convey its didactic point. Yet he was
curiously insensitive to his own achievement and to the comment of the one reader who tried to let him know what he
had done. The sign of his hardening intellectual habits came
in a reversal of his relation with his brother Brooks. During
the years of intense imaginative effort which produced his
two late masterpieces, Henry Adams tended to seal off his
historical theorizing in his correspondence with his younger
brother. He was capable of dodging Brooks across continents

on the expressed excuse that, being so much alike, they had little to give each other; unlike Brooks, who was ever ready to tackle the world for the sake of his newest idea, Henry avoided the one-track argument even in conversation. This adjustment by which the artist kept himself free for his daily tasks had the result that, from Brooks Adams' point of view, the single theme of his brother's later career was "The Degradation of the Democratic Dogma," the title he gave to his posthumous edition of Henry's speculative essays.* Brooks's perspective was special to himself: if the dissipation of force through entropy was an underlying idea in *Mont-Saint-Michel and Chartres* and the *Education*, it was transformed by the organic metaphor whereby the author showed cultures passing through the same naïve, mature, and intellectual stages as men. Henry Adams insisted that men do die, that the Middle Ages were dead, and that the modern era was flirting with catastrophe, but he also argued that society had hitherto been immortal and could maintain itself now by a new leap of mind. The continuing consultation of the two brothers did not have the central importance for the older of them which it had for the younger. Brooks's *esprit de géométrie* helped keep Henry on one track he chose to follow, but Henry's *esprit de finesse* refused to confine itself to that alone. The older brother defended the rights of his complex imagination, not without cruelty, when he wrote: "Brooks has helped me to catch on to the machine a little, but Brooks

---

The Degradation of the Democratic Dogma was published in 1919, when the public edition of the *Education* was running for the second consecutive year at the head of the non-fiction best-sellers. The difficulty of the *Education*, the postwar atmosphere of disillusionment, and the authority with which a brother could be assumed to speak combined to win general acceptance of Brooks's thesis, elaborated in his long introduction on "The Heritage of Henry Adams." Adams' letters, except for special series which did not reveal very much of his scope as a man and a writer, were to remain unpublished for more than a decade. It is therefore not surprising that this interpretation of Henry Adams' late career has yielded to change very slowly.

himself is as far from catching on as ever, I think . . . Brooks is too brutal, too blatant, too emphatic, and too intensely set on one line alone, at a time, to please any large number of people." But in 1909 it was Henry who was stuck too much on one line of thought. Brooks did not pretend to understand the science of the "Rule," but he recognized its art and wrote enthusiastically:

> You have, at last, overcome your obstacle. There is your unity whereby to measure your diversity. The Theorem which should precede the experiment. Your education has been the search for the "new mind." The contrast you wish to draw is the absolute gap between the thing nature demands and the human effort. If you can strip from your book all semblance of personal irritation against individuals, eliminate the apparent effort to write fragments of biography, and raise your story to the level in dignity of the vast conception against which you are to measure the result, you will have created one of the masterpieces of literature, psychology, and history.

Henry Adams could not rise to the point his brother made. Almost by return mail, he sent along his detailed and severe criticisms of Brooks's manuscript life of John Quincy Adams, apologizing in his old tone for the demands of clarity and proportion which he made on the book: "My mean nature led me, early in life, to aspire to be an artist rather than a gymnast; and my mean abilities shut me up within this narrow scope of art." At seventy-one, however, he was losing the right to condescend so, for he saw others' faults more clearly than his own. Brooks took the humiliation and manfully suppressed the biography of his grandfather, while Henry for reasons quite different suppressed the "Rule." A year later, Brooks reread his brother's essay and pleaded again, "Recast your memoirs and make it the base. That will satisfy me. Nothing else will." Meanwhile, Henry had been following his scientific line still farther, so that in the spring of 1910 he printed his *Letter to American Teachers of History* and circulated it to a carefully compiled list of educators and historians. Within so short a time, the high humor of the "Rule" was changed into the bad joke of the *Letter*. Thinking that history would die if not irritated, he performed the service with such indecorous zeal that he could honestly say, "I don't know that I should see the joke myself if I were not its author." He thought that if his basic argument about the tendencies of modern history were correct, it should be convertible to any set of terms from modern science that he might try to use; but when he switched from Gibbs's rule of phases to Kelvin's second law of thermodynamics, something more than translation occurred. So much bitterness spilled forth in his exposition of entropy in history, that the despair of wasted energy was much more obviously a reflection of the author than a successful projection of mind into objective nature. Successful metaphors are never interchangeable, and Adams should have been artist enough to know that. The scientific figure he now elaborated had a tenor of its own which brought to expression the most desperate and perverse aspect of his personality. He gave in to intellectual waywardness and, regarding his brother Brooks as a confidant for speculations but beyond the reach of art, he paid no heed to the most constructive criticism he had ever had.

The *Letter to American Teachers* provides disheartening evidence that Henry Adams' ingrained vice of self-depreciation had finally taken its toll. His belief that failure was the ultimate destiny of intellectual effort had always suggested more than its literal meaning that nature outreaches mind. He himself had constantly associated the pessimistic implications of this thesis with his own professional career until he became, as he said of his grandfather John Quincy Adams, incapable of drinking when the cup of triumph was offered. Having persuaded himself that not half a dozen people had ever read his *History*, almost from the first he ran from the honors his work brought to him. His saying in the *Education* that politics was "the systematic organization of hatreds" amounted to a personal disclosure: although he could graciously accept praise from the friends of his private circle, he instinctively felt the social forum to be a place for vigorous challenge and counterattack. Shyness and commitment to public life never mixed easily, but the eccentricity of 1910 was an extreme form of the personal quirk which, in 1894, still came to only venial proportions. When at that time he slipped out of giving a Presidential Address to the American Historical Association, he met his obligation by sending a written message from his hideout in Mexico. His self-consciousness as a public figure affected only the mode of delivery, but not the substance of what he had to say. The Adams of 1894, in his first letter to his professional colleagues, spoke out clearly and strongly: "That the effort to make history a science may fail is possible, and perhaps probable; but that it should cease, unless for reasons that would cause all science to cease, is not within the range of experience." In his mid-fifties, he took sides against his own impulse to quit the world and held that the mind could not quit its self-appointed tasks, even if it faced impossibility. His theoretical belief about the function of reason in a chaotic world was not to change. The difference from the older man lay not so much in metaphysics, as in social and individual attitudes. As the responsible head of his academic guild, he foretold that the great need of the future would be not simply intelligence, but intellectual courage: any conclusions that serious reasoning might lead to must necessarily put the reasoner at odds with some of the great conflicting forces of society. He outlined the situation and prospects of the historian so cogently, indeed, that his analysis ought to be followed in the detail of an extended quotation:

... Had history been converted into a science [at mid-century] it would perhaps have taken the form of cheerful optimism which gave to Darwin's conclusions the charm of a possible human perfectibility. Of late years the tone of European thought has been distinctly despondent among the classes which were formerly most hopeful. If a science of history were established to-day on the lines of its recent development I greatly fear it would take its tone from the pessimism of Paris, Berlin, London, and St. Petersburg, unless it brought into sight some new and hitherto unsuspected path for civilization to pursue.

If it pointed to a socialistic triumph it would place us in an attitude of hostility toward existing institutions. Even supposing that our universities would permit their professors in this country to announce the scientific certainty of communistic triumphs, could Europe be equally liberal? Would property, on which the universities depend, allow such freedom of instruction? Would the state suffer its foundation to be destroyed? Would society as now constituted tolerate the open assertion of a necessity which should affirm its approaching overthrow?

If, on the other hand, the new science required us to announce that the present evils of the world — its huge armaments, its vast accumulations of capital, its advancing materialism, and declining arts — were to be continued, exaggerated, over another thousand years, no one would listen to us with satisfaction. Society would shut its eyes and ears. If we proved the certainty of our results we should prove it without a sympathetic audience and without good effect. No one except artists and socialists would listen, and the conviction which we should produce on them could lead only to despair and attempts at anarchy in art, in thought, and in society.

If, finally, the science should prove that society must at a given time revert to the church and recover its old foundation of absolute faith in a personal providence and a revealed religion, it commits suicide.

In whatever direction we look we can see no possibility of converting history into a science without bringing it into hostility toward one or more of the most powerful organizations of the era. If the world is to continue moving toward the point which it has so energetically pursued during the last fifty years, it will destroy the hopes of the vast organizations of labor. If it is to change its course and become communistic, it places us in direct hostility to the entire fabric of our social and political system. If it goes on, we must preach despair. If it goes back, it must deny and repudiate science. If it goes forward, round a circle which leads through communism, we must declare ourselves hostile to the property that pays us and the institutions we are bound in duty to support.

A science cannot be played with. . . .

The moral consequences of intellectual seriousness, as Adams saw in 1894, were bound to subject the learned professions to severe public pressures. He urged upon his colleagues, in 1894, that historians as well as physicists should prepare to make Galileo's *"E pur si muove"* their rallying cry. In the privacy of his retirement, he himself plugged away at the problem he had set for younger men. He covered acres of paper with his analyses of international finance, demographical statistics, and geopolitical possibilities. Having flirted with the hopes of socialism, he learned to accept the continuance of the present order even though, in his view, such acceptance ought to lead to despair. The privacy of his speculations must be emphasized, however, for until 1910 the much vaunted pessimism of Henry Adams found expression in his personal correspondence rather than in what he wrote for circulation. Until the year of the *Letter*, Adams the author was more concerned with a dynamic theory of history than with a thermodynamic theory of calamity. The letter writer, on the other hand, was full of dire predictions that the world was going to smash. His fascination with the startling led him continually to guess that the bust-up would occur within a year — or, at any rate, five years sooner than he had last calculated. This strain in Adams was often clairvoyant, occasionally ludicrous, and eventually morbid. The compulsion to triangulate the future became so serious a vice that John Hay, as a practical statesman, felt compelled to cut himself clear of it by declaring to his friend: "Sufficient unto the day is the blunder thereof. . . . If I looked at things as you do in the light of reason, history and mathematics, I should go off after lunch and die, like Mouravieff." The attempt to make a science of history, responsibly undertaken, had somehow trailed off into a perversity which came to expression in the *Letter to American Teachers of History*.

Adams presented his *Letter* as an extension of his presidential message of 1894, a full-length report on the state of the profession and, in particular, its relations with the sciences. He elaborated his earlier remark on the change between midnineteenth-century optimism and the gloom of fifty years later, for he now observed society to be questioning its health as constantly as if it were a nervous invalid. He detached himself from the temper of his time by asserting that although "the intended effect of intellectual education is, — as Bacon, Descartes, and Kant began by insisting, — a habit of doubt, it is only in a very secondary sense a habit of timidity or despair." This was the challenge of the *Letter*. Adams knew all too well that no reader could entirely submit himself to the book without a sense that the educational experience was more unnerving than beneficial. If invalidism were not the whole story, it was because he hoped for, and thought society might produce, the reader who would react on behalf of healthy vigor. The gift which he offered to whoever would reject it, so to speak, was a detailed — and loaded — analysis of the scientific developments of half a century. He argued that his own generation had jumped at the idea that evolution must be synonymous with elevation, that they had proved to be exactly wrong, that the second law of thermodynamics was

in fact the one inclusive concept and degradation the one
necessary term for what instinctively hopeful men had wanted
to call progress. To escape his argument would require intellectual subtlety as well as moral vigor.

Adams' counterattack on Victorian optimism was somewhat
of a period piece in 1910. What dated the book was its logic
rather than its subject. Adams chose to undermine the naïve
idea of progress, not by criticizing its premises, but by accepting them. He preferred to turn the attitudes of popular
Darwinism upside down, even if Samson-like he brought the
whole structure down on his own head. Still loyal to the
generation of which he was a part, he valued the contribution
of Darwin toward an intellectual synthesis even though he
accepted none of the sanguine inferences his contemporaries
had drawn. His early review of Lyell's *Geology* had led him to
doubt, on scientific grounds, that evolution provided a basis
for regarding all the past as a single uniform upward progress,
but early and late he liked the idea of using science as a sanc-
tion for historical generalization. What Darwin meant to him
was distinct from the clichés of popular Darwinism and even
from the "personal" theories of Darwin himself, "which might
be all abandoned without affecting his credit for bringing
all vital processes under the law of development or evolution,
— whether upward or downward being immaterial to the
principle that all history must be studied as a science." Having begun his historical career with a study of John Smith and
Pocahontas and pursued it as an alternative to really handling
power, he had always had an educated doubt, a lurking fear
that history might come down to mere antiquarianism. To
find a general significance beyond the interest of the discreet
item of knowledge was the only possible safeguard. He now
asserted that for the first time since the Church had lost its
authority and "the historian's field had shrunk into narrow
limits of rigorously human action," post-Darwinian science

was making large generalizations available to the student of human affairs. If the "lugubrious plan" of the degradationist theory should seem too strong a medicine, the historian had "only to hold his tongue, and remain quietly in the pleasant meadows of antiquarianism, protected as heretofore by the convenient and sufficient axiom of the nineteenth century that history is not a science, and society not an organism; but if this resource should fail him, his first thought will be to find allies." Clearly, Adams had at last decided not to hold his tongue, but to look for allies in the one institutional group he had most seriously committed himself to. He appealed to the members of the American Historical Association to become not just metaphorically, but literally, a guild — a communal organization with a clear-cut function in society and a concerted dedication to knowing its place in a world larger than the merely human. As in a medieval cathedral, the humble crafts as well as the powers of this world could help to build a great, organic edifice. The conception of a unified science might be the clue to a modern synthesis. Or, as he put it with ironic modesty and deliberate obscurity, he wrote the *Letter* to ask American teachers of history what they were going to do about socialism.

Although Adams turned from the path of silence, he talked with a rhetoric of concealment and swamped his point in a mass of long quotations drawn from his wide reading in the sciences. What he tried to hide thus was the fact that the appeal for a community of scholars touched a tender nerve deep inside him. Ever since his Civil War experience of the clearly articulated society of England, in which he could see where a man stood and even where he himself might have found a place, he had keenly felt the lack of community which is an aspect of American individualism. In youth he had projected a "school" of reformers for America, a close-knit band of intellectuals who turned out later to be the Independents who were mostly independent of each other. His first professional efforts went into the collaborative volume on Anglo-Saxon law, where the absence of his name from the cover signified his participation in a group, not his seclusion from the public. During the intensely relished years of marriage and fruitful work in history, he enjoyed his place in the intimacy of "The Five of Hearts," in the larger world of Washington social life, and in the literary comradeship of Hay the biographer of Lincoln. In age, he meant it seriously when he submitted his memoirs for correction on the premise that history should be a work among workers. In his devious way, the old Henry Adams expressed the same social impulse in both the *Education* and the *Letter*. For all his splendid aggregation of nieces, he still thought of his ideal reader as a "son in wishes." Like his friend Justice Holmes with his succession of law clerks and his brother Brooks with his constant search for a new model administrator — both of them childless like himself — Adams hoped to see his work carried on. But not expecting that his plea would get an answer, he tried to sound as though he had never uttered it at all.

The teacher who would affect eternity hid himself behind the scholar who reported on the accumulating arguments that seemed to make degradation of energy the theoretical link between the mechanical and the vital sciences. Although he claimed not to take sides, his massed evidence in support of the thesis could have only one meaning. Even if the theory were true, the *Letter* could be said to weaken its chance for reasoned consideration. For, as William Jordy has shown, Adams' so-called report depended on biased selection, fallacious interpretation, and semantic ambiguity. Had he cared less for his rhetoric, he might have cleaned out most of the defects of his amateur scientism, but he willfully chose to appall his audience rather than persuade them. Where his "Rule of Phase" suggested a working hypothesis, his *Letter* insisted on inexorable and fearful law. Occasionally, his wit broke the momentum of his gloomy rhetoric. He dryly summed things up by saying that "man and beast can, at the best, look forward only to a diversified agony of twenty million years"; he reiterated his old moral that for man, who stood "convicted" of being a Vertebrate, a Mammal, a Monodelphe, and a Primate, there was no escape from the law of entropy "except through the loophole called Mind." Despite such reassertions of the brilliant fabulist, however, he mostly performed as the preacher of doom and expressed the despair which he had predicted must set in if the evils of the nineteenth century were to be continued and exaggerated in the twentieth.

If Adams didn't quite believe in his apocalyptic sermon, so much the worse. In private, he referred to the *Letter* as "about a hundred pages of no consequence, announcing the end of the Universe, as predicted by your friend Lord Kelvin"; but just to the extent that he made the work a practical joke, designed to worry universities and irritate professors, he confused the issues which he took most seriously. The old hell-fire preachers had used their catastrophic rhetoric for the purpose of converting those who would give heed, whereas even the best-intentioned readers of the *Letter* are forced to ask, Conversion to what? To deterministic science or vitalistic thought? To university reform or cowed silence? To co-operative effort or disillusion with democracy? And one feels that Adams would only have answered with the counter-question, Conversion of whom? He sent out several hundred copies of the *Letter* and, aside from those with whom he was already in correspondence, drew from the recipients hardly a score of replies, all of them polite, whether in gratitude or disagreement, but none of them quite what he was after. The response he most appreciated came from a member of his own generation. William James, almost at his dying breath, summoned all his youthful intellectual vigor to denounce the book. "To tell the truth," James wrote, "it doesn't impress me at all, save by its wit and erudition; and I ask you whether an old man soon about to meet his Maker can hope to save himself from the consequences of his life by pointing to the wit and learning he has shown in treating a tragic subject." Perhaps both James and Adams recognized that this was a paraphrase of the crucial sentence of the *Education* in which the old man refused to meet his maker without performing an act of intellectual responsibility as his final homage. The philosopher went on to criticize in detail both scientific and metaphysical fallacies, such as the inference that diminished energy could not do work effectively and the assumption that matters of value could be discussed in terms of measurable physical units. The historian, though he neither denied nor admitted his mistakes, accepted the criticism and shifted the question: "I calculated, on my data, that out of five hundred readers, I should get five reactions. I have got one; and he is almost my oldest teacher! 'Tis something; nay, 'tis much! but I must reform my statistics." He could maintain his elaborate joke only by recognizing how it turned upon himself.

Not only Adams' joke, but his despair turned inward. Technically, the *Letter* left it open whether the final stage of social development would be a utopia or a permanent twilight. With all its reckonings of disaster, there was only one catastrophe it announced as certain: "Between two equilibriums, each mechanical, and each insisting that history is at an end, lost forever in the ocean of statistics, the classical University teacher of history, with his intuitions of free-will and art, can exist only as a sporadic survival to illustrate for his colleagues the workings of their second law of thermodynamics." Like the *Education*, the *Letter* ended by killing off the projection of Henry Adams. As in the earlier work, the implicit suicide of the imagination contained an ambiguous and antagonizing note of pride. The figurative victim of his argument, Adams seemed to be the literal victim of his rhetoric as well. In the act of writing, he persuaded himself that society had entered the vast ocean of equipotential where there were neither distinctions of value nor vital relations among the infinity of separate particles that made up the mass. He began to echo "We are *there!*" as the insistent refrain of his letters. He tended to abandon rational criticism and noted the leveling-down processes of society in the language of snobbery — and worse: "I can't go out of my cheap garret here in Paris, for an hour, without being throttled by some infernal socialist, levelling, humanitarian regulation which is intended to kill me and keep some syphilitic abortion alive." The sense of personal affront reached its climax when he was rudely frisked and spiritually manhandled by customs agents on the New York docks. Given this fresh, though hardly unique, symbol for ascendant bureaucracy and degraded institutions, he let private outrage become his substitute for moral indignation. He cried out once more his revulsion at America and the age, vented some of his anxieties in a resurgence of antisemitic feeling, suffered without relief the grim nightly vigils of insomnia. Whatever had happened to society, he himself had entered, as in the nineties, the terrible backwash that followed a period of sustained solitary labor. The biographical incident provides a clue to the psychological environment in which the *Letter* was composed.

The most obscure and perhaps the most important side of Henry Adams in such a time was his desperate loneliness. He felt as a human being the isolation he expressed as a writer in his compulsive need and rejection of an audience. The *Letter*, his last attempt to seek intellectual allies, was predestined by its author to fail, but the statistics of negative response do not tell the whole story. The self-doomed effort of despair was set in perspective by the continuing effects of a labor of love, for the *Chartres* still existed with the power to reach the unknown reader whom Adams so badly wanted. Along with the sourest letters he ever wrote came the extremely cordial beginnings of his correspondence with two Yale medievalists who discovered, read, and thanked him for his earlier book. To one of them, Adams conveyed his gratitude with the humble pathos and involuted complexity of Proust's maiden aunts. Commenting on how few students could be expected to grasp medieval art, he said, "Indeed I sometimes think the Yale man is really more impressionable than the Harvard man, both as teacher and student. My own experience lies decidedly that way." Despite his self-conscious indirections, he showed himself still capable of simple sweetness; he enclosed with his letter a photograph of his favorite church at Mantes as an illustration to go with his book: "Perhaps it will help some of your students to begin to feel what we are driving at. One must live with these things to love them." To his other Yale correspondent, he offered the best rationale he ever made for the role he chose to play. Describing himself as "a normal-school instructor — a teacher of teachers," he explained his books since 1890 as a series of private suggestions to those still active in the classroom, suggestions that could be taken up by the few who felt their point:

> My idea is that the world outside — the so-called modern world — can only pervert and degrade the conceptions of the primitive instinct of art and feeling, and that our only chance is to accept the limited number of survivors — the one-in-a-thousand of born artists and poets — and to intensify the energy of feeling within that radiant centre. In other words, I am a creature of our poor old Calvinistic, St. Augustinian fathers, and am not afraid to carry out my logic to the rigorous end of regarding our present society, its ideals and purposes, as dregs and fragments of some primitive, essential instinct now nearly lost. . . .

You see, therefore, why I should be not merely indifferent [to], but positively repellent of, a popular following. It means to me a crowd of summer-tourists, vulgarizing every thought known to artists. In act, it is the Oberammergau Passion-play as now run for Cook's tourists.

It is hard to deny that art in our modern mass society has become an esoteric pursuit, but it is even harder to apply the argument to any given set of facts. Adams' affair with the New York Customs was but a crude instance of the classic difficulty: How to distinguish travelers from vulgar tourists? How to identify the saving remnant? Adams had full cause to know that the radiant center could not be defined as either of the groups to which he himself belonged, the upper middle class or the historical profession. Nevertheless, he gradually let these two groups stand for all and came to regard the dimensions of his shrinking personal world as the universal boundaries of art. Out of the double sifting — biographical accident as well as social process — survivors necessarily seemed to be far fewer than they actually were. When his contemporaries died off without being replaced *for him*, he assumed too easily that society also had no replacements. The list which included Richardson, Saint-Gaudens, La Farge, King, Hay, and the Jameses suggests how little Adams had been isolated from artists and intellectuals, how much vitality the American upper middle class had had in his generation. That the friend of Richardson was blind to Louis Sullivan and the friend of La Farge impervious to Cézanne was merely Adams' limitation, so long as Richardson and La Farge were making positive contributions to what he could see; but dead, they were a total loss to him. Given the limitation of a narrowing circle, his best hope for the next generation lay with George Cabot Lodge, the junior partner of his Conservative Christian Anarchism — a brilliant conversationalist, apparently, an accomplished linguist, and a dedicated writer of poetry. When

Lodge suddenly died in 1909, only thirty-five years old, Adams exaggerated but slightly in saying, "Bay was my last tie to active sympathy with men." As far as he was willing to see, politicians and writers, scholars and artists led solitary lives which confirmed the total disintegration of society. Apparently they could come together only through him, for one spring day of 1912 he wrote to Mrs. Cameron that he kept his house full and his table occupied "but not by men or by intellectuals." On the same day he wrote to one of the Yale correspondents he never met, that his memoir of Lodge expressed his sympathy for the teacher's lonely, unencouraged work: "There is, in our modern society, a singular want of solidarity, — a lack of purpose and direction, — which you and I are not responsible for, and cannot counteract." Although his plea for esoteric art had started by making a virtue of necessity, he now treated as absolute necessity the virtue by which the aristocratic *bourgeoisie* ought to have furnished the world with statesmen, artists, and intelligentsia. Too shrewd to be taken in by the ingenuous avant-gardism of the time, he was not quite wise enough to avoid its opposite. In *The Life of George Cabot Lodge*, he tried to establish an *arrière-garde* for literature.

In the memoir of Lodge, Adams gave his most serious attention to sketching the social conditions of art at the time of his old age and Lodge's youth. His primary contention was that "the Bostonian of 1900 differed from his parents and grandparents of 1850, in owning nothing the value of which, in the market, could be affected by the poet." Revolt itself became impossible when no one took it seriously. The rebellious artist was paralyzed by the passive unresistance of his declared enemy. Furthermore, the young poet of 1900 lacked "the combination of tradition, mental habit, association of ideas, labor of technique, criticism, instinct — that makes a school." He worked on his own, as isolated from his fellow craftsmen as from the public. He had to devise a system of self-training that would of course be slower than apprenticeship, yet he found himself compelled by the same conditions to publish prematurely, for "the artist, living in a vacuum without connection with free air, is forced by mere want of breath to cry out against the solitude that stifles him." Even so, the consequence of such an outcry, given the torpid reactions of the world at large, would tend to discouragement rather than relief. Adams wrote with the conviction that the ocean of degraded social energies had drowned Bay Lodge, and he tried to make the biography a manifesto for that thesis.

The irony of the *Lodge* rests on the fact that, despite the portentous language, the theme is much less general than that of the *Letter*. Adams was writing about Boston and not America, and to say that "society" could no longer be divided into hostile camps by intellectual issues was to use the term as equivalent to "polite society." Despite this restriction of subject, the biographer's tendency to self-projection had room to exercise itself: the heritage of Henry Adams included Boston as well as Quincy, just as Bay Lodge was the creature of Beacon Street as well as Nahant. Adams remorselessly depicted his subject as a boy whose primitive instincts germinated during summers by the sea and then found expression in verse that might have been "written after death instead of before the beginning of life." The bold outcry of Lodge's first volume proved to be, not a "violent outburst of self-assertion," not a "furious protest against the age he lived in," but a mild, diffident, and conventional statement of poetic intentions. The poet's fine-flowing Byronic garb was cut to size by expert New England tailoring:

> Love was to him a passion, and a very real one, not capable of dilution or disguise. Such passions generally have their own way, and force everything to yield. The marriage took place in Boston, August 18, 1900. True to his instinct of shrinking from

close and serious contact with the forms and conventions of a society which was to him neither a close nor a serious relation, he was married without previous notice, and without other than necessary witnesses, at the Church of the Advent. The officiating clergyman is said to have remarked that he had never seen a more beautiful wedding; but he was the only person present to appreciate its beauty.

They went off to Concord to pass the honeymoon, and thence to Tuckanuck. All the practical difficulties in their way were ignored, and remained ignored through life, without interfering with the young couple's happiness. The world is still kind to those who are young, and handsome, and in love, and who trample on respectability. Naturally, as soon as winter came, they set off for Paris.

Adams obviously knew that his book was as much a swan-song for the genteel tradition as a funeral oration for the arts, but he was unclear as to where one left off and the other began. As a result, he seemed to justify his own maxim that biographers murder their subjects. Though in private he called Lodge a genius, in the book he ventured to praise only by ambiguous innuendo. On the other hand, he had had the courage to tell his young friend that his language was his weakness, that his verse lacked poetry and his drama theatricality, but he skirted these matters in the memoir. Asserting that Lodge's tragic themes were the oldest and best resources of literature, he covered the poet's inability to exploit their dramatic strength by saying that "what he exacted from his readers was chiefly mind." As for Lodge's most ambitious work, an attempt to handle the combined myths of Herakles and Prometheus, he felt that where Euripedes had failed and Aeschylus had barely made the grade, "a critic can afford to keep silence." For Adams to say that Euripedes also failed as an artist (like Augustine in the *Confessions*) was a poor way to glorify his subject. Evasive archness disguised his perplexity without helping him get rid of it: "The better-informed and the more accomplished the critic may be, who reads 'Herakles' for the first time, knowing nothing of its author, the more disconcerted he is likely to be in reading it a second time. His first doubts of the poet's knowledge or merits will be followed by doubts of his own." These were doubts which made the mind timid rather than humble. Adams' diffidence before the task of serious criticism impels the reader to doubt the seriousness of Lodge's career. Despite his "ruthless requirement that anyone who challenges publicity, should stand up to it," Adams had good reason for being dissatisfied with this memoir of his friend. Dodging the essential issue, he incurred an unnecessary human expense: he made his book an interesting chapter of social history, but he neglected the harder job of making it seem a *Life*. The ruinous flaw of Lodge's art was to be found in the words he gave the Poet in his last play: "The animal will sing and drink and lust. . . . It is alone the spirit which is chaste." The artist was not merely isolated by society, but insulated by his particular culture; his frigidity of spirit was genuinely pathetic. "All of us must suffer," he wrote shortly before he died, "in the general human fate, and some must suffer of private wrongs. I've none such to complain of." And he went on as though he detected the chain of consequences: "You surely can't doubt that I deeply realize the value of human communion of any sort; but that does n't take me far toward getting it." But the individual was lost in what was at once a group picture and a self-portrait by the author:

> *Type bourgeois-bostonien!* A type quite as good as another, but more uniform. . . . God knows that we knew our want of knowledge! the self-distrust became introspection — nervous self-consciousness — irritable dislike of America, and antipathy to Boston. *Auch ich war in Arcadien geboren!*

Those were the words with which Adams had greeted Henry James a few years earlier on the occasion of a work against which the *Lodge* may be measured. *William Wetmore Story and His Friends* was not only an "official" biography like the memoir of Lodge, the record of a minor artist as presented by a major one, but, as its title indicates, it too was conceived as an essay on the social conditions of art. James was honoring the precursors of the liberated American in Europe where Adams memorialized a younger writer, the epigone of his own New England tradition, but the difference in subject does not really define the difference between the books. The novelist had his own terms for explaining that: "If it be the subject that makes the interest, it is the composition that makes, or at any rate expresses, the subject." He denied Adams' suggestion that the *Story* was intended to bring out the essential superficiality of its leading characters and insisted, rather, that it was the fault of the biographer if he did not "invest dull old Boston with a mellow, a golden glow." He had had not only a mediocre poet, but a pre-eminently mediocre sculptor to deal with, and he was quick to catch "drolleries" of missed ambition that were scarcely distinguishable from Adams' cosmic ironies. But where Adams saw failure, James saw good faith — the more to be respected in that Story sacrificed himself for a meager achievement rather than for an obvious great prize. Without being ungenerous, he could almost condescendingly report on a progress in the arts, whereas Adams, with dubious kindness, made Lodge the chief exhibit in his case for retrogression. There was no necessary contradiction in their facts. As Adams asserted, the personal and social difficulties which the artist had to overcome did increase greatly between 1850 and 1900, and as James pointed out, the possibilities of American culture had advanced correspondingly. At issue was a question of what James called "composition"; it was the same question Adams had defined in his *Chartres*, whether to see the death or feel the life in what the past bequeathed.

The continuing dialogue between the historian and the novelist provides a clear perspective on the later Adams, since Henry James kept to the end a fine balance of affection and judgment. James's discreet refusal to overrate his friend's travel sketches and, a decade later, his steadiness in the face of Adams' witty misinterpretation of the *Story* made all the more valuable his unreserved praise for the *Chartres* and the *Education*. Despite his touching letter of sympathy on the death of George Lodge, which made his silence the more evident, he apparently made no comment on the memoir which followed after a couple of years. But he still felt the life in his old friend and rose to the occasion of Adams' stroke in 1912 with the testimony of discerning love. "In these great stresses," he wrote, "friendship reaches out to the making of an image of the friend who has suffered assault — & I make one of you thus according to my sense of your rich & ingenious mind & your great resources of contemplation, speculation, resignation — a curiosity in which serenity is yet at home." Two more years passed before the novelist's autobiography prompted Adams to write in the old vein. When Adams lamented the dreamy, stuffy unreality of the New England past and went so far as to pity the isolated, unhonored old age of the writer, James replied with a declaration of what the will to life could still accomplish. His profession of artistic faith was all the stronger in that he accepted Adams' statement on the deadness of the past and insisted that Adams, despite himself, showed how the waste could be transcended:

> My dear Henry,
>   I have your melancholy outpouring of the 7th, and I know not how better to acknowledge it than by the full recognition of its unmitigated blackness. *Of course* we are lone survivors, of course

the past that was our lives is at the bottom of an abyss — if the abyss *has* any bottom; of course, too, there's no use talking unless one particularly *wants* to. But the purpose, almost, of my printed divagations was to show you that one *can*, strange to say, still want to — or at least can behave as if one did. Behold me therefore so behaving — and apparently capable of continuing to do so. I still find my consciousness interesting — under *cultivation* of the interest. . . . *Why* mine yields an interest I don't know that I can tell you, but I don't challenge or quarrel with it — I encourage it with a ghastly grin. You see I still, in the presence of life (or of what you deny to be such,) have reactions — as many as possible — and the book I sent you is a proof of them. It's, I suppose, because I am that queer monster, the artist, an obstinate finality, an inexhaustible sensibility. Hence the reactions — appearances, memories, many things, go on playing upon it with consequences that I note and "enjoy" (grim word!) noting. It all takes doing — and I *do*. I believe I shall do yet again — it is still an act of life. But you perform them still yourself — and I don't know what keeps me from calling your letter a charming one! There we are, and it's a blessing that you understand — I admit indeed alone — your all-faithful

HENRY JAMES

Adams had too few surviving friends like William and Henry James who stood up to him on behalf of his better self. It was perhaps a necessary condition that they be friends at a distance. Oliver Wendell Holmes, who liked Adams both for his distinction of mind and his great kindness of heart, explained the difficulties of living near at hand: "When I happened to fall in with him on the street he could be delightful, but when I called at his house and he was posing to himself as the old cardinal he would turn everything to dust and ashes. After a tiresome day's work one didn't care to have one's powers of resistance taxed by discourse of that sort, so I called rarely." For those with lesser powers of resistance, the cost of friendship came high. When George Cabot Lodge uttered his second-hand convictions on the degradation of modern society, the failure of the American man, or the need for art to be bad in order to succeed, the Adamsish phrases make the older man seem to have been a corrupter of youth. If there was to have been a school of Henry Adams, it died out because the chief pupil was overwhelmed by the teacher. A weak poet embalms the influences which shape his work; it takes a strong one to keep a tradition alive. How much so may be seen in the case of T. S. Eliot, who, even in his first volume, *Prufrock*, gave a far more vital extension to Adams' achievement than Lodge ever did. When the *Education* was finally published and Eliot reviewed it, he neither acknowledged debts nor made obeisance. Instead, he exorcised that side of Henry Adams which is the dominant projection of the Lodge memoir. He mocked the advantages of a pedigree that made Henry James seem "comparatively parvenu," denounced the Bostonian scepticism which was not destructive but dissolvent, and refashioned Arnold's dry lament for Shelley by speaking of an Adams "with the wings of a beautiful but ineffectual conscience beating vainly in a vacuum jar." Everything that Adams suggested of Lodge, Eliot said outright of Adams himself. He listed the weaknesses in relentless order: the quest for education (*vulgo*, culture in general) that left Adams as he was born, "well-bred, intelligent, and uneducated"; unawareness that education "is a by-product of being interested, passionately absorbed"; "extreme sensitiveness to all the suggestions that dampen enthusiasm or dispel conviction"; an emotional immaturity and a distended intellectuality that cut the mind off from the senses. Against the figure of Henry Adams which he was drawing, Eliot declared for Henry James and "the sensuous contributor to intelligence that makes the difference." Out of his resistance to Henry Adams, the creator of Gerontion and Tiresias was able to "use" the author of the *Education* to make poetry. As Adams himself had guessed, oversensitive and overtimid natures that could not regard the world without a shudder had to be rejected. Dust and ashes had to be buried before new life could come.

The crucial resistance to the morbidity of Adams' last years had to come from the man himself, and it did. He could never altogether cancel his interested awareness of what was going on in the arts and the sciences, so that he was constantly committing himself to life even though he felt himself ready for death. Having run out of copies of his *Chartres* to give away, he worked at correcting and retouching the volume for a second private edition. He looked around vainly for a young historian to tackle the current anthropology as he had once gone in for geologizing. For his own part, he could at least contribute indirectly to expanding the historical horizon: he helped finance the excavations of Henri Hubert and the hunt for Cro-Magnon remains in the caves of Dordogne. Reprinting the *Chartres* in 1912 was the last work he ever meant to do, but he reserved the right to play among the *chansons de geste* and began informing himself expertly on the newest problems of medieval literary history. In his will to assist at the accouchement of a 30,000-year-old baby and the solution of obscure problems in philology, he kept up a lively pursuit of science and art. He indulged his social instincts, too, enjoying the position of mild dignity at which he had arrived and the role of wise old man which he was expected to play. The social and the intellectual man, however, could not quite face down the student of power who dwelt obsessively in a world that seemed to mock the very notion of dignity or mildness. The bull-moose rampage of his friend Roosevelt struck him as the final blow to an already disrupted Taft regime, the last word on the subject of politics. The technological symbol was far more appalling than the political fact: as determined as ever to be in the front ranks of progress, he had bought passage for the return voyage of the *Titanic*, so that the great disaster struck him as a personal blow. He could not get "Taft, *Titanic*! *Titanic*, Taft!" out of his mind, for "only in history as a fairy-tale, does one like to see civilisations founder, and to hear the cries of the drowning." The collapse of our mechanical triumphs seemed to have been translated from the *Education* into a terrifying nightmare that was real. Ten days after the *Titanic* went down, on April 24, 1912, Adams suffered a stroke. During the slow and painful recovery, in which he fought against the threat of mental as well as physical crippling, he ventured the amateur diagnosis that it was the shock of the great steamship accident that had struck him down. What mattered more than the diagnosis was that after the climax of external events which he took as aimed personally at himself, he curbed his human tendency to project his ego on the world. Conceiving the reality outside as independent of himself, he won his own independence from the dominion of accident to which he had so dangerously submitted. Like the Bohemian journalist of the sixties, the reformer-professor of the seventies, the gentleman of letters, the fate-ridden traveler, and the secret artist at the center of the web, he arrived once more — and for the last time — at an individuality in which he could know himself and be content.

Actually to have come close to death reminded Adams of his true subjection to external things. Thereafter, his querulousness tended to subside and his sense of humor to revive. He picked up the vital threads with an equanimity that astonished him. The first day he was permitted to dictate letters, he resumed with Professor Raymond Weeks of Columbia his discussion of the *Chansons*. Adams, who had expressed surprise that we could "have a Romanist of that force in America without my knowing it," found in Weeks another younger scholar who drew his loyalty beyond the limits of his social circle. Obliged now to give up his own plan of tracing the poems of Catalonia and the Spanish March to Charlemagne's empire, he brought up the question of helping Weeks to get there. "I can imagine your difficulties," he said with noble tact, "because they are mostly those of my professorial friends in general." In an age when the giants of acquisitiveness were rifling Europe for their great collections, Adams became a patron of the arts for motives peculiarly his own. He explained his offer to Weeks as a matter of patriotic and professional pride, a chance for *American scholarship* to win a great triumph. Not that he did not become a collector, but he collected for individual motives, too. When Miss Aileen Tone became, not the companion of his invalidism, but the niece-in-residence of his household, she sang for him some Old French music which he did not know had survived. The lure of finding more music to the twelfth-century poetry he loved made him resolve to keep the old route for his spring migrations and go again to France. "I am not made for Boston, Mass.," he deliberately pronounced, "and would rather go to heaven another way." From a flat in Paris and then a rented château in the country, he supervised the research of his nieces and the two professional musicologists he kept on retainer. As the harvest of manuscript scores came in, Henry Adams listened with the happy fullness of sense that he had felt a few years before in his avid search for twelfth-century glass. He had finally by-passed Boston, and his other way was bright with music.

At seventy-five, Adams achieved his final role, by which he was enabled to endure in actual life the chaos he had foreseen in imagination. In the spring of 1914, he spoke in his own person what he had written in the *Education*: "The life is that of the fourth century, without St. Augustine." Convinced, all too rightly at last, that an end was approaching, he went ahead to take another apartment and another château and pressed his search for medieval songs. When the war in fact came, he shepherded his nieces through a series of last trains and last boats to Paris, Dieppe, England, and home. Staggered, not by his own discomforts and dangers but by the terrible event, he found that the resources of imagination were his chief refuge: "Throughout all the terrors and roars of German howitzers, we have lived on 'Seigneurs Sachez' and 'A vous amoants,' in France and England as here, and they alone have given us repose. Reims fell, but Thibaut rose." When the first Christmas of the war came round, with the world "just howling with peace and good will among men," he dryly noted: "I don't think we can stand much more. At least, Saint Augustine can't." For himself, he stood some three years more, listening to Thibaut of Chartres and the Châtelain of Coucy, helping friends who helped the war, resisting the failure of eyes and the decrepitude of age, mourning his own dead and living his own life. It remained true to the end that summer let him retreat from the order and disorder of the public world and view its events in the perspective of nature. Kept from revisiting the Ile de France, he settled for a hilltop in New Hampshire. Then, the following year, he took an immense and splendid house in the Massachusetts Berkshires, "the swellest house and the most guests I ever did have." Indulgence in life was his affirmation against the fact that life was failing. He lived more and more freely with his memories of the seventies and at last, in the summer of 1917, he was ready not only to endure the present, but to face the past. He returned to Beverly Farms, as he wrote Gaskell, "to the house which I built in 1876 and left in 1885, thinking that nothing on earth would ever bring me back."

From the tranquil center of his being, Adams could look on chaos without fear. He could even look for hope in the midst of destruction: America's entry into the war was for him the bewildering fulfillment of his one great object, the making of an Atlantic community. He concerned himself not with the prospect of military victory but with the constructive precedent. "Behind all the killing," he wrote, "comes the great question of what our civilization is to do next." When he went back to Washington, to the house he had built for Marian Adams and into which she had never moved, it was for the last time, but he was secure in the qualities that had furnished strength to his history and art and had proved to be his most enduring traits. One of those traits, inexplicably connected with his love for ancient music and colored glass, was the pugnacious irony which his last letter to his oldest friend, Gaskell, fittingly records:

> ... Your British aëroplanes are sailing up and down under my windows at all hours, as though I were myself a master of Aëroplane Horse in a new universe of winged bipeds. It is only twenty years since my friend, Professor Langley, at my table, talked about all these things as dreams of the future, and we're already wishing to heaven that they had remained dreams of the past. I am in a new society and a new world which is more wild and madder by far than the old one, and yet I seem to myself to be a part of it, and even almost to take share in it. I speculate on what is to happen as actively as I did at your table fifty years ago, and the only difference is that I terribly miss your father's conversation and his dry champagne. I no longer indulge in champagne or anything else, but I still look on at the British Secretaries of Legation enjoying their Pommery brut, even though we ordinary people in Washington are no longer permitted to have it. The world is improved! We kill each other by the hundred thousand, without remorse, but we are denied our dry champagne. ... Perhaps our next letters will grow more cheerful with the improvement of the world.

The long life which began under the shadow of the Boston State House was ended in Washington just across La Fayette Square from the White House. Henry Adams died quietly in his sleep sometime near dawn on March 27, 1918. To those who knew him he left the memory of the private man, and to the world at large he bequeathed what he had written. As passive as the figure in Rock Creek Cemetery beneath which he is buried, he offers "the consciousness that he and his people had a past, if they dared but avow it, and might have a future, if they could but divine it."

REFERENCES

References

THIS LIST of references uses the following abbreviations:

BA Brooks Adams   CFAjr Charles Francis Adams, Jr.
CFA Charles Francis Adams   HA Henry Adams

Cater Harold Dean Cater, comp. and author of biographical introduction, *Henry Adams and His Friends: A Collection of Hitherto Unpublished Letters* (Boston, 1947).

Chartres Henry Adams, *Mont-Saint-Michel and Chartres* (Boston and New York, 1933).

Cycle Worthington C. Ford, ed., *A Cycle of Adams Letters, 1861–1865* (2 vols., Boston and New York, 1920).

Degradation Henry Adams, *The Degradation of the Democratic Dogma* (New York, 1919). This includes "The Heritage of Henry Adams" by Brooks Adams and reprints Adams' presidential letter to the American Historical Association, "The Tendency of History" (1894), and *A Letter to American Teachers of History* (1910); it also includes first publication of "The Rule of Phase Applied to History" (1909).

Democracy Henry Adams, *Democracy: An American Novel* (New York, 1880).

Education Henry Adams, *The Education of Henry Adams: An Autobiography* (Boston and New York, 1918).

Esther Henry Adams (Frances Snow Compton, pseud.), *Esther: A Novel* (New York, 1884).

Ford Worthington C. Ford, ed., *Letters of Henry Adams*, Vol. I, 1858–1891, Vol. II, 1892–1918 (Boston and New York, 1930–38).

Gallatin Henry Adams, *The Life of Albert Gallatin* (Philadelphia and London, 1879).

History Henry Adams, *History of the United States of America during the Administrations of Thomas Jefferson and James Madison* (9 vols., New York, 1889–91).

Houghton   The Houghton Library at Harvard University.

Lodge   Henry Adams, *The Life of George Cabot Lodge* (Boston and New York, 1911).

MHS   The Library of the Massachusetts Historical Society.

Prayer   Henry Adams, *Letters to a Niece and Prayer to the Virgin of Chartres, with A Niece's Memories* by Mabel La Farge (Boston and New York, 1920).

Randolph   Henry Adams, *John Randolph* (Boston, 1882).

With standard books currently available in several editions, citation is made to the chapter rather than to the page of a particular edition.

Fuller bibliographical listings are to be found in: Ernest Samuels, *The Young Henry Adams* (Cambridge, Mass., 1948); Max I. Baym, *The French Education of Henry Adams* (New York, 1951); and William H. Jordy, *Henry Adams: Scientific Historian* (New Haven, 1952).

Chapter I
THE MAKING OF AN HISTORIAN

Page

1   "all I want." HA to Charles Milnes Gaskell, Jan. 29, 1882. Ford, I, 333.

2   "wrongly called 'An Autobiography.' " See page 306.

"to the railways." *Education*, p. 240.

"was change." *Education*, p. 230.

"build Chartres." *Education*, p. 388.

"passionate depravity." *Education*, p. 268.

3   "comparison with Gibbon's." Mr. Yvor Winters, to the best of my knowledge, is the first person to have insisted strongly on so high a valuation; see *The Anatomy of Nonsense* (Norfolk, Conn., 1943), pp. 68 ff.

"revive the dead." Thomas North, tr., *Plutarch's Lives*, "To the Reader."

6   "tapestry, and porcelain." CFA, ed., *Familiar Letters of John Adams and His Wife Abigail Adams* (New York, 1876), p. 381.

7   "but I failed in that." CFAjr, to HA, March 22, 1863. *Cycle*, I, 266.

"once lay beyond it." HA to CFAjr, May 1, 1863. *Cycle*, I, 278–79.

"must be my ladder." HA to CFAjr, Jan. 18, 1859. Ford, I, 13.

"call of public service." Samuel Flagg Bemis, *John Quincy Adams and the Foundations of American Foreign Policy* (New York, 1949), p. 14.

9   "of scale." *Education*, p. 6.

"the Washington of Italy." *Boston Courier*, July 10, 1860; reprinted in the *American Historical Review*, XXV (1919), 246.

11   "to the best uses." CFA to CFAjr, July 4, 1862. *Cycle*, I, 162.

13   "that we feel here." HA to CFAjr, July 4, 1862. *Cycle*, I, 163.

"the sensation was glorious." CFAjr to CFA, June 18, 1862. *Cycle*, I, 156.

"an old Betty." CFAjr to CFA, Feb. 28, 1862. *Cycle*, I, 117.

"in action, I suppose." HA to CFAjr, Feb. 14, 1862. *Cycle*, I, 113.

"perfectly fallow." CFAjr to CFA, Feb. 28, 1862. *Cycle*, I, 117.

14   "in the lurch." HA to CFAjr, Sept. 7, 1861. *Cycle*, I, 40.

"pugnacity that tells." HA to CFAjr, March 15, 1862. *Cycle*, I, 122.

"that they've raised." HA to CFAjr, April 11, 1862. *Cycle*, I, 133–34.

"no dealing with it." HA to CFAjr, May 8, 1862. *Cycle*, I, 140.

"of a drunken man." HA to CFAjr, May 16, 1862. *Cycle*, I, 146.

15   "tired of this life." HA to CFAjr, Dec. 28, 1861. *Cycle*, I, 93.

15n. "helpful encouragement." HA to CFAjr, Nov. 23, 1859, and March 26, 1860. Ford, I, 52, 57.

"it will do you good." CFAjr to HA, Jan. [?], 1862. *Cycle*, I, 102–3.

16   "an ideal cure." CFAjr to HA, Jan. 23, 1863. *Cycle*, I, 240.

"heal thyself." HA to CFAjr, Nov. 23, 1859. Ford, I, 51.

"keep it to yourself." CFAjr to HA, Jan. [?], 1862. *Cycle*, I, 103.

17   "a social animal." HA to CFAjr, Nov. 13, 1863. Ford, I, 111.

"the heavy society." HA to CFAjr, June 10, 1861. Ford, I, 92.

"radicals of England." HA to CFAjr, March 20, 1863. Ford, I, 97.

"invitation." HA to Henry Lee Higginson, Sept. 10, 1863. Ford, I, 110.

17n. "carrion—patronage." *Education*, p. 110.

18   "for all of me." HA to CFAjr, Dec. 18, 1863. Ford, I, 113.

"on the circle." HA to CFAjr, May 1, 1863. *Cycle*, I, 281–82.

"this last year." HA to CFAjr, July 23, 1863. *Cycle*, II, 62.

"high priests." HA to CFAjr, May 1, 1863. *Cycle*, I, 281.

19   "ablest man in England." HA to CFAjr, Feb. 13, 1863. *Cycle*, I, 253.

"model as well as a teacher." HA to CFAjr, May 1, 1863. *Cycle*, I, 282.

20   "full-grown statesman." CFA to CFAjr, Nov. 8, 1861. *Cycle*, I, 67.

21   "sin of family pride." *Democracy*, pp. 46–47.

"task of editing them." HA to CFAjr, March 13, 1859. Ford, I, 24.

22   "the cub." *Randolph*, p. 26.

"systematic way." How completely these phrases of his father's about John Quincy Adams (CFA to CFAjr, Nov. 8, 1861, cited above) apply to HA on Gallatin will be seen in Chapter II below.

23   "purest society in Europe." *Gallatin*, pp. 4–5.

25   "by the vulgar." HA to CFAjr, Oct. 23, 1863. *Cycle*, II, 95.

"of it all." HA to CFAjr, Oct. 2, 1863. *Cycle*, II, 90.

"world in general." HA to CFAjr, Sept. 5, 1862. *Cycle*, I, 183.

"experimento-philosophico-historico-progressiveness." HA to CFAjr, Oct. 2, 1863. *Cycle*, II, 90.

"one man and another." HA to CFAjr, Oct. 30, 1863. *Cycle*, II, 96–97.

26   "next best thing." *Education*, p. 225.

27 "ordained and executed." John Adams, *Discourses on Davila*, in CFA, ed., *The Works of John Adams . . . with a Life of the Author* (10 vols., Boston, 1850–56), VI, 395.

28 "a literary life." "Class Book of 1858," Harvard University Archives; reprinted in the *New England Quarterly*, XIV (1941), 684.

"their literary world." HA to CFAjr, Jan. 18, 1859. Ford, I, 13.

"*North American Review*." "Captain John Smith," CIV (1867), 1–30; "British Finance in 1816," CIV (1867), 354–86; "The Bank of England Restriction," CV (1867), 393–434; "Sir Charles Lyell's *Principles of Geology*," CVII (1868), 465–501.

29 "If not, why—so!" HA to CFAjr, Nov. 16, 1867. Ford, I, 136.

30 "for one's good." HA to Gaskell, Jan. 13, 1870. Ford, I, 177.

"like each other." HA to CFAjr, May 21, 1869. Ford, I, 160.

"course in writing." The bibliography of Adams' professional journalism is to be found in Ernest Samuels, *The Young Henry Adams* (Cambridge, Mass., 1948), pp. 317 ff. Adams reprinted some of the pieces in his *Historical Essays* (New York, 1891).

31 "do it well." HA to CFAjr, Jan. 22, 1869. Ford, I, 150.

"with a Dunciad." HA to Gaskell, Dec. 13, 1869. Ford, I, 176.

"latter-day Cleon." HA to Gaskell, March 7, 1870. Ford, I, 181.

"to firm ground." HA to CFAjr, Jan. 18, 1869. Ford, I, 149.

"our young men." HA to CFAjr, Nov. 13, 1863. Ford, I, 111.

32 "nerves are upset." HA to Gaskell, Nov. 23, 1869. Ford, I, 171.

" 'Bohemian' life." HA to Gaskell, Aug. 27, 1869. Ford, I, 166.

33 "and literary success." HA to Gaskell, May 17, 1869. Ford, I, 159.

"amusement of fighting." HA to Gaskell, March 28, 1870. Ford, I, 184.

"to bear." *Education*, p. 287.

34 "his father interposed." *Education*, p. 293.

"poor fallen one!" HA to Gaskell, Dec. 19, 1870. Ford, I, 199–200.

35 "at twenty-five." HA to Gaskell, Jan. 29, 1882. Ford, I, 333.

Chapter II
INTERPRETIVE SCHOLARSHIP

Page

40 "community of law." Edward A. Freeman, "An Introduction to American Institutional History," *Johns Hopkins University Studies in Historical and Political Science*, I (1882), 13.

41 "law of England?" Revised text; *Historical Essays* (New York, 1891), pp. 15–16. The lecture was delivered at the Lowell Institute on Dec. 9, 1876.

43 "of northern Germany." *Essays in Anglo-Saxon Law* (Boston, 1876) p. 1.

44 "form of transition." *Anglo-Saxon Law*, p. 4.

45 "difficulties of distance." *Anglo-Saxon Law*, p. 4.

46   "of the tenth." *Anglo-Saxon Law*, p. 19.

     "democratic starting-point." *Anglo-Saxon Law*, p. 22.

47   "the public wants." *Anglo-Saxon Law*, p. 25.

     "contradiction in terms." *History*, I, 116.

49   "and in France." *Anglo-Saxon Law*, p. 36.

     "circumstantial evidence." *Anglo-Saxon Law*, pp. 38 ff.

50   "took its place." *Anglo-Saxon Law*, p. 54.

     "EXPLICUIT SOCNAM." *Education*, p. 368.

51   "progressive lawgiver." *Anglo-Saxon Law*, p. 46.

53   "Jeffersonian point of view." HA to Charles W. Eliot, March 2, 1877. Cater, pp. 80–81.

     "or demagogic." Boston *Courier*, July 10, 1860; reprinted in the *American Historical Review*, XXV (1920), 247.

54   "to use one's mind." Henry Cabot Lodge, *Early Memories* (New York, 1913), p. 187.

55   "mission to close." HA to Lodge, June 2, 1872. Ford, I, 228.

56   "better-defined instruments." HA to Lodge, June 11, 1873. Ford, I, 253–54.

57   "fatal blunder." Lodge, *Life and Letters of George Cabot* (Boston, 1877), p. 475.

     "to withhold." *Documents*, p. v.

58   "family's private papers." The best concise history of this document is "Appendix I" of Samuel Flagg Bemis, *John Quincy Adams and the Foundations of American Foreign Policy* (New York, 1949). Professor Bemis points out the likelihood that Henry Adams did not know about another, briefer, and more persuasive account by John Quincy Adams of American party history, written later in 1829.

59   "long-expected 'crisis.'" *Nation*, XXV (1877), 13.

60   "was treason." *Nation*, XXV (1877), 13.

     "'plan' of secession." *Nation*, XXVI (1878), 11.

61   "L'univers t'abandonne." *Documents*, p. vi.

     "hereditary enmities." *Documents*, p. 331n.

     "universities and elsewhere." *Documents*, p. viii.

     "which is Democracy." Alexander Hamilton to Theodore Sedgwick, July 10, 1804. *Documents*, p. 365.

62   "best acquainted." HA to Charles William Eliot, March 2, 1877. Cater, p. 80.

     "drive him away." HA to Charles Milnes Gaskell, Sept. 8, 1876. Ford, I, 300.

62n. "not unnatural." *North American Review*, CXXIII (1876), 426.

     "cut loose." HA to Gaskell, Nov. 25, 1877. Ford, I, 302.

63   "Western engineers." Arnold J. Toynbee, *A Study of History* (2nd ed., London, 1935), I, 3–4.

64   "than finance." *Gallatin*, p. 399.

65   "to somebody." HA to Lodge, Aug. 31, 1879. Ford, I, 313.

66 "the 'scientific' historians." Donald E. Emerson, "Hildreth, Draper, and 'Scientific History,' " in Eric Goldman, ed., *Historiography and Urbanization: Essays in American History in Honor of W. Stull Holt* (Baltimore, 1941), pp. 139–70. The distinction between "the search for facts alone" and the "belief that there were historical laws or generalizations which could be formulated," applied intensively by Mr. Emerson, comes from W. Stull Holt, "The Idea of Scientific History in America," *Journal of the History of Ideas*, I (1940), 356–57.

67 "practical statesmanship." *Gallatin*, p. 268.
"business in hand." *Gallatin*, p. 172.
"sense of responsibility." *Gallatin*, pp. 180–81.

68 "American experience." *Gallatin*, pp. 154–55.

69 "the party 'machines.' " *North American Review*, CXXIII (1876), 429.
"in American politics." *Gallatin*, p. 214.

70 "in the end." *Gallatin*, p. 159.
"a partisan part." *Gallatin*, p. 87.
"popular convictions." *Gallatin*, p. 174.

71 "the body politic." *Gallatin*, p. 159.

72 "a new impulse." *Gallatin*, pp. 267–68.

73 "political objections." *Gallatin*, p. 322.
"passion for organization." *Gallatin*, p. 351.

74 "ideal of government." *Gallatin*, pp. 349–50.

75 "and inconsistencies." *Gallatin*, p. 352.
"that of peace." *Gallatin*, p. 271

76 "essential to its existence." *Gallatin*, p. 272.
"by circumstances." *Gallatin*, p. 273.

77 "surrender their power." *Gallatin*, p. 199.

78 "to Mr. Jefferson's Administration." *Gallatin*, p. 356.
"with his generation." *Gallatin*, p. 379.
"seeker of resources." *Gallatin*, p. 410.

79 "change of career." *Gallatin*, p. 478.
"made his strength." *Gallatin*, p. 559.
"of the past only." *Gallatin*, p. 379.

80 "their uncompleted task." *Gallatin*, p. 492.
"under which we labor." *Gallatin*, p. 650.
"to govern itself." *Gallatin*, p. 653.
"transcendental philosopher." HA to Lodge, Oct. 6, 1879. Ford, I, 314.

Chapter III
SATIRIC VIRTUOSITY
Page
83 "law of nature." HA to Charles Milnes Gaskell, Nov. 25, 1877. Ford, I, 302.
"to statesmen." *Education*, p. 317.

84 "invite the President." Henry James, *Novels and Tales* (26 vols., New York, 1907–17), XVIII, 131.
" 'ponderous' biography." HA to James Russell Lowell, May 3, 1880. Cater, p. 101.
"a leisure-class." James, *Novels and Tales*, XVIII, 130.
85 "and government." *Democracy*, p. 10.
86 "worth a sacrifice." *Democracy*, pp. 3–4.
87 "would manufacture." *Democracy*, p. 5.
"meanness of it." Henry David Thoreau, *Walden*, Chapter II.
"machinery of society." *Democracy*, p. 10.
"wheels of the machine." *Democracy*, p. 341.
88 "dance of Democracy." *Democracy*, pp. 86–88.
"democracy of life." *Democracy*, p. 342.
89 "of Peonia." *Democracy*, p. 23.
"a pleasure." *Democracy*, p. 35.
"public documents." *Democracy*, p. 37.
90 "with the dagger." *Democracy*, p. 158.
"and worse than that." *Democracy*, p. 107.
"eagerness to meddle." *Democracy*, p. 336.
91 "noblemen, he said." *Democracy*, p. 89.
"perverse or wicked." *Democracy*, pp. 38–39.
"into the shade." *Democracy*, pp. 72–73.
92 "level of brutes." *Democracy*, p. 102.
"what he calls 'badinaige.'" *Democracy*, p. 40.
93 "to eschew satire." *Democracy*, pp. 42–43.
"to be neutral." *Democracy*, pp. 75, 77.
"old Washington school." *Democracy*, p. 21.
94 "and not so wise." *Democracy*, p. 25.
" power was gone." *Democracy*, pp. 129–30.
95 "tipsy after dinner." *Democracy*, pp. 123–24.
"his next election." *Democracy*, pp. 137, 141.
"was facts." *Democracy*, p. 133.
"same old President." *Education*, p. 48.
96 "and your own good sense." HA to CFAjr, Jan. 18, 1869. Ford, I, 150.
"dragon's teeth." *Democracy*, p. 218.
98 "for the work's sake." HA to Henry Cabot Lodge, May 13, 1880. Ford, I, 322.
"drum and trumpet history." John Richard Green, *A Short History of the English People* (London, 1875), p. v.
99 "scandalous libel." HA to Henry Holt, Sept. 21, 1882. Cater, p. 122.
"be damned!" *Randolph*, pp. 17–18, 25.
100 "providential fact." Alexis de Tocqueville, *Democracy in America*, I, Introduction.
101 "its instinct." *Randolph*, pp. 6–7.

102 "arrogance seized him." *Randolph*, pp. 11–12.
 "bluff, brutal, blunt." *Education*, p. 181.
 "of American life." *Randolph*, pp. 4–5.
 "difficulty be restored." *Randolph*, p. 6.
103 "to one's self." *Randolph*, p. 14.
 "could have conceived." *Randolph*, pp. 12–13.
104 "enemies of liberty." *Randolph*, pp. 46–47.
105 "to think differently." *Randolph*, pp. 29–31.
 "experiences of Europe." *Randolph*, pp. 32–33.
106 "the surface of things." *Randolph*, p. 60.
 "renewing the extravagance." *Randolph*, p. 74.
107 "the executive power." *Randolph*, pp. 58–59.
 "New England farm-house." *Randolph*, p. 10.
108 "were masters." *Randolph*, pp. 65–66.
 "aristocratic democrat." *Randolph*, p. 95.
109 "general government." *Randolph*, p. 89.
110 "forgot their discipline." *Randolph*, p. 131.
 "logical method." *Randolph*, p. 143.
 "if not his own." *Randolph*, p. 129.
 "with coolness and skill." *Randolph*, p. 171.
111 "the slave power." *Randolph*, pp. 272–73.
 "politically sagacious." *Randolph*, p. 292.
112 "ruled supreme." *Randolph*, pp. 290–91.
 "lust for power." *Randolph*, p. 274.
 "helped to create." *Randolph*, p. 278.
113 "annals of the United States government." *Randolph*, pp. 295–96.
113n. "never actually made." William Cabell Bruce, *John Randolph of Roanoke* (New York and London, 1922), I, 650, 653.
114 "not to revenge." *Randolph*, pp. 258, 261.
 "cannot be recalled." *Randolph*, p. 306.
115 "bide his time." HA to John Hay, June 25, 1882. Ford, I, 337.

Chapter IV
HISTORY

Page
117 "became personal." *Education*, pp. 91–92.
118 "destiny of the United States." *History*, I, 30–31.
119 "the Roman Empire." Alfred North Whitehead, *Adventures of Ideas*, Chapter I.
 "greatest and most awful scene." Edward Gibbon, *The Decline and Fall of the Roman Empire*, Chapter 72.
120 "century before." *History*, I, 1–2.
 "of a continent." *History*, I, 1.
 "roads of their own." *History*, I, 5.

121 "agents of Destiny." Francis Parkman, *Pioneers of France in the New World. France and England in North America, Part First*, Introduction.
"of overcoming them." *History*, I, 40.
"5,308,483 persons." *History*, I, 1.
"democratic triumvirate." *History*, I, 190.
"a great democracy." *History*, IX, 222.

122 "for dramatists and poets." *History*, IX, 222, 223–24.

123 "were simply evil." John Richard Green, *A Short History of the English People* (London, 1875), pp. v–vii.
"its 'dulness.'" *History*, I, 49.

124 "the Roman Empire." *History*, I, 163.
"standards of greatness." *History*, I, 143.
"chiefly as types." *History*, IX, 222.
"for a new world." Alexis de Tocqueville, *Democracy in America*, I, Introduction.

125 "movement westward." *History*, V, 289.
"superintend its use." *History*, III, 216.

126 "as unconscious." HA to Francis Parkman, Dec. 21, 1884. Cater, p. 134.
"ruling over them." Tocqueville, *Democracy*, II, First Book, Chapter 20.

127 "a mechanical evolution." *History*, IX, 225, 224.
"master of economics." Max Lerner, ed., *The Mind and Faith of Justice Holmes* (Boston, 1943), p. 83.

128 "if it is a science." HA to Samuel Jones Tilden, Jan. 24, 1883. Cater, p. 126.
"sources of power." *History*, IX, 226.
"all he left." *History*, I, 267.
"want of ability." *History*, V, 11.

129 "the Duke of Bridgewater." *History*, I, 103.
"touch by touch." *History*, I, 277.
"in meaning well." *History*, III, 205.

130 "disease of omniscience." *History*, I, 145–46.
"*made* true by events." William James, *Pragmatism* (New York, 1907), p. 201.

131 "strain is put on it." HA to unknown correspondent, Oct. 6, 1899. Cater, p. 480.
"to do us justice." *History*, I, 216–17.

132 "society could comprehend." *History*, VI, 7.
"through political revolution." *History*, I, 310–11.
"because it was social." *History*, I, 163.
"had been felt." *Education*, p. 383.
"of the American people." *History*, I, 171.

133 "what it was really like." Noel Gilroy Annan, *Leslie Stephen* (London, 1951), p. 168n.

"drag your load." HA to Henry Osborn Taylor, Jan. 17, 1905. Cater, pp. 559–60.

134 "an independent empire." *History*, I, 3.
"centre of corruption." *History*, I, 196.
"with social distinctions." *History*, III, 441.

135 "end in confusion." *History*, V, 359.
"the reign of politics." *History*, IV, 135.

136 "be partially attained." *History*, III, 348.

137 "of the world." *History*, III, 370.
"a few visionaries." *History*, I, 69.

138 "engrossed public attention." *History*, III, 216–17.
"had ever engaged." *History*, V, 132, 215.
"ocean commerce." *History*, IX, 221.
"most striking success." *History*, IX, 236.

139 "of the people." *History*, IV, 134–35.

141 "of the Antonines." *History*, I, 8–9.
"images of time." William R. Taylor, "Historical Bifocals on the Year 1800," *New England Quarterly*, XXIII (1950), 179.
"ruled supreme." *History*, I, 15.
"the Aryan exodus." *History*, I, 17.
"Wall Street in 1875." *History*, I, 26.
"equality of condition." Tocqueville, *Democracy*, I, Introduction, and throughout.

142 "not yet in sight." *History*, I, 55, 57–60, 67, 72–73.

143 "schools of New England." *History*, I, 76, 86–87.
"reserved from exercise." *History*, I, 137, 143.

144 "prosperity of New York." *History*, I, 113–14.
"by political passions." *History*, I, 106.
"own political principles." *History*, I, 145.
"have lost Pennsylvania." *History*, I, 114.

145 "contradiction in terms." *History*, I, 114–16.
"could not penetrate." *History*, I, 172.

146 "they drove away." *History*, I, 177.
"in lowest esteem." *History*, I, 171.
"and tangible shape." *History*, I, 182–83.

147 "to the whole frame." Tocqueville, *Democracy*, II, First Book, Chapter XVII.

148 "the glowing continent." *History*, I, 170, 173–74.

150 "of human movement." *Education*, p. 382.

151 "rambling, vacant look." *History*, I, 185.
"of political importance." *History*, I, 187.
"of a corrupt man." *History*, I, 195.
"democratic triumvirate." *History*, I, 190.
"manners and appearance." *History*, I, 193.

152 "prove deeply interesting." *History*, I, 200–202.
153 "useless to them." *History*, I, 8.
"disturbed this dream." *History*, I, 212.
154 "not to be admitted." *History*, I, 242, 243, 245–46.
"of his only war." *History*, II, 425.
"Jefferson's republicanism." *History*, I, 230, 234.
155 "in the United States." *History*, I, 302.
"Callender's assertions." *History*, I, 322, 325.
"Paine, and Callender." *History*, I, 329.
156 "Secretary of State." *History*, I, 334–35.
157 "almost as enigmatical." *History*, I, 335.
"but not the thing." HA to Henry Cabot Lodge, May 21, 1881.
Ford, I, 328–29.
"over its captors." *History*, I, 340.
"government could govern." *History*, II, 115.
158 "force or fraud." *History*, V, 233, 321.
"not be enslaved." *History*, II, 121.
"waste paper." *History*, II, 94.
"France and Spain." *History*, II, 118.
"return within them." *History*, II, 208.
159 "'thing as intervention.'" *History*, II, 150.
"sat on a throne." *History*, II, 202.
160 "Peace was his passion." *History*, II, 376–77.
"without malignity." *History*, IX, 209.
"disappointment or war." *History*, II, 315.
161 "of the world." *History*, III, 2.
"dangerous than war." *History*, III, 59.
"without success." *History*, III, 71.
"throughout the world." *History*, III, 81.
162 "itself was lost." *History*, III, 115.
"of Northern men." *History*, III, 115.
163 "in numbers alone." *History*, III, 196.
164 "some violent test?" *History*, III, 211–13.
"a true democracy." *History*, III, 218.
165 "to allow it now." Cater, p. cv.
166 "than other people." *History*, III, 454.
"for such emergencies." *History*, III, 242.
167 "half the continent." *History*, III, 366–67.
"still less treason." *History*, I, 115.
"of its conspirators." *History*, IV, 184.
168 "of Burr." *History*, IV, 5.
"well worth making." *History*, IV, 272.
169 "enemy of the laws." *History*, IV, 276, 277.
"the opposite side." *History*, IV, 301.

170 "in the world." *History*, IV, 454–55.
"wholly upon Jefferson." *History*, IV, 454.
171 "cup of his defeats." *History*, V, 419–20.
172 "were none of his." *History*, V, 259.
"blind instinct of power." *History*, V, 354–56.
"no longer in force." *History*, V, 427–28.
"Court of London." *History*, VI, 21.
173 "proper self-control." *History*, VI, 11.
"unredressed outrage." *History*, VI, 26.
"wars of 1812." *History*, VI, 67.
"the Federalist rule." *History*, VI, 122.
174 "war with her." *History*, VI, 231.
"challenged confiscation." *History*, V, 408.
175 "of their own." *History*, IV, 136.
"not weld a nation." *History*, IV, 38.
"incompetence had caused." *History*, VIII, 145.
"panegyric upon war." *History*, VII, 365.
176 "possibility of war." *History*, VI, 376.
"civic honor." William James, *Memories and Studies* (London and New York, 1912), pp. 275, 289.
"not a single hero." *History*, IV, 277.
177 "with her manners." *History*, VII, 15.
"when he struck." *History*, VIII, 340, 342.
"artillery and muskets." *History*, IX, 234–35.
178 "competition among nations." *History*, IX, 227.
"down on her prey." *History*, IV, 75.
179 "prize-money scarce." *History*, VII, 336–37.
"a Yankee Schooner." *History*, VII, 319–20.
180 "debt of insult." *History*, VIII, 201.
"national misdemeanor." *History*, IX, 228.
181 "obstinately to her lips." *History*, IV, 281.
"Virginia legislation." *History*, VI, 447.
"of her neighbors." *History*, VIII, 14.
182 "hope or a despair." *History*, II, 292.
"responsibilities of government." *History*, VIII, 263–64.
183 "vigorous development." *History*, IV, 74.
"made war a duty." *History*, IV, 289.
"tests of popular intelligence." *History*, IX, 227.
184 "his 'haunting' dismay." HA to John Hay, July 22, 1888. Ford, I, 390–91.
"body of the text." *History*, IV, 289, in his discussion of the force which embargoes could apply in the realm of politics.
185 "acted on the Indian." *History*, VI, 69.
"were fixed." *History*, IX, 241.

186 "could not change." *History*, IX, 225.
"of its own end." *History*, IX, 224–25.
"intelligence and well-being." *History*, IX, 237.
"they were insuperable." *History*, IX, 185–86.

187 "to a conclusion." *History*, IX, 193.
"quickness of intelligence increased." *History*, IX, 218.
"its assumed powers." *History*, IX, 220.
"for moral progress?" *History*, I, 179.
"another century of experience." *History*, IX, 241–42.

188 "could but divine it." *Education*, p. 420.
"mythological antiquity." *The Works of John Adams . . . with a Life of the Author*, CFA, ed. (10 vols., Boston, 1850–56), I, 319.
"who write for citizens." Jacob Burckhardt, *The Civilization of the Renaissance in Italy* (London and New York, 1945), p. 148.

Chapter V
THE LAST LESSON OF EDUCATION

Page
191 "of his successors." *Education*, p. 26.

192 "of Maryland blood." *Education*, p. 19.
"ancient lady of our house." HA to Charles Milnes Gaskell, April 19, 1869. Ford, I, 157.
"preliminary materials." MS in Houghton.

193 "little pure satisfaction." *Education*, p. 19.
"meant by tone." *Education*, p. 9.

194 "caught on to an inheritance." *Education*, pp. 44–45.

195 "whited sepulchres." *Democracy*, p. 114.
"a temptation." HA to CFAjr, Feb. 9, 1859. Ford, I, 15.
"I shall be silly." HA to CFAjr, July 4, 1859. Ford, I, 46.
"moral bath." HA to Gaskell, Dec. 13, 1869. Ford, I, 176.

196 "twelfth-century window." HA to Henry Osborn Taylor, May 4, 1901. Ford, II, 332.
"and egotism fall away." HA to CFAjr, Sept. 3, 1863. Ford, I, 103; Elizabeth Stevenson, *Henry Adams* (New York, 1955), pp. 60–61.

197 "want of curiosity." Marian Adams to her father, Dr. Robert William Hooper, Jan. 1, 1873. Ward Thoron, ed., *The Letters of Mrs. Henry Adams* (Boston, 1936), p. 65.

198 "to play Ulysses." HA to Gaskell, Aug. 21, 1878. Ford, I, 308.
"without looking backwards." HA to Henry Cabot Lodge, Jan. 31, 1882. Ford, I, 334.

200 "trick of the imagination." *Esther*, p. 50.
"yacht in mid-ocean." *Esther*, p. 27.

201 "helped to increase." *Esther*, pp. 19–20.
"a way of spending money." *Esther*, p. 19.

202 "will not cling." *Esther*, p. 222.
"making it truer." *Esther*, p. 198.
"till it drew blood?" *Esther*, p. 203.
203 "to open it." *Esther*, p. 77.
204 "in his heart's blood." HA to Elizabeth Cameron, Aug. 23, 1886. Ford, I, 377.
205 "cut in halves." *Education*, p. 317
"most wanted on earth." HA to Edwin Lawrence Godkin, Dec. 16, 1885. Cater, p. 158.
206 "pleasantest jest of all." HA to John Hay, July 9, 1886. Ford, I, 367.
207 "never to return." HA to Gaskell, Dec. 12, 1886. Ford, I, 382.
"suppress the patriotic glow." CFAjr, marginal comment in privately printed draft, *History*, V, 287. MHS.
"party they belong." HA to Mrs. Cameron, Nov. 4, 1888. Ford, I, 396.
208 "always done so." HA to Gaskell, July 4, 1890. Ford, I, 403, 404.
"dull consciousness." HA to Mrs. Cameron, June 27, 1889. Ford, I, 400.
209 "from a human grave." MS in MHS. Filed with HA letters of Jan.–Aug., 1890.
"what the colors are." HA to Mabel Hooper La Farge, Aug. 20, 1890. Cater, p. 195.
"the last generation." HA to Mrs. Cameron, Aug. 31, Sept. 2, 1890. Ford, I, 407.
"another planet." HA to Mrs. Cameron, Sept. 27, 1890. MHS.
210 "proportionately less." HA to Oliver Wendell Holmes [Sr.], Jan. 4, 1885. Cater, p. 135.
"all the truth it has." HA to Mrs. Cameron, Oct. 22, 1890. Ford, I, 427.
"get by imagination." HA to Mrs. Cameron, Feb. 13, 1891. Ford, I, 468.
"only felt before." HA to Mrs. Cameron, March 29, 1891. Ford, I, 477.
"things—places—people." HA to Hay, Sunday, March 1891. MHS.
211 "ship or a house." HA to Mrs. Cameron, Oct. 27, 1890. Ford, I, 434.
"is not alike." HA to Anna Cabot Mills Lodge, Oct. 21, 1890. Ford, I, 431.
212 "feel so new again." HA to Mrs. Cameron, Oct. 9, 1890. Ford, I, 418.
"foundations of society." HA to Hay, Aug. 22, 1886. Ford, I, 377.
"Apollos to a man." HA to Hay, Oct. 16, 1890. Cater, pp. 198–99.
"with beauty itself." HA to Mrs. Cameron, Oct. 30, 1890. Ford, I, 439.
213 "what they have done." HA to Mrs. Cameron, Dec. 15, 1890. Ford, I, 450.

"or mean nothing." HA to Mrs. Cameron, Feb. 23, 1891. Ford, I, 469.

214 "exercise of the horse." HA to Mrs. Cameron, March 16, 1891. Ford, I, 475–76.

215 "when my wanderings end." HA to Mrs. Cameron, Oct. 22, 1890. Ford, I, 427.

"books or conversation." HA to Mrs. Cameron, May 13, 1891. Ford, I, 485.

"legends and love-songs." HA to Mrs. Cameron, May 31, 1891. Ford, I, 487.

216 "analytic and modern." HA to Hay, March 4, 1891. MHS.

"emotion of the moment." HA to Mrs. Cameron, March 1, 1891. Ford, I, 473–74.

217 "archaic woman was." HA to Mrs. Cameron, June 4, 1891. Ford, I, 489.

"to Gustave Flaubert." HA to Gaskell, Jan. 23, 1894. Ford, II, 35.

"including maps and indexes." HA to Mrs. Cameron, Feb. 13, 1891. Ford, I, 468.

"waiting for departure." HA to Mrs. Cameron, May 13, 1891. Ford, I, 485.

218 "on the tree trunks." HA to Mrs. Cameron, July 4, 1891. Ford, I, 500.

219 "as I regard snipe." HA to Mrs. Cameron, June 16, 1891. Ford, I, 492.

"of Benjamin Harrison." HA to Lodge, Aug. 4, 1891. Ford, I, 510.

"leads me." HA to Mrs. Cameron, Sept. 10, 1891. Ford, I, 523.

"without attaining Buddhaship." HA to Mrs. Cameron, Sept. 13, 1891. Ford, I, 526.

220 "*Think not! Strike!*" HA, "Buddha and Brahma," *Yale Review*, V (1915), 85.

"his mystic trances." *Yale Review*, V (1915), 89.

"what I cannot mend." *Yale Review*, V (1915), 86.

"but all are good." *Yale Review*, V (1915), 88.

221 "to the ewige woman." HA to Mrs. Cameron, June 18, 1889. Ford, I, 399.

"going to revive." HA to Mrs. Cameron, Oct. 8, 1891. Ford, I, 530.

"self—self—self." HA to Mrs. Cameron, Nov. 6, 1891. MHS.

"for a new avatar." HA to Mrs. Lodge, Nov. 25, 1891. Ford, I, 532.

221n. "his while to try." HA to Mrs. Cameron, June 18, 1889. Ford, I, 399–400.

222 "of the inevitable." Cater, p. cxviii, note 212.

"held up the mirror." *Education*, p. 329.

"look like favoritism." HA to Charles William Eliot, June 16, 1892. Ford, II, 10–11.

222n. "park a week earlier." HA to Hay, June 23, 1892. Ford, II, 12.

223 "candidate for honors." HA to Seth Low [March–April, 1894]. Ford, II, 44.

"made me work." HA to Mrs. Cameron, Feb. 9, 1902. MHS.

"melancholy little *Esther*." HA to Hay, Aug. 23, 1886. Ford, I, 377.

224 "national mind and ideals." HA to Mrs. Cameron, July 13, 1894. Ford, II, 53.

"thinks he rules us." HA to Gaskell, Nov. 26, 1893. Ford, II, 33.

"do in Paris anyhow." HA to Mrs. Cameron, Dec. 29, 1891. Ford, I, 534.

"the other refuse." HA to Gaskell, Aug. 24, 1896. Ford, II, 116.

"anti-semitic ravings." HA to Mrs. Cameron, July 27, 1896. Ford, II, 110.

"cautioning himself." *Democracy*, p. 46.

225 "the Jew scandal." HA to Mrs. Cameron, Jan. 13, 1898. Ford, II, 145.

226 "in Jew wars." HA to Mrs. Cameron, Sept. 5, 1899. Ford, II, 238.

"Dreyfusard or Anti." HA to Hay, April 11, 1899. Ford, II, 227.

"the great powers." HA to Hay, Aug. 20, 1899. Ford, II, 235.

227 "instantly to my ear." HA to Gaskell, March 29, 1900. Ford, II, 280.

"irritated or depressed." HA to Mrs. Cameron, Aug. 22, 1899. MHS.

"and mosquitoes." HA to Mrs. Cameron, Sept. 26, 1899. MHS.

"guide-book." HA to Mrs. Cameron, Oct. 15, 1899. MHS.

228 "classed as a style." HA to BA, Dec. 19, 1899. Ford, II, 251–52.

"without disturbing both." *Yale Review*, V (1915), 88.

229 "like himself." The marked passage from Adams' Michelet is transcribed in Max I. Baym, *The French Education of Henry Adams* (New York, 1951), p. 52.

"or three—ago." HA to Mrs. Cameron, June 4, 1891. Ford, I, 489.

"Norman paradise." HA to Mrs. Cameron, Aug. 29, 1895. Ford, II, 78.

230 "muck-heap life of Europe." HA to Hay, Aug. 4, 1895. Cater, p. 345.

"as I am of death." HA to Hay, Sept. 7, 1895. Cater, pp. 346–47.

231 "attic, in Paris." HA to Hay, Nov. 7, 1900. Ford, II, 299.

"solitude and absorption." HA to Taylor, May 4, 1901. Ford, II, 332.

"mission as teacher." HA to John Franklin Jameson, Nov. 17, 1896. Ford, II, 119.

"must not be agitated!" HA to Mrs. La Farge, July 18, 1899, and Sept. 5, 1899. Cater, pp. 468, 476.

"He alone sees." HA to Mrs. La Farge, May 29, 1900. Cater, p. 491.

"that one must please." HA to Mrs. La Farge, [?] 17, 1903. Cater, p. 536.

232 "Miracles of the Virgin." HA to Mrs. Cameron, April 22, 1901. Ford, II, 327.

"for want of training." *Education*, p. 370.

"Virgin of Chartres." HA to Mrs. Cameron, Feb. 18, 1901. Ford, II, 317.

"world without emotion." *Prayer*, pp. 128–30.

"Help me to bear!" *Prayer*, pp. 133–34.

233 "finished my dinner?" HA to Rebecca Gilman Rae, Dec. 21 [1897]. Cater, p. 426.

234 "except for Europe." HA to Mrs. Cameron, Dec. 6, 1898. MHS.

"as usual at 1603." HA to Mrs. Cameron, Feb. 3, 1901. Ford, II, 312.

Chapter VI
THE UNITY OF THE IMAGINATION

Page

235 "worth throwing in." HA to John Hay, Jan. 9, 1892. Cater, p. 263.

236 "with my nieces." HA to Elizabeth Cameron, May 13, 1905. Ford, II, 450.

"eyes *and* feet." HA to Henry Osborn Taylor, May 4, 1901. Ford, II, 333.

"and our ancestors." *Chartres*, p. 5.

237 "saints can pass." *Chartres*, p. 341.

238 "to carry a kodak." *Chartres*, pp. xiii–xiv.

"extinct like chivalry." *Education*, p. 443.

239 "in three centuries." *Chartres*, p. 60.

"facts are false." *Chartres*, p. 224.

"both militant." *Chartres*, p. 1.

"learn to feel it." *Chartres*, p. 2.

241 "majesty at Chartres." *Chartres*, p. 95.

"not to understand." *Chartres*, p. 226.

"is in architecture." *Chartres*, p. 12.

242 "of the relics." *Chartres*, p. 27.

"act of homage." *Chartres*, p. 29.

"art in France." *Chartres*, p. 11.

243 "of the Gothic." *Chartres*, p. 33.

244 "love is law." *Chartres*, p. 43.

"and silence." *Chartres*, p. 40.

"intelligence at rest." *Chartres*, p. 44.

"end of a world." *Chartres*, pp. 44–45.

245 "goes with the old." *Chartres*, p. 106.

"art, religion, and hope." *Chartres*, p. 45.

246 "as a work of art." Jacob Burckhardt, *The Civilization of the Renaissance in Italy* (London and New York, 1945). First Part.

"of our moral life." Oliver Wendell Holmes [Jr.], "The Path of the Law," reprinted in Max Lerner, ed., *The Mind and Faith of Justice Holmes* (Boston, 1943), p. 73.

247   "a well-rounded picture." Jacob Burckhardt, *The Age of Constantine the Great* (New York, 1949), p. 10.

"ways of saying it." *Chartres*, p. 60.

248   "difficulties of art." *Chartres*, p. 56.

250   "a pile of stones." James Russell Lowell, *The Cathedral* (Boston, 1870), p. 36.

"against the Revolution." *Education*, pp. 386–387.

251   "and 'grotesque.' " John Ruskin, *The Stones of Venice*, II, Chapter VI, "The Nature of Gothic."

"reasons, as final." *Chartres*, p. 63.

252   "Diane de Poitiers." *Chartres*, p. 66.

253   "Virgin's miracles." *Chartres*, p. 68.

"except misery." *Chartres*, p. 70.

254   "and the Imperial Crown." *Chartres*, p. 73.

"to Mary's feelings." *Chartres*, p. 84.

255   "usually meant 'fear.' " *Chartres*, p. 87.

256   "take refuge within." BA, *The Law of Civilization and Decay*, Chapter III.

"Queen of Heaven." *Chartres*, p. 88.

"every old peasant-woman." *Chartres*, p. 99.

"from ancient Greece." *Chartres*, p. 139.

257   "feeling the life." *Chartres*, p. 103.

"or a world's fair." *Chartres*, p. 104.

"poetry, or art." *Chartres*, p. 140.

"the fun of life." *Chartres*, p. 139, 140.

258   "truly American eye." *Chartres*, p. 89.

"practical reality." *Chartres*, p. 92.

"road to Paris." *Chartres*, p. 96.

259   " 'cash-value' of ideas." William James, *Pragmatism* (New York, 1907), several instances; see especially page 200.

"to them all." *Chartres*, pp. 140–41.

"building of it." *Chartres*, p. 101.

"unity of hearts." *Chartres*, p. 102.

260   "in the words." *Chartres*, p. 103.

"every touch they chiselled." *Chartres*, p. 97.

"phrase of Pascal." Passage from Adams' Pascal transcribed in Max I. Baym, *The French Education of Henry Adams* (New York, 1951), p. 198.

261   "mechanism and mathematics." *Chartres*, p. 103.

"knowledge can do." *Chartres*, p. 109.

"his imaginative genius." *Chartres*, p. 2.

262   "till she smiled." *Chartres*, p. 88.

"to feel Gothic art." *Chartres*, p. 106.

"technically perfect." *Chartres*, p. 120.

263 "did not even see." *Chartres*, p. 122.
"wine and women." *Chartres*, p. 29.

264 "vision or spirit." *Chartres*, p. 127.
"better not say it." *Chartres*, p. 138.
"English-speaking race." *Chartres*, pp. 29, 129.
"incapable of proof." *Chartres*, p. 129.

265 "pendants beneath." *Chartres*, p. 142.
"has rivalled." *Chartres*, p. 143.
"measure of his genius." *Chartres*, p. 142.
"even on infidels." *Chartres*, p. 143.

266 "colours of heaven." *Chartres*, pp. 144–45.
"are her guests." *Chartres*, p. 147.
"original documents." *Chartres*, p. 145.
"but in colour." *Chartres*, p. 169.
"that of the Virgin." *Chartres*, p. 170.

267 "motive of his own." *Chartres*, pp. 176–77.
"ephemeral pageant." *Chartres*, p. 182.

268 "what it felt." *Chartres*, p. 193.
"calms her child." *Chartres*, p. 194.
"as art, at least." *Chartres*, p. 195.

269 "in this world." *Chartres*, p. 97.
"pilgrim of art." *Chartres*, p. 191.
"on a dead faith." *Chartres*, p. 195.
"perfected form." *Chartres*, p. 196.

270n. "meaning of it all." BA to HA, Sept. 21, 1895. Houghton.
"cool reply." HA to BA, Oct. 3, 1895. Cater, pp. 348–49.
"this year of grace." HA to Mrs. Cameron, Jan. 22, 1915. Ford, II, 630.

271 "by broken glass." Quoted by Kenneth Clark, *The Gothic Revival* (London, 1928), p. 257.
"of believing it." T. S. Eliot, *Selected Essays* (New York, 1932), p. 349.
"gift of God." Blaise Pascal, *Pensées*, W. F. Trotter, tr. (New York, 1941), p. 88.
"but a stage." *Chartres*, p. 106.

273 "in the contradiction." *Chartres*, p. 211.
"as a phase of life." *Chartres*, p. 224.

274 "Queen of Heaven." *Chartres*, p. 226.
"is woman." *Chartres*, p. 196.
"poems of war." *Chartres*, p. 232.
"with the word: Despair." *Chartres*, pp. 247–48.

275 "only hope of despair." *Chartres*, p. 277.
"door of escape." *Chartres*, pp. 260–61, 273–74.
"effort in another." *Chartres*, p. 274.
"God the chaff." *Chartres*, p. 273.

"arbitrary acts of mercy." *Chartres*, p. 263.
276   "society that builds." *Chartres*, p. 67.
  "interlocutor of Aquinas." *Chartres*, p. 347.
277   "can afford to be." *Chartres*, pp. 196, 211, 224, 356.
  "not destroyed, a faith." *Chartres*, p. 252.
  "a single will." *Chartres*, p. 375.
  "as man moved." *Chartres*, p. 377.
279   "which is reason." *Chartres*, p. 317.
280   "veil of scepticism." *Chartres*, p. 321.
  "Adam loved." *Chartres*, p. 327.
281   "permit or avow." *Chartres*, p. 337.
  "and was silent." *Chartres*, p. 336.
  "repress anarchy." *Chartres*, pp. 365, 367.
282   "practically unchanged." *Chartres*, p. 345.
  "tended to fall." *Chartres*, p. 350.
283   "the ribalds laughed." *Chartres*, p. 364.
284   "justifies the church." *Chartres*, p. 373.
  "question of dates." HA to Frederick Bliss Luquiens, Feb. 27, 1911.
    Ford, II, 563.
  "very near decrepitude." Etienne Gilson, *The Spirit of Mediaeval
    Philosophy* (New York, 1940), p. 486.
  "under their own weight." Gilson, *Spirit*, p. 402.
285   "organic unity." *Chartres*, pp. 374–75.
  "into art at last." *Chartres*, p. 373
  "without logical violence." *Chartres*, p. 373.
286   "majesty of Chartres." *Chartres*, p. 281.
  "most complete expression." *Chartres*, pp. 376–77.
287   "this is all." *Chartres*, p. 377.

Chapter VII
MODERN MAN IN A MULTIVERSE
Page
289   "and seek another." HA to Charles Milnes Gaskell, April 28, 1894.
    Ford, II, 46.
  "division of time." HA to BA, July 29, 1900. Cater, p. 497.
  "cost of my comfort." HA to Gaskell, Nov. 10, 1901. Ford, II, 360.
291   "to any party." HA to Elizabeth Cameron, July 27, 1896. Ford,
    II, 109.
  "Bryan's campaign chest." The receipt from the Democratic National
    Chairman is among the Adams Papers for 1896. MHS.
292   "in a tight place." HA to Cecil Spring Rice, Feb. 12, 1897. Ford,
    II, 123.
  "concentrate and economise." HA to Mrs. Cameron, April 10, 1898.
    Ford, II, 164.

"do it at all." HA to BA, May 7, 1898. Ford, II, 177–78.

"estates cut up." HA to Sir Robert Cunliffe, May 19, 1898. Ford, II, 182.

293 "brother's historical theories." HA to BA, Oct. 31, 1899. Ford, II, 246.

"young men in America." HA to Mrs. Cameron, May 9, 1898. Ford, II, 178n.

"socialistic practices." HA to BA, Nov. 5, 1899. Ford, II, 248.

294 "but the anarchists." HA to Gaskell, Nov. 22, 1899. Ford, II, 249.

"there we stick." HA to John Hay, June 26, 1900. Ford, II, 290, 291.

295 "taken my seat." HA to John Franklin Jameson, Nov. 17, 1896. Ford, II, 119.

"save the pieces." HA to BA, April 2, 1898. Ford, II, 163.

"the same thing." HA to Hay, Dec. 16, 1900. Ford, II, 306.

"dead opposed." HA to Mrs. Cameron, April 6, 1902. Ford, II, 383.

"each other so often." HA to Gaskell, March 10, 1902. Ford, II, 378.

296 "always waste." HA to BA, Nov. 3, 1901. Ford, II, 359.

"Conservative Christian Anarchist." First instance in a letter is that in HA to Mrs. Cameron, Oct. 23, 1899. Ford, II, 244.

"of the universe." *Chartres*, pp. 366–67.

"reigns forever." Passage from Pascal is transcribed in Max I. Baym, *The French Education of Henry Adams* (New York, 1951), p. 196.

297 "and omnipotent." HA to BA, March 4, 1900. Ford, II, 271n.

298 "in the past." HA to BA, April 12, 1906. Cater, p. 583.

"and St. Thomas Aquinas." HA to BA, Aug. 10, 1902. Ford, II, 392.

299 "is overpowering." HA to BA, Feb. 7, 1900. Ford, II, 264.

"not 1920, but infinity." HA to Gaskell, March 29, 1900. Ford, II, 279–80.

300 "back of T. Jefferson." HA to Mrs. Cameron, April 1, 1901. Ford, II, 322n.

"to pray to them." HA to Spring Rice, Feb. 8, 1901. Ford, II, 315.

"from care and cant." HA to BA, March 8, 1903. Cater, 537.

"development of power." HA to BA, June 18, 1903. Houghton.

301 "lost their heads." HA to Mrs. Cameron, April 12, 1903. Ford, II, 405.

"which means the world." HA to Mrs. Cameron, Aug. 14, 1899. Ford, II, 234.

"Seneca to Theodonero?" HA to Mrs. Cameron, Jan. 10, 1904. Ford, II, 419.

"your, or my, automobile?" HA to Mrs. Cameron, Aug. 20, 1905. Ford, II, 459.

"anyhow consulted." HA to Mrs. Cameron, Aug. 27, 1905. Ford, II, 461.

302 "despotic socialism." HA to Worthington C. Ford, Dec. 19, 1898. Ford, II, 197.

"we are industrial." HA to Mrs. Cameron, Aug. 27, 1905. Ford, II, 461.

303 "explode or burn up." HA to Gaskell, June 26, 1904. MHS.
"mission as a teacher." HA to Jameson, Nov. 17, 1896. Ford, II, 119.
"broken off in 1877." HA to Gaskell, March 4, 1907. Ford, II, 472.
"go into a wall." HA to Mrs. Cameron, Aug. 20, 1905. Ford, II, 460.

304 "it must hurry." HA to Gaskell, Oct. 23, 1906. Ford, II, 469.
"men of the world." *Education*, p. x.
"twentieth-century multiplicity." *Education*, p. vii.
"active-minded young men." *Education*, p. x.

305 "politics, and economy." *Education*, p. 12.
"model of self-teaching." *Education*, p. ix.

306 "relation with ourselves." HA to Henry Osborn Taylor, Jan. 17, 1905. Cater, pp. 559–60.
"as I leave it." HA to Henry Cabot Lodge, March 1, 1915. Cater, p. 769.
"like a romance." HA to William James, Feb. 17, 1908. Ford, II, 490.
"against the Ego." *Education*, p. x.

307 "of human condition." *Education*, p. x.
"Boston Unitarianism." *Education*, p. 3.

308 "to reach perfection." *Education*, pp. 32–33.
"glacial epoch." *Education*, p. 15.
"social compact." *Education*, p. 13.

309 "silver mugs." *Education*, p. 15.
"to represent them." *Education*, p. 32.
"sum of all wickedness." *Education*, pp. 47–48.
"end of the vista." *Education*, p. 50.

310 "unconscious babyhood." *Education*, p. 4.
"in a long life." *Education*, p. 34.
"be alone respected." *Education*, p. 33.

311 "color of yellow." *Education*, p. 5.
"how to 'bear.'" *Educatino*, p. 4.

312 "had been stamped." *Education*, p. 55.
"had not begun." *Education*, p. 69.
"a very little education." *Education*, p. 71.
"practical education." *Education*, p. 73.
"not to be trusted." *Education*, pp. 80–81.

313 "lead to a sequence." *Education*, pp. 83–84, 90–91.
"something quite new." *Education*, p. 26.

314 "ignorance of men." *Education*, p. 94.
"outside of argument." *Education*, p. 182.

315 "without even an intrigue." *Education*, pp. 156–57.
"but themselves could run." *Education*, p. 49.

316 "he did not receive." *Education*, pp. 146–47.

"'by thinking so.'" *Education*, p. 147.
"perfection of human society." *Education*, p. 200.

317 "prove was change." *Education*, p. 230.
"one's earliest ancestor." *Education*, p. 229.
"religion of history." *Education*, p. 91.
"Common-Law deity." *Education*, p. 225.

318 "he had no Faith." *Education*, pp. 230–31.
"intelligible to him." *Education*, p. 236.
"Pullman civilization." *Education*, pp. 240, 245.
"friend lost." *Education*, p. 108; repeated with minor variation, p. 248.
"part of thought." *Education*, p. 252.

319 "end of its nose." *Education*, p. 239.
"enough to upset Darwin." *Education*, p. 266.

320 "mechanical motion." *Education*, pp. 287–88.

320n. "of the Education." R. P. Blackmur, "The Failure of Henry Adams," *Hound & Horn*, IV (1931), 442.

321 "new world to learn." *Education*, p. 289.
"grammes *per capita*." *Education*, p. 290.
"the word 'drift.'" *Education*, pp. 243, 254, 255, 259, 267.

322 "learning to see." *Education*, p. 398.
"when it was building." *Education*, p. 360.

323 "could not be a Person." *Education*, p. 289.

324 "Saint Thomas Aquinas." *Chartres*, p. 341.
"a clear idea." Henri Bergson, *Creative Evolution* (New York, 1911), p. 154.

325 "never seek them." *Creative Evolution*, p. 151.
"had taught him." *Education*, p. 403.
"or falsified." *Education*, p. 301.

326 "more complex still." *Education*, p. 300.
"for the view." HA to James Ford Rhodes, Feb. 10, 1908. MHS.
"world its shape." *Education*, pp. 36, 314.
"worked in the dark." *Education*, p. 315.

327 "deliberate belief." Joseph Conrad, *Heart of Darkness*, Chapter II.
"Youth needs illusions!" *Education*, p. 147.
"often contradictory things." *Education*, p. 373.
"exhausted auto-motion." *Education*, p. 426.

328 "thing called ignorance." *Education*, p. 297.
"wasted on thought." *Education*, p. 265.
"the closed entrance." *Education*, p. 302.
"improvement of society." *Education*, p. 352.

329 "ignorance of the past." *Education*, p. 328.

330 "lost sight of faith." *Education*, p. 329.
"twist towards ideals." *Education*, p. 341.
"centralizing, and mechanical." *Education*, p. 344.

331 "new sense of history." *Education*, pp. 354–55.
"common relation." *Education*, p. 376.
"real or imaginary." *Education*, p. 330.
"America adored." *Education*, p. 345.
"was arithmetic." *Education*, pp. 350–51.
"thirty years hence." *Education*, p. 352.

332 "the schoolboy $s = \frac{gt^2}{2}$." *Education*, p. 376.

"gravitation, or love." *Education*, pp. 380–81, 383.

333 "build Chartres." *Education*, p. 388.
"approached his end." *Education*, p. viii.
"suits it best." *Education*, p. 389.

334 "and John Hay." HA to Gaskell, May 10, 1907. Ford, II, 476.
"history 'in halves.'" *Education*, p. 392.
"the darkening prairie." *Education*, p. 396.
"*Ignoramus* before." *Education*, pp. 400–401.
"no one was to blame." *Education*, p. 408; *Chartres*, p. 339 and, by
    paraphrase, pp. 375–77.

335 "habit of permanence." *Education*, p. 409.
"better than the sun." *Education*, p. 413.
"empire were one." *Education*, pp. 414–15.

336 "the White House." *Education*, p. 416.
"wide as the world." *Education*, p. 422.
"stokers and pit-men." *Education*, p. 421.

337 "Jaurès and Bebel." *Education*, p. 423.
"falling forever in space." *Education*, p. 425.
"to my breast." *Education*, p. 427.
"weary pilgrim." *Education*, p. 433.

338 "should disappear." *Education*, p. 34.
"like chivalry." *Education*, p. 443.
"by imitating him." *Education*, p. 445.
"collectivist females." *Education*, p. 446.
"only a local one." *Education*, p. 441.

339 "dream of man." *Education*, p. 451.
"background of nature." *Education*, p. 458.
"or succumb to it." *Education*, p. 461.

340 "commonly called Death." *Education*, p. 431.
"so well acted." *Education*, p. 462.

341 "or the murdered?" *Education*, pp. 465–72.
"in face of a fear." *Education*, p. 457.
"education stopped." *Education*, p. 472.
"tortured history." *Education*, pp. 472, 473.

342 "helps to do work." *Education*, p. 474.
"the next life." *Education*, pp. 477–79.

343 "evolved thought." *Education*, p. 485.
"Cross of Christ." *Education*, pp. 486–87.
"correct its errors." *Education*, p. 488.
344 "unlimited power." *Education*, pp. 493, 496.
"than gravitation." *Education*, pp. 490–91.
"reconstruction of society." *Education*, pp. 494–96.
345 "also defies law." *Education*, p. 489.
"earth's atmosphere." *Education*, p. 496.
"would need to jump." *Education*, p. 498.
346 "was in sight." *Education*, pp. 499–500.
"soon pass perihelion." *Education*, p. 501.
"missing the catastrophe." *Education*, p. 503.
347 "a stage rôle." *Education*, p. 395.
"without a shudder." *Education*, p. 505.
"chances of a bomb." *Education*, p. 494.
"paring his fingernails." James Joyce, *A Portrait of the Artist as a Young Man* (New York, 1928), p. 252.
348 "may be thrown away." *Education*, p. x.
"climax of empire." *Education*, p. 367.
349 "shores of light." *Education*, pp. 384, 459.
"*suadere malorum.*" *De Rerum Natura*, Book I, line 83.
"reverse the method." *Education*, p. vii.
349n. "than the orthodox." Copy in MHS.
350 "*Leit motif* is flat." HA to Taylor, Sept. 9, 1909. Ford, II, 526.

Chapter VIII
THE DARKENING PRAIRIE

Page
352 "used to call electricity." HA to John Hay, Nov. 7, 1900. Ford, II, 301.
353 "the Mother,—You!" *Prayer*, p. 126.
"Me—the dead Atom-King!" *Prayer*, p. 130.
"of the year 1200." HA to Elizabeth Cameron, April 27, 1902. Ford, II, 387n.
354 "twelfth-centurian." HA to Cecil Spring Rice, Feb. 1, 1900. Ford, II, 261.
"return me the volume." HA to CFAjr, Feb. 20, 1907. Ford, II, 472.
355n. "of its sequel." HA to Henry Osborn Taylor, Jan. 17, 1905. Cater, pp. 558–59.
356 "I could reach." HA to Mrs. Cameron, May 13, 1905. Ford, II, 450.
"got hold of them!" HA to William James, Dec. 9, 1907. Ford, II, 485.
357 "failed too, as artist." HA to Edith Morton Eustis, [Feb.] 28, [1908?]. Cater, p. 615.

"work among workers." HA to CFAjr, Jan. 17, 1908. Ford, II, 487.

"of a long story." HA to Charles Milnes Gaskell, June 18, 1908. Ford, II, 501.

"Broca's convolution." HA to Mrs. Cameron, Sept. 15, 1908. Ford, II, 507.

358 "from noticing it." HA to George Cabot Lodge, April 22, 1903. Cater, p. 541.

"by one-fourth." HA to James Ford Rhodes, Feb. 10, 1908. MHS.

359 "taken too seriously." HA to BA, Feb. 10, 1909. Ford, II, 515n.

"amuse itself." HA to BA, Feb. 17, 1909. Cater, p. 640.

"by the form." HA to John Franklin Jameson, March 20, 1909. Cater, p. 650.

360 "absolutely dead." *Degradation*, p. 276.

361 "the rule itself." *Degradation*, p. 286.

"or even to think." *Degradation*, p. 282.

362 "by their modern airs." *Degradation*, p. 297.

"the whole world." *Degradation*, p. 298.

"or as science." *Degradation*, pp. 291, 295.

363 "radium to electrons." *Degradation*, p. 309.

"all that dread." *William Butler Yeats*, "Lapis Lazuli."

365 "number of people." HA to Mrs. Cameron, Jan. 14, 1902. Ford, II, 367.

"psychology, and history." BA to HA, Feb. 10, 1909. Houghton.

"narrow scope of art." HA to BA, March 5, 1909. Cater, p. 640.

"Nothing else will." BA to HA, April 2, 1910. Houghton.

366 "were not its author." HA to Mrs. Cameron, Jan. 24, 1910. Ford, II, 531.

367 "organization of hatreds." *Education*, p. 7.

"range of experience." *Degradation*, p. 126.

369 "cannot be played with." *Degradation*, pp. 130–31.

370 "like Mouravieff." Hay to HA, July 8, 1900. Ford, II, 292–93.

"timidity or despair." *Degradation*, p. 186.

371 "studied as a science." *Degradation*, p. 153.

"rigorously human action." *Degradation*, p. 146.

372 "to find allies." *Degradation*, p. 169.

"do about socialism." Cater, p. xcv.

" 'school' of reformers." HA to CFAjr, Nov. 21, 1862. *Cycle*, I, 196.

373 "and semantic ambiguity." William H. Jordy, *Henry Adams: Scientific Historian* (New Haven, 1952), pp. 131 ff., 216 ff.

374 "loophole called Mind." *Degradation*, pp. 185, 191.

"Lord Kelvin." HA to Gaskell, Nov. 28, 1909. Ford, II, 528.

375 "a tragic subject." William James to HA, June 17, 1910. Henry James, ed., *The Letters of William James* (Boston, 1920), II, 344.

"reform my statistics." HA to William James, June 20, 1910. Ford, II, 543.

"law of thermodynamics." *Degradation*, p. 249.

376 "We are *there!*" HA to CFAjr, Nov. 8, 1910. Ford, II, 553.

"abortion alive." HA to Raphael Pumpelly, May 19, 1910. Ford, II, 542.

377 "to love them." HA to Frederick Bliss Luquiens, July 5, 1910. Ford, II, p. 545.

378 "for Cook's tourists." HA to Albert Stanburrough Cook, Aug. 6, 1910. Ford, II, 546, 547.

379 "sympathy with men." HA to Anna Cabot Mills (Mrs. H. C.) Lodge, Aug. 29, 1909. Cater, p. 662.

"or by intellectuals." HA to Mrs. Cameron, April 11, 1912. Ford, II, 593.

"cannot counteract." HA to Luquiens, April 11, 1912, *Yale Review*, X (1920), 125–26.

"affected by the poet." *Lodge*, pp. 16–17.

"makes a school." *Lodge*, p. 30.

380 "that stifles him." *Lodge*, p. 62.

"beginning of life." *Lodge*, p. 14.

"age he lived in." *Lodge*, p. 64.

381 "set off for Paris." *Lodge*, pp. 98–99.

"chiefly mind." *Lodge*, p. 152.

"keep silence." *Lodge*, p. 166.

382 "doubts of his own." *Lodge*, p. 176.

"stand up to it." HA to Mrs. H. C. Lodge, June 21, 1910. Ford, II, 543n.

"is chaste." George Cabot Lodge, *Poems and Dramas* (Boston, 1911), II, 193.

"toward getting it." *Lodge*, p. 188.

"*in Arcadien geboren!*" HA to Henry James, Nov. 18, 1903. Ford, II, 414.

383 "expresses, the subject." Henry James, *William Wetmore Story and His Friends* (Boston, 1904), I, 16.

"a golden glow." Henry James to HA, Nov. 19, 1903. Percy Lubbock, ed., *The Letters of Henry James* (New York, 1920), I, 432.

384 "is yet at home." Henry James to HA, July 15, 1912. MHS.

"your all-faithful." Henry James to HA, March 21, 1914. *Letters*, II, 360–61.

385 "so I called rarely." Oliver Wendell Holmes to Sir Frederick Pollock, June 27, 1919. Mark DeWolfe Howe, ed., *Holmes-Pollock Letters* (Cambridge, Mass., 1946), II, 18.

386 "makes the difference." "A Sceptical Patrician," *The Athenaeum* (May 23, 1919), pp. 361–62.

388 "cries of the drowning." HA to Mrs. Cameron, April 16, April 21, 1912. Ford, II, 595.

"without my knowing it." HA to Luquiens, Jan. 25, 1912. Ford, II, 579.

389 "friends in general." HA to Raymond Weeks, July 15, 1912. Ford, II, 598.

"another way." HA to Mabel Hooper La Farge, Jan. 24, 1913. Cater, p. 752.

"without St. Augustine." HA to Gaskell, June 1, 1914. Ford, II, 625.

390 "but Thibaut rose." HA to Luquiens, *Yale Review*, X (1920), 130.

"Saint Augustine can't." HA to Mrs. Cameron, Dec. 20, 1914. Ford, II, 628.

"ever did have." HA to Gaskell, Oct. 3, 1916. Ford, II, 641.

"bring me back." HA to Gaskell, June 8, 1917. Ford, II, 643.

391 "to do next." HA to Mrs. Cameron, Sept. 5, 1917. Ford, II, 645.

"improvement of the world." HA to Gaskell, Feb. 19, 1918. Ford, II, 649–50.

392 "but divine it." *Education*, p. 420.

INDEX

Index